W9-BKA-791

# WEBSTER'S
# SPELLING
# DICTIONARY

# WEBSTER'S SPELLING DICTIONARY

PMC Publishing Company, Inc.

ISBN: 1-881275-15-9

Ever wonder why English spelling is so difficult? Why we don't just spell things the way they sound? Why different groups of letters sound the same? Or why one group gets pronounced in so many ways? How could anyone have come up with such a system?

Well, it wasn't done by just anyone, and certainly not by design. Like most languages, English began as a merging of primitive dialects, shaped and embellished by the speech of those with whom it came in contact. However, it didn't evolve in one place at one time, but in somewhat isolated pockets of fiercely independent peoples.

## ENGLISH - A BRIEF HISTORY

Picture this. It's the middle of the fifth century, on an island called Britain, occupied by Roman troops who rule the native Celts. The Roman Empire runs into trouble and the troops are called home. As the Celts watch the Romans leave, they in turn are being watched by the Germanic peoples of northern Europe who see a fine land, ripe for settlement. As far as we know, this is no sudden invasion, but rather a migration which takes place over a period of several generations. In the end, pockets of Angles, Saxons, Jutes, Friscians and others occupy the whole of Britain except for Scotland and Wales.

Consider the change which has taken place. The Romans invade, then inform the survivors that they are a part of the Roman Empire for which privilege they will be allowed to work their own land and pay taxes to Rome. The Romans, proud of their own language and culture, are content to rule and remain largely indifferent to the customs and culture of the peoples they rule. The Germanic tribes simply want the land and view anyone occupying it as an inconvenience. Unlike the Romans, there is no centralized authority and the Germanic dialects, though probably similar, are not the same, having been altered by contact with others through trade or war.

Germanic tribes are settling throughout the island. They interact in commerce and in war. Alliances for aggression and for protection are formed and broken. Dialects meet, blend, change and move from one part of the country to another. The Saxons emerge as the dominant group and so the language is called English after the more obscure Angles. Nobody knows why.

Enter the Vikings, attacking in such force that control of the northern part of England is ceded to them in the middle of the ninth century. They blend into the countryside and before long the addition of Scandinavian words further sharpens the differences between northern and southern dialects.

About the same time, another group of Vikings settle in the north of France adopting the local French provincial dialect. Called Normans, they invade England in 1066, changing the language of the aristocracy of England to a type of French; English is for the peasants.

English, left to the Englanders, changes dramatically. Regional differences become more pronounced, French words are adopted and adapted, but most important, it all becomes a lot simpler. Lacking the guidance of scholars to point out the error of their ways, peasants are dropping the arbitrary genders and inflectional endings, in short, the unnecessary complications to 'correct' speech.

As the Normans become increasingly isolated from the continent and assimilate into this land of England, they come to think of themselves more as Englishmen than Frenchmen. By the time Columbus makes his first voyage, English is again the dominant language in England, but not until the time of Shakespeare and the voyage of the Pilgrims is it a language that can be understood by most Englishmen.

When the language travels to America, it undergoes further change, much of it to describe the new environment and wildlife. Words like *moose, opossum* and *persimmon. Meadow* won't do for the Great Plains and *prairie* is borrowed from the French. Writers continue to borrow or create new words as they need them. Immigrants from around the world add theirs.

There you have it; 1500 years of linguistic evolution. The frustration we feel over the vagaries of English spelling must have been felt ten times over by any who attempted to standardize it. The effect of blending dialects, indiscriminate borrowing and arbitrary spelling is catastrophic.

Fortunately we now have in America a compendium of words that are mostly understood throughout the country. Unfortunately few can spell them, but the following pages contain some information which may help.

## A FEW SPELLING RULES

Reading this section will not make you an expert speller. It will, however, help you to become a better speller. Modern English, including scientific and technical terms, comprises well over a million words. We may have a nodding acquaintance with as many as 50,000 of those words, but we use, on a regular basis, a few thousand at most and are plagued by the spelling of a few hundred. Learning about the construction of words alerts you to patterns which tell when spelling is most likely right, and allows concentration on those most likely wrong. Don't be put off by the meager examples in each section. They are there only to illustrate the point; be assured that there are always more words which follow a rule than there are exceptions.

As much as I hate to admit it, your old English teacher was right: If you don't know how to spell a word, look it up. Naturally, if you don't know the first letter of the word, you may have to look in more than one place. Sure, it's a pain, but if you are really interested in using the right word, consider one other thing your teacher probably forgot to tell you. Looking up the word can often prevent a misunderstanding. For example, it's good news if you *brake* your car, but not so good if you *break* it. Among those words often misspelled are a number of similar sounding words which mean quite different things such as *affect/effect, ascent/assent, adapt/adopt, altar/alter* and *accept/except*. See what I mean?

### Dual Spelling

Matters are further complicated by the words which have acceptable dual spellings such as *endorse/indorse, adviser/advisor, enrolment/enrollment*, or *vender/vendor*. Common practice within our own sphere of influence (frequently requiring approval of instructor or supervisor) generally dictates which form we use. Many options such as *programme* are seldom used in America. The older forms of *-our* and *-re* as the last

vi

syllable of a word have generally been replace by *-or* and *-er* respectively. We tend to prefer *labor* to *labour*, *color* to *colour* and *center* to *centre*, but we use *theatre* as often as *theater*. Perhaps those in the theyatuh feel it smacks of culture. Common practice, however, does require consistency; whichever spelling you choose should be used all of the time.

## Pronunciation

Looking up a word occasionally is the mark of a conscientious, careful writer; looking up the same word over and over again may imply something quite different. These few pages are a small effort to assist in the quest to be identified as something other than "quite different". Like most of us, you have millions of unused brain cells lying fallow; it is time to put them to work.

Careless pronunciation is a trap. Perhaps you want to describe something clever or inventive as *ingenious*, only you get careless and pick up *ingenuous*. *Ingenuous* means frank or sincere. Not bad, really, but not what you wanted to say.

Pronunciation is definitely an aid to proper spelling. It's usually much easier to spell a word correctly when you pronounce it properly, or to look it up when you are not quite sure.

Pronunciation can help spelling in another way. When you look up a word, try pronouncing each syllable phonetically with a brief pause between syllables, taking care to pronounce each letter (even silent ones) and never varying the pronunciation of a particular letter. The result is a strange word which you wouldn't care to have another hear you say aloud, but one which will trigger your subconscious to tell you how to spell the word the next time you see it. Take *phonetically*, for example. Spelled the way it's normally pronounced, the results look like *fonetekly*, which could set the reader to looking for a German dictionary. Mentally sounded out one syllable at a time, however, it comes out *pho* (using a soft *f* or *p-ho* in our mental pronunciation to indicate *ph*), *net* (I can spell that), *i* (that, too), *cal* (and that), *ly* (and here's a bonus: pronouncing *cal* and *ly* separately insures that both *l*'s will get into the final spelling). You don't have to do this very many times before it becomes automatic and you stop looking up the same words over and over again.

## The A-B-C's Are Not For Children

Remember the cute rhyme in nursery school? See the colorful cards on the wall containing gaily decorated letters of the alphabet? You should have known what was to come when the colorful letters were replaced by stark black and white cards, capitals and lower case, with lines carefully drawn top, bottom and through the middle. You should have known that if you survived penmanship they would find another way to get you. And they are out there, singly and in groups.

We tend to concentrate on vowels because they give us the most problems. Just five vowels, *a, e, i, o, u* and one part-time vowel, *y*, are responsible for about twenty vowel sounds. Now any mathematician will tell you that it is no problem to create twenty distinct combinations out of five vowels. Unfortunately, this is English where any one of the sounds might come from several different spellings (*meat, meet, mete, deceit*) or any one spelling may engender a number of pronunciations (*rouge, rough, gouge, cough, thorough*).

Consonants are equally treacherous. The letter *s* masquerades part time as *z* (*suppose*), as *sh* (*sugar*), or quietly hides (*aisle*, *isle*). The *c* vacillates between being an *s* (*cede*) and a *k* (*care*) when it's not being an *sh* (*ocean*) or hiding behind a *k* (*acknowledge*). And the *k* - outrageous! Blatantly stands at the beginning of a word doing nothing (*knock*, *knee*, *know*). Almost as bad is the *p*, which normally well-behaved, when put with an *h*, thinks it's an *f* (*physician*, *phobia*). Association with *p* is not the only diversion of the *h*. Put it with a *g* and it can't decide whether to sound off like an *f* (*tough*) or be silent (*light*). Which brings us back to one of the same problems that exists with vowels, a single sound created by different spellings (*fool*, *photo*, *laugh*).

It's a wonder we can write this language at all. But these things have not been revealed to you to discourage you. By no means! They have been pointed out only to make you wary and to thirst for battle, so go forth and conquer - but be careful out there.

## Tips on Vowels

### Silent -e

Like most of the rules this works only part of the time. Usually words having a long vowel sound in the last syllable require a silent -*e* at the end (*cape*, *mope*, *slope*, *kite*, *cure*). There are, however, many exceptions such as *meet* and *feet* (long *e* marked by doubling), *achieve* and *piece* (silent *i* and silent *e*) or *chief* and *thief* (silent *i*, see -**ei- and -ie-**, below).

### -ei- and -ie-

In at least one Chinese dialect the long sound of *i-e* properly inflected is a cry of distress. It is also appropriate for English spelling.

Let's begin with the rule you learned in school - "*i* before *e* except after *c*." That's easy enough . . . when it works. What your teacher forgot to tell you is that it works (almost always) <u>only</u> with the long *e* sound. Words like *grief*, *piece*, *conceit* and *perceive* follow the rule.

Spellings pronounced with a sound other than the long *e* don't follow the rule (*weigh*, *veil*, *freight*, *their*).

Some words with the long *e* sound like *either*, *leisure*, *neither*, *seize*, *specie* and *weird* don't follow any rule.

## Prefixes

Normally a prefix added to a word changes its meaning without changing spelling. There are exceptions. (Who could have guessed?) The good news is that the exceptions are modest and clear cut or of no real concern to us here. Into the latter category fall words such as *inhabitable*, which means the same as *habitable*. The prefix *in-*, which means *not*, has been added without changing the spelling of the root word, but the meaning has not changed and both words are in common usage. Compare that with *human/inhuman*. It's another "nobody knows why" situation.

The exceptions which are of concern to us here all involve hyphens:

Hyphenate when joining *ex-*, *all-* or *self-* to a noun, such as *ex-president, all-inclusive*, or *self-proclaimed*.

Hyphenate when the prefix is used with a proper noun or adjective, such as *pro-American* or *un-American*.

Hyphenate to alleviate confusion such as creating a word which could be confused with another (*re-creation*, the act of creating again versus *recreation*, amusement) or to make the word easier to recognize (*re-emerge* rather than *reemerge*). You have some latitude with this one, but as in all things, be consistent.

There are about fifty prefixes in general use and nothing is to be gained by listing them all; however, it can be helpful to know the meaning of some which are similar:

> *ante-* means *before* as in *antedate*,
>> whereas *anti-* means *against* as in *antibody*
> *dis-* means *separation* as in *disgrace*,
>> whereas *dys-* means *ill* or *bad* as in *dysfunction*
> *hyper-* means *above* or *excessive* as in *hyperactive*,
>> whereas *hypo-* means *under* or *beneath* as in *hypodermic*
> *per-* means *through* as in *pervade*,
>> whereas *pre-* means *before* as in *precede*
>> and *pro-* means *forward* as in *proceed*

## Suffixes

### Dumping the Silent -e

Usually, when a suffix begins with a vowel (*-ed, -ing*), the final *-e* is dropped and the suffix is added (*mope, moping; kite, kited*). As usual there are exceptions. After *c* or *g* the *-e* is retained before a suffix beginning with *a* or *o* (are you with me so far?) in order to preserve the soft sound of the *c* or *g* (*notice, noticeable; outrage, outrageous*).

Words with the suffix *-ment* keep the silent *-e* (*place, placement*) unless the *-e* is preceded by two consonants in which case it is dropped (*judge, judgment; acknowledge, acknowledgment*). In England the *-e* is not dropped which makes it an optional spelling in many American dictionaries. Just keep in mind that if you opt for the English spelling, keep it that way all the time.

Finally there are some common exceptions just to make sure that no one gets an A on the exam (*true, truly; hoe, hoeing; singe, singeing; dye, dyeing; whole, wholly; mile, mileage*).

### Doubling Consonants

Following the silent *-e* rule, we drop the *-e* when adding endings like *-ed* and *-ing*. But how about their counterparts, the words with short vowel sounds which have no silent *-e*? How do we keep from confusing the two words? Simple. We double the consonant so that while *mope* becomes *moping, mop* becomes *mopping*. This usually works, but as you might have guessed, we don't get off that easily.

For one thing, the above rule applies only to syllables that contain a single vowel so that *scoop* changes to *scooping* (not *scoopping*).

Words of more than one syllable require a further consideration, namely which syllable is accented. Uh, oh!, we're back to pronunciation again. If the accent of the word created is on the last syllable, follow the doubling consonant rule above (*defer, defer´ring; refer, refer´ring*). If the accent of the word created is not on the last syllable, do not double the consonant (*credi cred´iting; refer, ref´erence*).

## -er versus -or ending

The *-er* ending indicates the person, thing or action related to the root word (*maker, speaker, driver*) and is the more common ending; when in doubt, use it. Some words take only the *-or* ending (*actor, creditor, elevator, visitor*), and a few words take either.

## -cede, -ceed, -sede endings

The most common of these three endings is *-cede* (*precede, secede*) and, glory be!, the exceptions are few (*supersede, exceed, proceed and succeed*). Memorize those four words and you will have one spelling lesson down pat.

## Y as a Vowel

We don't normally include *y* in our list of vowels, because it performs that function only part time. At the beginning of a word or syllable, it tends to function as a consonant; whereas, when it follows another consonant it functions as a vowel. If you wonder why anyone cares, read this sentence aloud, paying particular attention to the *y* sounds. In *you* and *paying*, exhibits a hard sound, while in *why* and *anyone* it sounds like the *i* in *while*. Never mind that phonetic spelling could eliminate the *y*, we're concerned here with how to get along with it.

A final *y* preceded by a consonant (*fry, copy, sixty*) changes to an *i* before a suffixes (*fried, copier, sixtieth*) except those suffixes beginning with i (*frying, copying, sixtyish*).

A final *y* preceded by a vowel (*pray, boy*) generally doesn't change when a suffix is added (*pray, prayed, praying; boy, boyish*) except sometimes (*day, daily, lay, laying, laid*). Go figure.

## Hard c

As mentioned earlier the letter *c* often hides behind a *k*; this time you get to put it there. Words ending in a hard *c* add a *k* before suffixes beginning with a vowel (*panic, panicky, panicking; mimic, mimicked, mimicker*).

# Plurals

Forming a plural offers another challenge to the writer. Most plurals are formed by adding *s*, but there are plenty of exceptions as you will see.

## Irregular Nouns

The bad news is that one group of irregular nounds changes spelling in a random fashion (*child, children; woman, women; man, men; goose, geese; mouse, mice*) while another doesn't change at all (*sheep, deer, fish*). The good news is that these are mostly words in common use and you should seldom encounter unfamiliar ones.

## Nouns Ending in -f and -fe

Another tricky group is comprised of nouns ending in *-f* and *-fe*; some take an *s* to make the plural (*chief, chiefs; dwarf, dwarfs*), whereas others change the *f* to *v* and add *s* or *es* (*calf, calves; knife, knives*).

## Yet Another Group

Forming the "yet another group" are nouns ending in *s, ss, z, sh, ch,* and *x*. If you can just remember that list of endings, you are home free - they all add *es*.

## Nouns Ending in -y

The letter *y* gets a little friendlier here. If the *-y* ending is preceded by a vowel simply add *s*; if it is preceded by a consonant, change the *y* to *i* and add *es*.

## Compound words

These offer an interesting challenge. Really! Most compound words are made up of a subject and a modifier. You only have to decide which is which and then apply the rules for making the subject plural.

Easiest are the one word compounds such as *fireman, firemen* or *congresswoman, congresswomen*.

Two word compound nouns are more fun. *Mother-in-law* becomes *mothers-in-law* because *mother* is the subject and *in-law* describes a relationship. The same principal applies to *editors in chief* and *ex-presidents*.

*Notary public* and *chairman of the board* offer a couple of unusual examples. The first is a *notary* who works in the public domain and a gathering of such men could be described as a group of *notaries public*; however, one might view the two words together as a title wherein each word carries equal weight in which case it would be a group of *notary publics*. In the second example, a strong argument can be made that the gathered titans of industry are collectively *chairmen*, but of a like number of *boards* as each board has only one chairman. Thus we have a meeting of the *chairmen of the boards*. (Except for boards which have co-chairmen). This is one of those places where there is no distinct right or wrong; we only hope that common sense will prevail and . . . you got it! . . . be consistent.

## Minding Your p's and q's

By this time you may be at 6's and 7's, but you should still be able to see where this rule is going with no if's, and's or but's. You have earned it; you

deserve it: an ironclad rule with no exceptions. THE PLURAL OF A NUM
BER, LETTER, WORD OR SYMBOL (+'s and -'s) IS CREATED BY ADDIN(
's.

## Nouns Ending in -o

Nouns ending in *o* and preceded by a consonant usually form the plural by
adding *-es* (*hero, heroes; potato, potatoes*); however, there are a number of
exceptions (*photo, photos; piano, pianos; solo, solo; silo, silos*)

Nouns ending in *o* preceded by a vowel take an *s* only (*radio, radios; zoo, zoos
trio, trios*)

Proper nouns ending in *o* always take an *s* only.

## Possessive Plurals

Finally, another easy one. When you want to form the plural possessive
form the plural by the applicable rule (or exception) and if the word ends in
an *s* add an apostrophe ('), otherwise add an apostrophe *s* (*'s*).

# Hyphenation

Most grammarians have one bit of advice about hyphenation. Don't do it
As we deal with ever more sophisticated writing tools such as word processors and
personal computers, we strive to turn out smarter looking documents which often
require hyphenation. Rather than get wrapped up in a lot of rules, follow just one
"Use common sense." When a word is broken at the end of a line, make sure that
enough of it is on the first line (at least three or four characters) so that the eye can
track it without the necessity of pausing or rereading. Otherwise your message loses
impact. Similarly, a stack of hyphens where words have been broken on line after
line makes tracking difficult. Most syllables follow pronunciation, but not all. This
dictionary has eliminated the non-breaking syllables except when they are accented
You'll recognize them in words like *a ̍ble*; you certainly wouldn't improve the look of
your document by leaving *a-* on one line and carrying *ble* to the next.

# And finally

Enjoy! Don't let the language intimidate you. The more you learn, the more fun it becomes. You feel in control, because you know that none of it was handed down on
stone tablets. You realize that words were coined and massaged by people like us
(Perhaps a little smarter . . . perhaps not.) Who knows but that you might introduce
something new into the language. Changing a word a little or combining a couple of
words to better suit your need strikes someone else who borrows and passes it on
and then someone else borrows it and then . . . fifty years from now someone will
agonize over its spelling and say "What fool . . .?"

**A**

aard´vark
Aa´ron
ab-a-ca´
aback
ab´a-cus
abaft
ab-a-lo´ne
aban´don
aban´doned
aban´don-er
aban´don-ment
abase
abased
abas´ed-ly
abase´ment
abash
abash´ment
aba´sia
abas´ing
abat´able
abate
abate´ment
ab´a-tis
aba´tor
ab´ba-cy
ab-ba´tial
ab´bey
ab-bre´vi-ate
ab-bre´vi-at-ed
ab-bre´vi-at-ing
ab-bre-vi-a´tion
ab´di-ca-ble
ab´di-cate
ab´di-cat-ing
ab-di-ca´tion
ab´di-ca-tor
ab´do-men
ab-dom´i-nal
ab-du´cent
ab-duct´
ab-duc´tion
ab-duc´tor
abeam
abe-ce-dar´i-an
abed
ab-en-ter´ic
Ab´er-deen

ab-er´rance
ab-er´ran-cy
ab-er´rant
ab-er-ra´tion
abet
abet´ted
abet´ting
abet´tor
abey´ance
abey´ant
ab-hor´
ab-horred´
ab-hor´rence
ab-hor´rent
ab-hor´ring
abid´ance
abide
abid´ing
ab´i-e-tate
abil´i-ties
abil´i-ty
ab-ject´, ab´ject
ab-jure´
ab-jur´ing
ab-late´
ab-la´tion
ab´la-tive
ablaze´
a´ble
a´ble—bod´ied
abloom
ab-lu´tion
ab-lu´tion-ary
a´bly
ab´ne-gate
ab-ne-ga´tion
ab´ne-ga-tive
ab-nor´mal
ab-nor-mal´i-ties
ab-nor-mal´i-ty
ab-nor´mal-ly
ab-nor´mi-ty
aboard
abode
abol´ish
ab-o-li´tion
ab-o-li´tion-ism
ab-o-li´tion-ist
ab-o-ma´sum

A´—bomb
abom´i-na-ble
abom´i-na-bly
abom´i-nate
abom´i-nat-ed
abom-i-na´tion
ab-o-rig´i-nal
ab-o-rig´i-ne
abort
abor´ti-cide
abor´ti-fa´cient
abor´tion
abor´tion-ist
abort´ive
abound
abound´ing
about
about—face´
above
above´board
ab-ra-ca-dab´ra
abrad´ant
abrade
abrad´ed
abrad´ing
A´bra-ham
abran´chi-an
abran´chi-ate
abra-si-om´e-ter
abra´sion
abra´sive
ab-re-ac´tion
abreast
abridge
abridge´a-ble
abridg´ing
abridg´ment
abroad
ab´ro-ga-ble
ab´ro-gate
ab´ro-gat-ed
ab´ro-gat-ing
ab´ro-ga´tion
ab´ro-ga-tive
ab´ro-ga-tor
ab-rupt´
ab-rup´tion
ab-rupt´ly
ab-rupt´ness

Ab´sa-lom
ab´scess
ab´scessed
ab-scond´
ab-scond´ed
ab´sence
ab´sent
ab-sen-tee´
ab-sen-tee´ism
ab´sent-ly
ab´sent-mind-ed
ab´sinthe
ab-sin´thi-an
ab´so-lute
ab´so-lute´ly
ab-so-lu´tion
ab´so-lut-ism
ab´so-lut-ist
ab´so-lu-tis´tic
ab´so-lu-tive
ab-sol´u-to-ry
ab-solv´a-ble
ab-solve´
ab-solved´
ab-sol´vent
ab-solv´er
ab-solv´ing
ab-sorb´
ab-sorb-a-bil´i-ty
ab-sorbed´
ab-sorb´ed-ly
ab-sor-be-fa´cient
ab-sorb´ent
ab-sorb´ing
ab-sorp´tion
ab-sorp´tive
ab-stain´
ab-stained´
ab-stain´er
ab-ste´mi-ous
ab-ste´mi-ous-ly
ab-sten´tion
ab-sten´tious
ab-ster´gent
ab-ster´sion
ab´sti-nence
ab´sti-nent
ab´stract
ab-stract´ed

ab-stract´ed-ly
ab-strac´tion
ab-strac´tive
ab´stract-ly
ab-stric´tion
ab-struse´
ab-struse´ly
ab-surd´
ab-surd´i-ty
ab-surd´ly
abu´lia
abu´lic
abun´dance
abun´dant
abun´dant-ly
abuse
abused
abus´er
abus´ing
abu´sive
abu´sive-ly
abu´sive-ness
abut
abu´ti-lon
abut´ment
abut´tal
abut´ted
abut´ter
Aby´dos
abysm´
abys´mal
abys´mal-ly
abyss
abyss´al
Ab-ys-sin´ia
aca´cia
ac´a-deme
ac-a-dem´ic
ac-a-dem´i-cal
ac-a-dem´i-cal-ly
ac-a-de-mi´cian
acad´e-my
Aca´dia
ac´a-leph
ac-a-na´ceous
ac-an-tha´ceous
acan-tho-ceph´a-lan
acan´thoid
acan´thous

acan´thus
acap-pel´la
acap´su-lar
ac-a-ri´a-sis
ac´a-roid
acar´pel-ous
acar´pous
acat-a-lec´tic
acau´dal
acau´date
acau-les´cent
acau´line
ac-cede´
ac-ced´ence
ac-ce-le-ran´do
ac-cel´er-ate
ac-cel´er-a´tion
ac-cel´er-a-tive
ac-cel´er-a-tor
ac-cel´er-a-to-ry
ac´cent
ac-cen-tu-al´i-ty
ac-cen´tu-ate
ac-cen-tu-a´tion
ac-cept´
ac-cept-a-bil´i-ty
ac-cept´a-ble
ac-cept´ance
ac-cep-ta´tion
ac-cept´ed
ac-cept´er
ac-cep´tor
ac´cess
ac-ces´sa-ri-ly
ac-ces´sa-ry
ac-ces-si-bil´i-ty
ac-ces´si-ble
ac-ces´sion
ac-ces-so´ri-al
ac-ces´so-ri-ly
ac-ces´so-ry
ac-ciac-ca-tu´ra
ac´ci-dence
ac´ci-dent
ac-ci-den´tal
ac-ci-den´tal-ly
ac-cip´i-tral
ac-cip´i-trine
ac-claim´

ac-claim´ing
ac-cla-ma´tion
ac-clam´a-to-ry
ac-cli´mat-a-ble
ac-cli´mate
ac-cli´mat-ed
ac-cli-ma´tion
ac-cli-ma-ti-za´tion
ac-cli´ma-tize
ae-cliv´i-ty
ac-cli´vous
ac-co-lade´
ac´co-lade
ac-com´mo-date
ac-com´mo-dat-ing
ac-com-mo-da´tion
ac-com´mo-da-tive
ac-com´pa-nied
ac-com´pa-nics
ac-com´pa-ni-ment
ac-com´pa-nist
ac-com´pa-ny
ac-com´plice
ac-com´plish
ac-com´plished
ac-com´plish-ment
ac-compt´
ac-cord´
ac-cord´a-ble
ac-cord´ance
ac-cord´ant
ac-cord´ed
ac-cord´ing
ac-cord´ing-ly
ac-cor´di-on
ac-cor´di-on-ist
ac-cost´
ac-couche-ment´
ac-cou-cheur´
ac-count´
ac-count-a-bil´i-ty
ac-count´a-ble
ac-count´an-cy
ac-count´ant
ac-count´ing
ac-cou´ter
ac-cou´ter-ment
ac-cred´it
ac-cres´cence

ac-cre´tion
ac-cre´tive
ac-cru´al
ac-crue´
ac-crue´ment
ac-cru´ing
ac-cum´ben-cy
ac-cum´bent
ac-cu´mu-late
ac-cu´mu-lat-ing
ac-cu´mu-la´tion
ac-cu´mu-la-tive
ac-cu´mu-la-tor
ac´cu-ra-cy
ac´cu-rate
ac´cu-rate-ly
ac´cu-rate-ness
ac-curs´ed
ac-cus´al
ac-cu-sa´tion
ac-cu´sa-tive
ac-cus´a-to-ry
ac-cuse´
ac-cused´
ac-cus´er
ac-cus´ing
ac-cus´ing-ly
ac-cus´tom
ac-cus´tomed
ac-e-naph´thy-lene
aceph´a-lous
ac´er-ate
acer´bi-ty
ac´er-ose
ac´er-ous
acer´vate
aces´cent
ac-e-tab´u-lum
ac-et-al´de-hyde
acet´a-mide
ac-et-an´i-lid
ac´e-tate
ace´tic
ace´ti-fy
ace´e-tone
ace´tous
ace´tum
ace´tyl
ace´tyl-ac´e-tone

acet-y-la´tion
acet´y-lene
ac-e-tyl´ic
ace´tyl-sal-i-cyl´ic
ached
ache´ni-al
Ach´er-on
achiev´able
achieve
achieved´
achieve´ment
achiev´ing
Achil´les
ach´ing-ly
ach-ro-mat´ic
ach-ro-mat´i-cal-ly
achro´ma-tism
achro´ma-tize
achro´ma-tous
acic´u-lar
ac´id
acid´ic
acid-i-fi-ca´tion
acid´i-fied
acid´i-fy
ac-i-dim´e-ter
acid-i-met´ric
acid´i-ty
ac´id-proof
acid´u-late
acid-u-la´tion
acid´u-lous
ac´i-er-ate
acin´i-form
ac-knowl´edge
ac-knowl´edge-a-ble
ac-knowl´edg-ing
ac-knowl´edg-ment
aclin´ic
ac´me
ac´ne
ac´o-lyte
acon´dy-lous
ac´o-nite
ac-o-ni´tum
acon´ti-um
a'corn
acot-y-le´don
acous´tic

acous´ti-cal
acous´ti-cal-ly
ac-ous-ti´cian
acous´tics
ac-quaint´
ac-quaint´ance
ac-quaint´ance-ship
ac-quaint´ed
ac-qui-esce´
ac-qui-es´cence
ac-qui-es´cent
ac-qui-esc´ing
ac-quire´
ac-quire´ment
ac-quir´er
ac-quir´ing
ac-qui-si´tion
ac-quis´i-tive
ac-quit´
ac-quit´tal
ac-quit´tance
ac-quit´ted
ac-quit´ting
a´cre
a´cre-age
ac´rid
ac´ri-dine
acrid´i-ty
ac´rid-ly
ac-ri-mo´ni-ous
ac´ri-mo-ny
ac´ro-bat
ac-ro-bat´ic
ac-ro-bat´ics
ac´ro-gen
acrog´e-nous
acro´le-in
ac´ro-lith
ac-ro-me-gal´ic
ac-ro-meg´a-ly
acro´mi-on
acron´i-cal
ac´ro-nym
acroph´o-ny
acrop´o-lis
across
acros´tic
acrot´ic
ac´ro-tism

ac´ry-late
acryl´ic
ac-ry-lo-ni´trile
ac´ti-nal
act´ing
ac-tin´ia
ac-tin´ic
ac´ti-nism
ac-tin´i-um
ac´ti-noid
ac-ti-nol´o-gy
ac-ti-no-my´cin
ac-ti-no-my-co´sis
ac´tion
ac´tion-able
Ac´ti-um
ac´ti-vate
ac-ti-va´tion
ac´ti-va-tor
ac´tive
ac´tive-ly
ac´tiv-ist
ac-tiv´i-ties
ac-tiv´i-ty
ac´tor
ac´tress
ac´tu-al
ac-tu-al´i-ty
ac´tu-al-ly
ac-tu-ar´i-al
ac´tu-ar-ies
ac´tu-ary
ac´tu-ate
ac´tu-at-ing
ac-tu-a´tion
ac´tu-a-tor
ac´u-ate
acu´i-ty
acu´le-ate
acu´men
acu´mi-nate
acu-mi-na´tion
ac´u-punc-ture
acute
acute´ly
acute´ness
acy´clic
ac´yl-ate
ad´age

ada´gio
Ad´am
ad´a-mant
ad-a-man´tine
Ad´ams
adapt
adapt-a-bil´i-ty
adapt´able
ad-ap-ta´tion
adapt´er
adapt´ive
adap´tor
ad-ax´i-al
add´a-ble
add´ed
ad-den´da
ad-den´dum
ad´der
add´i-ble
ad´dict
ad-dict´ed
ad-dic´tion
Ad´dis Ab´a-ba
Ad´di-son
ad-dit´a-ment
ad-di´tion
ad-di´tion-al
ad-di´tion-al-ly
ad´di-tive
ad´dle
ad´dled
ad-dress´
ad-dress-ee´
ad-dress´er
ad-dress´ing
Ad-dres´so-graph
ad-dres´sor
ad-duce´
ad-du´cent
ad-duc´i-ble
ad-duc´ing
ad-duct´
ad-duc´tion
ad-duc´tor
Ad´e-la
Ad´e-laide
Ad´el-bert
A´den
ade´nia

aden´i-form
ad-e-ni´tis
ad-e-no-fi-bro´ma
ad´e-noid
ad´e-noi´dal
ad-e-no´ma
adept
adept´ly
adept´ness
ad´e-qua-cy
ad´e-quate
ad´e-quate-ly
ad-here´
ad-her´ence
ad-her´ent
ad-he-res´cent
ad-her´ing
ad-he´sion
ad-he´sivc
ad-he´sive-ly
ad-hib´it
ad-hi-bi´tion
ad-i-a-bat´ic
ad-i-an´tum
ad-i-aph´o-rous
adi-a-ther´man-cy
adieu
ad in-fi-ni´tum
ad in´ter-im
adios
adip´ic
ad-i-poc´er-ous
ad´i-pose
ad-i-pos´i-ty
Ad-i-ron´dack
ad-ja´cen-cy
ad-ja´cent
ad-ja´cent-ly
ad-jec-ti´val
ad´jec-tive
ad-join´
ad-joined´
ad-join´ing
ad-journ´
ad-journed´
ad-journ´ment
ad-judge´
ad-judg´ing
ad-ju´di-cate

ad-ju´di-cat-ing
ad-ju-di-ca´tion
ad-ju´di-ca-tive
ad-ju´di-ca-tor
ad´junct
ad-junc´tive
ad-ju-ra´tion
ad-jur´a-to-ry
ad-jure´
ad-ju´ror
ad-just´
ad-just´a-ble
ad-just´er
ad-just´ment
ad-jus´tor
ad´ju-tant
ad´ju-tant gen´er-al
ad´ju-vant
ad—lib´
ad lib´i-tum
ad-mi-nic´u-lar
ad-min´is-ter
ad-min´is-trate
ad-min-is-tra´tion
ad-min´is-tra-tive
ad-min´is-tra-tor
ad-min´ls-tra-trlx
ad´mi-ra-ble
ad´mi-ra-bly
ad´mi-ral
ad´mi-ral-ty
ad-mi-ra´tion
ad-mire´
ad-mired´
ad-mir´er
ad-mir´ing
ad-mir´ing-ly
ad-mis-si-bil´i-ty
ad-mis´si-ble
ad-mis´sion
ad-mis´sive
ad-mit´
ad-mit´tance
ad-mit´ted
ad-mit´ted-ly
ad-mit´ting
ad-mix´ture
ad-mon´ish
ad-mon´ish-ment

ad-mo-ni´tion
ad-mon´i-to-ry
ado
ado´´be
ad-o-les´cence
ad-o-les´cent
adopt'
adopt´a-ble
adopt´er
adop´tion
adop´tive
ador´a-ble
ador´a-bly
ad-o-ra´tion
adored´
ador´er
ador´ing
adorn
adorned´
adorn´ing
adorn´ment
adown´
ad-re´nal
adrift
adroit
adroit´ly
ad-sci-ti´tious
ad-sorb´
ad-sorb´ent
ad-sorp´tion
ad-sorp´tive
ad-u-lar´ia
ad´u-iate
ad-u-la´tion
ad´u-la-to-ry
adult
adul´ter-ant
adul´ter-ate
adul-ter-a´tion
adul´ter-a-tor
adul´ter-er
adul´ter-ess
adul´ter-ous
adul´tery
adult´hood
adult´i-cide
ad-um´bral
ad-um´brant
ad´um-brate

ad va-lo´rem
ad-vance´
ad-vanced´
ad-vance´ment
ad-vanc´ing
ad-van´tage
ad-van-ta´geous
ad-van-ta´geous-ly
ad-ve´nience
ad´vent
ad-ven-ti´tious
ad-ven´tive
ad-ven´ture
ad-ven´tur-er
ad-ven´ture-some
ad-ven´tur-ess
ad-ven´tur-ous
ad´verb
ad-verb´i-al
ad´ver-sar-ies
ad´ver-sary
ad´verse
ad´verse-ly
ad-ver´si-ty
ad-vert´
ad-vert´ence
ad-vert´ent
ad-vert´ent-ly
ad´ver-tise
ad´ver-tise´ment
ad´ver-tis-er
ad´ver-tis-ing
ad-vice´
ad-vis-a-bil´i-ty
ad-vis´a-ble
ad-vise´
ad-vised´
ad-vis´ed-ly
ad-vise´ment
ad-vis´er
ad-vis´ing
ad-vi´sor
ad-vis´o-ry
ad´vo-ca-cy
ad´vo-cate
ad´vo-ca-tor
ad-voc´a-to-ry
Ae-ge´an
ae´gis

Ae-ne´as
Ae-ne´id
ae´ne-ous
Ae´o-lus
ae´on
aer´ate
aer-a´tion
aer´a-tor
aer´i-al
aer´i-al-ist
ae´rie
aer-if´er-ous
aer-i-fi-ca´tion
aer-o´bic
aero-do-net´ics
aero-dy-nam´ic
aero-dy-nam´ics
aer-og´ra-phy
aer-ol´o-gy
aer-om´e-ter
aer´o-mo-tor
aer´o-naut
aero-nau´ti-cal
aero-nau´ti-cal-ly
aero-nau´tics
aer´o-plane
aer´o-scope
aero-scop´ic
aer-os´co-py
ae´rose
aer´o-sol
aero-ther-a-peu´tics
ae-ru´gi-nous
a´ery
Aes-cu-la´pi-an
Ae´sop
aes´thete
aes-thet´ic
aes-thet´i-cal-ly
Aet´na
afar
af-fa-bil´i-ty
af´fa-ble
af´fa-bly
af-fair´
af-fect´
af-fec-ta´tion
af-fect´ed
af-fect´i-ble

af-fec´tion
af-fec´tion-ate
af-fec´tion-ate-ly
af-fec´tive
af´fer-ent
af-fi´ance
af-fi´anced
af-fi´ant
af-fi-da´vit
af-fil´i-ate
af-fil-i-a´tion
af-fin´i-ties
af-fin´i-ty
af-firm´
af-firm´a-bly
af-firm´ance
af-fir-ma´tion
af-firm´a-tive
af-firm´a-tive-ly
af-firm´a-to-ry
affix
af-fla´tus
af-flict´
af-flic´tion
af-flict´ive
af´flu-ence
af´flu-ent
af´flu-ent-ly
af-ford´
af-for-es-ta´tion
af-fray´
af´fri-cate
af-fric´a-tive
af-fright´
af-front´
af-front´ive
af-fu´sion
Af´ghan
Af-ghan´i-stan
afield´
afire
aflame
afloat
aflut´ter
afoot
afore´men-tioned
afore´said
afore´thought
a-fore´time

a for-ti-o´ri
afoul
afraid
afresh
Af´ri-ca
Af´ri-can
Af-ri-kan´der
af´ter
af´ter-birth
af´ter-burn-er
af´ter-care
af´ter-deck
af´ter-ef-fect
af´ter-glow
af´ter-life
af´ter-math
af-ter-noon´
af´ter-taste
af´ter-thought
af´ter-ward
af´ter-wards
again
against
Ag-a-mem´non
agape
a´gar
Ag´as-siz
ag´ate
ag´ate-ware
aga´ve
aged, ag´ed
age´less
a´gen-cies
a´gen-cy
agen´da
a´gent
ag-glom´er-ate
ag-glom-er-a´tion
ag-glu´ti-nant
ag-glu´ti-nate
ag-glu-ti-na´tion
ag-glu´ti-na-tive
ag-gran´dize
ag-gran´dize-ment
ag´gra-vate
ag´gra-vat-ed
ag´gra-vat-ing
ag´gra-va´tion
ag´gra-va-tor

ag´gre-gate
ag´gre-gate-ly
ag´gre-gat-ing
ag-gre-ga´tion
ag´gre-ga-tive
ag´gre-ga-to-ry
ag-gres´sion
ag-gres´sive
ag-gres´sive-ness
ag-gres´sor
ag-griev´ance
ag-grieve´
ag-grieved´
aghast´
ag´ile
ag´ile-ly
ag´ile-ness
agil´i-ty
ag´ing
ag´i-tate
ag´i-tat-ed
ag´i-tat-ed-ly
ag´i-tat-ing
ag-i-ta´tion
ag´i-ta-tive
ag´i-ta-tor
agleam´
ag´let
aglow
ag´mi-nat-ed
ag-na´tion
ag-no´men
ag-nom´i-nal
ag-no´sia
ag-nos´tic
ag-nos´ti-cal
ag-nos´ti-cal-ly
ago
agog
agon´ic
ag-o-nis´tic
ag´o-nize
ag´o-niz-ing
ag´o-ny
ag´o-ra
ag-o-ra-pho´bia
agraph´ia
agrar´i-an
agree

agree-a-bil´i-ty
agree´a-ble
agree´a-bly
agreed´
agree´ing
agree´ment
agres´tic
Agric´o-la
ag-ri-cul´tur-al
ag-ri-cul´tur-al-ist
ag´ri-cul-ture
ag-ri-cul´tur-ist
ag´ri-mo-ny
Agrip´pa
agrol-o-gy
ag-ro-nom´ic
ag-ro-nom´ics
agron´o-mist
agron´o-my
ag-ros-tol´o-gy
aground
ag-ryp-not´ic
a´gue
a´gue-weed
a´gu-ish
A´hab
ahcad
ahoy
Ai´da
aide´—de—camp
ai-grette´
ai-guille´
al-lan´thus
ai´le-ron
ail´ment
aim´less
Ai´nu
air base
air´borne
air brake
air´brush
air coach
air´—con-di´tion
air´—con-di´tioned
air´—cool
air´craft
air´drome
air´drop
Aire´dale

air ex-press´
air´field
air´foil
air force
air´freight
air hole
air´i-ly
air´i-ness
air´ing
air´less
air lift
air line
air´mail
air´man
air´—mind´ed
air-om´e-ter
air´plane
air pock´et
air´port
air pres´sure
air´proof
air pump
air raid
air ri´fle
air´ship
air´sickness
air space
air´speed
air´strip
air´tight
air´way
air well
air´wor-thy
air´y
aisle
Aix—la—Cha-pelle´
Ajac´cio
ajar
akin
Ak´ron
Al-a-bam´a
Al-a-bam´i-an
al-a-bam´ine
al´a-bas-ter
a la carte
alack
alac´ri-ty
Alad´din
a la king

Al-a-me´da
Al´a-mo
a la mode
al´a-nine
al´a-nyl
a´lar
alarm´
alarm´ing
alarm´ing-ly
alarm´ist
alar´um
a´la-ry
alas
Alas´ka
Alas´kan
Al-ba´nia
Al´ba-ny
al´ba-tross
al-be´it
Al´bert
al-bi´no
al-bi´nos
al´bo-lite
al´bum
al-bu´men
al-bu´min
al-bu´mi-nize
al-bu-mi-noi´dal
al-bu-mi-no´sis
al-bu´mi-nous
al-bu-min-u´ria
al-bu-min-u´ric
Al´bu-quer-que
al-bur´num
Al-cae´us
al-cal´de
al´ca-mine
Al´ca-traz
al-ca´zar
Al-ces´tis
al-chem´ic
al-chem´i-cal-ly
al´che-mist
al´che-my
Al-ci-bi´a-des
Al´ci-des
al´co-hol
al-co-hol´ic
al-co-hol-ic´i-ty

al´co-hol-ism
Al´cott
al´cove
al´der
al´der-man
al-der-man´ic
Al´der-ney
Al´drich
alert
alert´ly
alert´ness
Ales-san´dria
Aleut
Aleu´tian
Al-ex-an´der
Al-ex-an-dret´ta
Al-ex-an´dria
al-fal´fa
al-fres´co
al´ga
al´gae
al´ge-bra
al-ge-bra´ic
al-ge-bra´i-cal
al-ge-bra´i-cal-ly
Al-ge´ria
Al-giers´
al-go-lag´nia
al-gol´o-gy
al-gom´e-ter
al-go-met´ri-cal
Al-gon´quin
al´go-rithm
Al-ham´bra
a´li-as
A´li Ba´ba
al´i-bi
al´i-bi-ing
al-i-bil´i-ty
al´i-dade
al´ien
al´ien-a-ble
al´ien-ate
al´ien-at-ing
al´ien-a´tion
al´ien-ist
alif´er-ous
alight
align

align´ment
alike
al´i-ment
al-i-men´tal-ly
al-i-men´ta-ry
al-i-men-ta´tion
al´i-mo-ny
aline
aline´ment
al´i-ped
al´i-quant
al´i-quot
Al´i-son
alive
ali-vin´cu-lar
aliz´a-rin
al´ka-li
al-ka-lim´e-ter
al-ka-lim´e-try
al´ka-line
al-ka-lin´i-ty
al-ka-li-za´tion
al´ka-lize
al´ka-loid
al´ka-loid-al
al´ka-net
al´ke-nyl
al´kyl
al´kyl-ate
al´kyl-ene
al´kyl-ize
Al´lah
all—Amer´i-can
Al´lan
al-lan-to´ic
al-lan-toi´dal
all´—around´
al-lay´
al-lay´ing
al-le-ga´tion
al-lege´
al-lege´a-ble
al-leged´
al-leg´ed-ly
Al-le-ghe´nies
Al-le-ghe´ny
al-le´giance
al-leg´ing
al-le-gor´ic

al-le-gor´i-cal
al´le-go-ries
al´le-go-rist
al´le-go-rize
al´lego-ry
al-le´gro
al-le-lu´ia
Al´len-town
al´ler-gen
al-ler´gic
al´ler-gy
al-le´vi-ate
al-le´vi-at-ing
al-le-vi-a´tion
al-le´vi-a-tive
al´ley
al´leys
al´ley-way
al-li-a´ceous
al-li´ance
al-lied´
al-lies´
al´li-ga-tor
all´—im-por´tant
al-lit´er-ate
al-lit-er-a´tion
al-lit´er-a-tive
al´lo-ca-ble
al´lo-cate
al´lo-cat-ing
al-lo-ca´tion
al-log´a-mous
al-log´a-my
al-lot´
al-lot´ment
al-lo-troph´ic
al-lo-trop´ic
al-lot´ro-py
al-lot´ted
al-lot´ting
al-low´
al-low´a-ble
al-low´ance
al-lowed´
al-low´ed-ly
al´loy
all right
all´-spice
al-lude´

al-lure´
al-lured´
al-lure´ment
al-lur´ing
al-lu´sion
al-lu´sive
al-lu´sive-ly
al-lu´sive-ness
al-lu´vi-al
al-lu´vi-on
al-lu´vi-um
al´ly
al-ly´ing
al´lyl
al´lyl-amine´
al-lyl´ic
Al´ma
al´ma-gest
al´ma ma´ter
al´ma-nac
al-might´y
al´mond
al´mo-ner
al´most
alms´house
al´ni-co
alo´di-um
al´oe
al´oes
al´oes-ol
al-o-et´ic
aloft´
al´o-gism
alo´ha
al´o-in
alone
along
along-side´
Alon´so, Alon´zo
aloof
aloof´ness
al-o-pe´cia
aloud
al-pac´a
al´pha
al´pha-bet
al´pha-bet´ic
al´pha-bet´i-cal
al´pha-bet-ize

al´pha-nu-mer´ic
Al´phe-us
Al-phon´so
Al´pine
al-read´y
al-right´
Al´sace
Al´sace—Lor-raine´
Al-sa´tian
al´sike
al´tar
al´ter
al-ter-a-bil´i-ty
al´ter-a-ble
al´ter-a´tion
al´ter-cate
al-ter-ca´tion
al´ter e´go
al-ter´nant
al´ter-nate
al´ter-nat-ed
al´ter-nate-ly
al´ter-nat-ing
al-ter-na´tion
al-ter´na-tive
al´ter-na-tor
al-the´a
al-though´
al-tim´e-ter
al-tis´o-nant
al´ti-tude
al-ti-tu´di-nal
al-ti-tu-di-nar´i-an
al´to
al´-to-geth-er
Al´ton
Al-too´na
al´tru-ism
al´tru-ist
al-tru-is´ti-cal-ly
al´u-del
al´um
alu´mi-na
alu-mi-nif´er-ous
al-u-min´i-um
alu´mi-nize
alu´mi-nous
alu´mi-num
alum´na

alum´nae
alum´ni
alum´nus
al´u-nite
al´ways
alys´sum
a´mah
amal´gam
amal´ga-mate
amal-ga-ma´tion
amal´ga-ma-tor
Aman´da
Am-a-ril´lo
am-a-ryl´lis
amass
amass´-a-ble
amass´ment
am´a-teur
am´a-teur-ish
am´a-teur-ism
Ama´ti
am´a-tol
am´a-to-ry
am-au-ro´sis
amaze
amazed
amaz´ed-ly
amaze´ment
amaz´ing
amaz´ing-ly
Am´a-zon
Am-a-zo´ni-an
am´a-zon-ite
am-bas´sa-dor
am-bas-sa-do´ri-al
am-bas´sa-dress
am´ber
am´bi-ent
am-bi-gu´i-ty
am-big´u-ous
am-bi´tion
am-bi´tious
am-biv´a-lence
am-biv´a-lent
am´ble
am´bled
am´bling
am´bling-ly
am-blys´to-ma

Am´brose
am-bro´sia
am-bro´si-al
am´bry
am´bu-lance
am´bu-late
am´bu-la-to-ry
amb-ur´bi-al
am´bus-cade
am-bus-cad´er
am´bush
am´bushed
am´bush-er
am´bush-ment
ame´ba
Ame´lia
ame´lio-ra-ble
ame´lio-rate
ame-lio-ra´tion
ame´lio-ra-tive
ame´lio-ra-tor
a´men´
ame-na-bil´i-ty
ame´na-ble
amend
amend´a-ble
amend´ed
amend´ment
amends
amen´i-ties
amen´i-ty
Amer´i-ca
Amer´i-can
Amer´i-can´a
Amer´i-can-ism
Amer-l-can-i-za´tion
Amer´i-can-ize
am´e-thyst
am-e-trom´e-ter
am-e-tro´pia
Am´herst
ami-a-bil´i-ty
a´mi-a-ble
a´mi-a-bly
am-i-ca-bil´i-ty
am´i-ca-ble
am´i-ca-bly
am´ice
amid

am´ide
amid´ic
ami´do
ami´do-gen
amid´ships
amidst
Am´i-ens
ami´go
amine
ami´no
ami´no acid
ami-no-ben-zo´ic
Am´ish, A´mish
amiss
ami-to´sis
ami-tot´ic
am´i-ty
am´me-line
am´me-ter
am-mi-a´ceous
Am´mon
am-mo´nia
am-mo´ni-ac
am-mo´ni-ate
am-mon´ic
am´mo-nite
Am´mon-ite
am-mo´ni-um
am-mu-ni´tion
am-ne´sia
am´nes-ty
am-ni-ot´ic
amoe´ba
am-oe-bae´an
among
amongst
amor´al
amo-ral´i-ty
amor´al-ly
am´o-rous
amor´phism
amor´phous
am-or-ti-za´tion
am´or-tize
am´or-tiz-ing
A´mos
amount
amour
A´moy

am´per-age
am´pere
am´per-sand
am-phi-ar-thro´sis
Am-phib´ia
am-phib´i-an
am-phib´i-ous
am-phic´ty-on
am-phi-dip´loi-dy
am´phi-gen
am-phig´e-nous
am-phi-gor´ic
am´phi-go-ry
am-phip´o-da
am´phi-the-a-ter
am-phi-the´ci-um
Am´phi-tri-te
am´pho-ra
am´ple
am´ple-ness
am-pli-fi-ca´tion
am´pli fied
am´pli-fi-er
am´pli-fy
am´pli-fy-ing
am´pli-tude
am´ply
am´poule
am-pul´la
am´pu-tate
am´pu-tat-ed
am´pu-tat-ing
am-pu-ta´tion
am´pu-tee´
am-ri´ta
Am-rit´sar
Am´ster-dam
amuck
am´u-let
A´mund-sen
amus´a-ble
amuse
amused´
amus´ed-ly
amuse´ment
amu´sia
amus´ing
amus´ive
A´my

anach´ro-nism
anach-ro-nis´tic
anach´ro-nous-ly
an-a-clas´tic
an-a-con´da
Anac´re-on
an-aer-o´bia
an-aer-o´bic
an-aes-the´sia
an-a-glyph´ic
anag´ly-phy
an-a-glyp´tics
an-a-gog´i-cal
an´a-gram
an-a-gram-mat´ic
a´nal
an-al-ge´sia
an-al-ge´sic
an´a-log
an-a-log´i-cal
an-a-log´i-cal-ly
anal´o-gies
anal´o-gist
anal´o-gous
an´a-logue
anal´o-gy
anal´y-ses
anal´y-sis
an´a-lyst
an-a-lyt´ic
an-a-lyt´i-cal
an-a-lyt´i-cal-ly
an´a-lyze
an´a-lyz-ing
an-am-ne´sis
an-a-mor´pho-sis
an-an´drous
An-a-ni´as
an-a-paes´tic
anaph´o-ra
an-aph-ro-dis´i-ac
an-a-phy-lax´is
an´a-plas-ty
an-ap-tot´ic
an´arch
an-ar´chic
an-ar´chi-cal
an´ar-chism
an´ar-chist

an-ar-chis´tic
an´ar-chy
An-a-to´lia
an-a-tom´i-cal
anat´o-mist
anat´o-mize
anat´o-my
anat´ro-pous
an´ces-tor
an-ces´tral
an´ces-tress
anlces-try
An-chi´ses
an´chor
an´chor-age
an´cient
an´cient-ly
an´cil-lary
an´con
An-co´na
an-co´ne-al
an-cy-lo-sto-mi´a-sis
An-da-lu´sia
An´da-man
an-dan´te
An-de´an
An´der-sen
An´der-son
An´des
an´de-site
and´i-ron
An-dor´ra
An´do-ver
An-dre´
An´drew
An´drews
An´dro-clus
an-droe´ci-um
an´dro-gen
an-drog´y-nous
An-drom´a-che
An-drom´e-da
An´dros
an´dro-sin
an´ec-dot-al
an´ec-dote
an-ec-dot´ic
an-ec-dot´i-cal
an´ec-dot-ist

ane´mia
ane´mic
an-e-mo-log´i-cal
an-e-mom´e-ter
anem´o-ne
an-e-moph´i-lous
an-e-mo´sis
anent
an´er-oid
an-es-the´sia
an-es-the-si-ol´o-gist
an-es-thet´ic
anes´the-tist
anes´the-tize
aneu´ria
an´eu-rysm
anew
an-frac-tu-os´i-ty
an´ga-ry
an´gel
An´ge-la
an-gel´ic
an-gel´i-ca
an-gel´i-cal
an-gel´i-cal-ly
An´gell
An´ge-lo
An´ge-lus
an´ger
An´ge-vin
an-gi´na
an-gi´na pec´to-ris
an-gi-o-cyst
an-gi-o´ma
an-gi-om´a-tous
an-gi-op´-a-thy
an´gi-o-sperm
an´gi-o-sper´mous
an-gi-os´to-my
Ang´kor
an´gle
an´gler
an-gle-worm
An´gli-can
an´gli-cism
an-gli-ci-za´tion
an´gli-cize
an´gling
An´glo—Amer´i-can

An´glo-phile
An´glo—Sax´on
An-go´la
Am-go´ra
an´gri-ly
an´gri-ness
an´gry
ang´strom
An-guil´la
an´guish
an´guished
an´gu-lar
an-gu-lar´i-ty
An´gus
an-hi-dro´sis
An´hwei´
an´ile
an´i-lide
an´i-line
anil´i-ty
an´i-mate
an´i-mat-ed
an´i-mat-ing
an-i-ma´tion
an´i-mism
an-i-mos´i-ty
an´ion
an´ise
an´i-seed
An-jou´
an´kle
an´klet
an-ky-lo´sis
an-ky-los´to-ma
an´nal
an´nal-ist
an-nal-is´tic
an´nals
An´nam
An-nap´o-lis
Ann Ar´bor
an-neal´
an-nealed´
an´ne-lid
An-nette´
an-nex´
an-nex´a-ble
an-nex-a´tion
an-ni´hi-la-ble

an-ni´hi-late
an-ni-hi-la´tion
an-ni´hi-la-tor
An´nis-ton
an-ni-ver´sa-ries
an-ni-ver´sa-ry
An´no Dom´i-ni
an´no-tate
an-no-ta´tion
an´no-ta-tor
an-nounce´
an-nounce´ment
an-nounc´er
an-nounc´ing
an-noy´
an-noy´ance
an-noyed´
an´nu-al
an-nu´i-tant
an-nu´i-ty
an-nul´
an´nu-lar
an-nu-lar´i-ty
an´nu-let
an-nulled´
an-nul´ling
an-nul´ment
an-nun´ci-ate
an-nun-ci-a´tion
an-nun´ci-a-tor
an´ode
an´o-dyne
anoint
anoint´ed
anoint´er
anoint´ment
anom´a-lism
anom-a-lis´tic
anom´a-lous
anom´a-lous-ly
an´o-nym
an-o-nym´i-ty
anon´y-mous
anon´y-mous-ly
Anoph´e-les
an-oth´er
An´schluss
an´ser-ine
an´swer

an´swer-a-ble
ant-ac´id
An-tae´us
an-tag´o-nism
an-tag´o-nist
an-tag-o-nis´tic
an-tag´o-nize
Ant-arc´tic
Ant-arc´ti-ca
An-tar´es
an´te
ant´eat-er
an´te-bel´lum
an-te-ced´ent
an´te-cham-ber
an´te-date
an-te-di-lu´vi-an
an´te-lope
an´te me-rid´i-em
an-ten´na
an-te-pen´di-um
an-te-pe´nult
an-te-pe-nul´ti-mate
an-te´ri-or
an´te-room
ant-he´li-on
ant-hel-min´tic
an´them
an-the´mi-on
an´ther
an´ther-al
an-ther-id´i-um
an-the´sis
an-tho-cy´a-nin
an-tho´di-um
an-thog´e-nous
an-tho-log´i-cal
an-thol´o-gist
an-thol´o-gize
an-thol´o-gy
An´tho-ny
an´tho-taxy
an´thra-cene
an´thra-ces
an´thra-cite
an-thra-qui-none´
an-thra-qui-no´nyl
an´thrax
an-thro-po-gen´e-sis

an-thro-pog´e-ny
an-thro-pog´ra-phy
an´thro-poid
an-thro-po-log´i-cal
an-thro-pol´o-gist
an-thro-pol´o-gy
an-thro-pom´e-ter
an-thro-po-met´ric
an-thro-pom´e-try
an-thro-po-morph´ic
an´ti-air´craft
an-ti-bi-ot´ic
an´ti-bod-ies
an´ti-body
an-ti-cat´a-lyst
an-ti-cath´ode
an´ti-chlor
An´ti-christ
an-tic´i-pant
an-tic´i-pate
an-tic´i-pat-ed
an-tic´i-pat-ing
an-tic-i-pa´tion
an-tic´i-pa-tive
an-tic´i-pa-to-ry
an-ti-cler´i-cal
an ti-cli´max
an-ti-cli-no´ri-um
an-ti-cy´clone
an-ti-cy-clon´ic
an´ti-dot-al
an´ti-dote
an-ti-drom´ic
An-tie´tam
an´ti-freeze
An-ti´gua
an-ti-he´lix
an-ti-his´ta-mine
An-til´les
an-ti-log´a-rithm
an-til´o-gism
an-til´o-gy
an-ti-mis´sile
An´ti-och
An-ti´o-chus
an-ti-pas´to
an-ti-pa-thet´ic
an-ti-pa-thet´i-cal
an-tip´a-thy

an-ti-phlo-gis´tic
an´ti-phon
an-tiph´o-nal
an-tiph´o-nary
an-tiph´ra-sis
an-tip´o-dal
an´ti-pode
an-tip-o-de´an
an-tip´o-des
an-ti-quar´i-an
an´ti-quary
an´ti-quate
an´ti-quat-ed
an´ti-quat-ing
an-tique´
an-tiq´ui-ty
an-ti—Sem´i-tism
an-ti-sep´sis
an-ti-sep´tic
an-ti-se´rum
an-ti-slav´ery
an-ti-so´cial
an-tith´e-sis
an-ti-thet´ic
an-ti-tox´in
an-ti-tra´gus
an-ti-trust´
an-ti-typ´ic
an-ti-typ´i-cal
ant´ler
ant´lered
An-toi-nette´
An-to´nia
An-to´nio
An´to-ny
an´to-nym
ant´proof
An´trim
Ant´werp
an-u´rous
an´vil
anx-i´e-ty
anx´ious
anx´ious-ly
an´y
an´y-body
an´y-how
an´y-one
an´y-place

an´y-thing
an´y-way
an´y-where
aor´ta
aor´tic
apace
Apach´e
Ap-a-lach-i-co´la
apart
apart´heid
apart´ment
ap-a-tet´ic
ap-a-thet´ic
ap-a-thet´i-cal-ly
ap´a-thy
ape´like
ape´ri-ent
ape-ri-od´ic
aper-i-tif´
ap´er-ture
a´pex
aph´a-nite
aph-a-nit´ic
apha´sia
apha´si-ac
apha´sic
a´phid
A´phis
aphlo-gis´tic
apho´nia
aphon´ic
aph´o-rism
aph-o-ris´tic
apho´tic
aphra´sia
aph-ro-dis´i-ac
Aph-ro-di´te
a´pi-an
api-ar´i-an
a´pi-ary
ap´i-cal
ap´i-ces
apiece
ap´ish
ap´ish-ly
apiv´o-rous
ap-la-nat´ic
aplen´ty
aplomb

ap´nea
apoc´a-lypse
apoc-a-lyp´tic
Apoc´ry-pha
apoc´ry-phal
Ap´o-des
apod´o-sis
Apol´lo
apol-o-get´ic
ap-o-lo´gia
apol´o-gies
apol´o-gize
apol´o-gy
ap-o-neu-ro´sis
ap-o-phyl´lite
ap-o-plec´tic
ap-o-plec´ti-cal
ap´o-plexy
ap-o-si-o-pe´sis
apos´ta-sy
apos´tate
apos´ta-tize
apos-te-ri-o´ri
apos´tle
apos´tle-ship
apos´to-late
ap-os-tol´ic
ap-os-tol´i-cal
ap-os-tol´i-cism
apos-to-lic´i-ty
apos´tro-phe
ap-os-troph´ic
apos´tro-phize
apoth´e-car-ies
apoth´e-cary
Ap-pa-la´chi-an
ap-pall´
ap-palled´
ap-pall´ing
ap´pa-nage
ap-pa-rat´us
ap-par´el
ap-par´eled
ap-par´ent
ap-pa-ri´tion
ap-peal´
ap-peal´a-ble
ap-pealed´
ap-peal´er

ap-peal´ing
ap-pear´
ap-pear´ance
ap-peared´
ap-pear´ing
ap-peas´a-ble
ap-pease´
ap-pease´ment
ap-peas´er
ap-peas´ing
ap-peas´ing-ly
ap-pel´lant
ap-pel´late
ap-pel-la´tion
ap-pel´la-tive
ap-pend´
ap-pend´age
ap-pend´aged
ap-pend´an-cy
ap-pend´ant
ap-pen-dec´to-my
ap-pend´ed
ap-pen´di-cal
ap-pen-di-ci´tis
ap-pen-dic´u-lar
ap-pen´dix
ap-per-ceive´
ap-per-cep´tion
ap-per-cep´tive
ap´pe-tite
ap´pe-tiz-er
ap´pe-tiz-ing
Ap´pi-an
ap-plaud´er
ap-plaud´ing
ap-plause´
ap´ple
ap´ple-sauce
Ap´ple-ton
ap-pli´ance
ap-pli-ca-bil´i-ty
ap´pli-ca-ble
ap´pli-cant
ap´pli-ca´tion
ap´pli-ca-tive
ap-plied´
ap-pli´er
ap-pli-que´
ap-ply´

ap-ply´ing
ap-point´
ap-point´a-ble
ap-point´ed
ap-poin-tee´
ap-point´er
ap-point´ing
ap-point´ment
Ap-po-mat´tox
ap-por´tion
ap-por´tioned
ap-por´tion-er
ap-por´tion-ment
ap´po-site
ap-po-si´tion
ap-pos´i-tive
ap-prais´a-ble
ap-prais´al
ap-praise´
ap-praised´
ap-praise´ment
ap-prais´er
ap-prais´ing
ap-prais´ing-ly
ap-pre´cia-ble
ap-pre´ci-ate
ap-pre´ci-at-ed
ap-pre´ci-at-ing
ap-pre-ci-a´tion
ap-pre´cia-tive-ly
ap-pre´cia-to-ry
ap-pre-hend´
ap-pre-hend´ed
ap-pre-hend´ing
ap-pre-hen-si-bil´i-ty
ap-pre-hen´si-ble
ap-pre-hen´sion
ap-pre-hen´sive
ap-pren´tice
ap-pren´ticed
ap-pren´tice-ship
ap-prise´
ap-prised´
ap-pris´ing
ap-proach´
ap-proach-a-bil´i-ty
ap-pro-ba´tion
ap´pro-ba-tive
ap´pro-ba-tive-ness

ap-pro´pri-ate
ap-pro´pri-at-ed
ap-pro´pri-at-ly
ap-pro´pri-ate-ness
ap-pro´pri-at-ing
ap-pro-pri-a´tion
ap-prov´a-ble
ap-prov´al
ap-prove´
ap-proved
ap-prov´ing
ap-prov´ing-ly
ap-prox´i-mate
ap-prox´i-mat-ed
ap-prox´i-mate-ly
ap-prox´i-mat´ing
ap-prox-i-ma´tion
ap-pur´te-nance
ap-pur´te-nant
a´pri-cot
A´pril
a´pron
apse
ap´sis
Ap´tera
ap´ter-al
ap tc´ri-um
ap´ter-ous
ap´ti-tude
apt´ly
apt´ness
Apu´lia
aq´ua
aq´ua-lung
aq-ua-ma-rine´
aq´ua-plane
aq´ua-relle
aquar´i-um
Aquar´i-us
aquat´ic
aq´ue-duct
a´que-ous
Aq´ui-la
aq´ui-line
Aqui´nas
Aq´ui-taine
Aq-ui-ta´nia
Ar´ab
ar-a-besque´

Ara´bia
Ar´a-bic
Ar´ab-ist
Arach´ne
arach´noid
Ar´a-gon
Ar´al
Arap´a-ho
Ar´a-rat
ar´ba-lest
ar´bi-ter
ar´bi-tra-ble
ar´bi-trage
ar´bi-trag-er
ar´bi-tral
ar-bit´ra-ment
ar´bi-trar-i-ly
ar´bi-trary
ar´bi-trate
ar´bi-trat-ed
ar´bi-trat-ing
ar-bi-tra´tion
ar´bi-tra-tive
ar´bi-tra-tor
ar´bi-tress
ar´bor
ar-bo´re-al
ar-bo-res´cent
ar-bo-re´tum
ar´bo-rize
ar´bor-ous
ar´bor-vi´tae
ar-bu´tus
ar-cade´
Ar-ca´dia
Ar-ca´di-an
ar-chae-ol´o-gy
ar-cha´ic
ar-cha´i-cal-ly
ar´cha-ist
ar-cha-is´tic
art-cha-ism
arch´an´gel
arch´bish´op
arch-bish´op-ric
arch´dea´con
arch´di´o-cese
arch´du´cal
arch´duch´ess

arch´duch´y
arch´duke´
Ar-che´an
arched
arch´en´e-my
arch´er
arch´ery
arch´fiend´
Ar´chi-bald
Ar-chi-me´de-an
ar-chi-pel´a-go
ar´chi-tect
ar-chi-tec´tur-al
ar´chi-tec-ture
ar´chi-trave
ar-chi´val
ar´chive
ar´chi-vist
arch´way
arc´ing
Arc´tic
Arc´tic Cir´cle
ar´dent
ar´dent-ly
ar´dor
ar´du-ous
ar´du-ous-ly
ar´ea
ar´e-al
ar´ea-way
are´o-la
Ar-e-op´a-gus
A´res
Ar-gen-ti´na
Ar´gen-tine
ar´gil
Ar´give
Ar´go-lis
Ar´go-naut
Ar-gonne´
Ar´gos
ar´go-sy
ar´gue
ar´gu-ment
ar-gu-men-ta´tion
ar-gu-men´ta-tive
Ar´gus
Ar´gyle
Ar´gyll

a´ria
ar´id
arid´i-ty
Ar´i-el
A´ri-es
aright
arise
aris´en
aris´ing
Ar-is´ti-des
ar-is-toc´ra-cy
aris´to-crat
aris-to-crat´ic
Ar-is-toph´a-nes
Ar´is-tot-le
aris´to-type
arith´me-tic
ar-ith-met´i-cal
arith-me-ti´cian
Ar-i-zo´na
Ar´kan-sas
Ar´ling-ton
ar-ma´da
ar-ma-dil´lo
Ar-ma-ged´don
ar´ma-ment
ar´ma-ture
arm´chair
Ar-me´nia
Ar-me´ni-an
Ar-men-tieres´
arm´ful
arm´hole
ar´mies
ar´mi-stice
arm´let
ar´mor
ar´mored
ar´mor-er
ar´mo-ry
arm´pit
Arm´strong
ar´my
ar´ni-ca
Ar´nold
aro´ma
ar-o-mat´ic
arose
around

arous´al
arouse
arous´ing
ar-peg´gio
ar-raign´
ar-raign´ment
ar-range´
ar-range´ment
ar-rang´er
ar-rang´ing
ar´ras
ar-ray´
ar-rear´
ar-rest´
ar-rest´ed
ar-rest´er
ar-res´tive
ar-res´tor
ar-rive´
ar-riv´ing
ar´ro-gance
ar´ro-gan-cy
ar´ro-gant
ar´ro-gate
ar´ro-gat-ing
ar-ro-ga´tion
ar´row
ar´row-head
ar´row-root
ar´roy´o
ar´se-nal
ar´se-nate
ar´se-nic
ar´son
ar´son-ist
Ar´te-mis
ar-te´ri-al
ar´ter-ies
ar-te-ri-o-scle-ro´sis
ar´tery
ar-te´sian
art´ful
art´ful-ly
ar-thrit´ic
ar-thri´tis
ar´thro-pod
Ar-throp´o-da
ar-throp´o-dal
Ar´thur

Ar-thu´ri-an
ar´ti-choke
ar´ti-cle
ar-tic´u-lar
ar-tic´u-late
ar-tic´u-lat-ed
art´i-er
ar´ti-fact
ar´ti-fice
ar-tif´i-cer
ar-ti-fi´cial
ar-ti-fi-ci-al´i-ty
ar-ti-fi´cial-ly
ar-til´ler-ist
ar-til´lery
ar-til´lery-man
ar´ti-san
art´ist
ar-tiste´
ar-tis´tic
ar-tis´ti-cal
ar-tis´ti-cal-ly
ar´tist-ry
art´less
art´y
Ar´un-del
Ar´yan
as-bes´tos
As´bury
as-cend´
as-cend´an-cy
as-cend´ant
as-cend´ing
as-cen´sion
as-cent´
as-certain´
as-cer-tain´a-ble
as-cer-tain´ment
as-cet´ic
as-cet´i-cism
As´cham
ascor´bic
as-co-spor´ic
As´cot
as-cribe´
as-crib´ing
as-crip´tion
asep´sis
asep´tic

asex´u-al
asex-u-al´i-ty
As´gard
ashamed
asham´ed-ly
ash´en
Ashe´ville
ashore
ash´y
A´sia
A´sia Mi´nor
aside
as´i-nine
askance´
askew´
aslant´
asleep´
as-par´a-gus
as´pect
as´pen
as-per´i-ty
as-perse´
as-per´sion
as-per-so´ri-um
as´phalt
as´pho-del
as-phyx´ia
as-phyx´i-ate
as-phyx´i-at-ing
as-phyx-i-a´tion
as´pic
as-pi-dis´tra
as´pi-rant
as´pi-rate
as-pi-ra´tion
as´pi-ra-tor
as-pir´a-to-ry
as-pire´
as´pi-rin
as-pir´ing
as-pir´ing-ly
As-ple´ni-um
as-sail´
as-sail´a-ble
as-sail´ant
As-sam´
as-sas´sin
as-sas´si-nate
as-sas-si-na´tion

as-sas´si-na-tor
as-sault´
as´say
as-sem´bla-ble
as-sem´blage
as-sem´ble
as-sem´bling
as-sem´bly
as-sem´bly-man
as-sent´
as-sent´er
as-sert´
as-sert´er
as-ser´tion
as-ser´tive
as-ser´tor
as-ser´to-ry
as-sess´
as-sess´a-ble
as-sess´ment
ar´ses´sor
as´set
as-sev´er-ate
as-sev-er-a´tion
as-si-du´i-ty
as-sid´u-ous
as-sign´
as-sign-a-bil´i-ty
as-sign´a-ble
as-sig-na´tion
as-sign-ee´
as-sign´ment
as-sim´i-late
as-sim´i-lat-ing
as-sim-i-la´tion
as-sim´i-la-tive
as-sim´i-la-tor
as-sim´i-la-to-ry
as-sist´
as-sist´ance
as-sist´ant
as-sist´ed
as-sist´er
as-sist´ing
as-sis´tor
as-so´cia-ble
as-so´ci-ate
as-so´ci-at-ing
as-so-ci-a´tion

as-so´cia-tive
as-sort´
as-sort´ed
as-sort´ment
as-suage´
as-suage´ment
as-suag´ing
as-sua´sive
as-sum´a-ble
as-sum´a-bly
as-sume´
as-sum´ed-ly
as-sum´er
as-sum´ing
as-sump´tion
as-sur´ance
as-sure´
as-sured´
as-sur´ed-ly
as-sur´ed-ness
as-sur´ing
as-sur´gent
As-syr´ia
as´ter
as´ter-isk
astern
as´ter-oid
as´ter-oi´dal
asth´ma
asth-mat´ic
asth-mat´i-cal
astig´ma-tism
astir´
as-ton´ish
as-ton´ished
as-ton´ish-ing
as-ton´ish-ment
As´tor
As-to´ria
as-tound´
as-tound´ed
as-tound´ing
astrad´dle
as´tral
astray´
astride´
as-trin´gen-cy
as-trin´gent
as´tro-labe

as-trol´o-ger
as-tro-log´i-cal
as-trol´o-gy
as-trom´e-try
as´tro-naut
as-tron´o-mer
as-tro-nom´ic
as-tro-nom´i-cal
as-tro-nom´i-cal-ly
as-tron´o-my
as-tro-phys´i-cal
as-tro-phys´i-cist
as-tro-phys´ics
as-tute´
as-tute´ly
as-tute´ness
asun´der
asy´lum
asym-met´ric
asym-met´ri-cal
asym-met´ri-cal-ly
asym´me-try
as´ymp-tote
asyn-ap´sis
asyn´chro-nism
as-yn-det´i-cal-ly
asyn´de-ton
asys´to-le
at´a-bal
At-a-lan´ta
at´a-vic
at´a-vism
at´a-vist
at-a-vis´ti-cal-ly
atax´ia
atax´ic
Atch´i-son
ate-lier´
a´the-ism
a´the-ist
athe-is´tic
athe-is´ti-cal
athe-is´ti-cal-ly
Athe´na
Ath´ens
athirst´
ath´lete
ath-let´ic
ath-let´ics

Ath´os
athrep´sia
athwart´
atilt´
At-lan´tic
At´las
at´mo-sphere
at-mo-spher´ic
at-mo-spher´i-cal
at-mo-spher´i-cal-ly
at´oll
at´om
atom´ic
atom´i-cal
at-o-mic´i-ty
at´om-ize
at´om-iz-eraton´al
ato-nal´i-ty
atone
atone´ment
aton´ing
atop
a´tri-um
atro´cious
atro´cious-ly
atroc´i-ty
at´ro-phied
at´ro-phy
atrop´ic
at´ro-pine
At´ro-pos
at-tach´
at-tach´a-ble
at-ta-che´
at-tached´
at-tach´ment
at-tack´
at-tacked´
at-tack´er
at-tain´
at-tain-a-bil´i-ty
at-tain´a-ble
at-tain´a-ble-ness
at-tain´der
at-tain´er
at-tain´ment
at-taint´
at´tar
at-tempt´

at-tempt´a-ble
at-tempt´er
at-tend´
at-tend´ance
at-tend´ant
at-ten´tion
at-ten´tive
at-ten´tive-ly
at-ten´u-ate
at-ten-u-a´tion
at-test´
at-tes-ta´tion
at´tic
At´ti-ca
At´ti-la
at-tire´
at-tir´ing
at´ti-tude
at-ti-tu´di-nize
at-tor´ney
at-tor´ney gen´er-al
at-tract´
at-tract-a-bil´i-ty
at-tract´a-ble
at-tract´a-ble-ness
at-trac´tion
at-tract´ive
at-tract´ive-ly
at-trac´tor
at´tri-bute
at-tri-bu´tion
at-trib´u-tive
at-tri´tion
at-tune´
at-tun´ing
atyp´i-cal
au´burn
auc´tion
auc-tion-eer´
au-da´cious
au-dac´i-ty
au´di-ble
au´di-bly
au´di-ence
au´dio
au´dit
au-di´tion
au´di-tor
au-di-to´ri-um

au´di-to-ry
Au´du-bon
au´ger
aug-ment´
au gra´tin
Augs-burg
au´gur
au´gu-ry
Au´gust
Au-gus´ta
Au´gus-tine, Au-
  gus´tine
Au-gus´tus
auk
auld lang syne
au´ra
au´ral
au´re-ate
Au-re´lla
au´re-ole
Au-re-o-my´cin
au re-voir´
au´ri-cle
au´ri-cled
au-ric´u-lar
au-rif´er-ous
au-ro´ra
au-ro´ra bo-re-al´is
aus´oul tate
aus-cul-ta´tion
aus´pice
aus-pi´cious
aus-pi´cious-ly
aus-tere´
aus-ter´i-ty
Aus´ter-litz
Aus´tin
Aus-tra-la´sia
Aus-tra´lia
Aus´tria
au-then´tic
au-then´ti-cal-ly
au-then´ti-cate
au-then-ti-ca´tion
au-then-tic´i-ty
au´thor
au-thor-i-tar´i-an
au-thor´i-ta-tive
au-thor´i-ty

au-tho-ri-za´tion
au´tho-rize
au´tho-rized
au´tho-riz-ing
au´thor-ship
au´tism
au´to
au-to-bi-og´ra-pher
au-to-bi-o-graph´ic
au-to-bi-o-graph´i-cal
au-to-bi-og´ra-phy
au-toc´ra-cy
au´to-crat
au-to-crat´ic
au-to-crat´i-cal-ly
au´to—da—fé´
au-to-gen´ic
au´to-graph
au-tog´ra-pher
au-to-graph´ic
au-tog´ra-phy
au-to-ki-net´ic
au´to-mat
au-to-mat´ic
au-to-mat´i-cal
au-to-mat´i-cal-ly
au-to-ma´tion
au-tom´a-tism
au-tom´a-ton
au-to-mo-bile´
au-to-mo-bil´ist
au-to-mo´tive
au-ton´o-mous
au-ton´o-my
au´top-sy
au-to-sug-ges´tion
au´tumn
au-tum´nal
Au-vergne´
aux-il´ia-ry
avail
avail-a-bil´i-ty
avail´a-ble
availed´
av´a-lanche
Av´a-lon
avant´—garde´
av´a-rice
av-a-ri´cious

av-a-ri´cious-ly
av´a-tar
a´ve
A´ve Ma-ri´a
avenge
avenged
aveng´er
aveng´ing
Av´en-tine
av´e-nue
aver
av´er-age
averred´
aver´ring
averse
aver´sion
avert
avert´ed
a´vi-ary
a´vi-ate
avi-a´tion
a´vi-a-tor
avi-a´trix
av´id
avid´i-ty
av´id-ly
Avi-gnon´
A´vis
av-o-ca´do
av-o-ca´dos
av-o-ca´tion
avoid
avoid´a-ble
avoid´ance
avoid´ed
av-oir-du-pois´
A´von
avouch
avow
avow´al
avowed
avun´cu-lar
a´wait´
awake
awaked
awak´en
awak´en-ing
award
award´ed

aware
aware´ness
awash
away
awe
awea´ry
aweigh
awe´some
awe´stricken
awe´struck
aw´ful
aw´ful-ly
awhile
awk´ward
awk´ward-ly
awk´ward-ness
awl
aw´ning
awoke
awry
ax
ax´es
ax´il-lary
ax´i-om
ax-i-o-mat´ic
ax-i-o-mat´i-cal
ax-i-o-mat´i-cal-ly
ax´is
ax´le
ax-om´e-ter
aye
Ayr´shire
aza´lea
az-i-mi´no
az´i-muth
Azores
Az´tec
az´ure

### B

Ba´al
bab´bitt
bab´ble
bab´bler
bab´bling
Ba´bel
ba´bied
ba´bies

ba-boon´
ba´by
ba´by-hood
ba´by-ing
ba´by-ish
Bab´y-lon
Bab-y-lo´nia
Bab-y-lo´ni-an
bac-ca-lau´re-ate
bac´ca-rat
bac´cha-nal
bac-cha-na´lian
bac-chant´
bac-chant´e
Bac´chus
bach´e-lor
bach´e-lor-hood
bac´il-lary
ba-cil´li
ba-cil´lus
bac-i-tra´cin
back´ache
back´bite
back´bit-ing
back´bone
back´break-ing
back door
back´drop
back´er
back´field
back´fire
back´gam-mon
back´ground
back´hand
back´hand-ed
back´ing
back´lash
back´log
back´side
back´slide
back´slid-ing
back´stage´
back´stairs
back´stop
back´stroke
back´talk
back´track
back´ward
back´ward-ness

back´wash
back´wat-er
back-woods´
back-woods´man
back-yard´
ba´con
bac-te´ria
bac-te´ri-al
bac-te´ri-cide
bac´ter-id
bac-te-ri-o-log´i-cal
bac-te-ri-ol´o-gist
bac-te-ri-ol´o-gy
bac-te´rio-phage
bac-te´ri-um
badge
badg´er
bad-i-nage´
bad´ly
bad´min-ton
Bae´de-ker
baf´fle
baf´fler
baf´fling
bag´a-telle´
bag´gage
bag´gage-man
bag´gage room
bag´gy
Bagh´dad
ba´gnio
bag´pipe
bag´piper
ba-guette´
Ba-ha´i
Ba-ha´ma
Ba-hi´a
Bah-rain´
bai´liff
bai´li-wick
bail´ment
bails´man
bait
Ba´ke-lite
bak´er
bak´ery
bak´ing
Ba´laam
bal´ance

bal´anc-er
bal´anc-ing
Bal-bo´a
bal-brig´gan
bal´co-nies
bal´co-ny
bal´der-dash
bald´ness
bal´dric
Bald´win
baled
ba-leen´
bale´ful
Bal´four
Ba´li
balk
Bal´kan
balk´i-er
balk´ing
balk´y
bal´lad
bal-lade´
bal´lad-ry
bal´last
ball bear´ing
bal-le-ri´na
bal´let
bal-lis´tic
bal-lis-ti´cian
bal-lis´tics
bal´lo-net´
bal-loon´
bal-loon´ist
bal´lot
bal´lot box
ball´play-er
ball´room
bal´ly-hoo
balm
balm´i-ly
balm´i-ness
Bal-mor´al
balm´y
ba-lo´ney
bal´sa
bal´sam
Bal´tic
Bal´ti-more
Bal-zac´

bam-bi´no
bam-boo´
bam-boo´zle
bam-boo´zler
ban
ba´nal
ba-nal´i-ty
ba-nan´a
Ban´croft
ban´dage
ban´dag-ing
ban-dan´na
ban´dit
ban´dit-ry
ban-dit´ti
band´mas-ter
ban´do-leer´
bands´man
band´stand
band´wag-on
ban´dy
ban´dy-ing
ban´dy—leg-ged
bane´ful
Bang´kok
Ban-gla-desh´
ban´gle
Ban´gor
ban´ish
ban´ish-ment
ban´is-ter
ban´jo
bank´ ac-count
bank´book
bank´ draft
bank´er
bank´ing
bank´note
bank´rupt
bank´rupt-cy
banned
ban´ner
ban´quet
ban´quet-er
Ban´quo
ban´shee
ban´tam
ban´tam-weight
ban´ter

ban´ter-ing-ly
Ban´tu
ban´yan
ban-zai´
ba´o-bab
bap´tism
bap´tis´mal
Bap´tist
bap´tis-tery
bap-tize´
bap-tized´
bap-tiz´ing
Bar-ab´bas
Bar-ba´dos
Bar´ba-ra
bar-bar´i-an
bar-bar´ic
bar´ba-rism
bar-bar´i-ty
bar´ba-rize
Bar-ba-ros´sa
bar´ba-rous
Bar´ba-ry
bar´be-cue
barbed
barbed wire
bar´ber
bar´ber-ry
bar´ber-shop
bar´bi-tal
bar-bi´tu-rate
bar-bi-tu´ric
Bar´bi-zon
bar´ca-role
Bar-ce-lo´na
bare
bare´back
bared
bare´faced
bare´foot
bare´—hand-ed
bare´head-ed
bare´ly
bar´gain
bar´gain-er
barge
barge ca-nal´
barge´mas-ter
bar´i-tone

bar´i-um
bar´keep-er
bar´ken-tine
bark´er
bark´ing
bar´ley
bar´ley-corn
bar´maid
bar´man
Bar´na-bas
bar´na-cle
barn´dance
barn´storm-er
barn´storm-ing
Bar´num
barn´yard
bar´o-graph
ba-rom´e-ter
bar-o-met´ric
bar-o-met´ro-graph
bar´on
bar´on-age
bar´on-ess
bar-on-et´
bar-on-et´age
bar´on-et-cy
bar´ony
ba-roque´
bar´racks
bar-ra-cu´da
bar-rage´
barred
bar´rel
bar´ren
bar´ren-ness
bar-rette´
bar´ri-cade
bar´ri-cad´ing
bar´ri-er
bar´ring
bar´ris-ter
bar´room
bar´row
bar´tender
bar´ter
Bar-thol´o-mew
Ba-ruch´
ba´sal
ba´sal-ly

ba-salt´
base
base´ball
base´board
base´ hit
Ba´sel
base´less
base´ line
base´ly
base´ment
bash´ful
bash´ful-ness
ba´sic
ba´si-cal-ly
bas´il
ba-sil´i-ca
ba-sil´i-can
bas´i-lisk
ba´sin
ba´sis
bask
bas´ket
bas´ket-ball
bas´ket-ry
bas´ket-work
Basque
Bas´ra
bas´—re-lief´
bass
bas´set
bas-si-net´
bas´so
bas-soon´
bass´wood
bas´tard
bas´tardy
baste
bas-tille´
bast´ing
Ba-ta´via
bate
bat´fish
bath
bathe
bath´er
bath´ing
bath´robe
bath´room
Bath-she´ba

bath´y-sphere
ba-tik´
ba-tiste´
ba-ton´
Bat´on Rouge
bat-tal´ion
bat´ten
bat´ter
bat´ter-ies
bat´ter-ing
bat´tery
bat´tle
bat´tle cruis´er
bat´tle cry
bat´tle-field
bat´tle-ground
bat´ty
Ba-tum´
bau´ble
baux´ite
Ba-var´ia
bawd´y
bawl
Ba-yeux´
bay´o-net
Ba-yonne´
bay´ou
Bay´reuth
ba-zaar´
ba-zoo´ka
beach
beach´comb-er
beach´head
bea´con
bead´ed
bead´ing
bead´y
bea´gle
beaked
beak´er
beamed
beam´ing
bear
bear´able
beard´ed
beard´less
bear´er
bear´ing
bear´ish

bé-ar-naise´
bear´skin
beast´ly
beat´en
beat´er
be-at´i-fied
be-at´i-fy
beat´ing
be-at´i-tude
beau
Beau´fort
beau geste
Beau-mar-chais´
Beau´mont
Beau´re-gard
beau´te-ous
beau´ties
beau´ti-fi-ca´tion
beau´ti-fied
beau´ti-fi-er
beau´ti-ful
beau´ti-ful-ly
beau´ti-fy
beau´ti-fy-ing
beau´ty
beaux
beaux arts
bea´ver
be-calm´
be-cause´
Beck´et
beck´on
beck´on-ing
be-cloud´
be-come´
be-com´ing
be-daub´
be-daze´
be-daz´zle
be-daz´zling
bed´bug
bed´clothes
be-deck´
be-dev´il
be-dev´il-ment
be-dew´
bed´fast
bed´fel-low
Bed´ford

bed´jack-et
bed´lam
Bed´ou-in
bed´pan
bed´post
be-drag´gle
bed´rid-den
bed´rock
bed´room
bed´sheet
bed´side
bed´sore
bed´spread
bed´spring
bed´stead
bed´time
beech
beef
beef´eat-er
beef´steak
beef-y
bee´hive
bee´line
Beel´ze-bub
beer
Beer-she´ba
beer´y
bees´wax
beet
Bee´tho-ven
bee´tle
bee´tle-browed
be-fall´
be-fall´en
be-fell´
be-fit´
be-fit´ting
be-fog´
be-fogged´
be-fog´ging
be-fore´
be-fore´hand
be-foul´
be-friend´
be-fud´dle
be-get´
beg´gar
beg´gar-ly
beg´ging

be-gin´
be-gin´ner
be-gin´ning
be-gone´
be-go´nia
be-grime´
be-grudge´
be-grudg´ing
be-grudg´ing-ly
be-guile´
be-guil´er
be-guil´ing-ly
be-half´
be-have´
be-haved´
be-hav´ing
be-hav´ior
be-hav´ior-ism
be-hav-ior-is´tic
be-head´
be-held´
be-he´moth
be-hest´
be-hind´
be-hind´hand
be-hold´
be-hold´en
be-hold´er
be-hold´ing
be-hoove´
beige
be´ing
Bei´rut
be-la´bor
be-lat´ed
be-lay´
be-lea´guer
be-lea´guered
Bel´fast
Bel´fort
bel´fry
Bel´gian
Bel´gium
be-lie
belief´
be-li´er
be-liev´a-ble
be-lieve´
be-lieved´

be-liev´er
be-liev´ing
be-lit´tle
be-lit´tling
Be-lize´
bel-la-don´na
bell´boy
Bel-leau´
belles let´tres
bell´hop
bel´li-cose
bel-lig´er-ence
bel-lig´er-en-cy
bel-lig´er-ent
bel´low
bell´weth-er
bel´ly
bel´ly-band
Bel´mont
be-long´
be-longed´
be-long´ings
be-loved´, be-lov´ed
be-low´
Bel-shaz´zar
belt´ed
be-mire´
be-mir´ing
be-moan´
be-muse´
be-mused´
be-mus´ing
Be-na´res
bend´ed
bend´er
bend´ing
be-neath´
be-ne-di´ci-te
ben´e-dict
Ben-e-dic´tine
ben-e-dic´tion
ben-e-dic´to-ry
ben´e-fac-tion
ben´e-fac-tor
ben´e-fac-tress
be-nef´ic
ben´e-fice
ben´e-ficed
be-nef´i-cence

be-nef´i-cent
ben-e-fi´cial
ben-e-fi´cial-ly
ben-e-fi´cia-ries
ben-e-fi´cia-ry
ben´e-fit
ben´e-fit-ed
ben´e-fit-ing
Be´nes
be-nev´o-lence
be-nev´o-lent
Ben´gal
be-night´ed
be-nign´
be-nig´nant
be-nig´nant-ly
be-nig--ni-ty
be-nign´ly
ben´i-son
Ben´ja-min
Bent´ley
be-numb´
Ben´ze-drine
ben´zene
ben´zine
ben´zo-ate
ben´zol
Be´o-wulf
be-queath´
be-quest´
be-rate´
be-rat´ed
be-rat´ing
Ber´ber
be-reave´
be-reaved´
be-reave´ment
be-reav´ing
be-reft´
Ber´es-ford
be-ret´
ber´ga-mot
Ber´gen
Ber´-ge-rac´
beri-ber´i
Ber´ing
Berke´ley
Berk´ley
Berk´shires

Ber-lin´
Ber-mu´da
Bern´hardt
ber´ries
ber´ry
ber-serk´
ber-serk´er
berth
Ber´tha
ber´yl
be-ryl´li-um
be-seech´
be-seeched´
be-seech´ing
be-set´
be-set´ting
be-side´
be-sides´
be-siege´
be-sieg´er
be-sieg´ing-ly
be-smear´
be-smirch´
be´som
be-sot´
be-sot´ted
be-spat´ter
be-speak´
be-spoke´
Bes-sa-ra´bia
Bes´se mer
bes´tial
bes-ti-al´i-ty
bes´tial-ly
be-stir´
be-stow´
be-stow´al
be-strew´
be-stride´
be-strode´
be´ta
be-take´
be´tel
Be´tel-geuse
Beth´a-ny
Beth´el
Be-thes´da
Beth´le-hem
Beth-sa´i-da

be-tide´
be-to´ken
be-tray´
be-tray´al
be-tray´er
be-troth´
be-troth´al
be-throthed´
bet´ter
bet´ter-ment
be-tween´
be-twixt´
bev´el
bev´eled
bev´el-ing
bev´er-age
bev´ies
bev´y
be-wail´
be-ware´
be-wil´der
be-wil´dered
be-wil´dered-ly
be-wil´der-ing
be-wil´der-ing-ly
be-wil´der-ment
be-witch´
be-witch´ing
be-witch´ment
be-yond´
be-zique´
Bhu-tan´
bi-an´nu-al
bi-an´nu-al-ly
bi´as
bi´ased
bi´as-ing
bi-ax´i-al
Bi´ble
Bib´li-cal
Bib´li-cal-ly
bib´li-o-graph
bib-li-og´ra-pher
bib´li-o-graph´ic
bib-li-og´ra-phy
bib-li-o-ma´nia
bib´li-o-phile
bib-li-oph-i-lis´tic
bib´li-o-pol´ic

bib´u-lous
bi-cam´er-al
bi-car´bon-ate
bi-cen-ten´a-ry
bi-cen-ten´ni-al
bi´ceps
bi-chlo´ride
bick´er
bick´er-ing
bi-con´vex
bi-cus´pid
bi-cus´pi-date
bi´cy-cle
bi´cy-cler
bi´cy-clist
bid´da-ble
Bid´de-ford
bid´den
bid´der
bid´ding
bid´dy
bide
Bid´e-ford
bid´ing
bi-en´ni-al
bi-en´ni-al-ly
bier
bi-fa´cial
bi-far´i-ous-ly
bi´fid
bi´fo-cal
bi´fur-cate
bi´fur-cat-ed
bi-fur-ca´tion
big´a-mist
big´a-mous
big´a-mous-ly
big´a-my
big´ger
big´heart-ed
big´horn
big´ot
big´ot-ed
big´ot-ry
bi-ki´ni
bi-la´bi-al
bil´an-der
bi-lat´er-al
bi-lat´er-al-ly

Bil-ba´o
bil´ber-ry
bil´i-ary
bi-lin´gual
bil´ious
bill´board
bil´let
bil´let—doux
bill´fish
bill´fold
bil´liards
Bil´lings
bil´lion
bil´lion-aire
bil´low
bil´lowy
bi-met´al-list
bi-month´ly
bi´na-ry
bin-au´ral
Bing´ham-ton
bin´go
bin´na-cle
bin-oc´u-lar
bi-no´mi-al
bio-chem´i-cal
bi´o-chem´ist
bio-chem´is-try
bio-de-grad´a-ble
bio-de-grade´
bio-ecol´o-gy
bio-gen´e-sis
bi´o-graph
bi-og´ra-pher
bio-graph´ic
bio-graph´i-cal
bi-og´ra-phy
bio-log´ic
bio-log´i-cal
bi-ol´o-gist
bi-ol´o-gy
bi-om´e-try
bi-on´ic
bio-nom´ics
bi´op-sy
bi´o-sphere
bio-tox´in
bi-par´ti-san
bi-par´tite

bi-par-ti´tion
bi´ped
bi´plane
bi-po´lar
bi-quar´ter-ly
birch´bark
birch´en
bird´call
bird´lime
bird´man
bird's´—eye
bi-ret´ta
Bir´ming-ham
birth
birth´day
birth´mark
birth´place
birth´stone
Bis´cay
bis´cuit
bi´sect´
bi-sec´tion
bi´sec´tor
bish´op
bish´op-ric
bis´muth
bi´son
bisque
bis´ter
bi-sul´fide
bitch
bite
bit´er
bit´ing
bit´ten
bit´ter
bit´ter-ly
bit´tern
bit´ter-ness
bit´ter-root
bit´ters
bit´ter-sweet
bi-tu´men
bi-tu´mi-nous
bi-va´lent
bi´valve
bi-val´vu-lar
biv´ouac
biv´ouacked

biv´ouack-ing
bi-week´ly
bizarre´
bi-zarre´ness
Bizet
blab
blab´ber
black´ball
black´ber-ry
black´bird
black´board
black´cap
black´en
black´ened
black´en-er
black´—eyed
Black´feet
Black´foot
black´guard
black´head
Black Hills
black´ing
black´jack
black´list
black´ly
black´mail
black´out
black sheep
black´smith
black´thorn
blad´der
blade
blade´less
blame´wor-thy
blam´ing
blanch
blanch´er
blanch´ing
blanc-mange´
bland
blan´dish
blan´dish-ment
bland´ly
bland´ness
blank´book
blan´ket
blank´ly
blank´ness
blare

blar´ney
bla-sé´
blas´pheme
blas´phem-er
blas´phem-ing
blas´phe-mous
blas´phe-my
blast´ed
blas´tu-la
bla´tant
bla´tant-ly
blath´er-skite
blaze
blazed
blaz´er
blaz´ing
bleach´er
bleak
bleak´ly
blear´i-ness
blear´y
bleat´ing
bleed´ing
blem´ish
blem´ish-er
blend´er
blend´ing
Blen´heim
bless
blessed, bless´ed
bless´ed-ly
bless´ed-ness
bless´ing
blind´er
blind´fold
blind´ing
blind´ly
blind´ness
blink´er
blink´ing
bliss´ful
bliss´ful-ly
blis´ter
blis´tery
blithe
blithe´ly
blithe´some
blitz´krieg
bliz´zard

block
block-ade´
block-ad´ed
block-ad´ing
block´buster
block´head
block´house
blond´ness
blood bank
blood´cur-dling
blood´hound
blood´i-ness
blood´less
blood´let-ting
blood pres´sure
blood´shed
blood´shot
blood´stain
blood´stained
blood´stone
blood´suck-er
blood´thirst-i-ly
blood´thirsty
blood´ vessel
blood´y
bloom´ers
bloom´ing
bloom´ing-ly
blos´som
blotch
blotch´y
blot´ted
blot´ter
blow´er
blow´fly
blow´gun
blow´hole
blow´i-ness
blown
blow´out
blow´pipe
blow´torch
blow´up
blub´ber
blub´bery
bludg´eon
blue
Blue´beard
blue´bell

blue´berry
blue´bird
blue´bon-net
blue book
blue´coat
blue´—eyed
blue´fish
blue´grass
blue´jacket
blue´ jay
blue laws
blue moon
blue´print
blue´stock-ing
blue´stone
blu´et
bluff´er
bluff´ing
blu´ing
blun´der
blun´der-buss
blun´der-er
blun´der-ing
blur
blurred
blur´ring
blushed
blush´ing
blus´ter
blus´ter-ing
blus´ter-ous
blus´tery
bo´a
boar
board´er
board´walk
boast´er
boast´ful
boast´ing-ly
boat´build-er
boat club
boat´hook
boat´house
boat´ing
boat´man
boat´swain
bobbed
bob´bin
bob´bing

bob´cat
bob´o-link
bob´sled
bob´tail
bob´white´
Boc-cac´cio
bod´ice
bod´i-ly
bod´kin
bod´y
bod´y-guard
bo´gey
bog´gish
bog´gle
bog´gy
Bo-go-ta´
bo´gus
bo´gy
Bo-he´mia
boil´er
boil´ing
Boi´se
bois´ter-ous
bois´ter-ous-ly
bold´face
bold´ly
bold´ness
Bo-li´var
Bo-liv´ia
boll
boll´ wee´vil
bo´lo
Bo-lo´gna
Bol´she-vik
Bol´she-vism
bol´ster
bolt´er
bomb
bom-bard´
bom´bar-dier´
bom-bard´ment
bom´bast
bom-bas´tic
bom-bas´ti-cal
Bombay´
bomb bay
bomb´er
bomb´proof
bomb´shell

bomb´sight
bo´na fide
bo-nan´za
Bo´na-parte
Bo-na-ven-tu´ra
bon´bon
bond´age
bond´ed
bond´man
bonds´man
bond´wom-an
bone´dry
bone´less
bon´er
bon´fire
Bon´i-face
bon jour
bon´net
bon vi-vant´
bon vo-yage´
boo´dle
book
book a´gent
book´bind-er
book´bind-ery
book´case
book club
book col-lec´tor
book´dealer
book´end
book´ie
book´ish
book´keep-er
book´keep-ing
book´let
book´mak-er
book´mark
book´plate
book´rack
book re-view´
book´sell-er
book´shelf
book´shop
book´store
book´worm
boo´mer-ang
boon´dog-gle
boor´ish
boost´er

boot´black
boot´ed
boo´tee´
booth
boot´leg
boot´leg-ger
boot´leg-ging
boot´less
boot tree
boo´ty
booze
booz´er
booz´y
bo´rax
Bor-deaux´
bor´der
bor´dered
bor´der-land
bor´der-line
bore
bore´dom
Bor´gia
bo´ric
bor´ing
born
borne
Bor´neo
bo´ron
bor´ough
bor´row
bor´row-er
borsch
bos´om
boss´ism
boss´y
Bos´ton
bo´sun
Bos´well
bo-tan´i-cal
bot´a-nist
bot´a-nize
bot´a-ny
botch
botch´y
both´er
both´er-some
Bo-tswa´na
Bot-ti-cel´li
bot´tle

bot´tle-neck
bot´tle—nosed
bot´tler
bot´tle wash´er
bot´tling
bot´tom
bot´tom-land
bot´tom-less
bot´u-lism
bou-clé´
bou-doir´
bou-gain-vil´lea
bough
bought
bouil´la-baisse´
bouil´lon
boul´der
bou´le-vard
Bou-logne´
bounce
bounc´er
bounc´ing
bound
bound´a-ries
bound´a-ry
bound´ed
bound´less
boun´te-ous
boun´ti-ful
boun´ty
bou-quet´
bour´-bon
bour´geois
bour´geoise
bour´geoi-sie´
bourne
bourse
bou´ton-niere´
bo´vine
bow´el
bow´er
bow´ery
bow´ie
bow´knot
bowl
bow´leg
bow´leg-ged
bowl´er
bow´line

bowl´ing
bow´man
bow´string
box´car
box´er
box´ing
box kite
box´wood
boy
boy´cott
boy´cott-er
boy´hood
boy´ish
boy´ish-ness
Boyle
boy´sen-ber-ry
brace´let
brac´er
brach´i-al
brac´ing
brack´en
brack´et
brack´ish
brag´gart
bragged
brag´ger
brag´ging
Brah´ma
Brah´min
Brahms
Braille
brain cell
brain´i-er
brain´less
brain´wash-ing
brain´work
brain´y
braise
braised
brais´ing
brake
brake´man
bram´ble
bram´bly
Bran´deis
Bran´den-burg
bran´died
brand´—new
bran´dy

Bran´dy-wine
bran´ni-gan
Bra-sí´lia
brass´ie
bras-siere´
brass´y
bra-va´do
brave´heart-ed
brave´ly
brav´ery
brav´est
bra´vo
bra-vu´ra
brawl
brawl´er
brawn
brawn´i-er
brawn´i-est
brawn´i-ness
brawn´y
bra´zen
bra´zier
Bra-zil´
bra-zil´wood
braz´ing
breach
bread
bread´pan
breadth
bread´win-ner
break
break´able
break´age
break´down
break´er
break´fast
break´neck
break´through
break´up
break´wa-ter
breast
breast´bone
breast´plate
breath
breathe
breath´er
breath´ing
breath´less
breath´less-ly

breath´taking
bred
breech
breech´es
breed
breed´er
breed´ing
breeze
breeze´way
breez´y
Bre´men
Bren´ner
breth´ren
Bret´on
bre-vet´
bre-vet´ted
bre´via-ry
brev´i-ty
brew´er
brew´ery
brew´ing
bri´ar
bribed
brib´er
brib´ery
bric´—a—brac
brick´lay-er
brick´work
brick´yard
brid´al
bride´groom
brides´maid
bridge´head
Bridge´port
Bridge´wa-ter
bridge´work
bri´dle
bri´dling
brief´ing
brief´ly
bri´er
brig´a-dier
brig´an-dine
brig´an-tine
bright´—eyed
bright´ly
bright´ness
Brigh´ton
bril´liance

bril´lian-cy
bril´liant
brim´stone
bring
bring´er
bring´ing
brink
bri´o-lette
bri-quet´
bri-quette´
bris´ket
brisk´ly
brisk´ness
bris´tle
bris´tling
Bris´tol
Brit´ain
Bri-tan´nia
Brit´ish
Brit´on
Brit´ta-ny
brit´tle
broach
broad
broad´brim
broad´cast
broad´cloth
broad´en
broad´loom
broad´ly
broad´—mind-ed
broad´—mind-ed-ness
broad´side
broad´tail
Broad´way
bro-cade´
bro-cad´ed
broc´co-li
bro-chette´
brochure´
Brock´ton
bro´gan
brogue
broi´dery
broil
broil´er
bro´kage
broke
bro´ken

bro´ken-heart-ed
bro´ker
bro´ker-age
bro´mide
bro´mine
bro´mo-form
bro-mom´e-try
bron´chi-al
bron-chi´tis
bron´chus
bron´co
Bron´te
bron´to-saur
bronze
bronz´ing
brooch
brood´er
brood´ing
brook´let
Brook´line
Brook´lyn
broom´stick
broth
broth´el
broth´er
broth´er-hood
broth´er—in—law
broth´er-ly
brougham
brow´beat
brow´beat-ing
brown´ie
brown´out
brown´stone
browse
brows´ing
bruise
bruised
bruis´er
bruis´ing
bru-net´
Bruns´wick
brunt
brusque´ly
Brus´sels
bru´tal
bru-tal´i-ty
bru´tal-ize
bru´tal-ly

brute
brut´ish
Bru´tus
bub´ble
bub´bling
bub´bling-ly
bub´bly
bu-bon´ic
buc´ca-neer
Bu-chan´an
Bu´cha-rest
buck´a-roo
buck´board
buck´et
buck´et-ful
buck´eye
Buck´ing-ham
buck´le
buck´ler
buck´ling
buck´saw
buck´shot
buck´skin
buck´thorn
buck´tooth
buck´wheat
bu-col´ic
Bu´da-pest
Bud´dha
Bud´dhism
Bud´dhist
bud´dy
budge
bud´get
bud´get-ary
bud´get-ed
bud´ge-teer
bud´get-er
bud´get-ing
Bue´na Vis´ta
Bue´nos Ai´res
buf´fa-lo
buf´fa-loes
buff´er
buf´fet
buf-foon´
buf-foon´ery
bug´a-boo
bug´bear

bug´gy
bu´gle
bu´gler
bu´gling
build´er
build´ing
build´up
built´—in
bul-ba´ceous
bul´bar
bul´bous
Bul-gar´ia
bulge
bulg´er
bulg´ing
bulk´head
bulk´i-er
bulk´i-ness
bulk´y
bull´dog
bull´doze
bull´doz-er
bull´doz-ing
bul´let
bul´le-tin
bul´let-proof
bull´fight
bull´fight-er
bull´finch
bull´frog
bull´head
bull´head-ed
bul´lied
bul´lion
bull´ish
bull´lock
bull´pen
Bull Run
bull's´—eye
bull´whip
bul´ly
bul´ly-ing
bul´ly-rag
bul´rush
bul´wark
bum´ble-bee
bum´bling
bum´boat
bump´er

bump´i-er
bump´kin
bump´tious
bump´y
bunch
bunch´i-er
bunch´y
bun´co
bun´der
bun´dle
bun´dling
bun´ga-low
bung´hole
bun´gle
bun´gled
bun´gler
bun´gling
bun´gling-ly
bun´ion
bun´ker
bunk´house
bun´ko
bun´ny
Bun´sen
bunt´er
bunt´ing
Bun´yan
buoy
buoy´age
buoy´an-cy
buoy´ant
Bur´bank
bur´den
bur´den-some
bu´reau
bu-reauc´ra-cy
bu´reau-crat
bu-reau-crat´ic
bu-rette´
bur´geon
bur´gess
bur´glar
bur´gla-ries
bur-glar´i-ous
bur´glar-ize
bur´glar-proof
bur´gla-ry
Bur-goyne´
Bur´gun-dy

bur´i-al
bur´ied
bur´ies
bur´lap
Bur´leigh
bur´lesque´
bur´lesqued´
bur-lesqu´er
bur´ley
bur´li-ness
Bur´ling-ton
bur´ly
Bur´ma
burned
burn´er
bur-net´
Bur´ney
burn´ing
burn´ish
bur-noose´
burn´sides
burnt
bur´ro
Bur´roughs
bur´row
bur´row-er
bur´sa
bur´sar
bur-sar´i-al
bur´sa-ry
bur-si´tis
burst
burst´ing
Bur´ton
Bu-run´di
bur´y
bur´y-ing
bur´y-ing ground
bus´es
bush´el
bush´i-er
Bush´man
bush´mas-ter
bush´rang-er
bush´whack-er
bush´y
bus´ied
bus´i-er
bus´i-est

bus´i-ly
bus´i-ness
bus´i-ness-like
bus´i-ness-man
bus´kin
bus´ses
bus´tard
bus´tle
bus´tled
bus´tler
bus´tling
bus´tling-ly
bus´y
bus´y-body
bus´y-ness
bu´tane
butch´er
butch´ery
but´ler
butte
but´ter
but´ter-cup
but´ter-fat
but´ter-fin-ger
but´ter-fish
but´ter-fly
but´ter-milk
but´ter-nut
but´ter-scotch
but´tery
but´tocks
but´ton
but´ton-hole
but´ton-wood
but´tress
bu-tyr´ic
bux´om
bux´om-ness
buy´er
buy´ing
buz´zard
buzz´er
buzz saw
by´gone
by´law
by´—line
by´pass
by´path
by´play

by´—prod-uct
Byrd
by´road
By´ron
bys´sus
by´stand-er
by´way
by´word
Byz´an-tine
By-zan´tium

### C

ca-bal´
cab´a-la
cab-a-lis´tic
cab-a-lis´ti-cal
ca-bal-le´ro
ca-ban´a
cab-a-ret´
cab´bage
cab´by
ca´ber
ca-ber-net´
cab´in
cab´in boy
cab´i-net
cab´i-net-mak-er
cab´i-net-work
ca´ble
ca´ble-gram
ca´bling
cab´man
cab´o-chon
ca-boose´
Cab´ot
cab´ri-ole
cab-ri-o-let´
cab´stand
ca-ca´o
cach´a-lot
cache
cached
ca-chet´
ca-cique´
cack´le
cack´ling
ca-coph´o-ny
cac´ti

cac´tus
ca-dav´er
ca-dav´er-ous
cad´die
cad´dis
cad´dish
cad´dy
ca´dence
ca´den-cy
ca-den´za
ca-det´
Cad´il-lac
Ca-diz´
Cad´me-an
cad´mi-um
Cad´mus
cad´re
ca-du´ce-us
Cae´sar
Cae-sar´e-an
cae-su´ra
ca-fe´
caf-e-te´ria
caf´feine
caf´tan
Ca-ga-yan´
cage´ling
ca´gey
ca´gi-er
cai´man
cairn
Cai´ro
cais´son
cai´tiff
Ca´ius
ca-jole´
ca-jol´ery
Ca´jun
cake´box
cake mix´er
cake pan
cake´walk
cal´a-boose
Ca-la´bria
Ca-lais´
cal´a-mine
cal´a-mite
ca-lam´i-tous
ca-lam´i-ty

cal-cif´er-ous
cal-ci-fi-ca´tion
cal´ci-fy
cal-cim´e-ter
cal´ci-mine
cal-ci-na´tion
cal´cine
cal´cin-er
cal´cite
cal´ci-um
cal´cu-la-ble
cal´cu-late
cal´cu-lat-ing
cal-cu-la´tion
cal´cu-la-tive
cal´cu-la-tor
cal´cu-lus
Cal-cut´ta
Cal-de-ron´
cal´dron
Ca´leb
Cal-e-do´nia
cal´en-dar
cal´en-der
Cal´ends
ca-len´du-la
cal´en-ture
calf
calf´skin
Cal´ga-ry
Cal-houn´
Cal´i-ban
cal´i-ber
cal´i-brate
cal-i-bra´tion
cal-i-bra-tor
cal´i-co
Cal-i-for´nia
Ca-lig´u-la
cal´i-per
ca´liph
cal-is-then´ics
calk
calk´ing
call´able
Cal-la´o
call´er
Cal´les
cal-lig´ra-pher

cal-li-graph´ic
cal-lig´ra-phy
call´ing
cal-li´o-pe
Cal-lis´to
cal-los´i-ty
cal´lous
cal´low
cal´lus
cal´lus-es
calm
calm´ly
calm´ness
ca-lor´ic
cal-o-ric´i-ty
cal´o-rie
cal´o-ries
cal-o-rif´ic
cal-o-rim´e-ter
cal´o-rize
ca-lotte´
cal´u-met
ca-lum´ni-ate
ca-lum-ni-a´tion
ca-lum´ni-a-tor
cal´um-nies
ca-lum´ni-ous
ca-lum´ni-ous-ly
cal´um-ny
Cal´va-ry
calve
Cal´vert
calves
Cal´vin
Cal´vin-ism
cal-vi´ti-es
calx
Cal´y-don
ca-lyp´so
ca-lyp´tra
ca´lyx
ca-ma-ra´de-rie
cam-a-ril´la
cam´ber
cam´bi-um
Cam-bo´dia
Cam´bria
Cam´bri-an
cam´bric

Cam´bridge
Cam´den
cam´el
ca-mel´lia
Cam´e-lot
Cam´em-bert
cam´eo
cam´era-man
Cam´er-oon
Ca-mil´la
Ca-mille´
ca-mion´
cam´i-sole
cam´o-mile
Ca-mor´ra
cam´ou-flage
Cam-pa´gna
cam-paign´
cam-paign´er
cam-pa-ni´le
Camp´bell
camp´er
camp´fire
camp´ground
cam´phor
cam-phor´ic
cam´pus
Ca´naan
Can´a-da
ca-nal´
ca-nal´boat
ca-nal-i-za´tion
ca-nal´ize
ca´na-pé
ca-nard´
ca-nar´ies
ca-nar´y
ca-nas´ta
Can´ber-ra
can´can
can´cel
can´celed
can´cel-er
can´cel-ing
can-cel-la´tion
can´cer
can´cer-ous
can-de-la´bra
can-de-la´brum

can-des´cence
can-des´cent
can´did
can´di-da-cy
can´di-date
can´did-ly
can´did-ness
can´died
can´dies
can´dle
can´dle-light
Can´dle-mas
can´dle-nut
can´dle-pow-er
can´dor
can´dy
Can´field
ca´nine
Ca´nis
can´is-ter
can´ker
can´ker-ous
canned
can´ner
can´nery
Cannes
can´ni-bal
can´ni-bal-ism
can-ni-bal-is´tic
can´ni-bal-ize
can´ni-ly
can´ni-ness
can´ning
can´non
can´non-ade´
can´non-ball
can´non-eer
can´not
can´nu-la
can´ny
ca-noe´
ca-noe´ing
ca-noe´ist
ca-noes´
can´on
ca´ñon
can´on-ness
ca-non´i-cal
can-on-i-za´tion

can´on-ize
can´on-ry
can´ o´pen-er
can´o-pies
can´o-py
can´ta-loupe
can-tan´ker-ous
can-ta´ta
can-teen´
can´ter
Can´ter-bury
can´ti-le-ver
can´to
Can´ton
Can´ton-ese´
can´tor
Ca-nuck´
Ca-nute´
can´vas
can´vas-back
can´vass
can´vass-er
can´yon
ca-pa-bil´i-ties
ca-pa-bil´i-ty
ca´pa-ble
ca´pa-bly
ca-pa´cious
ca-pac´i-tance
ca-pac´i-ty
Ca-pel´la
ca´per
Ca-per´na-um
Ca-pet´
cap´ful
ca´pi-as
cap-il-la´ceous
cap-il-lar´i-ty
cap´il-lary
cap´i-ta
cap´i-tal
cap´i-tal-ism
cap´i-tal-ist
cap-i-tal-is´tic
cap-i-tal-i-za´tion
cap´i-tal-ize
cap´i-tan´
cap´i-tate
cap-i-ta´tion

cap´i-tol
ca-pit´u-lar
ca-pit´u-late
ca´pon
ca-pote´
Cap-pa-do´cia
Ca-pri´
ca-pric´cio
ca-price´
ca-pri´cious
Cap´ri-corn
cap´ri-ole
cap´size
cap´siz-ing
cap´su-lar
cap´sule
cap´tain
cap´tain-cy
cap´tion
cap´tious
cap´ti-vate
cap´ti-vat-ing
cap-ti-va´tion
cap´ti-va-tor
cap´tive
cap-tiv´i-ty
cap´tor
cap´ture
cap´tur-ing
cap´u-chin
Cap´u-let
Car´a-cal´la
Ca-ra´cas
car´a-cole
car´a-cul
ca-rafe´
car´a-mel
car´a-pace
car´at
car´a-van
car-a-van´sa-ry
car´a-vel
car´a-way
car´bide
car´bine
car´bi-nol
car-bo-hy´drate
car-bol´ic
car´bo-lize

car´bon
car-bo-na´ceous
car´bon-ate
car-bon-a´tion
car´bon di-ox´ide
car-bon´ic
car-bon-if´er-ous
car´bon-ize
car-bo-run´dum
car´boy
car´bun-cle
car´bu-ret-or
car´ca-jou
car´cass
car-cin´o-gen
car-ci-no´ma
car´da-mom
card´board
Car´de-nas
car´di-ac
Car´diff
car´di-gan
car´di-nal
card´ing
car´dio-gram
car-di-og´ra-phy
Car-do´zo
card´play-er
card´room
card ta´ble
ca-reen´
ca-reer´
care´free
care´ful
care´ful-ly
care´ful-ness
care´less
care´less-ly
care´less-ness
ca-ress´
ca-ress´ive
ca-ress´ive-ly
car´et
care´tak-er
Ca-rew´
care´worn
car´fare
car´go
car´goes

Car´ib
car´i-bou
car´i-ca-ture
car´i-ca-tur-ist
car´ies
car´il-lon
car´il-lon-neur´
car-i-o´ca
car´i-ous
Car-lisle´
car´load
Car-lot´ta
Car-lyle´
car´man
Car´mel
car´mine
car´nage
car´nal
car-nal´i-ty
car´nall-ite
car´nal-ly
car-na´tion
Car´ne-gie
car-ne´lian
car´ni-val
car´ni-vore
car-niv´o-rous
car´ol
car´ol-er
Car-o-li´na
car´om
ca-rot´id
ca-rous´al
ca-rouse´
ca-rous´ing
car´pal
Car-pa´thi-an
car´pen-ter
car´pen-try
car´pet
car´pet-bag
car´pet-bag´ger
car´pet-ing
car´riage
car´ri-er
car´ri-on
car´rot
car´roty
car-rou-sel´

car´ried
car´ry
car´ry-all
car´ry—o´ver
cart´age
Car-ta-ge´na
carte blanche
car-tel´
cart´er
Car´ter
Car´thage
Car-thu´sian
Car-tier´
car´ti-lage
car-ti-lag´i-nous
car-tog´ra-pher
car-to-graph´ic
car-tog´ra-phy
car´ton
car-toon´
car-toon´ist
car´tridge
cart´wheel
Ca-ru´so
carv´er
carv´ing
car-y-at´id
car-y-at´id-al
car-y-op´sis
ca-sa´ba
Ca-sa-blan´ca
Cas-a-no´va
cas-cade´
case´ hard´en
ca-sein´
case´mate
case´ment
cash´book
cash´ew
cash-ier´
cash´mere
cas´ing
ca-si´no
cask
cas´ket
Cas´per
Cas-san´dra
Cas´sius
cas´sock

cas´so-wary
cast
cas-ta-net´
cast´a-way
caste
cast´er
cas´ti-gate
cas-ti-ga´tion
Cas-tile´
cast´ing
cast iron
cas´tle
cas´tor
cas´trate
cas-tra´tion
ca´su-al
ca´su-al-ly
ca´su-al-ness
ca´su-al-ty
ca´su-ist
ca´su-is´tic
ca-su-is´ti-cal-ly
ca´su-is-try
cat´a-clysm
cat-a-clys´mic
cat´a-comb
cat´a-falque
cat´a-lep-sy
cat-a-lep´tic
Cat-a-li´na
cat´a-log
cat´a-log-er
cat´a-log-ing
ca-tal´pa
ca-tal´y-sis
cat´a-lyst
cat-a-lyt´ic
cat´a-lyze
cat´a-lyz-er
cat-a-ma-ran´
cat´a-mount
cat´a-pult
cat´a-ract
ca-tarrh´
ca-tas´tro-phe
cat-a-stroph´ic
cata-ton´ic
Ca-taw´ba
cat´bird

cat´boat
cat´call
catch´all
catch´er
catch´i-er
catch´word
catch´y
cat-e-che´sis
cat´e-chism
cat-e-chis´mal
cat´e-chist
cat-e-chi-za´tion
cat´e-chize
cat-e-chu´men
cat-e-chu´men-al
cat-e-gor´i-cal
cat-e-gor´i-cal-ly
cat´e-go-rize
cat´e-go-ry
ca´ter
ca´ter-er
cat´er-pil-lar
cat´fish
cat´gut
ca-thar´sis
ca-thar´tic
Ca-thay´
ca-the´dral
Cath´er
Cath´er-ine
cath´e-ter
cath´ode
Cath´o-lic
Ca-thol´i-cism
cath-o-lic´i-ty
ca-thol´i-cize
cat´kin
cat´like
cat´nap
cat´nip
Ca´to
cat—o´—nine´—tails
cat's´—eye
Cats´kill
cat's´—paw
cat´sup
cat´tail
cat´tle
cat´tle-man

cat´ty
cat´walk
Cau-ca´sian
cau´cus
cau´dal
cau´dle
caught
cau´li-flow-er
caus´al
cau-sa´tion
caus´a-tive
cause´less
caus´er
cause´way
caus´ing
caus´tic
caus´ti-cal-ly
cau-ter-i-za´tion
cau´ter-ize
cau´tery
cau´tion
cau´tion-ary
cau´tious
cau´tious-ly
cav´al-cade´
cav´a-lier´
cav´al-ry
cav´al-ry-man
Cav´en-dish
cav´ern
cav´ern-ous
cav´i-ar
cav´il
cav´i-ties
cav´i-ty
cavort´
ca-vort´ing
cay´enne´
cay´man
cay´use
cease
ceased
cease´less
cease´less-ly
ceas´ing
ce´dar
cede
ced´ed
ce-dil´la

ced´ing
ceil
ceil´ing
Cel´a-nese
cel´e-brant
cel´e-brate
cel´e-brat-ed
cel-e-bra´tion
cel´e-bra-tor
ce-leb´ri-ty
ce-ler´i-ty
cel´ery
ce-les´tial
cel´i-ba-cy
cel´i-bate
cel´lar
cel´lar-age
cel´list
cel´lo
cel´lo-phane
cel´lu-lar
cel´lule
cel´lu-loid
cel´lu-lose
Cel´si-us
Celt´ic
ce-ment´
cem´e-ter-ies
cem´e-tery
cen´o-bite
cen´o-taph
Ce-no-zo´ic
cen´ser
cen´sor
cen-so´ri-al
cen´sor-ship
cen´sur-a-ble
cen´sure
cen´sured
cen´sur-ing
cen´sus
cen´tare
cen´taur
cen-ta´vo
cen-te-nar´i-an
cen-ten´a-ry
cen-ten´ni-al
cen´ter
cen´ter-board

cen´ter-piece
cen´ti-grade
cen´ti-gram
cen´ti-li-ter
cen´ti-me-ter
cen´ti-pede
cen´tral
cen-tral-i-za´tion
cen´tral-ize
cen-trif´u-gal
cen´tri-fuge
cen-trip´e-tal
cen´trum
cen-tu´ri-al
cen-tu´ri-on
cen´tu-ry
Ce´phe-id
ce-ram´ic
ce-ram´ics
ce-ram´ist
Cer´ber-us
ce´re-al
cer-e-bel´lar
cer-e-bel´lum
cere´bral
cere´brum
cer-e-mo´ni-al
cer´e-mo-nies
cer-e-mo´ni-ous
cer´e-mo-ny
Ce´res
ce´ric
ce-rise´
ce´rite
cer´tain
cer´tain-ly
cer´tain-ties
cer´tain-ty
cer-ti-fi-a-ble
cer-tif´i-cate
cer-ti-fi-ca´tion
cer´ti-fied
cer´ti-fies
cer´ti-fy
cer´ti-fy-ing
cer´ti-tude
ce-ru´le-an
ce-ru´men
Cer-van´tes

cer´ve-lat
cer´vi-cal
cer´vix
ce-sar´e-an
ces-sa´tion
ces´sion
cess´pit
cess´pool
ce´tyl
Cey-lon´
Ce-zanne´
Cha´blis
Cha´co
chafed
cha´fer
chaf´fer
chaf´ing
chaf´ing dish
Cha´gres
cha-grin´
cha-grined´
chain gang
chain re-ac´tion
chain´—smoke
chain stitch
chain store
chain´work
chair´man
chair´man-ship
chaise longue
Chal´ce-don
Chal-de´a
cha´let
chal´ice
chalk´i-ness
chalk´y
chal´lenge
chal´lenge-a-ble
chal´leng-er
chal´leng-ing
cham´ber
cham´bered
cham´ber-maid
cha-me´leon
cham´ois
cham-pagne´
cham-pi´gnon
cham´pi-on
cham´pi-on-ship

Cham-plain´
Champs Ely-sées
chance´ful
chan´cel
chan´cel-lery
chan´cel-lor
chan´cel-lor-ship
Chan´cel-lors-ville
chan´cery
chanc´y
chan´de-lier´
chan´dler
chan´dlery
change´able
changed
change´ful
change´less
chang´er
chang´ing
chan´nel
chan´neled
chan´nel-ing
Chan´ning
chant´er
chan´ti-cleer
cha´os
cha-ot´ic
cha-peau´
cha-peaux´
chap´el
chap´er-on
chap´i-ter
chap´lain
chap´let
Chap´lin
chap´ter
char´ac-ter
char-ac-ter-is´tic
char-ac-ter-is´ti-cal-ly
char-ac-ter-i-za´tion
char´ac-ter-ize
char´ac-tery
charade´
char´coal
charge´able
char´gé d'af-faires´
charged
charg´er
charg´ing

char´i-ot
char´i-o-teer´
cha-ris´ma
char´is-mat´ic
char´i-ta-ble
char-i-ties
char´i-ty
char´la-tan
Char´le-magne
Charles´ton
Charles´town
Char´ley
Char´lotte
Char´lottes-ville
Char´lotte-town
charm´er
charm´ing
charm´ing-ly
char´nel
chart´er
chartreuse´
chart room
char´wom-an
char´y
Cha-ryb´di-an
Cha-ryb´dis
chased
chas´er
chas´ing
chasm
chas´mal
chasm´y
chasse´pot
chas-seur´
chas´sis
chaste
chas´ten
chas-tise´
chas-tise´ment
chas-tis´er
chas´ti-ty
cha-teau´
cha-teaux´
Cha-teau-bri-and´
Cha-teau—Thier-ry´
cha´te-laine
Chat´ham
Chat-ta-hoo´chee
Chat-ta-noo´ga

chat´tel
chat´ter
chat´ter-box
chat´ter-er
Chat´ter-ton
chat´ti-ly
chat´ting
chat´ty
Chau´cer
chauf´fer
chauf´feur
chau´vin-ism
chau´vin-ist
cheap´en
cheap´ened
cheap´ly
cheap´ness
cheat´er
check´book
cheek´er
check´er-board
check´ered
check´ers
check girl
check´mate
check´—out
check´rein
check´room
check´up
ched´dar
cheek´bone
cheek´y
cheer´er
cheer´ful
cheer´ful-ly
cheer´ful-ness
cheer´i-ly
cheer´less
cheer´y
cheese´cake
cheese´cloth
cheese knife
cheese´par-ing
chees´i-ness
chees´y
chee´tah
chef
chef d'oeu´vre
Che´khov

Chel´sea
Chel´ten-ham
chem´i-cal
che-mise´
chem´ist
chem´is-try
chemo-ther´a-py
che-nille´
che´quer
Cher´bourg
cher´ish
Cher´o-kee
che-root´
cher´ries
cher´ry
cher´ub
che-ru´bic
cher´u-bim
Ches´a-peake
Chesh´ire
chess´board
chess´man
Ches´ter
Ches´ter-field
Ches´ter-ton
chest´nut
chest´y
che-va-lier´
Chev´i-ot
Chev´ro-let´
chev´ron
chew´ing
Chey-enne´
Cheyne
Chiang´ Kai-shek´
Chi-an´ti
Chi-ca-go
chi-cane´
chi-ca´nery
chick´a-dee
Chick-a-hom´i-ny
Chick-a-mau´ga
Chick´a-saw
chick´en
chick´en-heart´ed
chicken pox
chick´pea
chick´weed
chi´cle

chic´o-ry
chide
chid´ing
chief´ly
chief´tain
chif-fon´
chif´fo-robe
chig´ger
chi´gnon
Chi-hua´hua
child´bear-ing
child´bed
child´birth
child´hood
child´ish
child´ish-ly
child´ish-ness
child´less
child´like
chil´dren
Chil´e
chil´i
chill´i-ness
chill´ing
Chil-lon´
chill´y
chimed
chim´er
chim´ing
chim´ney
chim´ney-piece
chim´ney pot
chim´ney sweep
chim´pan-zee
Chi´na
chi´na-ber-ry
Chi´na-man
Chi´na-town
chi´na-ware
chin-chil´la
Chi-nese´
Chin-kiang
chinned
chin´ning
chi-nook´
chintz
Chi´os
chip´munk
chipped

Chip´pen-dale
chip´per
Chip´pe-wa
chip´ping
chi-rog´ra-pher
chi´ro-graph´ic
chi-rog´ra-phy
chi´ro-man-cy
chi-rop´o-dist
chi-rop´o-dy
chi´ro-prac´tic
chi´ro-prac´tor
chis´el
chis´eled
chis´el-er
chis´el-ing
chit´chat
chi-val´ric
chiv´al-rous
chiv´al-ry
chlor-am´ide
chlor-am´ine
chlo´rate
chlor´dane
chlo´ric
chlo´ride
chlo´ri-dize
chlo´ri-nate
chlo-rin-a´tion
chlo´rine
chlo´rite
chlo´ro-form
chlo´ro-my-ce´tin
chlo´ro-phyll
chock´—full´
choc´o-late
Choc´taw
choice´ly
choic´est
choir
choked
choke´damp
chok´er
chok´ing
chol´er
chol´era
chol´er-ic
choose
choos´ing

chop´house
Cho´pin
chop´per
chop´ping
chop´py
chop´stick
chop su´ey
cho´ral
chord
chord´al
chore
cho-re´a
chore´man
cho-re-og´ra-pher
cho-re-og´ra-phy
cho´ric
cho´ri-on
cho´ris-ter
cho-rog´ra-phy
cho´roid
chor´tle
chor´tling
cho´rus
chose
cho´sen
chow´der
chrism
Chris´ta-bel
chris´ten
chris´ten-dom
chris´ten-ing
Chris´tian
chris-ti-an´ia
Chris-tian´i-ty
chris´tian-ize
Christ´like
Christ´ly
Christ´mas
Christ´mas-tide
Chris´to-pher
chro´ma
chro´mate
chro-mat´ic
chro-mat´i-cal-ly
chro´ma-tin
chro´ma-tism
chro-mat´o-gram
chro-ma-tog´ra-phy
chro-mat´o-scope

chrome
chro´mic
chro´mite
chro´mi-um
chro´mo-gen
chro-mom´e-ter
chro´mo-some
chro´mo-sphere
chron´ic
chron´i-cal-ly
chron´i-cle
chron´i-cler
chron´i-cling
chron´o-graph
chro-nog´ra-pher
chron-o-log´ic
chron-o-log´i-cal
chro-nol´o-gist
chro-nol´o-gy
chro-nom´e-ter
chron-o-met´ric
chrys´a-lis
chry-san´the-mum
chrys´o-lite
chub´by
chuck´le
chuck´led
chuck´le-head
chuck´ling
chuff´y
chuk´ker
chum´mi-ly
chum´my
Chung-king
chunk´y
church´go-er
Church´ill
church´ly
church´man
church´ward-en
church´yard
churl´ish
churl´ish-ly
churl´ish-ness
churn´er
chute
chut´ney
ci-bo´ri-um
ci-ca´da

cic´a-tri-ces
cic-a-tri´cial
cic´a-trix
cic´a-trize
Cic´e-ro
cic-e-ro´ne
ci´der
ci-gar´
cig-a-rette´, cig-a-ret´
ci-gar´—shaped
cil´ia
cil´i-ary
cil´i-ate
Ci-li´cia
cin-cho´na
Cin-cin-nat´i
cinc´ture
cin´der
Cin-der-el´la
cin´e-ma
cin-e-mat´o-graph
cin-e-ma-tog´ra-pher
cin-e-ma-tog´ra-phy
cin´er-a-tor
cin´na-bar
cin´na-mon
cinque´foil
ci´on
ci´pher
cir´ca
Cir-cas´sian
Cir´ce
cir´cle
cir´cled
cir´clet
cir´cling
cir´cuit
cir-cu´i-tous
cir´cu-lar
cir-cu-lar-i-za´tion
cir´cu-lar-ize
cir´cu-late
cir-cu-la´tion
cir´cu-la-tive
cir´cu-la-tor
cir´cu-la-to-ry
cir´cum-am´bi-ent
cir´cum-cise
cir´cum-ci´sion

cir-cum´fer-ence
cir-cum-fer-en´tial
cir´cum-flex
cir-cum´flu-ent
cir-cum-lo-cu´tion
cir-cum-loc´u-to-ry
cir-cum-nav´i-gate
cir-cum-nav-i-ga´tion
cir-cum-nu-ta´tion
cir´cum-po´lar
cir´cum-scis´sile
cir´cum-scribe
cir´cum-scrip-tion
cir´cum-spect
cir´cum-spec´tion
cir´cum-stance
cir´cum-stanced
cir´cum-stan´tial
cir´cum-stan´tial-ly
cir-cum-stan´ti-ate
cir´cum-vent
cir-cum-ven´tion
cir-cum-vo-lu´tion
cirque
cir-rho´sis
cir-rhot´ic
Cis-ter´cian
cis´tern
cit´a-del
ci-ta´tion
ci´ta-to-ry
cite
cith´a-ra
cit´ies
cit´i-fy
cit´ing
cit´i-zen
cit´i-zen-ry
cit´i-zen-ship
cit´ral
cit´rate
cit´re-ous
cit´ric
cit´rin
cit´ron
cit-ro-nel´la
cit´rous
cit´rus
cit´y

42

cit´y—state
civ´et
civ´ic
civ´ics
civ´il
ci-vil´ian
ci-vil´i-ty
civ-i-li-za´tion
civ´i-lize
civ´i-lized
civ´i-liz-ing
civ´il-ly
civ´il serv´ice
clab´ber
claim´ant
claim´er
clair-voy´ance
clair-voy´ant
cla´mant
clam´bake
clam´ber
clam´mi-ness
clam´my
clam´or
clam´or-ous
clam´shell
clan-des´tine
clang´or
clang´or-ous
clan´nish
clans´man
clap´board
clapped
clap´per
clap´ping
clap´trap
claque
Clar´ence
Clar´en-don
clar´et
clar-i-fi-ca´tion
clar´i-fied
clar´i-fy
clar´i-fy-ing
clar´i-net´
clar´i-on
clar´i-ty
clas´sic
clas´si-cal

clas´si-cal-ly
clas´si-cism
clas´si-cist
clas-si-fi-a-ble
clas-si-fi-ca´tion
clas´si-fi-ca-to-ry
clas´si-fied
clas´si-fy
clas´si-fy-ing
clas´sis
class´mate
class´room
clas´tic
clat´ter
clat´tered
Clau´di-us
claus´al
clause
claus-tro-pho´bia
clav´i-chord
clav´i-cle
cla-vic´u-lar
cla-vier´
claw´like
clay´ey
clay´more
clean—cut
clean´er
clean´li-ness
clean´ly
clean´ness
cleanse
cleansed
cleans´er
cleans´ing
clean´up
clear´ance
clear´—cut
clear´—eyed
clear´head-ed
clear´ing
clear´ing-house
clear´ly
clear´ness
clear´—sight-ed
cleav´age
cleaved
cleav´er
cleav´ing

clem´a-tis
Cle-men-ceau´
clem´en-cy
Clem´ens
clem´ent
Clem´en-tine
Cle-o-pat´ra
cler´gy
cler´gy-man
cler´ic
cler´i-cal
Cler´mont
Cleve´land
clev´er
clev´er-ly
clev´er-ness
clev´is
clew
cli-che´
click
click´er
cli´ent
cli´en-tele´
Clif´ford
Clif´ton
cli-mac´ter-ic
cli-mac´tic
cli´mate
cli-mat´ic
cli´max
climbed
climb´er
climb´ing
clinch´er
cling´ing
cling´stone
cling´y
clin´ic
clin´i-cal
clink´er
Clin´ton
clipped
clip´per
clip´ping
clique
clit´o-ris
clo-a´ca
cloak´room
clob´ber

cloche
clock´mak-er
clock tow´er
clock´wise
clock´work
clod´hopper
clois´ter
clois´tral
closed
close´—fist-ed
close´—fit-ting
close´—hauled
close´—lipped
close´y
close´mouthed
close´ness
clos´est
clos´et
close´—up
clo´sure
cloth
clothe
clothes
clothes´line
cloth´ier
cloth´ing
cloth´yard
clo´ture
cloud´burst
cloud´i-ness
cloud´y
clo´ven
clo´ver
Clo´vis
clown´ish
cloy´ing
cloy´ing-ly
club´ba-ble
clubbed
club´bing
club´foot
club´house
club´man
club´room
club´wom-an
clum´si-er
clum´si-ly
clum´si-ness
clum´sy

Clu´ny
clus´ter
clut´ter
Clydes´dale
coach´man
co-ad´ju-tant
co-ad-ju´tor
co-ad´u-nate
co-ag´u-la-ble
co-ag´u-late
co-ag-u-la´tion
co-ag´u-la-tive
co-ag´u-la-tor
coal barge
coal bin
coal box
coal car
coal cel´lar
coal chute
coal deal´er
co-a-lesce´
co-a-les´cence
co-a-les´cent
co-a-lesc´ing
coal´field
coal gas
coal hod
oo a li´tion
coal mine
coal scut´tle
coal shov´el
coal tar
coal yard
coarse
coarse´ly
coarse´ness
coast´al
coast´er
coast guard
coast´line
coast´wise
coat´ing
coat of arms
coat of mail
coat´room
coat´tail
co´au´thor
coax
co-ax´i-al

coax´ing
coax´ing-ly
co´balt
cob´ble
cob´bler
cob´ble-stone
co´bra
Co´burg
cob´web
cocaine
coc´cus
coc-cyg´e-al
coc´cyx
coch´lea
cock-ade´
cock´a-too
cock´crow
cock´er
cock´er-el
cock´eyed
cock´le
cock´le-shell
Cock´ney
Cock´ney-ism
cock´pit
cock´sure
cock´tail
cock´y
co´co
co´coa
co´co-nut
co-coon´
cod´dle
cod´ed
co-de-fend´ant
co´deine
cod´fish
codg´er
cod´i-cil
cod-i-fi-ca´tion
cod´i-fied
cod´i-fy
cod´ling
co´—ed´
co-ed-u-ca´tion
co-ed-u-ca´tion-al
co´ef-fi´cient
co-e´qual
co-erce´

co-erc´i-ble
co-erc´ing
co-er´cion
co-er´cive
co-ex-ist´
co-ex-is´tence
co-ex-is´tent
co-ex-ten´sive
cof´fee
cof´fee-house
cof´fee-pot
cof´fer
cof´fin
co´gen-cy
co´gent
cog´i-ta-ble
cog´i-tate
cog´i-tat-ing
cog-i-ta´tion
cog´i-ta-tive
co´gnac
cog-ni´tion
cog´ni-za-ble
cog´ni-zance
cog´ni-zant
cog´wheel
co-hab´It
co-hab´i-tant
co´heir
co-here´
co-her´ence
co-her´ent
co-her´er
co-he´sion
co-he´sive
co-he´sive-ness
co´hort
coif-feur´
coif-fure´
coin
coin´age
co-in-cide´
co-in´ci-dence
co-in´ci-dent
co-in-ci-den´tal
co-in-cid´ing
coin´er
co-in-sure´
co´i-tus

coked
cok´ing
col´an-der
Col´bert
Col´by
Col´ches-ter
Col´chis
cold´—blood-ed
cold cream
cold´heart-ed
cold´ly
cold´ness
cold´proof
cole´slaw
Col´gate
col´ic
col´icky
col-i-se´um
co-li´tis
col-lab´o-rate
col-lab´o-rat-ing
col-lab-o-ra´tion
col-lab´o-ra-tor
col-lage´
col-lapse´
col-lapsed´
col-laps´i-ble
col-laps´ing
col´lar
col´lar-band
col´lar-bone
col´lar but-ton
col-late´
col-lat´er-al
col-lat´ing
col-la´tion
col-la´tor
col´league
col-lect´
col-lect´ed
col-lect´i-ble
col-lec´tion
col-lec´tive
col-lec´tive-ly
col-lec´tiv-ist
col-lec´tor
col´leen
col´lege
col´leg-er

col-le´gi-al
col-le´gian
col-le´giate
col-lide´
col-lid´ing
col´lie
col´lier
co´liery
col´li-gate
col´li-ma-tor
col-li´sion
col´lo-cate
col-lo-ca´tion
col´loid
col-loi´dal
col-lo-qui-al
col-lo´qui-al-ism
col-lo´qui-al-ly
col´lo-quy
col-lude´
col-lud´ing
col-lu´sion
col-lu´sive
col-lu´sive-ly
co-logne´
Co-lom´bia
Co-lom´bo
co´lon
co-lon´
col´o-nel
co-lo´ni-al
co-lon´ic
col´o-nies
col´o-nist
col-o-ni-za´tion
col´o-nize
col-on-nade´
col´o-ny
col´o-phon
col´o-pho-ny
col´or
Col-o-rad´o
col-or-a´tion
col-or-a-tu´ra
col´or—blind
col´or-cast
col´ored
col´or-ful
col´or-ing

col´or-ist
col´or-less
co-los´sal
Col-os-se´um
Co-los´si-an
co-los´sus
colt´ish
Co-lum´bia
col´um-bine
Co-lum´bus
col´umn
co-lum´nar
col´um-nist
co´ma
Co-man´che
co´ma-tose
co´ma-tose-ly
com´bat
com-bat´ant
com-bat´ing
com-bat´ive
comb´er
com-bi-na´tion
com´bi-na-tive
com-bine´
com-bin´ing
com-bus´ti-ble
com-bus´tion
co-me´dl-an
co-me´di-enne
com´e-dies
com´e-dy
come´li-ness
come-ly
com´er
com´et
com´fit
com´fort
com´fort-able
com´fort-ably
com´fort-er
com´fort-less
com´ic
com´i-cal
com´ing
com´i-ty
com´ma
com-mand´
com´man-dant

com´man-deer´
com-mand´er
com-mand´ing
com-mand´ment
com-man´do
com-man´dos
com-mea´sure
com-mem´o-rate
com-mem´o-rat-ing
com-mem´o-ra´tion
com-mem´o-ra-tive
com-mence´
com-mence´ment
com-menc´ing
com-mend´
com-mend´able
com-men-da´tion
com-men´da-to-ry
com-men-su-ra-bil´i-
  ty
com-men´su-rate
com-men´su-rate-ly
com-men-su-ra´tion
com´ment
com´men-tary
com´men-ta-tor
com´merce
com-mer´cial
com-mer´cial-ism
com-mer´cial-ize
com-mer´cial-ized
com-mer´cial-ly
com-min´gle
com-min´gling
com-mis´er-a-ble
com-mis´er-ate
com-mis-er-a´tion
com´mis-sar
com´mis-sar´i-at
com´mis-sary
com-mis´sion
com-mis´sion-aire´
com-mis´sioned
com-mis´sion-er
com-mit´
com-mit´ment
com-mit´tal
com-mit´ted
com-mit´tee

com-mit´tee-man
com-mit´ting
com-mode´
com-mo´di-ous
com-mod´i-ties
com-mod´i-ty
com´mo-dore
com´mon
com´mon-al-ty
com´mon-er
com´mon-ly
com´mon-place
com´mon sense
com´mon-wealth
com-mo´tion
com-mu´nal
com-mune´
com-mu´ni-ca-ble
com-mu´ni-cant
com-mu´ni-cate
com-mu´ni-cat-ing
com-mu´ni-ca´tion
com-mu´ni-ca-tive
com-mu´ni-ca-tor
com-mu´nion
com-mu´ni-qué
com´mu-nism
com´mu-nist
com´mu-nis´tic
com-mu´ni-ties
com-mu´ni-ty
com-mut´able
com´mu-tate
com-mu-ta´tion
com´mu-ta-tor
com-mute´
com-mut´er
com-mut´ing
Co´mo
Com´o-ros
co´mose
com´pact
com-pa-nies
com-pan´ion
com-pan´ion-able
com-pan´ion-ship
com-pan´ion-way
com´pa-ny
com´pa-ra-ble

com-par´a-tive
com-par´a-tive-ly
com-par´a-tor
com-pare´
com-par´ing
com-par´i-son
com-part´ment
com´pass
com´pass-es
com-pas´sion
com-pas´sion-ate
com-pat-i-bil´i-ty
com-pat´i-ble
com-pa´tri-ot
com´peer
com-pel´
com-pelled´
com-pel-ling
com-pen´di-ous
com-pen´di-um
com-pen´sa-ble
com´pen-sate
com´pen-sat-ing
com´pen-sa´tion
com´pen-sa-tive
com´pen-sa-tor
com´pen-sa-to-ry
com-pete´
com´pe-tence
com´pe-tent
com-pet´ing
com-pe-ti´tion
com-pet´i-tive
com-pet´i-tive-ly
com-pet´i-tor
com-pi-la´tion
com-pile´
com-pil´er
com-pil´ing
com-pla´cence
com-pla´cen-cy
com-pla´cent
com-pla´cent-ly
complain´
com-plain´ant
com-plaint´
com-plai´sance
com-plai´sant
com´ple-ment

com-ple-men´tal
com-ple-men´ta-ry
com-plete
com-plete´ly
com-plete´ness
com-ple´tion
com´plex
com-plex´ion
com-plex´ioned
com-plex´i-ty
com-pli´a-ble
com-pli´ance
com-pli´ant
com´pli-cate
com´pli-cat-ed
com´pli-ca´tion
com-plic´i-ty
com-plied´
com´pli-ment
com-pli-men´ta-ry
com-ply´
com-ply´ing
com-po´nent
com-port´
com-port´ment
com-pose´
com-posed´
com-pos´ed-ly
com-pos´er
com-pos´ite
com-po-si´tion
com-pos´i-tor
com´post
com-po´sure
com´pote
com´pound
com-pre-hend´
com-pre-hend´ible
com-pre-hen´si-ble
com-pre-hen´sion
com-pre-hen´sive
com´press
com-pressed´
com-press´ible
com-press´ing
com-pres´sion
com-pres´sive
com-pres´sor
com-prise´

com-pris´ing
com´pro-mise
comp-tom´e-ter
comp-trol´ler
com-pul´sion
com-pul´sive
com-pul´so-ry
com-punc´tion
com-put´able
com-pu-ta´tion
com-pute´
com-put´er
com-put´ing
com-put´ist
com´rade
com´rade-ship
con´cave
con-ceal´
con-ceal´ment
con-cede´
con-ced´ed
con-ced´er
con-ced´ing
con-ceit´
con-ceit´ed
con-ceit´ed-ly
con-ceiv-abil´i-ty
con-ceiv´able
con-ceiv´ably
con-ceive´
con-ceiv´ing
con´cen-trate
con´cen-trating
con´cen-tra´tion
con´cen-tra-tor
con-cen´tric
con-cen´tri-cal
con-cen-tric´i-ty
con´cept
con-cep´ta-cle
con-cep´tion
con-cep´tual
con-cern´
con-cerned´
con-cern´ing
con-cern´ment
con´cert
con-cert´ed
con-cer-ti´na

con-cer´to
con-ces´sion
con-ces´sion-aire´
con-ces´sion-ary
conch
con-cierge´
con-cil´i-a-ble
con-cil´i-ate
con-cil´i-at-ing
con-cil´i-a´tion
con-cil´i-a-tor
con-cil´ia-to-ry
con-cise´
con-cise´ly
con-cise´ness
con-ci´sion
con´clave
con-clude´
con-clud´ing
con-clu´sion
con-clu´sive
con-clu´sive-ly
con-coct´
con-coct´er
con-coc´tion
con-com´i-tant
con´cord
con-cor´dance
con-cor´dant
con´course
con´crete, con-crete´
con-crete´ly
con-cre´tion
con´cu-bine
con-cur´
con-curred´
con-cur´rence
con-cur´rent
con-cur´ring
con-cus´sion
con-demn´
con-dem-na´tion
con-dem´na-to-ry
con-demned´
con-demn´er
con-demn´ing
con-den´sate
con-den-sa´tion
con-dense´

con-dens´er
con-dens´ing
con-de-scend´
con-de-scend´ence
con-de-scend´ing
con-de-scend´ing-ly
con-de-scen´sion
con-dign´
con´di-ment
con-di´tion
con-di´tion-al
con-di´tion-al-ly
con-di-tioned
con-dole´
con-do´lence
con-dol´ing
con-do-min´i-um
con-don´ance
con-do-na´tion
con-done´
con´dor
con-duce´
con-du´cive
con´duct
con-duct´ance
con-duct´ed
con-duc´tion
con-duc´tive
con-duc´tor
con´duit
cone´—shaped
con-fec´tion
con-fec´tion-ary
con-fec´tion-er
con-fec´tion-ery
con-fed´er-a-cy
con-fed´er-ate
con-fed-er-a´tion
con-fer´
con´fer-ee´
con´fer-ence
con-ferred´
con-fer´ring
con-fess´
con-fessed´
con-fess´ed-ly
con-fes´sion
con-fes´sion-al
con-fes´sor

con-fet´ti
con´fi-dant
con´fi-dante
con-fide´
con-fid´ed
con´fi-dence
con´fi-dent
con-fi-den´tial
con-fi-den´tial-ly
con´fi-dent-ly
con-fid´ing
con-fig-u-ra´tion
con-fine´
con-fine´ment
con-fin´er
con-fin´ing
con-firm´
con-firm´able
con-fir-ma´tion
con-fir´ma-to-ry
con-firmed´
con-fis´ca-ble
con´fis-cate
con´fis-cat-ing
con-fis-ca´tion
con-fis´ca-to-ry
con-fla-gra´tion
con´flict
con-flic´tion
con-flic´tive
con´flu-ence
con´flu´ent
con´flux
con-form´
con-form´ance
con-for-ma´tion
con-form´ist
con-form´i-ty
con-found´
con-found´ed-ly
con-fra-ter´ni-ty
con-front´
con-fron-ta´tion
Con-fu´cius
con-fuse´
con-fused´
con-fus´ed-ly
con-fus´ing
con-fu´sion

con-fu-ta´tion
con-fu´ta-tive
con-fute´
con-geal´
con-geal´ment
con-ge-la´tion
con-ge´nial
con-ge-nial´i-ty
con-gen´i-tal
con´ger
con-gest´
con-gest´ed
con-ges´tion
con-glom´er-ate
con-glom-er-a´tion
con-glu-ti-na´tion
Con´go
con-grat´u-lant
con-grat´u-late
con-grat´u-lat-ing
con-grat-u-la´tion
con-grat´u-la-tor
con-grat´u-la-to-ry
con´gre-gate
con-gre-ga´tion
con-gre-ga´tion-al
Con-gre-ga´tion-al-ist
con´gress
con-gres´sio-nal
con´gress-man
con´gress-wom-an
con-gru´ence
con-gru´en-cy
con-gru´ent
con-gru´i-ty
con´gru-ous
con´ic
con´i-cal
con´i-fer
con-jec´tur-al
con-jec´tur-al-ly
con-jec´ture
con-join´
con-joint´
con´ju-gal
con´ju-gal-ly
con´ju-gate
con-ju-ga´tion
con´ju-ga-tor

con-junc´tion
con-junc´tive
con-junc-ti-vi´tis
con-junc´ture
con-ju-ra´tion
con´jure, con-jure´
con´jur-er
con´ju-ror
con-nect´
con-nect´ed
con-nect´ed-ly
con-nect´er
Con-nect´i-cut
con-nec´tion
con-nec´tive
con-nec-tiv´i-ty
con-nec´tor
conn´ing
conn´ing tower
con-niv´ance
con-nive´
con´nois-seur´
con-no-ta´tion
con´no-ta-tive
con´no-ta-tive-ly
con-note´
con-not´ing
con´quer
con´quered
con´quer-ing
con´quer-or
con´quest
con-quis´ta-dor
con-san´guine
con-san-guin´eous
con-san-guin´i-ty
con´science
con´science-less
con´science—
  strick´en
con-sci-en´tious
con-sci-en´tious-ly
con´scious
con´scious-ly
con´scious-ness
con´script
con-scrip´tion
con´se-crate
con´se-crat-ing

con-se-cra´tion
con-sec´u-tive
con-sec´u-tive-ly
con-sen´su-al
con-sen´sus
con-sent´
con-sent´er
con´se-quence
con´se-quent
con-se-quen´tial
con´se-quent-ly
con-serv´an-cy
con-ser-va´tion
con-serv´a-tism
con-serv´a-tive
con´ser-va-tor
con-serv´a-to-ry
con-serve´
con-serv´ing
con-sid´er
con-sid´er-a-ble
con-sid´er-a-bly
con-sid´er-ate
con-sid´er-ate-ly
con-sid-er-a´tion
con-sid´ered
con-sid´er-ing
con-sign´
con-sig-na´tion
con´sign-ee´
con-sign´ment
con-sign´or
con-sist´
con-sist´ence
con-sist´en-cy
con-sist´ent
con-sist´ent-ly
con-sis-to´ri-al
con-sis´to-ry
con-so-la´tion
con-sol´a-to-ry
con-sole´
con-sol´i-date
con-sol´i-dat-ing
con-sol-i-da´tion
con-sol´ing
con-sol´ing-ly
con´som-mé´
con´so-nance

con´so-nant
con´so-nan´tal
con´so-nant-ly
con-sort´
con-sor´ti-um
con-spic´u-ous
con-spic´u-ous-ly
con-spir´a-cy
con-spir´a-tor
con-spir´a-to´ri-al
con-spire´
con-spir´ing
con´sta-ble
con-stab´u-lary
Con´stance
con´stan-cy
con´stant
Con´stan-tine
Con´stan-ti-no´ple
con´stant-ly
con´stel-late
con-stel-la´tion
con´ster-nate
con-ster-na´tion
con´sti-pate
con´sti-pat-ed
con-sti-pa´tion
con-stit´u-en-cy
con-stit´u-ent
con´sti-tute
con-sti-tu´tion
con-sti-tu´tion-al
con-sti-tu-tion-al´i-ty
con-sti-tu´-tion-al-ly
con-sti-tu-tive
con-strain´
con-strained´
con-straint´
con-strict´
con-stric´tion
con-stric´tive
con-stric´tor
con-strin´gent
con-struct´
con-struc´tion
con-struc´tive
con-struc´tive-ly
con-struc´tor
con-strue´

con-strued´
con-stru´ing
con´sul
con´sul-ar
con´sul-ate
con-sult´
con-sul´tant
con-sul-ta´tion
con-sum´able
con-sume´
con-sumed´
con-sum´er
con-sum´ing
con-sum´mate
con-sum-ma´tion
con-sump´tion
con-sump´tive
con´tact
con´tac-tor
con-ta´gion
con-ta´gious
con-tain´
con-tain´er
con-tain´ing
con-tain´ment
con-tam´i-nant
con-tam´i-nate
con-tam´i-nat-ed
con-tam´i-nat-ing
con-tam-i-na´tion
con-tem´pla-ble
con´tem-plate
con´tem-plat-ing
con-tem-pla´tion
con´tem-pla-tive
con-tem-po-ra´ne-ous
con-tem´po-rary
con-tem´po-rize
con-tempt´
con-tempt´ible
con-tempt´ibly
con-temp´tu-ous
con-temp´tu-ous-ly
con-tend´
con-tend´er
con-tent´
con-tent´ed
con-tent´ed-ly
con-ten´tion

con-ten´tious
con-ten´tious-ly
con-tent´ment
con´tents
con-ter´mi-nous
con´test
con-test´able
con-tes´tant
con´text
con-ti-gu´i-ty
con-tig´u-ous
con-tig´u-ous-ly
con´ti-nence
con´ti-nent
con-ti-nen´tal
con-tin´gen-cy
con-tin´gent
con-tin´u-al
con-tin´u-al-ly
con-tin´u-ance
con-tin-u-a´tion
con-tin´u-a-tive
con-tin´ue
con-tin´u-ing
con-ti-nu´i-ty
con-tin´u-ous
con-tin´u-ous-ly
con-tin´u-um
con-tort´
con-tor´tion
con-tor´tive
con´tour
con´tra-band
con´tra-cep´tion
con´tra-cep´tive
con´tract
con-tract´ed
con-tract´ile
con-trac´tion
con´trac-tor
con-trac´tu-al
con-tra-dict´
con-tra-dic´tion
con-tra-dic´to-ri-ly
con-tra-dic´to-ry
con-tra-dis-tinc´tion
con-tral´to
con-trap´tion
con-tra-pun´tal

con-tra-ri´e-ty
con´trar-i-ness
con´trary
contrast´
con-tra-vene´
con-tra-ven´tion
con-trib´ute
con-trib´ut-ing
con-tri-bu´tion
con-trib´u-tor
con-trib´u-to-ry
con-trite´
con-trite´ly
con-tri´tion
con-triv´ance
con-trive´
con-triv´er
con-triv´ing
con-trol´
con-trol´la-ble
con-trol-led´
con-trol´ler
con-trol´ling
con-tro-ver´sial
con´tro-ver-sy
con´tro-vert
con-tuse´
con-tu´sion
co-nun´drum
con-va-lesce´
con-va-les´cence
con-va-les´cent
con-va-lesc´ing
con-vect´
con-vec´tion
con-vec´tor
con-vene´
con-ve´nience
con-ve´nient
con-ve´nient-ly
con-ven´ing
con´vent
con-ven´tion
con-ven´tion-al
con-ven´tion-al´i-ty
con-ven´tu-al
con-verge´
con-ver´gence
con-ver´gent

con-verg´ing
con-vers´able
con-ver´sant
con-ver-sa´tion
con-ver-sa´tion-al
con-ver-sa´tion-al-ist
con-verse´
con-verse´ly
con-vers´ing
con-ver´sion
con-ver´sive
con´vert
con-vert´er
con-vert´ible
con-ver´tor
con´vex
con-vex´i-ty
con-vey´
con-vey´ance
con-vey´ing
con´vict
con-vic´tion
con-vince´
con-vinc´ing
con-vinc´ing-ly
con-viv´i-al
con-viv-i-al´i-ty
con-vo-ca´tion
con-voke´
con-vok´ing
con´vo-lute
con-vo-lu´tion
con´voy
con´voyed
con-vulse´
con-vul´sion
con-vul´sive
con-vul´sive-ly
coo´ing
cook´book
cook´er
cook´ery
cook´ie
cook´stove
cool´er
Coo´lidge
coo´lie
cool´ly
cool´ness

coop´er
coop´er-age
co-op´er-ate
co-op-er-a´tion
co-op´er-a-tive
co-op´er-a-tor
co—opt´
co-or´di-nate
co-or-di-na´tion
co-or´di-na-tor
coot´ie
Co-pen-ha´gen
Co-per´ni-can
cop´i-er
cop´ies
co-pi´lot
cop´ing
co´pi-ous
co´pi-ous-ly
co´pi-ous-ness
cop´per
cop´per-head
cop´per-plate
cop´pice
co´pra
copse
Cop´tic
cop´u-la
cop´u-late
cop-u-la´tion
cop´u-la-tive
cop´y
cop´y-book
cop´y-ing
cop´y-ist
cop´y-right
co-quet´
co´quet-ry
co-quette´
co-quet´ting
co-quett´ish
co-qui´na
cor´a-cite
cor´al
cor´bel
cord
cord´age
cor´date
cord´ed

Cor-de´lia
cor´dial
cor-dial´i-ty
cor´dial-ly
cor-dil-le´ra
cord´ite
Cór´do-ba
cor´don
cor´do-van
cor´du-roy
cord´wood
core
co-re-la´tion
cor´er
co-re-spon´dent
co-ri-an´der
Cor´inth
Co-rin´thi-an
cork´screw
corn bread
corn´cob
cor´nea
cor´ne-al
Cor-ne´lia
cor´ner
cor´ner-stone
cor-net´
cor-net´ist
corn´flower
cor´nice
Cor´nish
corn´stalk
corn´starch
cor-nu-co´pia
Corn´wall
Corn-wal´lis
co-rol´la
cor´ol-lary
co-ro´na
Cor-o-na´do
cor´o-nary
cor-o-na´tion
cor´o-ner
cor´o-net´
cor´po-ral
cor-po-ral´i-ty
cor´po-rate
cor-po-ra´tion
cor-po´re-al

cor-po-re´i-ty
corps
corpse
cor´pu-lence
cor´pu-lent
cor´pus
Cor´pus Chris´ti
cor´pus-cle
cor-pus´cu-lar
cor-ral´
cor-rect´
cor-rec´tion
cor-rec´tion-al
cor-rec´tive
cor-rect´ly
Cor-reg´i-dor
cor´re-late
cor-re-la´tion
cor-rel´a-tive
cor-re-spond´
cor-re-spon´dence
cor-re-spon´dent
cor-re-spond´ing
cor-re-spon´sive
cor´ri-dor
cor´ri-gi-ble
cor-rob´o-rate
cor-rob-o-ra´tion
cor-rob´o-ra-tive
cor-rob´o-ra-tor
cor-rob´o-ra-to-ry
cor-rode´
cor-rod´i-ble
cor-rod´ing
cor-ro´sion
cor-ro´sive
cor´ru-gate
cor´ru-gat-ed
cor-ru-ga´tion
cor-rupt´
cor-rupt´er
cor-rup´tion
cor-rup´tive
cor-sage´
cor´sair
corse´let
cor-se-let´
cor´set
Cor´si-ca

cor´tege
cor´tex
cor´ti-cal
cor-ti-cos´ter-one
cor´ti-sone
co-sig´na-to-ry
cos-met´ic
cos´mic
cos´mi-cal-ly
cos-mog´ra-pher
cos-mog´ra-phy
cos-mo-log´-i-cal
cos-mol´o-gy
cos´mo-naut
cos-mo-pol´i-tan
cos´mos
Cos´sack
cos´tal
Cos´ta Ri´ca
cos´ter
cost´li-ness
cost´ly
cos´tume
cos´tum-er
co´te-rie
co-til´lion
cot´tage
cot´tag-er
cot´ter
cot´ton
cot´ton-seed
cot´ton-tail
cot´ton-wood
cou´gar
cou´lee
coun´cil
coun´cil-man
coun´sel
coun´sel-or
coun´te-nance
coun´ter
coun´ter-act´
coun´ter-at-tack
coun´ter-bal-ance
coun´ter-check
coun´ter-claim
coun´ter-clock´wise
coun´ter-es-pi-o-nage
coun´ter-feit

coun´ter-feit-er
coun´ter-foil
coun´ter-ir´ri-tant
coun´ter-mand
coun´ter-march
coun´ter-mine
coun´ter-pane
coun´ter-part
coun´ter-plot
coun´ter-point
coun´ter-poise
coun´ter-rev-o-lu´tion
coun´ter-sign
coun´ter-sink
coun´ter-weight
count´ess
coun´ties
count´less
coun´tries
coun´tri-fied
coun´try
coun´try-man
coun´try-side
coun´try-wom-an
coun´ty
coup´ d´etat´
cou-pé´
coupe
cou´ple
cou´pler
cou´plet
cou´pling
cou´pon
cour´age
cou-ra´geous
cou´ri-er
course
cours-er
cour´te-ous
cour´te-sy
court´house
cour´tier
court´li-ness
court´ly
court´—mar-tial
court´room
court´ship
court´yard
cous´in

cou-ture´
cou-tu´rier
cov´e-nant
cov´e-nan-ter
cov´e-nan-tor
Cov´en-try
cov´er
cov´er-age
cov´ered
cov´er-let
cov´ert
cov´er-ture
cov´et
cov´e-tous
cov´e-tous-ness
cov´ey
cow´ard
cow´ard-ice
cow´bell
cow´boy
cow´er
cow´hide
cow´lick
cowl´ing
co´—work´er
cow´pox
cow´rie
cox´comb
cox´swain
coy´ness
coy´ote
coz´en
coz´en-age
co´zi-est
co´zi-ly
co´zy
crab ap´ple
crab´bed
crab´bing
crab´by
crab´grass
crack´down
crack´er
crack´ing
crack´le
crack´ling
crack´—up
Cra´cow
cra´dle

cra´dling
craft´i-ly
craft´i-ness
crafts´man
crafts´man-ship
craft´y
crag´gi-ness
crag´gy
cram
crammed
cram´ming
cramped
cran´ber-ry
craned
cra´ni-al
cran´ing
cra-ni-ol´o-gy
cra´ni-um
crank´case
crank´i-ness
crank´y
Cran´mer
cran´nied
cran´ny
crashed
crass´ly
Cras´sus
cra´ter
crat´ing
cra-vat´
cra´ven
crav´ing
craw´fish
crawl´ing
crawl´y
cray´fish
cray´on
crazed
cra´zi-ly
cra´zi-ness
craz´ing
cra´zy
creak
creak´y
cream´er
cream´ery
cream´y
creased
creas´ing

cre-ate´
cre-at´ing
cre-a´tion
cre-a´tive
cre-a´tive-ly
cre-a´tor
crea´ture
cre´dence
cre-den´tial
cred-i-bil´i-ty
cred´i-ble
cred´it
cred´it-able
cred´i-tor
cre´do
cre´dos
cred´u-lous
creek
creep´er
creep´ing
creep´y
cre´mate
cre-ma´tion
cre´ma-to-ry
Cre´ole
cre´o-sol
cre´o-sote
crepe
cre-scen´do
cres´cent
cres´set
Cres´si-da
crest´ed
crest´fall-en
cre-ta´ceous
Cre´tan
cre´tin-isin
cre´tonne
cre-vasse´
crev´ice
crew´el
crib´bage
crib´bing
crib´work
crick´et
crick´et-er
cried
cri´er
Cril´lon

Cri-me´a
crim´i-nal
crim-i-nal´i-ty
crim-i-no-log´i-cal
crim-i-nol´o-gist
crim-i-nol´o-gy
crim´son
cringe
cringed
cring´ing
crin´gle
cri´nite
crin´kly
crin´o-line
crip´ple
crip´pled
crip´pling
cri´ses
cri´sis
crisp´ing
crisp´ly
crisp´ness
crisp´y
criss´cross
Cris-to´bal
cri-te´ri-on
crit´ic
crit´i-cal
crit´i-cism
crit´i-cize
crit´i-ciz-ing
cri-tique´
croak´er
Croat
Cro-a´tia
cro-chet´
cro-cheted´
cro-chet´er
cro-chet´ing
crock´ery
Crock´ett
croc´o-dile
cro´cus
Croe´sus
Croix de guerre
crom´lech
Crom´well
cro´ny
crook´ed

crooked
croon´er
crop´per
cro-quet´
cro-quette´
cross´bar
cross´bill
cross´bones
cross´bow
cross´bred
cross´breed
cross´—coun´try
cross´cut
cross—ex-am-i-
   na´tion
cross´—ex-am´ine
cross´—eyed
cross´—grained
cross´ing
cross´—leg-ged
cross´let
cross´ly
cross´over
cross´piece
cross´—pol´li-nate
cross´—pol-li-na´tion
cross´—ref´er-ence
cross´road
cross sec´tion
cross´—stitch
cross´walk
cross´ways
cross´wise
cross´word
crotch´et
crotch´ety
crou´pi-er
crou´ton
crow´bar
crowd´ed
crow´foot
crow´ing
crowned
cru´cial
cru´ci-ble
cru´ci-fer
cru-cif´er-ous
cru´ci-fied
cru´ci-fix

cru-ci-fix´ion
cru´ci-fy
crude´ly
cru´di-ty
cru´el
cru´el-ly
cru´el-ty
cru´et
cruised
cruis´er
cruis´ing
crul´ler
crum´ble
crum´bling
crum´bly
crum´pet
crum´ple
crum´pling
crunch´ing
cru-sade´
cru-sad´er
cru-sad´ing
Cru´soe
crus-ta´cean
crust´ed
crust´y
crux
cru-zei´ro
cry
cry´ing
cry´o-gen
cry-o-gen´ics
crypt-anal´y-sis
cryp´tic
cryp´to-gam
cryp´to-gram
cryp-tog´ra-pher
cryp-tog´ra-phy
crys´tal
crys´tal-line
crys´tal-lin´i-ty
crys´tal-lite
crys-tal-li-za´tion
crys´tal-lize
Cu´ba
cub´by-hole
cubed
cu´bic
cu´bi-cal

cu´bi-cal-ly
cu´bi-cle
cub´ism
cu´bit
cu´bi-tal
cuck´old
cuck´oo
cu´cum-ber
cud´dle
cud´dled
cud´dling
cud´gel
cud´gel-er
cui-sine´
cuisse
cul—de—sac
cul´i-nary
cull´ing
cul´mi-nate
cul-mi-na´tion
cu-lotte´
cul-pa-bil´i-ty
cul´pa-ble
cul´prit
cul´ti-va-ble
cul´ti-vate
cul´ti-vat-ed
cul-ti-va´tion
cul´ti-va-tor
cul´tur-al
cul´ture
cul´tured
cul´vert
cum´ber
Cum´ber-land
cum´ber-some
cum lau´de
cum´mer-bund
cu´mu-late
cu-mu-la´tion
cu´mu-la-tive
cu´mu-lus
cun´ning
cup´bear-er
cup´board
cup´cake
cu-pel´
cup´ful
Cu´pid

cu-pid´i-ty
cup´like
cu´po-la
cup´ping
cur-abil´i-ty
cur´able
Cu´ra-cao´
cu-ra´re
cu´rate
cu´ra-tive
cu-ra´tor
curb´ing
curb´stone
cur´dle
cur´dling
cure
cure´—all
cure´less
cur´few
cu´ria
Cu-rie´
cur´ing
cu´rio
cu-ri-os´i-ty
cu´ri-ous
cur´lew
cur´li-cue
curl´i-ness
curl´ing
curl´y
cur´rant
cur´ren-cy
cur´rent
cur´ri-cle
cur-ric´u-lar
cur-ric´u-lum
cur´ried
cur´ri-er
cur´ry
cur´ry-ing
cursed
curs´ing
cur´so-ry
cur-tail´
cur-tail´ment
cur´tain
cur´tal
curt´ly
curt´sy

cur-va´ceous
cur´va-ture
curved
curv´ing
cush´ion
cus´pi-dal
cus´pi-dor
cus´tard
Cus´ter
cus-to´di-al
cus-to´di-an
cus´to-dy
cus´tom
cus´tom-ar´i-ly
cus´tom-ary
cus´tom-er
cus´tom-house
cus´tom—made
cut´away
cut glass
cu´ti-cle
cut´lass
cut´ler
cut´lery
cut´let
cut´off
cut´out
cut´ter
cut´ting
cut´tle
cut´tle-fish
cut´wa-ter
cut´worm
cy´a-nide
cy-a-no´sis
cy-ber-net´ics
Cyc´la-des
cy´cle
cy´clic
cy´cli-cal
cy´cling
cy´clist
cy´clone
cy-clo-pe´dia
Cy´clops
cy´clo-tron
cyg´net
cyl´in-der
cy-lin´dri-cal

cy´ma-rose
cy-ma´ti-um
cym´bal
cyn´ic
cyn´i-cal
cyn´i-cism
cy´no-sure
cy´press
cyp´ri-noid
Cyp´ri-ot
Cy´prus
Cy´ra-no
Cyr´il
Cy´rus
cyst
cys´tic
cy-tol´o-gy
cy´to-plasm
czar
czar´e-vitch
cza-rev´na
cza-ri´na
czar´ism
Czech
Czech´o-slo´vak
Czech´o-slo-va´kia

### D

dab´bling
dab´ble
dab´bling
Dac´ca
dachs´hund
Da´cron
dac´tyl
dac-tyl´ic
dac-ty-li´tis
dad´dy
daf´fo-dil
dag´ger
da-guerre´o-type
dahl´ia
dai´lies
dai´ly
dain´ties
dain´ti-ly
dain´ti-ness
dain´ty

dair´ies
dair´y
dair´y-ing
dair´y-man
da´is
dai´sies
dai´sy
Da-kar´
Da-ko´ta
Dal´las
dal´li-ance
dal´lied
dal´ly
dal´ly-ing
Dal-ma´tian
dam
dam´age
dam´ag-ing-ly
dam´a-scene
Da-mas´cus
dam´ask
dammed
dam´ming
damn
dam´na-ble
dam-na´tion
damned
damn´ing
damn´ing-ly
Dam´o-cles
Da´mon
damp´en
damp´en-er
damp´er
damp´ing
dam´sel
Da´na
danced
danc´er
danc´ing
dan´de-li-on
dan´der
dan´dle
dan´druff
dan´dy
dan´ger
dan´ger-ous
dan´ger-ous-ly
dan´gle

dan´gled
dan´gler
dan´gling
Dan´iel
Dan´ish
dank´ness
dan-seuse´
Dan´te
Dan´ube
Dan´ville
Dan´zig
dap´per
dap´ple
Dar-da-nelles´
dare´dev-il
Dar-i-en´
dar´ing
Dar-jee´ling
dark´en
dark horse
dark´ly
dark´ness
dark´room
dar´ling
Darm´stadt
Dart´mouth
Dar´win
dash´board
dashed
dash´er
dash´ing
das´tard
das´tard-ly
da´ta
dat´ed
date´less
dat´ing
da´tum
daub´er
daub´ery
daugh´ter
daugh´ter—in—law
daunt´less
daunt´less-ly
dau´phin
dav´en-port
Da´vid
Da´vis
da´vit

daw´dle
daw´dler
daw´dling
Daw´son
day´break
day´dream
day let´ter
day´light
day´star
day´time
Day´ton
Day-to´na
dazed
daz´ed-ly
daz´ing
daz´zle
daz´zling
daz´zling-ly
dea´con
dead´en
dead´eye
dead´fall
dead´li-er
dead´line
dead´li-ness
dead´lock
dead´ly
dead´wood
deaf´en
def´en-ing
deaf´en-ing-ly
deaf´—mute
deaf´ness
deal´er
deal´ing
dealt
Dear´born
dear´ie
dear´ly
dear´ness
dearth
death´blow
death´like
death´ly
death rate
death's´—head
death´watch
de-ba´cle
de-bar´

de-bar-ka´tion
de-bar´ment
de-bar´ring
de-base´
de-based´
de-base´ment
de-bas´ing
de-bat´able
de-bate´
de-bat´er
de-bat´ing
de-bauch´
de-bauch´ee
de-bauch´er
de-bauch´ery
de-ben´ture
de-bil´i-tate
de-bil´i-tat-ed
de-bil-i-ta´tion
de-bil´i-ty
deb´it
deb´o-nair´
Deb´o-rah
dé-bou-ché´
debt´or
de-bunk´
de´but
deb´u-tante
dec´ade
dec´a-dence
dec´a-dent
dec´a-logue
de-camp´
de-camp´ment
de-cant´
de-cant´er
de-cap´i-tate
de-cap-i-ta´tion
dec´a-pod
De-cap´o-lis
de-cath´lon
De-ca´tur
de-cay´
de-cayed´
de-cay´ing
de-cease´
de-ceased´
de-ce´dent
de-ceit´

de-ceit´ful
de-ceit´ful-ness
de-ceive´
de-ceiv´er
de-ceiv´ing-ly
de-cel´er-ate
de-cel-er-a´tion
De-cem´ber
de´cen-cy
de´cent
de-cen´ter
de´cent-ly
de-cen-tral-i-za´tion
de-cen´tral-ize
de-cep´tion
de-cep´tive
dec´i-bel
de-cide´
de-cid´ed-ly
dec´i-mal
dec´i-mate
dec-i-ma´tion
dec´i-me-ter
de-ci´pher
de-ci´pher-able
de-ci´sion
de-ci´sive
de-ci´sive-ly
de-claim´
dec-la-ma´tion
dec-la-ra´tion
de-clar´a-tive
de-clar´a-to-ry
de-clare´
de-clas´si-fy
de-clin´able
dec-li-na´tion
de-clin´a-to-ry
de-cline´
de-clined´
de-clin´ing
de-cliv´i-ty
de-cli´vous
de-code´
de-cod´ing
dé-col-le-tage´
dé-col-le-té´
de-col´or-ize
de-com-pose´

de-com-po-si´tion
de-con-tam´i-nate
de-con-tam-i-na´tion
de-cor´
dec´o-rate
dec-o-ra´tion
dec´o-ra-tive
dec´o-ra-tor
dec´o-rous
de-co´rum
de-coy´
de-coyed´
de-coy´ing
de´crease´
de-cree´
de-creed´
de-cree´ing
dec´re-ment
de´crem-e-ter
de-crep´it
de-crep´i-tate
de-crep´i-tude
de´cre-scen´do
de-cres´cent
de-cry´
ded´i-cate
ded-i-ca´tion
ded´i-ca-to-ry
de-duce´
de-duced´
de-duc´i-ble
de-duc´ing
de-duct´
de-duct´ible
de-duc´tion
de-duc´tive
deep´en
deep´—root-ed
deep´—seat-ed
deer´skin
de-face´
de-faced´
de-fac´ing
de fac´to
def-a-ma´tion
de-fam´a-to-ry
de-fame´
de-fault´
de-fault´er

de-fea´si-ble
de-feat´
de-feat´ed
de-feat´ist
def´e-cate
def-e-ca´tion
de´fect
de-fect´ed
de-fec´tion
de-fec´tive
de-fend´
de-fend´ant
de-fend´er
de-fense´
de-fense´less
de-fen-si-bil´i-ty
de-fen´si-ble
de-fen´sive
de-fer´
def´er-ence
def´er-ent
def-er-en´tial
de-fer´ra-ble
de-ferred´
de-fer´ring
de-fi´ance
de-fi´ant
de-fi´ant-ly
de-fi´cien-cy
de-fi´cient
def´i-cit
de-fied´
de-file´
de-file´ment
de-fil´ing
de-fin´able
de-fine´
de-fin´ing
def´i-nite
def´i-nite-ly
def-i-ni´tion
de-fin´i-tive
de-flate´
de-fla´tion
de-fla´tion-ary
de-flect´
de-flec´tion
de-flec´tive
de-flec´tor

De-foe´
de-fo´li-ate
de-for´est
de-form´
de-form-abil´i-ty
de-form´able
de-for-ma´tion
de-for´ma-tive
de-formed´
de-for´mi-ty
de-fraud´
de-frau-da´tion
de-fraud´ed
de-fray´
de-frayed´
de-fray´ing
de-frost´
de-frost´er
deft´ly
deft´ness
de-funct´
de-fy´
de-fy´ing
De-gas´
de-gen´er-a-cy
de-gen´er-ate
de-gen-er-a´tion
de-gen´er-a-tive
deg-ra-da´tion
de-grade´
de-grad´ed
de-grad´ing
de-gree´
de-hu-mid´i-fi-er
de-hy´drate
de-hy-dra´tion
de-ic´er
deic´tic
de-i-fi-ca´tion
de´i-fied
deign
de´ist
de´i-ties
de´i-ty
de-ject´ed
de-ject´ed-ly
de-jec´tion
de ju´re
Del´a-ware

de-lay´
de-layed´
de-lay´ing
de´le
de-lec´ta-ble
de-lec-ta´tion
del´e-ga-cy
del´e-gate
del-e-ga´tion
de´le-ing
de-lete´
de-let´ed
de-le´tion
Del´hi
De´lia
de-lib´er-ate
de-lib-er-a´tion
de-lib´er-a-tive
del´i-ca-cies
del´i-ca-cy
del´i-cate
del´i-cate-ly
del-i-ca-tes´sen
de-li´cious
de-light´
de-light´ed
de-light´ful
De-li´lah
de-lin´e-ate
de-lin-e-a´tion
de-lin´e-a-tor
de-lin´quen-cy
de-lin´quent
de-lir´i-ous
de-lir´i-um
de-liv´er
de-liv´er-able
de-liv´er-ance
de-liv´er-er
de-liv´er-ies
de-liv´er-y
Del´phi
del´phi-nine
del´ta
del´toid
de-lude´
de-lud´ed
de-lud´ing
del´uge

del´uged
de-lu´sion
de-lu´sive
de-lu´so-ry
de-luxe´
delve
delved
delv´ing
de-mag´net-ize
dem´a-gog´ic
dem´a-gogue
dem´a-gogu-ery
dem´a-gogy
de-mand´
de-mand´ed
de-mean´
de-mean´or
de-ment´ed
de-men´tia
de-mer´it
De-me´tri-us
dem´i-god
dem´i-john
de-mil-i-ta-ri-za´tion
de-mil´i-ta-rize
de-mise´
dem´i-tasse
de-mo-bi-li-za´tion
de-mo´bi-lize
de-moc´ra-cy
dem´o-crat
dem´o-crat´ic
de-moc´ra-tize
de-mog´ra-pher
de´mo-graph´ic
de-mog´ra-phy
de-mol´ish
dem-o-li´tion
de´mon
de-mon-e-ti-za´tion
de-mon´e-tize
de-mo´ni-ac
de-mo-ni´a-cal
de-mon´ic
de´mon-ism
de-mon-ol´a-try
de-mon-ol´o-gy
de-mon´stra-ble
de-mon´stra-bly

dem´on-strate
dem´on-strat-ing
dem-on-stra´tion
de-mon´stra-tive
dem´on-stra-tor
de-mor-al-iza´tion
de-mor´al-ize
de-mor´al-iz-ing
De-mos´the-nes
de-mote´
de-mot´ed
de-mo´tion
de-mur´
de-mure´
de-mur´rage
de-mur´ral
de-murred´
de-mur´rer
de-mur´ring
de-na´tion-a-lize
de-nat´u-ral-ize
de-na´tur-ant
de-na´tured
den-e-ga´tion
de-ni´al
de-nied´
de-ni´er
de-nies´
den´i-grate
den´im
den´i-zen
Den´mark
Den´nis
de-nom´i-nate
de-nom-i-na´tion
de-nom-i-na´tion-al
de-nom-i-na´tion-al-
  ism
de-nom´i-na-tive
de-nom´i-na-tor
de-no-ta´tion
de-note´
de-not´ing
de-noue-ment´
de-nounce´
de-nounced´
de-nounce´ment
de-nounc´ing
dense

dense´ly
den´si-ty
den´tal
den-ta-tion
den´ti-cle
den´ti-frice
den´til
den´tin
den´tist
den´tis-try
den-ti´tion
den´ture
de-nude´
de-nun´ci-ate
de-nun-ci-a´tion
de-nun´ci-a-to-ry
Den´ver
de-ny´
de-ny´ing
de-o´dor-ant
de-o´dor-ize
de-o´dor-iz-er
de-on-tol´o-gy
de-part´
de-part´ed
de-part´ment
de-part-men´tal
de-par´ture
de-pend´
de-pend-abil´i-ty
de-pend´able
de-pen´dence
de-pen´den-cy
de-pen´dent
de-pict´
de-pic´tion
dep´i-late
de-pil´a-to-ry
de-plete´
de-plet´ed
de-ple´tion
de-plor´able
dep-lo-ra´tion
de-plore´
de-plored´
de-plor´ing
de-ploy´
de-ploy´ment
de-po´lar-ize

de-pop´u-late
de-pop-u-la´tion
de-port´
de-por-ta´tion
de-port´ed
de-port-ee´
de-port´ment
de-pos´al
de-pose´
de-posed´
de-pos´ing
de-pos´it
de-pos´i-tary
de-pos´it-ed
dep-o-si´tion
de-pos´i-tor
de-pos´i-to-ry
de´pot
dep-ra-va´tion
de-prave´
de-praved´
de-prav´i-ty
dep´re-cate
dep´re-cat-ing
dep-re-ca´tion
dep´re-ca-to-ry
de-pre´cia-ble
de-pre´ci-ate
de-pre-ci-a´tion
dep´re-date
dep-re-da´tion
dep´re-da-tor
dep´re-da-to-ry
de-press´
de-pres´sant
de-pressed´
de-press´ible
de-press´ing
de-pres´sion
de-pres´sor
de-priv´al
dep-ri-va´tion
de-prive´
de-prived´
de-priv´ing
depth
dep-u-ta´tion
de-pute´
dep´u-ties

dep´u-tize
dep´u-ty
de-rail´
de-rail´ment
de-range´
de-range´ment
de-rang´ing
der´by
der´e-lict
der-e-lic´tion
de-ride´
de-rid´ing
de-ri´sion
de-ri´sive
de-ri´sive-ly
de-ri´so-ry
der-i-va´tion
de-riv´a-tive
de-rive´
de-rived´
de-riv´ing
der´ma-toid
der-ma-tol´o-gist
der-ma-tol´o-gy
der´mis
der-nier´
de-rog´a-to-ry
der´rick
der´rin-ger
der´vish
des´cant
Des-cartes´
de-scend´
de-scend´ant
de-scend´ed
de-scend´er
de-scend´ible
de-scent´
de-scrib´able
de-scribe´
de-scribed´
de-scrip´tion
de-scrip´tive
des-cry´
des-cry´ing
Des-de-mo´na
des´e-crate
des-e-cra´tion
des´e-cra-tor

de-seg´re-gate
de-seg-re-ga´tion
de-sen´si-tize
des´ert´
de-sert´er
de-ser´tion
de-serve´
de-served´
de-serv´ed-ly
de-serv´ing
des´ic-cate
des-ic-ca´tion
des´ic-ca-tor
de-sid-er-a´ta
de-sid-er-a´tum
de-sign´
de-sign´able
des´ig-nate
des-ig-na´tion
des´ig-na-tive
des´ig-na-tor
de-sign´ed-ly
des´ig-nee´
de-sign´er
de-sign´ing
de-sir-abil´i-ty
de-sir´able
de-sire´
de-sir´ous
de-sist´
de-sis´tance
Des Moines
des´o-late
des-o-la´tion
De So´to
de-spair´
de-spaired´
de-spair´ing
des-per-a´do
des-per-a´does
des´per-ate
des´per-ate-ly
des-per-a´tion
de-spic´a-ble
de-spis´able
de-spise´
de-spised´
de-spis´ing
de-spite´

de-spite´ful
de-spoil´
de-spoil´er
de-spoil´ing
de-spo-li-a´tion
de-spond´
de-spon´dence
de-spon´den-cy
de-spon´dent
des´pot
des-pot´ic
des-pot´i-cal
des´po-tism
des-sert´
des-ti-na´tion
des´tine
des´ti-nies
des´ti-ny
des´ti-tute
des-ti-tu´tion
de-stroy´
de-stroyed´
de-stroy´er
de-struc´ti-ble
de-struc´tion
de-struc´tive
de-struc´tive-ness
de-tach´
de-tach´able
de-tached´
de-tach´ment
de-tail´
de-tain´
de-tect´
de-tect´able
de-tec´ta-phone
de-tec´tion
de-tec´tive
de-tec´tor
de-ten´tion
de-ten´tive
de-ter´
de-ter´gent
de-te´ri-o-rate
de-te´ri-o-ra´tion
de-te´ri-o-ra-tive
de-ter´min-able
de-ter´mi-nant
de-ter´mi-nate

de-ter-mi-na´tion
de-ter´mine
de-ter´mined
de-ter´mined-ly
de-ter´mi-nism
de-ter´mi-nist
deterred´
de-ter´rent
de-ter´ring
de-ter´sive
de-test´
de-test´able
de-tes-ta´tion
de-throne´
det´o-na-ble
det´o-nate
det-o-na´tion
det´o-na-tor
de´tour
de-tract´
de-trac´tion
de-trac´tor
de-trac´to-ry
det´ri-ment
det-ri-men´tal
De-troit´
deuc´ed
Deutsch´land
de´va
De Va-le´ra
de-val´u-ate
de-val-u-a´tion
dev´as-tate
dev´as-tat-ed
dev´as-tat-ing
dev-as-ta´tion
de-vel´op
de-vel´oped
de-vel´op-er
de-vel´op-ing
de-vel´op-ment
de-vel´op-men´tal
de´vi
de´vi-ate
de-vi-a´tion
de-vice´
dev´il
dev´il-fish
dev´il-ish

dev´il-ment
dev´il-ry
dev´il-try
de´vi-ous
de´vi-ous-ly
de-vis´able
de-vise´
dev´i-sor´
de-vi-tal-iza´tion
de-vi´tal-ize
de-vo´cal-ize
de-void´
de-voir´
dev-o-lu´tion
de-volve´
de-volve´ment
de-volv´ing
Dev´on
Dev´on-shire
de-vote´
de-vot´ed
de-vot´ed-ly
dev´o-tee´
de-vo´tion
de-vo´tion-al
de-vour´
de-vout´
de-vout´ly
dew´ber-ry
dew´drop
Dew´ey
dew´i-ness
De Witt´
dew´lap
dew´point
dew´y
dex´ter
dex-ter´i-ty
dex´ter-ous
dex´ter-ous-ly
dex´trose
dex´trous
di-a-be´tes
di´a-bet´ic
di-a-bol´ic
di-a-bol´i-cal
di-ab´o-lism
di´a-caus´tic
di-a-crit´ic

di-a-crit´i-cal
di´a-dem
di´ag-nose
di-ag-no´sis
di-ag-nos´tic
di-ag-nos-ti´cian
di-ag´o-nal
di-ag´o-nal-ly
di´a-gram
di´a-gram-mat´ic
di´a-gram-mat´i-cal
di´al
di´a-lect
di´a-lec´tal
di´a-lec´tal-ly
di-a-lec´tic
di-a-lec´ti-cal
di-a-lec´ti-cism
di´aled
di´al-ing
di´a-log
di´a-logue
di-al´y-sis
di´a-lyt´ic
di-a-lyt´-i-cal-ly
dia-mag-net´ic
di-am´e-ter
di-am´e-tral
di-a-met´ric
di-a-met´ri-cal
di´a-mond
Di-an´a
di-a-net´ic
di-a-no-et´ic
di´a-per
di-aph´a-nous
di´a-phragm
di´a-phrag-mat´ic
di-aph´y-sis
di´a-ries
di´a-rist
di-ar-rhe´a
di´a-ry
Di´as
di´a-stat´ic
di´a-stol´ic
di´a-sto-mat´ic
di´a-ther-my
di-ath´e-sis

di´a-thet´ic
di´a-tom
di-atom´ic
di-at´om-ite
di´a-ton´ic
di´a-tribe
Di-az´
dib´ble
di-chro-mat´ic
dick-cis´sel
Dick´ens
Dick-en´si-an
dick´er
dick´ey
Dick´in-son
Dic´ta-phone
dic´tate
dic´tat-ing
dic-ta´tion
dic´ta-tor
dic-ta-to´ri-al
dic-ta´tor-ship
dic´tion
dic´tio-nar-ies
dic´tio-nary
Dic´to-graph
dic´tum
did´dle
die cut´ter
died
Di-e´go
die´mak-er
Dieppe
di´et
di´e-tary
di´et-er
di-e-tet´ic
di-e-ti´tian
dif´fer
dif´fered
dif´fer-ence
dif´fer-ent
dif-fer-en´tia-ble
dif-fer-en´tial
dif-fer-en´ti-ate
dif-fer-en-ti-a´tion
dif´fi-cult
dif´fi-cul-ties
dif´fi-cul-ty

dif´fi-dence
dif´fi-dent
dif-fract´
dif-frac´tion
dif-fuse´
dif-fus´ible
dif-fu´sion
dif-fu´sive
dig´a-my
di-gas´tric
di´gest
di-gest-ibil´i-ty
di-gest´ible
di-ges´tion
di-ges´tive
dig´ger
dig´ging
dig´it
dig´i-tal
dig-i-tal´is
dig´i-ta-lize
dig´ni-fied
dig´ni-fied-ly
dig´ni-fy
dig´ni-fy-ing
dig´ni-tar-ies
dig´ni-tary
dig´ni-ties
dig´ni-ty
di-gress´
di-gres´sion
di-lap´i-date
di-lap´i-dat-ed
di-lap-i-da´tion
dil-a-ta´tion
di-late´
di-lat´ing
di-la´tion
dil´a-to-ry
di-lem´ma
dil-et-tante´
dil-et-tant´ism
dil´i-gence
dil´i-gent
dil´u-ent
di-lute´
di-lut´ing
di-lu´tion
di-men´sion

dim´er-ous
dim´e-ter
di-min´ish
di-min-u-en´do
dim-i-nu´tion
di-min´u-tive
dim´ly
dimmed
dim´ming
dim´ness
dim´ple
dim´pling
di-nar´
dined
din´er
di-nette´
dingh´y
din´gi-ness
din´gle
din´gy
din´ing
din´ing room
din´ner
din´ner-time
din´ner-ware
di-noc´er-as
di´no-saur
di-oc´e-san
di´o-cese
Di-o-cle´tian
Di-og´e-nes
di-ox´ide
diph-the´ria
diph´thong
di-plo´ma
di-plo´ma-cy
dip´lo-mat
dip-lo-mat´ic
dip-lo-mat´i-cal-ly
dipped
dip´per
dip-so-ma´nia
di-rect´
di-rec´tion
di-rect´ly
di-rect´ness
di-rec´tor
di-rec´tor-ate
di-rec´to-ry

dirge
dir´i-gi-ble
dirt´i-er
dirt´i-ly
dirt´i-ness
dirt-y
dis-abil´i-ty
dis-a´ble
dis-a´bled
dis-a´bling
dis-ad-van´tage
dis-ad-van-ta´geous
dis-af-fect´ed
dis-af-fec´tion
dis-af-firm´ance
dis-af-fir-ma´tion
dis-agree´
dis-agree´able
dis-agree´ment
dis-al-low´
dis-al-low´ance
dis-ap-pear´
dis-ap-pear´ance
dis-ap-peared´
dis-ap-point´
dis-ap-point´ed
dis-ap-point´ment
dis-ap-prov´al
dis´ap-prove´
dis´ap-prov´ing
dis´ap-prov´ing-ly
dis-arm´
dis-ar´ma-ment
dis-ar-range´
dis-ar-range´ment
dis-ar-ray´
di-sas´ter
di-sas´trous
di-sas´trous-ly
dis-avow´
dis-avow´al
dis-band´
dis-bar´
dis-bar´ment
dis-bar´ring
dis-be-lief´
dis-be-lieve´
dis-be-liev´er
dis-bur´den

dis-burse´
dis-burse´ment
dis-burs´ing
disc
dis´card
dis-cern´
dis-cern´ible
dis-cern´ibly
dis-cern´ing
dis-cern´ment
dis´charge
dis-ci´ple
dis´ci-plin´able
dis´ci-pli-nar´i-an
dis´ci-pli-nary
dis´ci-pline
dis´ci-plin-er
dis-claim´
dis-claim´er
dis-cla-ma´tion
dis-close´
dis-clo´sure
dis-col´or
dis-col-or-a´tion
dis-com´fort
dis-com´fort-able
dis´con-cert´
dis-con-nect´
dis-con-nect´ed
dis-con-nec´tion
dis-con´so-late
dis-con´so-late-ly
dis-con-tent´
dis-con-tent´ed
dis-con-tin´u-ance
dis-con-tin-u-a´tion
dis-con-tin´ue
dis-con-ti-nu´i-ty
dis-con-tin´u-ous
dis´cord
dis-cor´dance
dis-cor´dant
dis´count
dis-coun´te-nance
dis-cour´age
dis-cour´age-ment
dis-cour´ag-er
dis-cour´ag-ing
dis´course

dis-cour´te-ous
dis-cov´er
dis-cov´er-er
dis-cov´er-ies
dis-cov´ert
dis-cov´ery
dis-cred´it
dis-cred´it-able
dis-creet´
dis-creet´ly
dis-crep´an-cy
dis-crete´
dis-cre´tion
dis-cre´tion-ary
dis-crim´i-nate
dis-crim´i-nat-ing
dis-crim-i-na´tion
dis-crim´i-na-to-ry
dis´cus
dis-cuss´
dis-cussed´
dis-cuss´ible
dis-cus´sion
dis-dain´
dis-dain´ful
dis-dain´ful-ly
dis ease´
dis-eased´
dis-eas´es
dis-em-bark´
dis-em-bar-ka´tion
dis-em-bar´rass
dis-em-bod´i-ment
dis-em-bod´y
dis-em-bogue´
dis-em-bow´el
dis-en-a´ble
dis-en-chant´
dis-en-chant´ment
dis-en-cum´ber
dis-en-gage´
dis-en-tan´gle
dis-es-tab´lish
dis-es-tab´lish-ment
dis-fa´vor
dis-fig´ure
disfig´ur-ing
dis-gorge´
dis-grace´

dis-grace´ful
dis-grun´tle
dis-grun´tled
dis-guise´
dis-guis´ed-ly
dis-gust´
dis-gust´ed
dis-gust´ed-ly
dis-gust´ing
dis-gust´ing-ly
dis-ha-bille´
dis-har-mo´ni-ous
dis-har´mo-ny
dis-heart´en
di-shev´el
di-shev´eled
dis-hon´est
dis-hon´es-ty
dis-hon´or
dis-hon´or-able
dish´wash-er
dis-il-lu´sion
dis-il-lu´sion-ment
dis-in-cli-na´tion
dis-in-clined´
dis-in-fect´
dis-in-fec´tant
dis-in-fec´tion
dis-in-gen´u-ous
dis-in-her´it
dis-in´te-grate
dis-in-te-gra´tion
dis-in-ter´
dis-in´ter-est-ed
dis-in´ter-est-ed-ness
dis-join´
dis-joint´
dis-joint´ed
dis-junct´
dis-junc´tion
dis-junc´tive
disk
dis-like´
dis´lo-cate
dis-lo-ca´tion
dis-lodge´
dis-loy´al
dis-loy´al-ty
dis´mal

dis´mal-ly
dis-man´tle
dis-man´tling
dis-mast´
dis-may´
dis-mem´ber
dis-mem´ber-ment
dis-miss´
dis-mis´sal
dis-mis´sion
dis-mount´
dis-obe´di-ence
dis-obe´di-ent
dis-obey´
dis-obeyed´
dis-or´der
dis-or´dered
dis-or´der-li-ness
dis-or´der-ly
dis-or-ga-ni-za´tion
dis-or´ga-nize
dis-own´
dis-par´age
dis-par´age-ment
dis-par´ag-ing-ly
dis-par´ate
dis-par´i-ty
dis-pas´sion-ate
dis-patch´
dis-patch´er
dis-pel´
dispelled´
dis-pel´ling
dis-pens´abil´i-ty
dis-pens´able
dis-pen´sa-ry
dis-pen-sa´tion
dis-pense´
dis-pens´er
dis-per´sal
dis-per´sant
dis-perse´
dis-pers´ible
dis-per´sion
di-spir´it
di-spir´it-ed
dis-place´
dis-placed´
dis-place´ment

dis-play´
dis-please´
dis-pleas´ing
dis-plea´sure
dis-pos´able
dis-pos´al
dis-pose´
dis-pos´er
dis-po-si´tion
dis-pos-sess´
dis-pro-por´tion
dis-pro-por´tion-al
dsi-pro-por´tion-ate
dis-prove´
dis-put´able
dis-pu´tant
dis-pu-ta´tion
dis-pu-ta´tious
dis-pu´ta-tive
dis-pute´
dis-qual-i-fi-ca´tion
dis-qual´i-fied
dis-qual´i-fy
dis-qui´et
Dis-rae´li
dis-re-gard´
dis-re-pair´
dis-rep´u-ta-ble
dis-rep´u-ta-bly
dis-re-pute´
dis-re-spect´
dis-re-spect´able
dis-re-spect´ful
dis-robe´
dis-rupt´
dis-rup´tion
dis-sat-is-fac´tion
dis-sat´is-fied
dis-sat´is-fy
dis-sect´
dis-sect´ed
dis-sec´tion
dis-sec´tor
dis-sem´blance
dis-sem´ble
dis-sem´bler
dis-sem´i-nate
dis-sem-i-na´tion
dis-sem´i-na-tor

dis-sen´sion
dis-sent´
dis-sent´er
dis´ser-tate
dis´ser-ta´tion
dis´ser-ta-tive
dis-serv´ice
dis-sev´er
dis´si-dence
dis´si-dent
dis-sil´ien-cy
dis-sil´ient
dis-sim´i-lar
dis-sim-i-lar´i-ty
dis-sim-i-la´tion
dis-sim´u-late
dis-sim-u-la´tion
dis´si-pate
dis´si-pat-ed
dis´si-pa´tion
dis´si-pa-tor
dis-so´ci-ate
dis-so´ci-a´tion
dis-sol-u-bil´i-ty
dis-sol´u-ble
dis´so-lute
dis-so-lu´tion
dis-solv´able
dis-solve´
dis-sol´vent
dis-solv´ing
dis´so-nance
dis´so-nan-cy
dis´so-nant
dis-suade´
dis-sua´sive
dis-sua´sive-ly
dis´taff
dis-tain´
dis´tal
dis´tance
dis´tant
dis´tant-ly
dis-taste´
dis-taste´ful
dis-tem´per
dis-ten´tion
dis-till´
dis-till´able

dis´til-late
dis-til-la´tion
dis-till´er
dis-till´ery
dis-till´ing
dis-tinct´
dis-tinc´tion
dis-tinc´tive
dis-tinct´ly
dis-tinct´ness
dis-tin´guish
dis-tin´guish-able
dis-tin´guish-ably
dis-tin´guished
dis-tort´
dis-tort´ed
dis-tor´tion
dis-tor´tive
dis-tract´
dis-tract´ible
dis-trac´tion
dis-trac´tive
dis-traught´
dis-tress´
dis-tress´ful
dis-tress´ing
dis-trib´u-tary
dis-trib´ute
dis-tri-bu´tion
dis-trib´u-tive
dis-trib´u-tor
dis´trict
dis-trust´
dis-trust´ful
dis-turb´
dis-tur´bance
dis-turb´er
dis-un´ion
dis-unite´
dis-use´
dith´er
dit´to
dit´ty
di-uret´ic
di-ur´nal
di´va
di-van´
div´er
di-verge´

di-ver´gence
di-ver´gen-cy
di-ver´gent
di-ver´gent-ly
di´vers
di-verse´
di-verse´ly
di-ver-si-fi-ca´tion
di-ver´si-fied
di-ver´si-fy
di-ver´sion
di-ver´si-ty
di-vert´
di-ver-tic´u-lum
di-ver´tise-ment
Di´ves
di-vest´
di-vide´
di-vid´ed
div´i-dend
di-vid´er
di-vid´u-al
div-i-na´tion
di-vin´a-to-ry
di-vine´
di-vine´ly
di-vin´er
div´ing
di-vin´i-ty
di-vis-i-bil´i-ty
di-vis´i-ble
di-vi´sion
di-vi´sion-al
di-vi´sive
di-vi´sor
di-vorce´
di-vor´cee´
di-vorce´ment
div´ot
di-vul´gate
di-vulge´
di-vulge´ment
di-vulg´ing
Dix´ie
Dix´on
diz´zi-ly
diz´zi-ness
diz´zy
dob´bin

Do´ber-man pin´scher
doc´ile
doc´ile-ly
dock´et
dock fore´man
dock´hand
dock´man
dock´mas-ter
dock rent
dock´side
dock´yard
doc´tor
doc´tor-al
doc´tor-ate
doc´tri-naire´
doc´tri-nal
doc´trine
doc´u-ment
doc´u-men´ta-ry
doc-u-men-ta´tion
dod´der
do-dec´a-gon
dodg´er
dodg´ing
do´er
doe´skin
does´n't
dog´bite
dog´cart
dog´catch-er
dog col´lar
dog days
doge
dog´—eared
dog´fight
dog´fish
dog´ged
dog´ged-ly
dog´ger-el
dog´gery
dog´ging
dog´gy
dog´house
do´gie
dog´ma
dog-mat´ic
dog-mat´i-cal
dog-mat´i-cal-ly
dog´ma-tism

dog´ma-tist
dog´ma-tize
dog rose
dog´wood
doi´lies
doi´ly
do´ing
dol´ce
dol´drum
dole´ful
dole´ful-ly
dol´lar
dol´ly
dol´man
dol´men
do´lo-mite
Do-lo´res
dol´phin
do-main´
Domes´day
do-mes´tic
do-mes´ti-cate
do-mes-ti-ca´tion
do-mes-tic´i-ty
dom´i-cal
dom´i-cile
dom´i-nance
dom´i-nant
dom´i-nate
dom-i-na´tion
dom´i-neer´
dom´i-neer´ing
Dom´i-nic
Do-min´i-can
do-min´ion
Dom´i-nique
dom´i-no
dom´i-noes
Don´ald
do-nate´
Don-a-tel´lo
do-nat´ing
do-na´tion
Don´a-tism
do-nee´
Don´e-gal
Don Ju´an
don´key
don´na

Donne
do´nor
Don Qui-xo´te
don't
doo´dle
doo´dling
dooms´day
door´bell
door´keep-er
door´knob
door´man
door´nail
door´plate
door´post
door´sill
door´step
door´stone
door´way
door´yard
doped
dop´ing
Dor´ches-ter
Dor´ic
dor´man-cy
dor´mant
dor´mer
dor´mi-ent
dor´mi-to-ries
dor´mi-to-ry
Dor´o-thy
dor´sal
Dor´set-shire
Dort´mund
do´ry
dos´age
dosed
do-sim´e-try
dos´ing
dos´ser
dos´sier
dot´age
dot´ed
dot´ing
dot´ish
dot´ted
dot´ty
dou´ble
dou´ble—bar´reled
dou´ble cross

dou´ble en-ten´dre
dou´ble-head´er
dou´ble—quick´
dou´blet
dou´bling
dou-bloon´
dou´bly
doubt
doubt´able
doubt´ful
doubt´ful-ly
doubt´less
douche
douch´ing
dough´boy
Dough´er-ty
dough´nut
dough´ty
dough´y
Doug´las
doused
dous´ing
Do´ver
dove´tail
dow´a-ger
dowd´y
dow´el
dow´er
down´cast
down´fall
down´heart-ed
down´hill´
down´pour
down´right
down´stairs´
down´stream
down´throw
down´town´
down´trod´den
down´ward
down´y
dow´ries
dow´ry
dows´er
dox´y
doz´en
doz´ing
drab´ness
drach´ma

Dra´co
draft
draft-ee´
draft´i-ly
drafts´man
draft´y
dragged
drag´ging
drag´gle
drag´net
drag´on
drag´on-et´
drag´on-fly
dra-goon´
drag´rope
drain´age
drain´er
drain´pipe
drain pump
drain valve
dra´ma
dra-mat´ic
dra-mat´i-cal-ly
dram´a-tist
dram-a-ti-za´tion
dram´a-tize
dram´shop
drap´er
drap´ery
drap´ing
dras´tic
dras´ti-cal-ly
draught
draught´y
draw´back
draw´bar
draw´bridge
draw-ee´
draw´er
draw´ing
drawl´ing
dray´age
Dray´ton
dread´ful
dread´ful-ly
dread´nought
dream´er
dream´i-ly
dream´i-ness

dream´ing
dream´land
dream´less
dreamt
dream´y
drear´i-ly
drear´i-ness
drear´y
dredg´er
dredg´ing
Drei´ser
Dres´den
dress´er
dress´ing
dress´ing gown
dress´ing room
dress´mak-er
dress´mak-ing
dress´y
Drey´fus
drib´ble
drib´bled
dri´er
drift´age
drift´er
drift´ing
drift´wood
drift´y
drilled
drill´er
drill´ing
drill´mas-ter
dri´ly
drink´able
drink´er
Drink´water
dripped
drip´ping
driv´el
driv´en
driv´er
drive´way
driv´ing
driz´zle
driz´zly
drom´e-dary
droop´ing
droop´y
drop´let

dropped
drop´per
drop´ping
drop´sy
drought
dro´ver
drowned
drows´i-ly
drows´i-ness
drows´y
drub´bing
drudge
drudg´ery
drudg´ing
drug clerk
drugged
drug´ging
drug´gist
drug´store
drummed
drum´mer
drum´ming
Drum´mond
drum´stick
drunk´ard
drunk´en
drunk´en-ness
Dry´den
dry-dock
dry´er
dry´goods
dry´ing
dry´ly
dry´ness
du´al
du´al-ism
du-al´i-ty
du´al-ly
dub´bing
du´bi-ous
du´bi-ous-ly
du´bi-ta-ble
Dub´lin
Du-buque´
du´cal
duc´at
duch´ess
duck´bill
duck´ling

duck´weed
duck´y
duct´less
dud´geon
due bill
du´el
du´el-ist
du-et´
duf´fel
duf´fer
dug´out
duke´dom
dul´lard
dull´ness
dul´ly
Du-luth´
du´ly
Du´ma
Du-mas´
Du Mau-rier´
dumb´bell
dumb´wait-er
dum´dum
dum´found
dum-my
dump´i-ness
dump´ling
dump´y
Dun´bar
Dun´can
dunce
Dun-dee´
dun-ga-ree´
Dun´ge-ness´
dun´geon
dunk´er
Dun´kirk
dun´nage
dun´ning
du´o
du´o-dec´i-mal
du-o-dec´i-mo
du´o-de´nal
du´o-den´ary
du-o-de´num
dup´able
duped
dup´ery
dup´ing

du´plex
du-plex´i-ty
du´pli-cate
du-pli-ca´tion
du´pli-ca-tive
du´pli-ca-tor
du-plic´i-ty
Du-quesne´
du-ra-bil´i-ty
du´ra-ble
du´rance
du-ra´tion
du-ress´
Dur´ham
dur´ing
dusk´i-ness
dusk´y
Dus´sel-dorf
dust bowl
dust´cloth
dust cov´er
dust´er
dust´pan
dust´proof
dust´y
Dutch´man
du´te-ous
du´te-ous-ly
du´ti-able
du´ties
du´ti-ful
du´ty
Dvo´rak
dwarf´ish
dwell´er
dwell´ing
dwell´ing place
dwelt
dwin´dle
dwin´dling
dyed
dye´ing
dy´ing
dyke
dy-nam´ic
dy-nam´i-cal
dy-nam´ics
dy´na-mism
dy´na-mite

dy´na-mo
dy´na-mos
dy-na-mom´e-ter
dy-nas´tic
dys´en-tery
dys-func´tion
dys-pep´sia
dys-pep´tic
dysp´nea

E

ea´ger
ea´ger-ly
ea´ger-ness
ea´gle
ea´gle—eyed
ea´glet
ea´gre
ear´ache
ear´drop
ear´drum
earl´dom
car´li-cr
ear´li-est
ear´ly
ear´mark
ear´muff
earn´er
ear´nest
ear´nest-ly
ear´nest-ness
earn´ing
ear´phone
ear´ring
ear´shot
earth´born
earth´en
earth´en-ware
earth´i-er
earth´i-ness
earth´li-ness
earth´ly
earth´quake
earth´ward
earth´work
earth´worm
earth'y
ear trum´pet

ear´wax
ear´wig
eased
ea´sel
ease´ment
eas´i-er
eas´i-est
eas´i-ly
eas´i-ness
eas´ing
Eas´ter
east´er-ly
east´ern
east´ern-er
Eas´ter-tide
Eas´ton
east´ward
eas´y
eas´y chair
eas´y-go-ing
eat´able
eat´en
eat´er
eat´ing
eaves
eaves´drop
eaves´drop-per
eaves´drop-ing
ebbed
ebb´ing
Eb-e-ne´zer
eb´o-ny
ebul´lience
ebul´lient
eb-ul-li´tion
ec´ce ho´mo
ec-cen´tric
ec-cen´tri-cal
ec-cen´tri-cal-ly
ec-cen-tric´i-ty
Ec-cle-si-as´tes
ec-cle-si-as´tic
ec-cle-si-as´ti-cal
ec-dys´i-al
ec-dys´i-ast
ec´dy-sis
ech´e-lon
ech´o
ech´oed

ech´oes
ech´o-ing
é´clair
ec-lec´tic
ec-lec´ti-cal
ec-lec´ti-cism
eclipse´
eclips´ing
eclip´tic
ecole´
ec-o-log´i-cal
ecol´o-gist
ecol´o-gy
econ´o-met´ric
ec-o-nom´ic
ec-o-nom´i-cal
ec-o-nom´i-cal-ly
econ´o-mies
econ´o-mist
econ´o-mize
econ´o-miz-ing
econ´o-my
ec´o-sphere
ec´ru
ec´sta-sies
ec´sta-sy
ec-stat´ic
ec-stat´i-cal-ly
ec´to-plasm
ec´to-plas-mic
Ec´ua-dor
Ec´ua-dor an
Ec´ua-dor´i-an
ec-u-men´i-cal
ec-u-me-nic´i-ty
ec-ze´ma
edac´i-ty
ed´died
ed´dies
ed´dy
ed´dy-ing
e´del-weiss
ede´ma
E´den
Ed´gar
edge´ways
edge´wise
edg´ing
edg´y

ed-i-bil´i-ty
ed´i-ble
e´dict
e´dic´tal
ed-i-fi-ca´tion
ed´i-fice
ed´i-fied
ed´i-fies
ed´i-fy
ed´i-fy-ing
Ed´in-burg
Ed´i-son
ed´it
edi´tion
ed´i-tor
ed-i-to´ri-al
ed-i-to´ri-al-ize
ed-i-to´ri-al-ly
ed´i-tor-ship
ed´u-ca-ble
ed´u-cate
ed´u-cat-ing
ed-u-ca´tion
ed-u-ca´tion-al
ed-u-ca´tion-al-ist
ed-u-ca´tion-al-ly
ed´u-cat-ive
ed´u-ca-tor
ed´u-ca-to-ry
educe´
educ´ible
educ´tion
educ´tive
educ´tor
eel´y
ee´rie
ee´ri-ly
ee´ri-ness
ef-face´
ef-face´able
ef-face´ment
ef-fac´ing
ef-fect´
ef-fect´ible
ef-fec´tive
ef-fec´tive-ly
ef-fec´tive-ness
ef-fec´tu-al
ef-fec-tu-al´i-ty

ef-fec´tu-al-ly
ef-fec´tu-ate
ef-fec-tu-a´tion
ef-fem´i-na-cy
ef-fem´i-nate
ef´fer-ent
ef-fer-vesce´
ef-fer-ves´cence
ef-fer-ves´cent
ef-fer-vesc´ible
ef-fer-vesc´ing
ef-fete´
ef-fi-ca´cious
ef´fi-ca-cy
ef-fi´cien-cy
ef-fi´cient
ef-fi´cient-ly
ef-fig´ial
ef´fi-gy
ef´flo-resce´
ef-flo-res´cence
ef-flo-res´cent
ef´flu-ence
ef´flu-ent
ef-fo´di-ent
ef´fort
ef-fron´tery
ef-ful´gence
ef-ful´gent
ef-fuse´
ef-fu´sion
ef-fu´sive
ef-fu´sive-ly
eft-soon´
egad´
egg´head
egg´nog
egg´plant
egg´shaped
egg´shell
e´go
e´go-cen´tric
ego-cen-tric´i-ty
ego-cen´trism
e´go-ism
e´go-ist
e´go-is´tic
e´go-is´ti-cal
e´go-tism

e´go-tist
e´go-tis´tic
e´go-tis´ti-cal
e´go-tis´ti-cal-ly
e´gress
egres´sion
e´gret
E´gypt
Egyp´tian
ei´der
ei´der-down
ei´do-graph
ei´do-lon
Eif´fel
eight
eigh-teen´
eigh-teenth´
eight´fold
eighth
eight´i-eth
eight´y
Ein´stein
Ei´sen-how-er
ei´ther
ejac´u-late
ejac´u-lat-ing
ejac-u-la´tion
ejac´u-la-tive
ejac´u-la-to-ry
eject
ejec´tion
ejec´tive
ejec´tor
eked
ek´ing
elab´o-rate
elab´o-rate-ly
elab´o-rate-ness
elab´o-rat-ing
elab-o-ra´tion
elab´o-ra-tive
élan´
e´land
elapse
elaps´ing
elas´tic
elas-ti-cal-ly
elas-tic´i-ty
elas-tom´e-ter

elate
elat´ed
el´a-ter
elat´er-id
elat´er-in
el-a-te´ri-um
ela´tion
El´ba
el´bow
el´bow-room
el´der
el´der-ber-ry
el´der-ly
el´dest
El Do-ra´do
El´ea-nor
El-e-a´zar
elect
elec´tion
elec´tion-eer´
elec´tive
elec´tor
elec´tor-al
elee´tor-ate
Elec´tra
elec´tric
elec´tri-cal
elec´tri-cal-ly
elec-tri´cian
elec-tric´i-ty
elec-tri-fi-ca´tion
elec´tri-fied
elec´tri-fy
elec´tro
elec-tro-anal´y-sis
elec-tro-car´dio-gram
elec-tro-car´dio-graph
elec-tro-chem´i-cal
elec-tro-chem´is-try
elec´tro-cute
elec-tro-cu´tion
elec´trode
elec-tro-dy-nam´ics
elec-tro-graph´ic
elec-trog´ra-phy
elec-trol´y-sis
elec´tro-lyte
elec-tro-lyt´ic
elec-tro-lyt´i-cal

elec´tro-lyze
elec´tro-mag-net
elec´tro-mag-net´ic
elec-tro-mag´net-ism
elec-trom´e-ter
elec´tro-met´ric
elec´tro-mo-tive
elec´tron
elec-tron´ic
elec-tro-os-mo´sis
elec-troph´o-rus
elec´tro-plate
elec´tros
elec´tro-scope
elec-tro-scop´ic
elec-tro-stat´ic
elec-tro-ther´a-py
elec-tro-ton´ic
elec-trot´o-nus
elec´tro-type
elec´tro-typ-er
elec´trum
elec´tu-ary
cl-ee-mos´y-nary
el´e-gance
el´e-gan-cy
el´e-gant
el´e-gant-ly
el´e-gi´ac
el´e-gist
el´e-gize
el´-e-gy
el´e-ment
el-e-men´tal
el-e-men-tar´i-ly
el-e-men´ta-ry
el´e-phant
el-e-phan-ti´a-sis
el´e-phan´tine
El-eu-sin´i-an
Eleu´sis
el´e-vate
el´e-vat-ed
el-e-va´tion
el´e-va-tor
elev´en
elev´enth
elf´in
elf´ish

El´gin
E´li
Eli´as
elic´it
elic-i-ta´tion
elic´i-tor
elide´
elid´ible
elid´ing
el-i-gi-bil´i-ty
el´i-gi-ble
Eli´hu
elim´i-nant
elim´i-nate
elim-i-na´tion
elim´i-na-tor
El´i-ot
Eli´sha
elite
elix´ir
Eliz´a-beth
Eliz-a-be´than
Elk´hart
El´li-ot
el-lipse´
el-lips´es
cl-lip´sis
el-lip´soid
el-lip´soi´dal
el-lip´-tic
el-lip´ti-cal
el-lip-tic´i-ty
El-mi´ra
el-o-cu´tion
el-o-cu´tion-ary
el-o-cu´tion-ist
El-o-him´
El-o-his´tic
eloign´er
elon´gate
elon-ga´tion
elope´
elope´ment
elop´er
elop´ing
el´o-quence
el´o-quent
el´o-quent-ly
El Pas´o

El Sal´va-dor
else´where
elu´ci-date
elu-ci-da´tion
elu-ci-da-tive
elude´
elud´ible
elud´ing
elu´sion
elu´sive
elu´so-ry
El´vis
el´vish
El´wood
Ely-see´
ema´ci-ate
ema-ci-a´tion
em´a-nate
em-a-na´tion
em´a-na-tive
eman´ci-pate
eman-ci-pa´tion
eman´ci-pa-tor
emas´cu-late
emas-cu-la´tion
em-balm´
em-balm´er
em-balm´ment
em-bank´
em-bank´ment
em-bar-ca-de´ro
em-bar´go
em-bar´goed
em-bar´goes
em-bark´
em-bar-ka´tion
em´bar-ras´
em´bar´rass
em-bar´rassed
em-bar´rass-es
em-bar´rass-ing
em-bar´rass-ing-ly
em-bar´rass-ment
em´bas-sies
em´bas-sy
em-bat´tle
em-bed´
em-bed´ded
em-bel´lish

em-bel´lish-ment
em´ber
em-bez´zle
em-bez´zled
em-bez´zle-ment
em-bez´zler
em-bit´ter
em-bla´zon
em-bla´zon-ment
em-bla´zon-ry
em´blem
em´blem-at´ic
em-blem-at´i-cal
em-blem-at´i-cal-ly
em-blem´a-tize
em´ble-ment
em-bod´i-ment
em-bod´y
em-bold´en
em-bol´ic
em´bo-lism
em-bo-lis´mic
em´bo-lus
em-bos´om
em-boss´
em-bossed´
em-boss´er
em-boss´ing
em-bow´el
em-bow´er
em-brace´
em-brac´er
em-brac´ery
em-brac´ing
em-broi´der
em-broi´der-er
em-broi´dery
em-broil´
em-broil´ment
em-brown´
em´bryo
em-bry-og´e-ny
em-bry-ol´o-gy
em´bry-o-nal
em-bry-on´ic
em´bry-os
emend
em´er-ald
emerge

emer´gence
emer´gen-cies
emer´gen-cy
emer´gent
emerg´ing
emer´i-tus
emer´sion
Em´er-son
em´ery
em´i-grate
em´i-grat-ing
em-i-gra´tion
emi-gre´
E´mil
Emile
Em´i-ly
em´i-nence
em´i-nen-cy
em´i-nent
em´i-nent-ly
emir
emir´ate
em´is-sar-ies
em´is-sary
emis´sion
emis´sive
emit
emit´ted
emit´ter
emit´ting
Em-man´u-el
emol´lient
emol´u-ment
emote
emot´er
emot´ing
emo´tion
emo´tion-al
emo´tion-al-ism
emo´tion-al-ly
emo´tive
em-pan´el
em-pan´el-ing
em-path´ic
em´pa-thy
em´per-or
em´pery
em´pha-ses
em´pha-sis

em´pha-size
em´pha-siz-ing
em-phat´ic
em-phat´i-cal-ly
em-phy-se´ma
em´pire
em-pir´i-cal
em-pir´i-cism
em-pir´i-cist
em-place´ment
em-ploy´
em-ploy-ee´
em-ploy´er
em-ploy´ment
em-po´ri-um
em-pow´er
em´press
em-prise´
cmp´tied
emp´ti-er
emp´ties
emp´ti-ness
emp´ty
emp´ty—hand-ed
emp´ty—head-ed
emp´ty-heart-ed
emp´ty-ing
e´mu
cm´u-late
em-u-la´tion
em´u-la-tive
em´u-la-tive-ly
em´u-la-tor
em´u-la-to-ry
em´u-lous
em´u-lous-ly
emul-si-fi-ca´tion
emul´si-fied
emul´si-fi-er
emul´si-fy
emul´sion
emul´sive
en-a´ble
en-a´bling
en-act´
en-ac´tive
en-act´ment
en-am´el
en-am´eled

en-am´el-er
en-am´el-ware
en-am´or
en-am´ored
en-camp´
en-camp´ment
en-cap´su-late
en-car´nal-ize
en-case´
en-cas´ing
en-caus´tic
en´ce-phal´ic
en-ceph´a-lit´ic
en-ceph-a-li´tis
en-ceph´a-lo-gram
en-ceph-a-lo-graph´ic
en-ceph-a-log´ra-phy
en-ceph´a-loid
en-ceph´a-lon
en-ceph-a-lop´a-thy
en-chain´
en-chant´
en-chant´er
en-chant´ing
en-chant´ment
en-chant´ress
en-chase´
en-chi-la´da
en-cir´cle
en-cir´cle-ment
cn-cir´cling
en´clave
en-clit´ic
en-close´
en-clos´er
en-clos´ing
en-clo´sure
en-coi´gnure
en-co´mi-ast
en-com´pass
en´core
en-coun´ter
en-cour´age
en-cour´age-ment
en-cour´ag-ing
en-crat´ic
en-croach´
en-croach´ment
en-crust´

en-crus-ta´tion
en-cum´ber
en-cum´brance
en-cyc´lic
en-cyc´li-cal
en-ey-clo-pe´dia
en-cy-clo-pe´dic
en-cy-clo-pe´dism
en-cy-clo-pe´dist
en-cyst´
en-cys-ta´tion
en-cyst´ment
en-dear´
en-dear´ing
en-dear´ment
en-deav´or
en-deav´ored
en-de´mi-al
en-dem´ic
en-dem´i-cal-ly
en-de-mic´i-ty
en-de-mi-ol´o-gy
en´de-mism
En´di-cott
end´ing
en´dive
end´less
end´less-ly
end´long
eud man
end´most
en-do-car´di-um
en´do-carp
en´do-cri´nal
en´do-crine
en´do-crin-o-log´ic
en´do-cri-nol´o-gy
en´do-crin´o-path´ic
en´do-cri-nop´a-thy
en-doc´ri-nous
en´do-der´mal
en´do-gam´ic
en-do-ge-net´ic
en-do-ge-nic´i-ty
en-dog´e-nous
en-dog´e-nous--ly
en-do-me-tri´tis
en-do-me´tri-um
en´do-mor´phic

en´do-plasm
en´do-plas´ma
en´do-plas´mic
en-dors´able
en-dorse´
en-dors´ee´
en-dorse´mcnt
en-dors´er
en-dors´ing
en´do-sperm
en-dow´
en-dow´ment
en´drin
en-due´
en-dur´able
en-dur´ance
en-dure´
en-dur´ing
end´ways
end´wise
en´e-ma
en´e-mies
en´e-my
en-er-gei´a
en-er-get´ic
en-er-get´i-cal
en-er-get´i-cal-ly
en´er-gies
en´er-gism
en´er-gize
en´er-giz-er
en´er-gy
en´er-vate
en´er-va´tion
en´er-va-tor
en-face´
en-fant´
en-fee´ble
en-fee´bling
en-fold´
en-force´
en-force´able
en-forc´ed-ly
en-force´ment
en-forc´er
en-forc´ing
en-fran´chise
en-fran´chise-ment
en-gage´

en-gaged´
en-gage´ment
en-gag´ing
en-gen´der
en´gine
en-gi-neer´
eu-gl-neer´ing
en´gine room
en´gine-ry
En´gland
En´glish
En´glish-man
En´glish-wom-an
en-graft´
en-grave´
en-grav´er
en-grav´ing
en-gross´
en-gross´ing
en-gross´ment
en-gulf´
en-hance´
en-hance´ment
en-hanc´ing
en-har-mon´ic
enig´ma
enig-mat´ic
enig-mat´i-cal
enig-mat´i-cal-ly
enig´ma-tize
En-i-we´tok
en-join´
en-join´der
en-joy´
en-joy´able
en-joy´ably
en-joy´ment
en-kin´dle
en-lace´
en-large´
en-large-ment
en-light´en
en-light´en-ment
en-list´
en-list-ee´
en-list´ment
en-liv´en
en-mesh´
en´mi-ties

en´mi-ty
en-no´ble
en-no´bling
en-nui´
enor´mi-ty
enor´mous
enor´mous-ly
E´nos
enough´
en-phy-tot´ic
en-quire´
en´quiry
en-rage´
en rap-port´
en-rapt´
en-rap´ture
en-rav´ish
en-rich´
en-rich´ment
en-robe´
en-roll´
en-rolled´
en-roll´ing
en-roll´ment
en route
en-sam´ple
en-sconce´
en-sem´ble
en-shrine´
en-shroud´
en´sign
en-slave´
en-slave´ment
en-slav´er
en-slav´ing
en-snare´
en-sue´
en-su´ing
en-sure´
en-tail´
en-tail´ment
en-tan´gle
en-tan´gle-ment
en-tan´gler
en-tan´gling
en´ta-sis
En-teb´be
en´ter
en-ter-al´gia

en-ter´ic
en-ter-i´tis
en´ter-on
en´ter-prise
en´ter-pris-ing
en´ter-pris-ing-ly
en-ter-tain´
en-ter-tain´er
en-ter-tain´ing
en-ter-tain´ment
en-thet´ic
en-thrall´
en-thrall´ing
en-thrall´ing-ly
en-throne´
en-thuse´
en-thu´si-asm
en-thu´si-ast
en-thu-si-as´tic
en-thu-si-as´ti-cal-ly
en-tice´
en-tice´ment
en-tic´ing
en-tire´
en-tire´ly
en-tire´ty
en´ti-ties
en-ti´tle
en´ti-ty
en-tomb´
en-tomb´ment
en-to-mol´o-gist
en-to-mol´o-gy
en´tou-rage´
en´trails
en-train´
en´trance
en´trance-way
en-tranc´ing
en-tranc´ing-ly
en´trant
en-trap´
en-trap´ment
en-trap´ping
en´tre
en-treat´
en-treat´ies
en-treat´ing
en-treat´ing-ly

en-treat´y
en´trée
en-trench´
en-trench´ment
en´tre-nous
en´tre-pre-neur´
en-tre-pre-neur´i-al
en´tries
en-trust´
en´try
en´try-way
en-twine´
enu´mer-ate
enu-mer-a´tion
enu´mer-a-tive
enun´ci-ate
enun-ci-a´tion
enun´cia-tive
enun´ci-a-tor
en-vel´op
en´ve-lope
en-vel´oped
en-vel´op-ing
en-vel´op-ment
en´vi-able
en´vi-ably
en´vied
en´vies
en´vi-ous
en´vi-ous-ly
en-vi´ron
en-vi´ron-ment
en-vi´ron-men´tal
en-vi´rons
en-vis´age
en-vi´sion
en´voy
en´vy
en´vy-ing
en´vy-ing-ly
en-wrap´
en´zyme
e´on
ep´au-let
é´pée
é´pée-ist
ephed´rine
ephem´era
ephem´er-al

ephem´er-id
ephem´er-is
ephem´er-on
eph´od
eph´or
E´phra-im
Eph´ra-ta
ep´i-bol´ic
ep´ic
ep´i-cal
ep´i-cal-ly
ep´i-can´thic
ep´i-can´thus
ep´i-carp
ep´i-cede
ep´i-cene
ep´i-cen´ter
ep´i-cen´trum
ep´i-crit´ic
ep´i-cure
Ep´i-cu-re´an
ep´i-cur-ism
Ep´i-cu-rus
ep´i-dem´ic
ep-i-dem´i-cal
ep-i-de-mic´i-ty
ep-i-de-mi-o-log´i-cal
ep-i-de-mi-ol´o-gy
ep´i-der´mal
ep-i-du´ral
ep´i-gas´tric
ep-i-gas´tri-um
ep´i-ge´al
ep-i-glot´tis
ep´i-gone
ep´i-gram
ep-i-gram-mat´ic
ep-i-gram-mat´i-cal
ep-i-gram´ma-tist
ep´i-graph
epig´ra-pher
ep´i-graph´ic
epig´ra-phy
ep-i-la´tion
ep´i-la-tor
ep´i-lep-sy
ep´i-lep´tic
ep´i-logue
ep´i-mer

ep-i-mer-i-za´tion
ep´i-mer-ize
ep´i-nas-ty
ep-i-neph´rine
ep-i-neu´ri-um
ep´i-nine
Epiph´a-ny
epis´co-pa-cy
epis´co-pal
Epis´co-pa´lian
epis´co-pal-ism
epis´co-pate
ep´i-sode
ep-i-sod´ic
ep-i-sod´i-cal
ep-i-sod´i-cal-ly
epis´tle
ep´i-stome
ep´i-taph
epit´a-sis
ep-i-tha-la´mi-on
ep-l-tha-la´mi-um
ep-i-the´li-al
ep-i-the-li-o´ma
ep´i-the-li-om´a-tous
ep-i-the´li-um
ep´i-them
epith´e-sis
ep´i-thet
epit´o-me
ep´i-tom´i-cal
epit-o-mize
epit´ro-phy
e plu´ri-bus u´num
ep´och
ep´och-al
ep´ode
ep´o-nym
ep´o-nym´ic
ep´os
ep-ox´y
ep´si-lon
Ep´som
eq-ua-bil´i-ty
eq´ua-ble
e´qual
e´qualed
e´qual-ing
equal´i-ty

e´qual-i-za´tion
e´qual-ize
e´qual-iz-er
e´qual-ly
equa-nim´i-ty
equate´
equa´tion
equat´ive
equa´tor
equa-to´ri-al
eq´uer-ry
eques´tri-an
eques´tri-enne´
e´qui-an´gu-lar
equi-an-gu-lar´i-ty
e´qui-dis´tant
e´qui-lat´er-al
equil´i-brant
equil´i-brate
equil-i-bra´tion
equi-lib´rist
equi-lib´ri-stat
equi-lib´ri-um
eq´ui-lin
e´quine
e´qui-noc´tial
e´qui-nox
equip´
eq´ui-page
equip´ment
eq´ui-poise
equi-pol´lence
equipol´lent
equi-pon´der-ate
e´qui-po-ten´tial
equipped´
equip´ping
eq´ui-ta-ble
eq´ui-tes
eq´ui-ties
eq´ui-ty
equiv´a-lence
equiv´a-len-cy
equiv´a-lent
equiv´o-cal
equiv´o-cate
equiv´o-ca´tion
e´ra
era-di-a´tion

erad´i-ca-ble
erad´i-cate
erad-i-ca´tion
erad´i-ca-tive
erad´i-ca-tor
eras´able
erase´
erased
eras´er
eras´ing
Eras´mus
era´sure
Er´a-to
Er-a-tos´the-nes
er´bi-um
erect
erec´tile
erec-til´i-ty
erec´tion
erect´ly
erec´tor
erect´ness
er´e-mite
er-e-mit´i-cal
er´ga-tive
er´go
er´gone
er´got
er-got´ic
er´go-tism
er´go-tize
Er´ic
E´rie
erig´er-on
Er´in
erin´e-um
er´in-ite
er´i-nose
er´mine
erode´
erod´ible
erog´e-nous
Er´os
ero´sion
ero´sive
erot´ic
erot´i-cism
err-abil´i-ty
er´rand

er´rant
er´rant-ry
er-ra´ta
er-rat´ic
er-rat´i-cal-ly
er-ra´tum
erred
er´rhine
err´ing
err´ing-ly
er-ro´ne-ous
er-ro´ne-ous-ly
er´ror
er´ror—proof
er´satz
erst´while´
eruct´
eruc´tate
eruc-ta´tion
er´u-dite
er-u-di´tion
erupt´
erup´tion
erup´tive
er-y-sip´e-las
er-y-the´ma
er´y-thrinc
eryth´ro-blast
eryth´ro-scope
er´y-throse
eryth´ro-sin
er-y-thro´sis
eryth´ru-lose
es´ca-drille
es´ca-lade
es´ca-la-tor
es-cal´lop
es-cal´loped
es-cam´bio
es-cap´able
es´ca-pade
es-cape´
es-caped´
es´cap-ee´
es-cape´ment
es-cap´ing
es-ca´pism
es-cap´ist
es´ca-role

es-carp´ment
es´char
es´cha-rot´ic
es-cheat´
es-chew´
es-chew´al
es´cort´
es´cri-toire
es´crow
es-cu´do
es´cu-lent
es´cu-lin
es-cutch´eon
Es´ki-mo
esoph´a-ge´al
esoph´a-go-scope
esoph´a-gus
es´o-ter´ic
es-o-ter´i-cal-ly
es-pe´cial
es-pe´cial-ly
Es-pe-ran´to
es´pi-o-nage
es´pla-nade
es-pous´al
es-pouse´
es-pous´er
es-pous´ing
es-prit´
es-py´
es´quire
es´say
es´say-ist
es´sence
es-sen´tial
es-sen-ti-al´i-ty
es-sen´tial-ly
Es´sex
es-tab´lish
es-tab´lished
es-tab´lish-ment
es-tate´
es-teem´
es´ter
es-ter´i-fy
es´ter-ize
Es´ther
es-thet´ic
es-thet´ics

Es-tho´nia
es´ti-ma-ble
es´ti-mate
es-ti-ma´tion
es´ti-ma-tor
es´ti-va-tor
Es-to´nia
es-top´
es-trange´
es-trange´ment
es-trang´ing
es-tray´
es´tro-gen
es´tro-gen´ic
es´trous
es´tu-a-rine
es´tu-ary
et cet´era
etch´ing
eter´nal
eter´nal-ly
eter´ni-ty
ete´sian
E´than
eth´ane
eth´a-nol
Eth´el
eth´ene
e´ther
ethe´re-al
ethe-re-al´i-ty
ethe´re-al-ize
ethe´re-ous
ether´i-fy
ether-iza´tion
e´ther-ize
eth´ic
eth´i-cal
eth´ics
eth-i-on´ic
Ethi-o´pia
eth´moid
eth-moi´dal
eth´nic
eth´ni-cal
eth´ni-cal-ly
eth-nic´i-ty
eth´no-cen´tric
eth-no-graph´ic

eth-no-graph´i-cal
eth-nol´o-gist
eth-nol´o-gy
eth´yl
eth´yl-ate
eth´yl-ene
eth´yl-e´nic
ethyl´ic
ethyl´i-dene
ethy´nyl
e´ti-o-late
e´ti-o-log´i-cal
et´i-quette
Etrus´can
e´tude
et-y-mo-log´i-cal
et-y-mol´o-gist
et-y-mol´o-gy
eu´ca-lypt
eu´ca-lyp´tic
eu-ca-lyp´tole
eu-ca-lyp´tus
eu´cha-ris
Eu´cha-rist
Eu-cha-ris´tic
Eu´clid
Eu-clid´e-an
Eu-do´ra
Eu´gene
eu-gen´ic
eu´ge-nol
eu-he´mer-ism
eu-lo´gia
eu´lo-gies
eu´lo-gist
eu-lo-gis´tic
eu-lo-gis´ti-cal
eu´lo-gize
eu´lo-gy
Eu´nice
eu-on´y-mous
eu-on´y-my
eu-pep´tic
eu´phe-mism
eu´phe-mis´tic
eu´phe-mize
eu-phon´ic
eu-pho´ni-ous
eu-pho´ni-um

eu´pho-ny
eu-phor´bia
eu-pho´ria
eu-phor´ic
Eu-phra´tes
Eur-a´sian
Eu-re´ka
Eu-rip´i-des
Eu´rope
Eu-ro-pe´an
eu-ryth´mics
Eu-sta´chian
eu-then´ics
evac´u-ate
evac-u-a´tion
evac´u-ee´
evade´
evad´ing
eval´u-ate
eval-u-a´tion
ev-a-nes´cence
ev´a-nes´cent
evan´gel
e´van-gel´ic
e´van-gel´i-cal
Evan´ge-line
evan´ge-lism
evan´ge-list
evan´ge-lis´tic
evan´ge-lize
Ev´ans-ton
Ev´ans-ville
evap´o-ra-ble
evap´o-rate
evap´o-rat-ing
evap-o-ra´tion
evap´o-ra-tive
evap´o-ra-tor
eva´sion
eva´sive
evec´tion
e´ven
e´ven-fall
e´ven-hand-ed
e´ven-ing
e´ven-ly
e´ven-ness
e´ven-song
event´

event´ful
e´ven-tide
even´tu-al
even´tu-al´i-ty
even´tu-al-ly
even´tu-ate
ev´er
Ev´er-est
Ev´er-ett
Ev´er-glades
ev´er-green
ev-er-last´ing
ev-er-last´ing-ly
ev-er-more´
ever´sion
evert´
ever´tor
ev´ery
ev´ery-body
ev´ery-day
ev´ery-one
ev´ery-thing
ev´ery-where
evict´
evic´tion
evic´tor
ev´i-dence
ev´i-denc-ing
ev´i-dent
ev´i-den´tial
ev´i-dent-ly
e´vil
e´vil-do-er
e´vil-ly
e´vil—mind-ed
e´vil-ness
evince´
evinc´ible
evinc´ing
evis´cer-ate
evis-cer-a´tion
evis´cer-a-tor
ev´i-ta-ble
ev´o-ca-ble
evo-ca´tion
evoc´a-tive
e´vo-ca-tor
evoc´a-to-ry
evoke´

evok´ing
ev´o-lute
ev-o-lu´tion
ev-o-lu´tion-ary
ev-o-lu´tion-ist
evolve´
evolve´ment
evolv´ing
evul´sion
ewe
ew´er
ex-ac´er-bate
ex-ac´er-bat-ing
ex-ac-er-ba´tion
ex-act´
ex-act´able
ex-act´ing
ex-ac´tion
ex-ac´ti-tude
ex-act´ly
ex-act´ness
ex-ag´ger-ate
ex-ag´ger-at-ed
ex-ag-ger-a´tion
ex-ag´ger-a-tive
ex-ag´ger-a-tor
ex-alt´
ex-al-ta´tion
ex-alt´ed
ex-alt´er
ex-am´
ex-am´in-able
ex-am-i-na´tion
ex-am´ine
ex-am´in-er
ex-am´ple
ex-an´i-mate
ex-an-the´ma
ex-as´per-ate
ex-as´per-at-ing
ex-as´per-at-ing-ly
ex-as-per-a´tion
Ex-cal´i-bur
ex´ca-vate
ex-ca-va´tion
ex´ca-va-tor
ex-ceed´
ex-ceed´ing
ex-ceed´ing-ly

ex-cel´
ex-celled´
ex´cel-lence
ex´cel-len-cy
ex´cel-lent
ex´cel-lent-ly
ex-cel´ling
ex-cel´si-or
ex-cept´
ex-cept´able
ex-cept´ing
ex-cep´tion
ex-cep´tion-able
ex-cep´tion-al
ex-cep´tion-al-ly
ex´cerpt
ex-cerpt´er
ex-cerpt´ible
ex-cess´
ex-ces´sive
ex-ces´sive-ly
ex-change´
ex-change´able
ex-chang´ing
ex´che-quer
ex-cip´i-ent
ex´cis-able
ex´cise
ex-ci´sion
ex-cit-abil´i-ty
ex-cit´able
ex-cit´ant
ex-ci-ta´tion
ex-cit´a-tive
ex-cite´
ex-cit´ed-ly
ex-cite´ment
ex-cit´er
ex-cit´ing
ex-ci´tor
ex-claim´
ex-cla-ma´tion
ex-clam´a-to-ry
ex-clud´able
ex-clude´
ex-clud´ing
ex-clu´sion
ex-clu´sive
ex-clu´sive-ly

ex-clu´sive-ness
ex-cog´i-tate
ex-com-mu´ni-cate
ex-com-mu-ni-ca´tion
ex-co´ri-ate
ex-co-ri-a´tion
ex´cre-ment
ex-cres´cence
ex-cres´cen-cy
ex-cres´cent
ex-cre´ta
ex-crete´
ex-cre´tion
ex´cre-to-ry
ex-cru´ci-ate
ex-cru´ci-at-ing
ex-cru-ci-a´tion
ex-cul-pa´tion
ex-cul´pa-to-ry
ex-cur´rent
ex-cur´sion
ex-cur´sion-ist
ex-cur´sive
ex-cus´able
ex-cu´sa-to-ry
ex-cuse´
ex-cus´ing
ex´e-crate
ex-e-cra´tion
ex-e-cur-able
ex-ec´u-tant
ex´e-cute
ex-c-cu´tion
ex-e-cu´tion-er
ex-ec´u-tive
ex-ec´u-tor
ex-ec´u-to´ri-al
ex-ec´u-to-ry
ex-ec´u-trix
ex-em´plar
ex-em´pla-ry
ex-em´pli-fy
ex-empt´
ex-empt´ible
ex-emp´tion
ex-emp´tive
ex´er-cis-able
ex´er-cise
ex´er-cis-er

ex-ert´
ex-er´tion
ex-ert´ive
Ex´e-ter
ex-fo-li-a´tion
ex´hal´ant
ex-ha-la´tion
ex´hale
ex-haust´
ex-haust´ed
ex-haust´er
ex-haust´ible
ex-haus´tion
ex-haus´tive
ex-liaus´tive-ly
ex-haust´less
ex-hib´it
ex-hi-bi´tion
ex-hi-bi´tion-er
ex-hi-bi´tion-ism
ex-hi-bi´tion-ist
ex-hib´i-tive
ex-hib´i-tor
ex-hib´i-to-ry
ex-hil´a-rant
ex-hil´a-rate
ex-hil-a-ra´tion
ex-hil´a-ra-tive
ex-hil´a-ra-to-ry
ex-hort´
ex-hor-ta´tion
ex-hort´a-to-ry
ex-hu-ma´tion
ex-hume´
ex´i-gen-cies
ex´i-gen-cy
ex´i-gent
ex´ile
ex-il´ic
ex-ist´
ex-is´tence
ex-is´tent
ex-is-ten´tial
ex-is-ten´tial-ism
ex-is-ten´tial-ist
ex´it
ex-o-don´tist
ex´o-dus
ex´o-gam´ic

ex-og´e-nous
ex-og´a-my
ex-on´er-ate
ex-on-er-a´tion
exo-pep´ti-dase
ex-oph´a-gy
ex-oph-thal´mic
ex-or´bi-tance
ex-or´bi-tant
ex-or-ci-sa´tion
ex´or-cise
ex´or-cis-er
ex´or-cism
ex´or-cist
exo-skel´e-tal
exo-skel´e-ton
ex-os-to´sis
ex´o-ter´ic
ex´o-ther´mic
ex-ot´ic
ex-ot´i-cal-ly
ex-ot´i-cism
ex-pand´
ex-pand´able
ex-pand´er
ex-panse´
ex-pan-si-bil´i-ty
ex-pan´si-ble
ex-pan´sion
ex-pan´sive
ex par´te
ex-pa´ti-ate
ex-pa-ti-a´tion
ex-pa´tri-ate
ex-pa-tri-a´tion
ex-pect´
ex-pect´able
ex-pect´an-cy
ex-pect´ant
ex-pect´ant-ly
ex-pec-ta´tion
ex-pect´a-tive
ex-pec´to-rant
ex-pec´to-rate
ex-pec-to-ra´tion
ex-pec´to-ra-tor
ex-pe´di-en-cy
ex-pe´di-ent
ex-pe´di-ent-ly

ex´pe-dite
ex´pe-dit-er
ex´pe-dit-ing
ex-pe-di´tion
ex-pe-di´tion-ary
ex-pe-di´tious
ex-pe-di´tious-ly
ex-pel´
ex-pel´la-ble
ex-pel´lant
ex-pelled´
ex-pel-lee´
ex-pel´ling
ex-pend´
ex-pend´able
ex-pend´i-ture
ex-pense´
ex-pen´sive
ex-pen´sive-ly
ex-pe´ri-ence
ex-pe´ri-enced
ex-pe´ri-enc-ing
ex-pe´ri-en´tial
ex-per´i-ment
ex-per´i-men´tal
ex-per´i-men´tal-ly
ex-per-i-men-ta´tion
ex-per´i-ment-er
ex-pert´
ex-per-tise´
ex´pert-ly
ex´pert-ness
ex´pi-ate
ex-pi-a´tion
ex´pi-a-tor
ex´pi-a-to-ry
ex-pi-ra´tion
ex-pir´ato-ry
ex-pire´
ex-pired´
ex-pir´ing
ex-pi´ry
ex-plain´
ex-plain´able
ex-pla-na´tion
ex-plan´a-tive
ex-plan´a-to-ry
ex´ple-tive
ex-plic´a-ble

ex´pli-cate
ex-pli-ca´tion
ex-plic´a-tive
ex´pli-ca-tor
ex-plic´a-to-ry
ex-plic´it
ex-plic´it-ly
ex-plode´
ex-plod´er
ex-plod´ing
ex-ploit´
ex-ploit´able
ex-ploi-ta´tion
ex-ploit´ative
ex-ploit´er
ex-plo-ra´tion
ex-plor´ative
ex-plor´a-to-ry
ex-plore´
ex-plor´er
ex-plor´ing
ex-plo´sion
ex-plo´sive
ex-plo´sive-ly
ex-po´nent
ex-po-nen´tial
ex-po-nen´tial-ly
ex-po´ni-ble
ex´port
ex-port´able
ex-por-ta´tion
ex-port´er
ex-pose´
ex po-sé´
ex-posed´
ex-pos´er
ex-pos´ing
ex-po-si´tion
ex-pos´i-tive
ex-pos´i-tor
ex-pos´i-to-ry
ex post fac´to
ex-pos´tu-late
ex-pos-tu-la´tion
ex-pos-tu-la-to-ry
ex-po´sure
ex-pound´
ex-pound´er
ex-press´

ex-press´age
ex-press´er
ex-press´ible
ex-press´ing
ex-pres´sion
ex-pres´sion-ism
ex´pres´sion-less
ex-pres´sive
ex-pres´sive-ly
ex-press´ly
ex-press´man
ex-pres´sor
ex-press´way
ex-pro´pri-ate
ex-pro-pri-a´tion
ex-pro´pri-a-tor
ex-pul´sion
ex-pul´sive
ex-punge´
ex´pur-gate
ex´pur-ga´tion
ex´pur-ga´tor
ex-pur´ga-to-ry
ex-quis´ite
ex-quis´ite-ly
ex-sert´
ex-sert´ed
ex-ser´tile
ex-ser´tion
ex´sic-cate
ex-sic-ca´tion
ex-stip´u-late
ex´tant
ex-tem´po-ral
ex-tem´po-rary
ex tem´po-re
ex-tem-po-ri-za´tion
ex-tem´po-rize
ex-tem´po-riz-er
ex-tend´
ex-tend´ed
ex-tend´er
ex-tend´ible
ex-ten-si-bil´i-ty
ex-ten´si-ble
ex-ten´sion
ex-ten´si-ty
ex-ten´sive
ex-ten´sive-ly

ex-ten´sor
ex-tent´
ex-ten´u-ate
ex-ten´u-at-ing
ex-ten-u-a´tion
ex-ten´u-a-tor
ex-ten´u-a-to-ry
ex-te´ri-or
ex-te´ri-or-ize
ex-ter´mi-nate
ex-ter-mi-na´tion
ex-ter´mi-na-tive
ex-ter´mi-na-tor
ex-ter´mi-na-to-ry
ex-ter´nal
ex-ter-nal´i-ty
ex-ter´nal-ize
ex-ter´nal-ly
ex´ter-o-cep´tive
ex´ter-o-cep´tor
ex-tinct´
ex-tinc´tion
ex-tinc´tive
ex-tin´guish
ex-tin´guish-able
ex-tin´guish-er
ex-tol´
ex-tolled´
ex-tol´ling
ex-tor´sion
ex-tort´
ex-tort´ed
ex-tor´tion
ex-tor´tion-ate
ex-tor´tion-er
ex-tor´tion-ist
ex-tort´ive
ex´tra
ex´tract
ex-tract´able
ex-trac´tion
ex-trac´tive
ex-trac´tor
ex´tra-cur-ric´u-lar
ex´tra-dit-able
ex´tra-dite
ex´tra-dit-ing
ex´tra-di´tion
ex´tra-ju-di´cial

ex-tral´i-ty
ex´tra-mar´i-tal
ex´tra-mu´ral
ex-tra´ne-ous
ex-traor´di-nar´i-ly
ex-traor´di-nary
ex-trap´o-late
ex´tra-sen´so-ry
ex´tra-ter-ri-to´ri-al
ex-trav´a-gance
ex-trav´a-gant
ex-trav´a-gan´za
ex-trav-a-sa´tion
ex-treme´
ex-treme´ly
ex-tre´mism
ex-trem´ist
ex-trem´i-ty
ex-tric´a-ble
ex´tri-cate
ex-tri-ca´tion
ex-trin´sic
ex-trin´si-cal-ly
ex-tro-ver´sion
ex´tro-vert
ex´tro-vert-ish
ex-tro-ver´tive
ex-trude´
ex-trud´er
ex-trud´ing
ex-tru´si-ble
ex-tru´sion
ex-tru´sive
ex-tu´ber-ance
ex-u´ber-ance
ex-u´ber-ant
ex-u´ber-ate
ex´u-date
ex-u-da´tion
ex-ude´
ex-ult´
ex-ult´ance
ex-ult´ant
ex-ul-ta´tion
ex-ult´ing-ly
ex´urb
ex-ur´ban-ite
eye´ball
eye´bright

eye´brow
eye´cup
eyed
eye´glass
eye´hole
eye´ing
eye´lash
eye´let
eye´lid
eye´piece
eye´shade
eye´sight
eye´sore
eye´spot
eye´strain
eye´strings
eye´tooth
eye´wash
eye´wa-ter
eye´wink
eye´wit-ness
Eze´ki-el
Ez´ra

## F

Fa´bi-an
fa´ble
fa´bled
fab´ric
fab´ri-cant
fab´ri-cate
fab-ri-ca´tion
fab´ri-ca-tor
fab´u-list
fab´u-lous
fab´u-lous-ly
fa-çade´
face´able
faced
fac´er
fac´et
fac´et-ed
fa-ce´tious
fa´cial
fa´ci-end
fa´cient
fa´ci-es
fac´ile

fac´ile-ness
fa-cil´i-tate
fa-cil´i-ties
fa-cil´i-ty
fac´ing
fac-sim´i-le
Fac´tice
fac-tic´i-ty
fac´tion
fac´tion-al
fac´tious
fac´tious-ly
fac-ti´tious
fac-ti´tious-ly
fac´ti-tive
fac´tor
fac´tor-age
fac-to´ri-al
fac´to-ries
fac-tor-i-za´tion
fac´tor-ize
fac´to-ry
fac´tu-al
fac´tu-al-ly
fac´ul-ties
fac´ul-ty
fad
fad´dist
fade
fade´—out
fad´er
fa-e´na
Fa-en´za
fa´er-ie
fa´ery
Fa´gin
fag´ot
fag´ot-ing
Fahr´en-heit
fail´ing
fail´ing-ly
faille
fail´ure
fai´ne-ance
fai´ne-an-cy
fai´ne-ant
faint
faint´ed
faint´heart-ed

faint´ish
faint´ly
faint´ness
fair´ies
fair´lead
fair´ly
fair´—mind-ed
fair´ness
fair´sized
fair´—spo-ken
fair´way
fair´y
fair´y-hood
fair´y-land
fair´y-like
fair´y tale
fait ac-com-pli´
faith´ful
faith´ful-ly
faith´ful-ness
faith´less
fak´er
fa-kir´
fal´con
fal´con-er
fal´con-et´
fal´con-ry
fal´de-ral
Falk´land
fal´la-cies
fal-la´cious
fal-la´cious-ly
fal´la-cy
fall´en
fal-li-bil´i-ty
fal´li-ble
fall´ing
Fal-lo´pi-an
fall´out
fal´low
false´heart-ed
false´hood
false´ly
false´ness
fal-set´to
fal-set´tos
false´work
fal-si-fi-ca´tion
fal´si-fied

fal´si-fi-er
fal´si-fy
fal´si-fy-ing
fal´si-ty
Fal´staff
fal´ter
fal´ter-ing
famed
fa-mil´ial
fa-mil´iar
fa-mil-iar´i-ty
fa-mil-iar-iza´tion
fa-mil´iar-ize
fa-mil´iar-ly
fam´i-lies
fam´i-ly
fam´ine
fam´ish
fa´mous
fa´mous-ly
fa-nat´ic
fa-nat´i-cal
fa-nat´i-cism
fan´cied
fan´ci-er
fan´cies
fan´ci-ful
fan´ci-ful-ly
fan´cy
fan´cy—free
fan´cy-ing
fan´cy-work
fan-dan´go
Fan´euil
fan´fare
fanged
fanned
fan´ning
Fan´ny
fan´on
fan´tail
fan-ta´sia
fan´ta-size
fan-tas´tic
fan-tas´ti-cal
fan-tas´ti-cal-ly
fan´ta-sy
fan´tod
fan´wise

far´away
farce
far´cial
far´ci-cal
far-ci-cal´i-ty
far´cy
far´del
fare-well´
far´—famed
far´fetched
far´—flung
Far´go
fa-ri´na
farm´er
farm´house
farm´ing
farm´stead
farm´yard
far´—off
Fa-rouk´
Far´ra-gut
far´—reach-ing
far´row
far´see-ing
far´sight-ed
far´ther
far´ther-most
far´thest
far´thing
fas-cic´u-lar
fas-cic´u-late
fas´ci-nate
fas´ci-nat-ed
fas´ci-nat-ing
fas´ci-nat-ing-ly
fas-ci-na´tion
fas´ci-na-tor
fas-cine´
fas´cism
Fas´cist
fash´ion
fash´ion-able
fash´ion-ably
fast-ten
fas´ten-er
fas´ten-ing
fas-tid´i-ous
fas-tid´i-ous-ness
fas-tig´i-ate

fas-tig´i-at-ed
fas-tig´i-um
fast´ing
fast´ness
fa´tal
fa´tal-ism
fa´tal-ist
fa-tal-is´tic
fa-tal-is´ti-cal-ly
fa-tal´i-ty
fa´tal-ly
fat´ed
fate´ful
fa´ther
fa´ther-hood
fa´ther—in—law
fa´ther-land
fa´ther-less
fa´ther-like
fa´ther-li-ness
fa´ther-ly
fath´om
fath´om-able
Fa-thom´e-ter
fath´om-less
fat´i-ga-ble
fa-tigue´
fa-tigued´
fa-tigu´ing
fa-tigu´ing-ly
Fat´i-ma
fat´ling
fat´ness
fat´ten
fat´ten-er
fat´ter
fat´tish
fat´ty
fa-tu´i-ty
fau´cal
fau´cal-ize
fau´ces
fau´cet
fau´cial
fault´find-ing
fault´i-er
fault´i-ly
fault´i-ness
fault´less

fault´y
faun
fau´na
fau´nal
fau´vism
faux pas
fa´vism
fa´vor
fa´vor-able
fa´vor-ably
fa´vored
fa´vor-er
fa´vor-ite
fa´vor-it-ism
fa´vus
fawn
faze
fe´al-ty
fear´ful
fear´ful-ly
fear´less
fear´less-ly
fear´less-ness
fear´some
fea´sance
fea-si-bil´i-ty
fea´si-ble
feath´er
feath´er-bed-ding
feath´er-brain
feath´ered
feath´er-edge
feath´er-head
feath´er-ing
feath´er-less
feath´er-weight
feath´ery
fea´ture
fea´tured
fea´ture-less
feb-ri-fa´cient
fe-brif´er-ous
fe-brif´ic
fe-brif´u-gal
feb´ri-fuge
feb´rile
fe-bril´i-ty
Feb´ru-ary
fe´cal

fe´ces
feck´less
fec´u-la
fec´u-lence
fec´u-lent
fe´cund
fed´er-a-cy
fed´er-al
fed´er-al-ese
fed´er-al-ism
fed´er-al-ist
fed-er-al-is´tic
fed-er-al-iza´tion
fed´er-al-ize
fed´er-ate
fed-er-a´tion
fed´er-a-tive
fe-do´ra
fee´ble
fee´ble-heart-ed
fee´ble-mind-ed
fee´ble-ness
fee´bly
feed´er
feed´ing
feed pipe
feed´stuff
feed valve
feel´er
feel´ing
feel´ing-ly
feign
feigned
feign´er
feint
feld´spar
feld´spath-ic
fe-lic´i-tate
fe-lic-i-ta´tion
fe-lic´i-tous
fe-lic´i-ty
fe´lid
fe´line
fe-lin´i-ty
fell´er
fell´ness
fel´low
fel´low-ship
fel´on

fe-lo´ni-ous
fe-lo´ni-ous-ly
fel´o-ny
felt´er
felt´ing
fe´male
fe-mal´i-ty
fem´i-na-cy
fem-i-nal´i-ty
fem-i-ne´i-ty
fem´i-nine
fem-i-nin´i-ty
fem´i-nism
fem´i-nist
fe-min´i-ty
fem´i-nize
femme fa-tale´
fem´o-ral
fe´mur
fence
fenced
fence´less
fenc´er
fen´ci-ble
fenc´ing
fend´er
fen-es-tel´la
fe-nes´tra
fen´es-trat-ed
fen-es-tra´tion
fen´nel
fe-ra´cious
fe-rac´i-ty
fe´ral
Fer´ber
fer´—de—lance´
Fer´di-nand
fer´e-to-ry
fer´i-ty
fer-ment´
fer-ment´able
fer-men-ta´tion
fer-ment´a-tive
fer-ment´er
fer-men´tive
Fer-nan´dez
fe-ro´cious
fe-ro´cious-ness
fe-roc´i-ty

Fer-ra´ra
fer´ret
fer´ret-er
fer´ri-age
fer´ric
fer´ried
fer´ries
fer-rif´er-ous
fer-ri-na´trite
Fer´ris wheel
fer´ro-cene
fer-ro-mag-net´ic
fer-ro-mag´net-ism
fer-rom´e-ter
fer´rous
fer´rule
fer´ry
fer´ry-boat
fer´ry-ing
fer´ry-man
fer´tile
fer-til´i-ty
fer´til-iz-able
fer-til-iza´tion
fer´til-ize
fer´til-iz-er
fer´u-la
fer´ule
fer´ven-cy
fer´vent
fer´vent-ly
fer´vid
fer´vor
fes´cue
fes´tal
fes´ter
fes´ti-val
fes´tive
fes-tiv´i-ty
fes-toon´
fe´tal
fe-ta´tion
fetch´ing
fete
fe´tial
fe´ti-ci´dal
fe´ti-cide
fet´id
fe-tid´i-ty

fe-tip´a-rous
fet´ish
fet´ish-ism
fet´lock
fe´tor
fet´ter
fet´tle
fe´tus
feud
feu´dal
feu´dal-ism
feu-dal-iza´tion
feu´dal-ize
feu´dal-ly
feu´da-to-ry
feud´ist
fe´ver
fe´vered
fe´ver-ish
fe´ver-ish-ly
fe´ver-ous
few´ness
fi-an-cé´
fi-an-cée´
fi-as´co
fi´at
fib´bing
fi´ber
fi´ber-board
Fi´ber-glas
fi´ber-ize
fi´bril
fi´bril-lary
fib-ril-la´tion
fi´bril-lous
fi´brin
fi´broid
fi´bro-in
fi-bro´ma
fi-bro´sis
fi-bro-si´tis
fi´brous
fib´u-la
fib´u-lar
fick´le
fick´le-ness
fic´tile
fic´tion
fic´tion-al

fic-ti´tious
fic-ti´tious-ly
fid´dle
fid´dler
fid´dle-sticks
fid´dling
fi-del´i-ty
fid´get
fid´gety
fi-du´cial
fi-du´cial-ly
fi-du´ci-ary
field day
field´er
field glass
Field´ing
field mar´shal
field´piece
field´work-er
fiend
fiend´ish
fierce
fierce´ly
fierce´ness
fierc´er
fi´eri-ness
fi´ery
fi-es´ta
fif-teen´
fif-teenth´
fif´ti-eth
fif´ty
fight´er
fight´ing
fig´ment
fig´ur-al
fig´u-rant
fig´u-rate
fig´u-rate-ly
fig´u-ra´tion
fig´u-ra-tive
fig´u-ra-tive-ly
fig´ure
fig´ured
fig´ure-head
figu-rine´
fil´a-ment
fil-a-men´ta-ry
fil´a-men´tous

fi´lar
fi-lar´ia
fi-lar´i-al
fil-a-ri´a-sis
fil´a-ture
fil´bert
filch´er
fil´er
fi-let´
fi-let´ mi-gnon´
fil´i-al
fil-i-a´tion
fil´i-bus-ter
fil´i-ci´dal
fil´i-cide
fil´i-gree
fil´ing
Fil-i-pi´no
fill´er
fil´let
fill´ing
fil´lip
fil´ly
film´i-er
film´y
fil´ter
fil-ter-abil´i-ty
fil´ter-able
fil´ter-er
filth´i-er
filth´i-ly
filth´i-ness
filth-y
fil-tra-bil´i-ty
fil´tra-ble
fil´trate
fil-tra´tion
fin´able
fi-na´gle
fi-na´gling
fi´nal
fi´nal´e
fi´nal-ist
fi-nal´i-ty
fi´nal-ly
fi-nance´
fi-nan´cial
fi-nan´cial-ly
fin-an-cier´

fi-nanc´ing
fin´back
find´er
find´ing
fine´ly
fine´ness
fin´er
fin´ery
fine´spun´
fi-nesse´
fin´ger
fin´ger-nail
fin´ger-print
fin´ger-tip
fin´i-al
fin´i-cal
fin´ick-ing
fin´icky
fin´is
fin´ish
fin´ished
fin´ish-er
fi´nite
Fin´land
Finn´ish
fin´ny
fiord
fire ant
fire´arm
fire´ball
fire´box
fire´brand
fire´brick
fire´bug
fire´crack-er
fire´dog
fire´—eat-er
fire en´gine
fire´fly
fire´less
fire´light
fire´man
fire´place
fire´plug
fire´pow-er
fire´proof
fire´—re-sist´ant
fire´side
fire´stone

fire tow´er
fire´trap
fire wall
fire´wa-ter
fire´wood
fire´works
fir-ing
fir´kin
fir´ma-ment
fir-ma-men´tal
fir-man´
firm´er
firm´ly
firm´ness
fir´ry
first aid
first´born
first´hand
first´ling
first´ly
first´—rate
first wa´ter
fis´cal
fis´cal-ly
fish´er
fish´er-man
fish´ery
fish´hook
fish´i-ly
fish´i-ness
fish´ing
fish´line
fish´mon-ger
fish´tail
fish´wife
fish´worm
fish´y
fis´sile
fis´sion
fis´sion-able
fis´sure
fis´sur-ing
fist´ic
fist´i-cuff
fis´tu-la
fis´tu-lous
fitch´et
fit´ful
fit´ful-ly

fit´ly
fit´ness
fit´ted
fit´ter
fit´ting
fit´ting-ly
Fitz-ger´ald
Fitz-pat´rick
five´fold
fiv´er
fix´able
fix´ate
fix-a´tion
fix´a-tive
fixed
fix´ed-ly
fix´ed-ness
fix´ing
fix´ture
fizz´er
fiz´zle
fiz´zling
fjord
flab´ber-gast
flab´bi-er
flab´bi-ness
flab´by
flac´cid
flac´cid-ly
flac´on
flag´el-lant
flag´el-latc
flag-el-la´tion
flag-el-la-tor
fla-gel´lum
flagged
flag´ging
flag´man
flag´on
flag´pole
fla´grance
fla´gran-cy
fla´grant
fla´grant-ly
flag´ship
flag´staff
flag´stone
flail
flair

flaked
flak´i-er
flak´ing
flak´y
flam´beau
flam-boy´ance
flam-boy´an-cy
flam-boy´ant
flamed
fla´men
fla-men´co
flame´proof
flam´ing
fla-min´go
fla-min´gos
flam´ma-ble
flam´y
Flan´ders
flange
flank´er
flan´nel
flap´er-on
flap´jack
flapped
flap´per
flap´ping
flare
flare´—up
flar´ing
flash´board
flash´i-ly
flash´i-ness
flash´ing
flash´light
flash´y
flat´boat
flat´—bot´tomed
flat´foot
flat´head
flat´iron
flat´ness
flat´ten
flat´ter
flat´ter-er
flat´ter-ing
flat´tery
flat´top
flat´ware
flat´worm

flaunt
flaunt´er
flaunt´ing
flau´tist
Fla´via
fla´vin
fla´vone
fla´vor
fla´vor-ing
flaw´less
flax´en
flax´seed
flax´y
flay´er
flea´bite
flec´tion
flec´tion-al
fledged
fledg´ing
fledg´ling
fleece
fleec´i-er
fleec´i-ness
fleec´y
flee´ing
fle´er
fleet´ing
fleet´ly
fleet´ness
Flem´ing
Flem´ish
flesh´—col-ored
flesh´i-ness
flesh´less
flesh´ly
flesh´pot
flesh´y
fletch´er
fletch´er-ize
fleur—de—lis´
flew
flex-i-bil´i-ty
flex´i-bi-lize
flex´ible
flex´ion
flex-om´e-ter
flex´or
flex-u-os´i-ty
flex´u-ous

flex´ur-al
flex´ure
flib´ber-ti-gib-bet
flick´er
flick´er-ing-ly
flick´ery
fli´er
flight
flight´i-ness
flight´less
flight´y
flim´si-ly
flim´si-ness
flim´sy
flinched
flinch´ing
fling´ing
flint´lock
flint´y
flip´pan-cy
flip´pant
flipped
flip´per
flip´ping
flir-ta´tion
flir-ta´tious
flirt´er
flirt´ing-ly
flit´ter
flit´ting
fliv´ver
float´able
float´er
float´ing
floc´cu-lence
floc´cu-lent
flocked
flock´y
flogged
flog´ging
flood´gate
flood´light
flood´proof
floor´ing
floor´walk-er
flopped
flop´pier
flop´ping
flop´py

flo´ral
Flor´ence
Flor´en-tine
flo-res´cence
flo-res´cent
flo´ret
flo-ri-at-ed
flo-ri-cul´tur-al
flo´ri-cul-ture
flor´id
Flor´i-da
flo-rid´i-ty
flor´id-ly
flor´id-ness
flor´u-lent
floss´y
flo´tage
flo-ta´tion
flo-til´la
flot´sam
flounce
flounced
flounc´ing
floun´der
floun´dered
floun´der-ing
flour´ish
flour´ished
flour´ish-ing
flout´ed
flout´ing
flow´er
flow´ered
flow´er-et
flow´er-i-ly
flow´er-ing
flow´er-pot
flow´ery
flown
fluc´tu-ant
fluc´tu-ate
fluc´tu-at-ed
fluc´tu-at-ing
fluc-tu-a´tion
flu´en-cy
flu´ent
fluff´i-er
fluff´i-ly
fluff´i-ness

fluff´y
flu´id
flu-id´ic
flu-id´i-ty
fluk´y
flun´ky
fluo-chlo´ride
flu-or-ap´a-tite
flu´o-rene
flu´o-re-nyl
flu-o-resce´
flu-o-res´ce-in
flu-o-res´cence
flu-o-res´cent
flu-o-resc´ing
flu-or´ic
flu´o-ri-date
flu´o-ri-da´tion
flu´o-ride
flu´o-ri-dize
flu´o-ri-nate
flu´o-rine
flu´o-rite
flu´o-ro-ace´tic
flu´o-ro-graph´ic
flu-o-rog´ra-phy
flu-o-ro´sis
flu´or-spar
flur´ried
flur´ries
flur´ry
flur´ry-ing
Flush´ing
flus´ter
flus-ter-a´tion
flus-tra´tion
flut´ed
flut´er
flut´ing
flut´ist
flut´ter
flut´tered
flut´ter-ing
flut´tery
flu´vi-al
flu´vi-a-tile
flu-vi-ol´o-gy
flux´ible
fly´away

fly´catcher
fly´er
fly´ing
fly´ing fish
fly´leaf
fly´speck
fly´trap
fly´weight
fly´wheel
foamed
foam´i-er
foam´ing
Foam´ite
foam´y
fo´cal
fo-cal-iza´tion
fo´cal-ize
fo´cused
fo´cus-er
fo´cus-ing
fod´der
fog´gi-er
fog´gi-ly
fog´gy
fog´horn
fo´gy
foiled
foil´ing
foist´ed
fold´ed
fold´or
fold´ing
fo´li-age
fo´li-ate
fo´li-at-ed
fo-li-a´tion
fo´lic
fo´lio
fo´li-o-late
folk´lore
folksy
folk´way
fol´li-cle
fol-lic´u-lar
fol-lic´u-lin
fol-lic-u-li´tis
fol´low
fol´lowed
fol´low-er

fol´low-ing
fol´low—through
fol´low—up
fol´ly
fo-ment´
fo-men-ta´tion
fo-ment´er
fon´dant
fon´dle
fon´dled
fon´dler
fon´dling
fond´ly
fond´ness
fon-du´
fon-due´
Fon-taine-bleau´
food´stuff
fool´ery
fool´har-di-ness
fool´har-dy
fool´ing
fool´ish
fool´ish-ly
fool´ish-ness
fool´proof
fools´cap
foot´age
foot´ball
foot´bath
foot´board
foot´bridge
foot´ed
foot´fall
foot´hill
foot´hold
foot´ing
foot´less
foot´light
foo´tling
foot´loose
foot´man
foot´mark
foot´note
foot´pad
foot´path
foot´print
foot´room
foot´ rule

foot´sore
foot´step
foot´stool
foot´walk
foot´wear
foot´work
foot´worn
for´age
for´aged
for´ag-er
for´ag-ing
for-as-much
for´ay
for-bade´
for-bear´
for-bear´ance
for-bid´
for-bid´dance
for-bid´den
for-bid´der
for-bid´ding
for-bore´
forced
force´ful
force´meat
for´ceps
forc´er
forc´ible
forc´ibly
forc´ing
ford´able
for-do´
fore´arm
fore´bear
fore-bode´
fore-bod´ing
fore´cast
fore´cast-er
fore´cas-tle
fore-close´
fore-clo´sure
fore-doom´
fore´fa-ther
fore´fin-ger
fore´foot
fore´front
fore´go-ing
fore´gone´
fore´ground

fore´hand
fore´hand-ed
fore´head
for´eign
for´eign-er
fore-judge´
fore´know´
fore´knowl-edge
fore´la-dy
fore´land
fore´leg
fore´lock
fore´man
fore´mast
fore´most
fore´name
fore´noon
fo-ren´sic
fo-ren´si-cal
fo-ren´si-cal-ly
fore-or-dain´
fore-or´di-nate
fore-or-di-na´tion
fore´part
fore´paw
fore´quar-ter
fore-run´
fore´run-ner
fore´sail
fore-saw´
fore-see´
fore-see´able
fore-see´ing
fore-seen´
fore-shad´ow
fore-short´en
fore´sight
fore´skin
fore-stall´
fore´stay
for´est-ed
for´est-er
for´est-ry
fore´taste
fore-tell´
fore-tell´er
fore-tell´ing
fore´thought
fore-told´

for-ev´er
for-ev-er-more´
fore-warn´
fore´wom-an
fore´word
for´feit
for´feit-er
for´feit-ure
for´fi-cate
for-gath´er
for-gave´
forge
forge´able
forg´er
for´gery
for-get´
for-get´ful
for-get´ful-ness
for´ge-tive
for-get´—me—not
for-get´ta-ble
for-get´ting
forg´ing
for-give´
for-giv´en
for-give´ness
for-giv´ing
for-go´
for-go´ing
for-gone´
for-got´
for-got´ten
fo´rint
forked
fork´ed-ly
for-lorn´
for-lorn´ly
for´mal
for´mal-ism
for´mal-ist
for-mal-is´tic
for-mal´i-ty
for´mal-ize
for´mal-iz-er
for´mal-iz-ing
for´mal-ly
form-am´ide
form-am´i-dine
for´mat

for´mate
for-ma´tion
form´a-tive
form´a-zan
for´mer
for´mer-ly
for´mic
For-mi´ca
for´mi-cary
for´mi-cate
for´mi-cide
for-mi-da-bil´i-ty
for´mi-da-ble
form´less
For-mo´sa
for´mu-la
for´mu-la-ri´zable
for´mu-lar-iza´tion
for´mu-lar-ize
for´mu-late
for-mu-la´tion
for´mu-la-tor
for-nent´
for´ni-cate
for-ni-ca´tion
for´ni-ca-tor
for´nix
for-sake´
for-sak´en
For´se-ti
for-sook´
for-sooth´
for-swear´
for-sworn´
for-syth´ia
fort
for´ta-lice
forte
forth
forth´com-ing
forth´right
forth-with´
for´ti-eth
for-ti-fi-ca´tion
for´ti-fied
for´ti-fi-er
for´ti-fy
for-tis´si-mo
for´ti-tude

fort´night
fort´night-ly
for´tress
for-tu´i-tism
for-tu´i-tous
for-tu´i-ty
For-tu´na
for´tu-nate
for´tu-nate-ly
For-tu-na´tus
for´tune
for´ty
fo´rum
for´ward
for´ward-er
for´ward-ly
for´ward-ness
fos´sa
fos´sick
fos´sil
fos-sil-if´er-ous
fos-sil-i-za´tion
fos´sil-ize
fos-so´ri-al
fos´ter
foul
fou-lard´
foul´ly
foul´ness
foun-da´tion
found´er
found´ling
found´ries
found´ry
foun´tain
foun´tain-head
foun´tain pen
four´fold
four´—foot-ed
Fou´ri-er
four´—post-er
four´ score
four´some
four´square
four-teen´
four-teenth´
fourth
fowl
Fow´ler

fowl´er
fox´glove
fox´hole
fox´hound
fox´i-ness
fox´tail
fox ter´ri-er
fox´—trot
fox´y
foy´er
fra´cas
frac´tion
frac´tion-al
frac´tion-ary
frac´tion-ate
frac-tion-a´tion
frac´tious
frac-tog´ra-phy
frac´tur-al
frac´ture
frag´ile
fra-gil´i-ty
frag´ment
frag-men´tal
frag´men-tary
frag-men-ta´tion
frag´ment-ed
frag´ment-ize
fra´grance
fra´gran-cy
fra´grant
frail
frail´ties
fram-be´sia
framed
fram´er
frame´—up
frame´work
fram´ing
franc
fran-çais´
Fran´ces
fran´chise
Fran´cis
fran´co-lin
Fran-co´nia
Fran´co-phile
Fran-co-pho´bia
fran-gi-bil´i-ty

fran´gi-ble
fran-gi-pan´i
frank
Frank´en-stein
Frank´fort
frank´furt-er
fran´kin-cense
Frank´ish
Frank´lin
frank´lin-ite
frank´ly
frank´ness
fran´tic
fran´ti-cal-ly
frap-pé´
fra´ter
fra-ter´nal
fra-ter´ni-ty
frat-er-ni-za´tion
frat´er-nize
frat´ri-ci-dal
frat´ri-cide
frau
fraud´u-lence
fraud´u-len-cy
fraud´u-lent
fraud´u-lent-ly
fräu´lein
Fraun´ho-fer
frayed
fraz´zle
fraz´zling
freak´ish
freck´le
freck´led
Fred-er-i´ca
Fred´er-ick
Fred´er-icks-burg
free´board
free´boot-er
free´born
freed´man
free´dom
free´hand
free´hold
free´ly
free´man
free´martin
Free´mason

fre´er
fre´est
free´stone
free´think-er
free´way
free-wheel´ing
free´will
freez´er
freez´ing
freight´age
freight´er
frem´i-tus
Fre´mont
fre´nal
French´man
Fre-neau´
fre-net´ic
fre´num
fren´zied
fren´zy
Fre´on
fre´quen-cy
fre´quent
fre-quen-ta´tion
fre´quent-ly
fres´co
fres´co-er
fres´coes
fresh´en
fresh´et
fresh´ly
fresh´man
fresh´ness
fresh´wa´ter
Fres´no
fret´ful
fret´ful-ly
fret´saw
fret´ted
fret´ty
fret´work
Freud´i-an
fri´ar
fri´ary
Fri´bourg
fric-as-see´
fric´tion
fric´tion-al
Fri´day

fried´cake
friend´less
friend´li-er
friend´li-ly
friend´li-ness
friend´ly
friend´ship
friczc
frig´ate
fright
fright´en
fright´ened
fright´en-ing
fright´ful
fright´ful-ly
fright´ful-ness
frig´id
fri-gid´i-ty
frill´ing
frill´y
fringed
fring´ing
fring´y
Fris´co
Fri´sian
fris´ket
frisk´i-er
frisk´i-ly
frisk´y
frit´il-lary
frit´ter
friv´ol
fri-vol´i-ty
friv´o-lous
frizz´ing
friz´zle
friz´zling
friz´zly
frock
frog´bit
frog´man
frol´ic
frol´icked
frol´ick-ing
frol´ic-some
front´age
fron´tal
fron-ta´lis
fron-tier´

fron-tiers´man
fron´tis-piece
front´less
front´let
front—page
frost´bite
frost´bit-ten
frost´i-ness
frost´ing
frost´proof
frost´y
froth´i-er
froth´i-ly
froth´y
fro´ward
frowned
frown´ing
frow´zi-er
frow´zi-ness
frow´zy
froze
fro´zen
fruc´tose
fru´gal
fru-gal´i-ty
fru´gal-ly
fru´gal-ness
fruit´age
fruit´er
fruit´er-er
fruit´ful
fruit´ful-ness
fruit´i-ness
fru-i´tion
fruit´less
fruit-y
frump´y
frus´trate
frus´trat-ed
frus´trat-er
frus´trat-ing
frus-tra´tion
fru´ti-cose
fry´er
fuch´sia
fu´cu-lose
fu´cus
fud´dle
fud´dling

fudge
fu´el
fu´el-er
fu-ga´cious
fu-ga´cious-ly
fu-gac´i-ty
fu´gi-tive
fu´gle
fu´gle-man
fugue
Füh´rer
Fu-ji-ya´ma
ful-fill´
ful-fill´ing
ful-fill´ment
ful´gu-rant
ful-gu-ra´tion
ful´gu-rite
ful´gu-rous
fu-lig´i-nous
full´back
full´—blown´
full´—dress´
Ful´ler
fuller
full´—fledged´
full´ness
ful´ly
ful´mar
ful´mi-nate
ful´mi-nat-ing
ful´mi-na´tion
ful´mi-na-tor
ful´mi-na-to-ry
ful-min´ic
ful´mi-nous
ful-min-u´ric
ful´some
ful´some-ness
Ful´ton
fu-mar´ic
fu´ma-role
fu´ma-to-ry
fum´ble
fum´bler
fum´bling
fumed
fu´mi-gate
fu´mi-gat-ing

fu-mi-ga´tion
fu´mi-ga-tor
fum´ing
fum´y
func´tion
func´tion-al
func´tion-ary
func´tion-ate
fun-da-men´tal
fun-da-men´tal-isin
fun-da-men´tal-ist
fun-da-men´tal-ly
fu´ner-al
fu´ner-ary
fu-ne´re-al
fu-nest´
fun´gal
fun´gi
fun-gi-bil´i-ty
fun´gi-ble
fun´gi-ci-dal
fun´gi-cide
fun-gif´er-ous
fun-giv´o-rous
fun´goid
fun-gos´i-ty
fun´gous
fun´gus
fun´gus—proof
fu-nic´u-lar
fun´nel
fun´neled
fun´nel-ing
fun´ni-er
fun´ni-ly
fun´ny
fur
fur´bish
fur´bish-er
fur´cal
fur´cu-lum
fu´ri-bund
fu´ri-ous
fu´ri-ous-ly
fur´long
fur´lough
fur´nace
fur´nish

fur´nish-er
fur´nish-ings
fur´ni-ture
fu´ror
fu´rore
furred
fur´ri-er
fur´ri-ness
fur´ring
fur´row
fur´ry
fur´ther
fur´ther-ance
fur´ther-more
fur´ther-most
fur´thest
fur´tive
fur´tive-ly
fu´run-cle
fu-run-cu-lo´sis
fu´ry
fu´ryl
furze
fu´sain
fus´cous
fuse
fused
fu-see´
fu´sel
fu´se-lage
fu-si-bil´i-ty
fu´si-ble
fu´sil
fu´si-lier
fu´sil-lade
fus´ing
fu´sion
fuss´i-ly
fuss´y
fus´tic
fus´ti-er
fus´ti-ly
fus´ty
fu´tile
fu´tile-ly
fu-til´i-ty
fut´ur-al
fu´ture
fu´tur-ism

fu´tur-ist
fu-tu´ri-ty
fuze
fuzz´i-ness
fuzz´y

**G**

gab´ar-dine
ga´ba-rit´
gab´bing
gab´ble
gab´bro
gab´by
ga-belle´
gab´er-dine
ga´bi-on
ga´ble
ga´bled
ga´bling
Ga-bon´
Ga´bri-el
ga´by
gad´about
gad´ding
gad´fly
gad´get
gad´ge-teer´
gad´get-ry
ga´did
ga´doid
Gael´ic
gaff´er
gage
gag´er
gagged
gag´ging
gai´ety
gai´ly
gai´ner
gain´ful
gain´said
gain´say
Gains´bor-ough
gait
gait´ed
gait´er
Ga´ius
ga´la

ga-lac´tic
Gal´a-had
gal´an-tine
ga-lan´ty
Ga-la´pa-gos
Gal-a-te´a
Ga-la´tia
Ga-la´tian
ga´lax
ga-lax´i-al
gal´axy
ga´lea
ga-le-ate
ga-le´gine
ga-le´i-form
Ga´len
ga-le´na
ga-le´nic
ga-len´i-cal
Ga-li´cia
Gal´i-lee
gal´in-gale
gal´lant
gal´lant-ly
gal´lant-ries
gal´lant-ry
gal´lery
gal´ley
gal´leys
gal´liard
Gal´lic
gall´ing
gal´li-ot
gal´li-um
gal´li-vant
gal´lon
gal-loon´
gal´lop
gal´loped
gal´lop-er
gal´lop-ing
Gal´lo-way
gal´lows
gall´stone
gal´op
ga-lore´
ga-losh´
ga-losh´es
Gals´wor-thy

gal-van´ic
gal´va-nism
gal-va-ni-za´tion
gal´va-nize
gall-va-niz-ing
gal-va-nom´e-ter
gal´va-no-met´ric
gal-va-nom´e-try
gal-van´o-scope
gal-va-not´ro-pism
Gal´ves-ton
Gal´way
gam-ba´do
gam´be-son
Gam´bia
gam´bier
gam´bit
gam´ble
gam´bler
gam´bling
gam´bol
gam´boled
gam´bol-ing
gam´brel
game´cock
game´keep-er
game´ness
game´some
game´ster
ga-met´ic
ga-met´i-cal-ly
gam´e-toid
gam´ic
gam´i-ly
gam´in
gam´i-ness
gam´ing
gam´ma
gam´mer
gam´mon
gam´ut
gam´y
gan´der
Gan´dhi
gan´dy danc-er
Gan´ges
gan´gly
gang´plank
gan´grene

gan´gre-nous
gang´ster
gang´way
gan´net
gant´let
gan-try
gaol
gaped
gap´er
gap´ing
gapped
gap´ping
ga-rage´
Ga-rand´
gar´bage
gar´ble
gar´bled
gar´bling
gar-çon´
gar´den
gar´den-er
gar-de´nia
Gar´di-ner
gar´di-nol
Gard´ner
Gar´eth
Gar´field
gar´fish
Gar-gan´tua
gar-gan´tu-an
gar´gle
gar´gled
gar´gling
gar´goyle
Gar-i-bal´di
gar´ish
gar´land
gar´lic
gar´licky
gar´ment
gar´ner
gar´net
gar´ni-er-ite
gar´nish
gar-nish-ee´
gar-nish-ee´ing
gar´nish-er
gar´nish-ment
gar´ni-ture

gar´ret
Gar´rick
gar´ri-son
gar-rote´
gar-rot´ed
gar-rot´ing
gar-ru´li-ty
gar´ru-lous
gar´ru-lous-ly
gar´ter
Gar´y
gas´con-ade´
gas´e-ous
gashed
gas´house
gas´i-fi-able
gas-i-fi-ca´tion
gas´i-fy
gas´ket
gas´light
gas mask
gas-o-line´
gas-om´e-ter
gas´o-met´ric
gas´ser
gas´sing
gas sta´tion
gas´sy
gas´tight
gas-trec´to-my
gas´tric
gas-tri´tis
gas-tro-en-ter-i´tis
gas-tro-in-tes´ti-nal
gas-trol´o-ger
gas-tro-nom´ic
gas-tro-nom´i-cal
gas-tron´o-my
gas´tro-pod
gas´tru-la
gas´works
gate
gate´post
gate´way
gath´er
gath´ered
gath´er-ing
gat´ing
Gat´ling

gauche
gauche´ly
gau´cho
gau´chos
gaud´ery
gaud´i-er
gaud´i-ly
gaud´i-ness
gaud´y
gauge
gauged
gaug´er
gaug´ing
Gau-guin´
gau´lei-ter
Gaull´ist
gaunt´let
gaunt´ly
gauss
Gau-tier´
gauze
gauz´i-ness
gauz´y
ga-vage´
gav´el
gav´el-er
ga´vi-al
ga-votte´
Ga-wain´
gawk´i-ly
gawk´i-ness
gawk´y
gay´ness
Ga´za
ga-ze´bo
gazed
ga-zelle´
gaz´er
ga-zette´
gaz´et-teer´
gaz´ing
gear´ing
gear´ shift
gear´ wheel
gee´zer
Gei´ger
gei´sha
gel
gel´a-tin

gel´a-tin-ase
ge-lat´i-nate
ge-lat-i-ni-za´tion
ge-lat´i-nize
ge-lat´i-niz-er
ge-lat´i-no-chlo´ride
ge-lat´i-nous
ge-la´tion
geld´ed
geld´ing
gel´id
ge-lid´i-ty
gel´ig-nite
gelled
gel´ling
gel´ose
gel-se´mic
gel-se´mi-um
Ge-ma´ra
gem´i-nate
gem-i-na´tion
gem´i-na-tive
Gem´i-ni
gem´ma
gem´mate
gem-ma´tion
gemmed
ge-mot´
gen´darme
gen´der
gene-a-log´i-cal
gene-a-log´i-cal-ly
gene-al´o-gist
gene-al´o-gy
gen-ecol´o-gy
gen´era
gen´er-al
gen-er-a-lis´si-mo
gen-er-al´i-ty
gen-er-al-iza´tion
gen´er-al-ize
gen´er-al-ly
gen´er-al-ship
gen´er-ate
gen´er-at-ing
gen-er-a´tion
gen´er-a-tive
gen´er-a-tor
gen´er-a´trix

ge-ner´ic
ge-ner´i-cal
ge-ner´i-cal-ly
gen-er-os´i-ty
gen´er-ous
gen´er-ous-ly
gen´e-sis
ge-net´
ge-net´ic
ge-net´i-cal
ge-net´i-cist
ge-net´ics
Ge-ne´va
Gen´e-vese´
Gen´e-vieve
Gen´ghis Khan
ge´nial
ge-ni-al´i-ty
ge´nial-ly
gen´ic
ge-nic´u-late
ge´nie
gen´in
gen´i-tal
gen´i-ti´val
gen´i-tive
gen´i-ture
ge´nius
Gen´oa
gen´o-ci´dal
gen´o-cide
Gen´o-ese´
ge´nome
ge´no-type
ge´no-typ´ic
gen´re
gen-teel´
gen-teel´ly
genth´ite
gen´tian
gen´tian-in
gen´tile
gen-til´i-ty
gen-tis´ic
gen´ti-sin
gen´tle
gen´tle-man
gen´tle-ness
gen´tle-wom-an

gen´tlest
gent´ly
gen´trice
gen´try
gen´u-flect
gen´u-flec´tion
gen´u-flec´to-ry
gen´u-ine
gen´u-ine-ly
gen´u-ine-ness
ge´nus
ge´o-des´ic
ge-od´e-sy
ge´o-det´ic
ge´o-det´i-cal
ge-od´ic
Ge-o-dim´e-ter
Geoff´rey
ge-og´e-nous
ge´og-nos´tic
ge-og´ra-pher
ge-o-graph´ic
ge-o-graph´i-cal
ge-o-graph´i-cal-ly
ge-og´ra-phy
ge-o-log´ic
ge-o-log´i-cal
ge-ol´o-gist
ge-ol´o-gy
ge-o-mag-net´ic
ge-o-mag´net-ism
ge-om´e-ter
ge-o-met´ric
ge-o-met´ri-cal
ge-om-e-tri´cian
ge-om´e-triz-er
ge-om´e-try
ge-o-phys´i-cal
ge-o-phys´i-cist
ge´o-phys´ics
ge-o-po-lit´i-cal
ge-o-pol-i-ti´cian
ge-o-pol´i-tics
George´town
Geor´gia
ge-o-tech-nol´o-gy
ge-ot-ri-cho´sis
ge´o-trop´ic
Ge-raint´

Ger´ald
Ger´al-dine
ge-ran´ic
ge-ra´ni-ol
ge-ra´ni-um
ge-ra´nyl
Ge-rard´
ge-rat´ic
ge´rent
Ger´hard
ger-i-a-tri´cian
ger-i-at´rics
Ger´man
ger-man´der
ger-mane´
Ger-man´ic
ger´ma-nite
ger-ma´ni-um
Ger´ma-ny
ger´mi-ci´dal
ger´mi-cide
ger´mi-nal
ger´mi-nant
ger´mi-nate
ger-mi-na´tion
ger´mi-na-tor
germ´proof
Ge-ron´i-mo
ger´ry-man-der
Ger´trude
ger´und
ge-run´di-al
ger´un-di´val
ge-run´dive
Ge´ry-on
ges´so
ge-sta´po
ges´tate
ges´tat-ing
ges-ta´tion
ges´tic
ges-tic´u-late
ges-tic-u-la´tion
ges-tic´u-la-tive
ges-tic´u-la-to-ry
ges´ture
ges´tur-ing
get´away
get´ta-ble

get´ting
Get´tys-burg
get´up
gey´ser
Gha´na
ghar´ry
ghast´li-ness
ghast´ly
gha´zi
gher´kin
ghet´to
ghost
ghost´like
ghost´li-ness
ghost´ly
ghost´write
ghost´writ-ten
ghoul´ish
gi´ant
giaour
gib´ber
gib´ber-ish
gib´bet
gib´bon
Gib´bons
gibe
gib´ing
gib´let
Gi-bral´tar
Gib´son
gid´di-ly
gid´di-ness
gid´dy
Gid´e-on
gift´ed
gi-gan-te´an
gi-gan-tesque´
gi-gan´tic
gi-gan´tism
gig´gle
gig´gling
gig´o-lo
gig´ot
Gil´bert
gild
gil´der
gild´ing
gilled
gil´ly-flow-er

gilt
gilt´—edged
gim´bal
gim´baled
gim´let
gim´mal
gim´mick
gin´ger
gin´ger-bread
gin´ger-li-ness
gin´ger-ly
gin´ger-snap
gin´gery
ging´ham
gin-gi´val
gin-gi-vi´tis
gink´go
gin´seng
Gio-van´ni
gi-raffe´
Gi-rard´
gir´a-sol
gird´er
gird´ing
gir´dle
gir´dler
gir´dling
girl´hood
girl´ish
girl´ish-ly
girth
gist
gi-tal´in
gi-tox-i-gen´in
git´tern
give´away
giv´en
giv´er
giv´ing
giz´zard
gla-bel´la
gla´brate
gla´brous
gla-cé´
gla´cial
gla´cial-ist
gia´cial-ly
gla´ci-ate
gla-ci-a´tion

gla´cier
gla-ci-ol´o-gy
gla´cis
glad´den
glad´i-ate
glad´i-a-tor
glad´i-a-to´ri-al
gia-di-o´lus
glad´ly
glad´ness
glad´some
Glad´stone
Glad´ys
glair
glam´o-rous
glam´our
glance
glanc´ing
glan´ders
glan´du-lar
glan´du-lous
glare
glar´ing
glar´y
Glas´gow
glass´es
glass´ful
glass´i-ly
glass´ine´
glass´i-ness
glass´ware
glass´y
Glas-we´gian
glau-co´ma
glau-co´ma-tous
glau´co-nite
glau´cous
glazed
glaz´er
gla´zier
glaz´ing
gleam
gleam´ing
gleam´y
glean´er
glean´ing
glebe
glee´ful
glee´man

Glen-gar´ry
glen´oid
gli´al
glib´best
glib´ly
glide
glid´er
glid´ing
glim´mer
glim´mer-ing
glim´mer-ing-ly
glimpse
glimps´ing
glis´ten
glis´ter
glit´ter
glit´ter-ing
glit´ter´y
gloam´ing
gloat´ing
glob´al
gio-bal´i-ty
glob´al-ly
glo´boid
glo´bose
glob´u-lar
glob-u-lar´i-ty
glob´ule
glob´u-lin
glom´er-ate
glom-er-a´tion
glo-mer´u-lar
glom´er-ule
gloom´i-ly
gloom´i-ness
gloom´ing
gloom´y
glo´ria
glo-ri-fi-ca´tion
glo´ri-fied
glo´ri-fi-er
glo´ri-fy
glo´ri-fy-ing
glo´ri-ole
glo´ri-ous
glo´ri-ous-ly
glo´ry
glos´sal
glos-sar´i-al

glos´sa-rist
glos´sa-ry
gloss´er
glos´si-ly
glos´si-ness
gloss´me-ter
gloss´y
Glouces´ter
Glouces´ter-shire
gloved
glov´er
glov´ing
glow´er
glow´er-ing
glow´er-ing-ly
glow´ing
glow´worm
glu-car´ic
glu´ci-num
glu´ci-tol
glu´ci-tyl
glu´co-nate
glu´con´ic
glu-co-pro´tein
glu-co´sa-mine
glu´cose
glu-co´si-dase
glu-co-sidc
glu-cu-ron´ic
glu-cu´ro-nide
glue
glued
glu´ey
glu´i-ness
glu´ing
glum´ly
glum´ness
glut´acon´ic
glu´ta-mate
glu-tam´ic
glu´ta-mine
glu´ten
glu´te-nin
glu´ti-nous
glu´ti-nous-ly
glut´ted
glut´ton
glut´ton-ous
glut´tony

gly-ce´mia
gly-ce´mic
glyc´er-ate
gly-cer´ic
glyc´er-ide
glyc´er-in
glyc´er-ol
glyc´er-yl
gly-cid´ic
glyc´i-dol
gly´cine
gly´co-gen
gly´co-gen´ic
gly-co-gen-ol´y-sis
gly-co-gen-o-lyt´ic
gly´col
gly-col´y-sis
gly-co-lyt´ic
gly-co-pro´tein
gly´cyl
glyph´ic
glyp´tic
gnarl
gnarled
gnarl´y
gnash
gnat
gnat´like
gnaw
gnawed
gnaw´ing
gneiss
gneiss´oid
gnome
gno´mic
gnom´ish
gno´sis
gnos´tic
gnos´ti-cism
gnu
Go´a
goad´ed
goal´keep-er
goa-tee´
goat´herd
goat´skin
goat´suck-er
gob´bet
gob´ble

gob´bler
gob´bling
Go´bi
gob´let
gob´lin
go´by
god´child
god´daugh-ter
god´dess
god´fa-ther
god´—fear-ing
god´—giv-en
god´head
Go-di´va
god´less
god´less-ness
god´like
god´li-ness
god´ly
god´moth-er
god´par-ent
god´send
god´ship
god´son
God´speed´
God´win
Goeb´bels
go´cr
Goe´thals
Goe´the
go-et´ic
gog´gle
gog´gling
gog´let
Goi-del´ic
go´ing
goi´ter
goi´tro-gen´ic
goi-tro-ge-nic´i-ty
Gol-con´da
gold´beat-er
gold´brick
gold´en
gold´en—haired
gold´en-rod
gold´—filled
gold´finch
gold´fish
gold´i-locks

gold´smith
gold stick
golf´er
Gol´gi
gol´iard
Go-li´ath
gom´bo
gom´er-al
Go-mor´rah
go´nad
go-na´di-al
gon´do-la
gon-do-lier´
Gon´er-il
gon´fa-lon
gon-fa-lon-ier´
gon´fa-non
go-nid´i-al
go-nid´i-um
go-ni-om´e-ter
go-ni-o-met´ric
go-ni-om´e-try
go´ni-on
go´ni-um
gon´of
gon-or-rhe´a
gon-or-rhe´al
goo´ber
good—by´
good—for—noth´ing
good´—heart-ed
good hu´mor
good—hu´mored
good´ies
good´ish
good´li-ness
good´ly
good´man
good´ness
good night
good´wife
good will
good´y
Good´year
goof´y
goo´gly
goo´gol
goose
goose´ber-ry

goose´flesh
goose´foot
goose´herd
goose´neck
goose´—step
go´pher
Gor´di-an
Gor´don
gored
gorge
gor´geous
gor´geous-ly
gorg´er
gor´ger-in
gor´get
gorg´ing
Gor´gon
gor´gon-ize
Gor-gon-zo´la
gor´hen
go-ril´la
gor´ing
gor´lic
gor´y
gos´ling
gos´pel
gos´pel-er
gos´sa-mer
gos´san
gos´sip
gos´sip-ing
gos´sip-red
gos´sipy
gos-soon´
gos-syp´i-trin
Goth´am
Goth´ic
got´ten
goug´ing
gou´lash
gourd
gour´mand
gour´mand-ism
gour´man-diz-er
gour´met
gout
gout´y
gov´ern
gov´ern-able

gov´ern-ance
gov´er-nante
gov´er-ness
gov´ern-ment
gov-ern-men´tal
gov´er-nor
gov´er-nor—gen´er-al
gov´er-nor-ship
gow´an
gowned
grab´bing
grab´ble
Grac´chi
grace´ful
grace´ful-ly
grace´ful-ness
grace´less
grac´ile
grac´ing
gra´cious
gra´cious-ly
grack´le
gra´date
gra-da´tion
gra-da´tion-al
grad´a-to-ry
grad´ed
grad´er
gra´di-ent
gra´dine
grad´ing
grad´u-al
grad´u-al-ism
grad´u-al-ist
grad´u-al-ly
grad´u-ate
grad´u-at-ing
grad-u-a´tion
grad´u-a-tor
graf-fi´to
graft´age
graft´er
graft´ing
gra´ham
Grain´ger
grain´ing
grain´y
gral-la-to´ri-al
gram

gram´a
gra-mer´cy
gram´ine
gra-min´e-ous
gram´mar
gram-mar´i-an
gram´mar school
gram-mat´i-cal
gram´pus
Gra-na´da
gran-a-dil´la
gra´na-ry
gran´dam
grand´aunt
grand-child
grand´chil-dren
grand-daugh-ter
gran´deur
grand´fa-ther
gran-dil´o-quence
gran-dil´o-quent
gran´di-ose
gran-di-os´i-ty
gran-di-o´so
grand´moth-er
grand´par-ent
Grand Rap´ids
grand´son
grand´stand
grang´er
gran´ger-ize
gran´ite
gran´ite-ware
gra-nit´ic
gran´it-ite
gran´ny
grant-ee´
grant´er
Gran´tha
grant´or
grants´ite
gran´u-lar
gran-u-lar´i-ty
gran´u-late
gran´u-lat-ed
gran´u-lat-er
gran´u-lat-ing
gran-u-la´tion
gran´u-la-tor

gran´ule
grape´fruit
grape juice
grap´ery
grape´shot
grape´skin
grape´vine
graph´ic
graph´i-cal
graph´i-cal-ly
graph´ite
gra-phit´ic
graph´i-tize
grap´nel
grap´ple
grap´pling
grap´y
grasped
grasp´er
grasp´ing
grasp´ing-ly
grass´hop-per
grass´land
grass´y
grate
grate´ful
grate´ful-ly
grat´er
Gra´tian
grat-i-fi-ca´tion
grat´i-fied
grat´i-fi-er
grat´i-fy
grat´i-fy-ing
grat´in
grat´ing
gra´tis
grat´i-tude
gra-tu´i-ties
gra-tu´i-tous
gra-tu´i-ty
grat´u-late
grat-u-la´tion
grat´u-la-to-ry
grave´dig-ger
grav´el
grav´eled
grav´el-ly
grave´ly

grav´en
grave´ness
Gra´ven-stein
grav´er
grave´stone
grave´yard
grav´i-cep´tor
grav´id
gra-vid´i-ty
grav-i-met´ric
gra-vim´e-try
grav´i-sphere
grav´i-tate
grav´i-tat-er
grav´i-tat-ing
grav-i-ta´tion
grav-i-ta´tion-al
grav´i-ta-tive
grav-i-tom´e-ter
grav´i-ton
grav´i-ty
gra-vure´
gra´vy
gray
gray´beard
gray´ish
gray´ling
gray´ness
graze
graz´er
gra´zier
graz´ing
grease´wood
greas´i-ly
greas´i-ness
greas´y
great
Great Brit´ain
great´coat
great gross
great´heart-ed
great´ly
great´ness
greave
Gre´cian
greed´i-ly
greed´i-ness
greed´y
Gree´ley

green´back
green´bri-er
green´ery
green´—eyed
green´horn
green´house
green´ing
green´ish
Green´land
green´ling
green´ness
green´room
green´sward
Green´wich
green´wood
greet´ing
greg´a-rine
gre-gar´i-ous
gre-gar´i-ous-ness
Gre-go´ri-an
Greg´o-ry
grem´lin
Gre-na´da
gre-nade´
gren´a-dier
gren´a-dine´
Gre-no´ble
Gresh´am
Gre´ta
Gret´chen
Gret´na
grey
grey´hound
grib´ble
grid´dle
grid´dle cake
grid´iron
grief
grief´strick-en
griev´ance
grieve
griev´ing
griev´ing-ly
griev´ous
griev´ous-ly
grif´fin
grif´fon
grift´er
grill

gril´lage
grille
grill´room
grim´ace
gri-mal´kin
grime
grim´i-er
grim´ly
grim´mer
grim´ness
grim´y
grin
grin-de´lia
grind´er
grind´ery
grind´ing
grind´stone
grin´go
grin´gos
grinned
grin´ning
grip
gripe
griph´ite
grip´ing
grippe
grip´ping
Gri-sel´da
gri-sette´
gris´kin
gris´li-er
gris´li-ness
gris´ly
gris´tle
gris´tly
grist´mill
grit´ting
grit´ty
griz´zle
griz´zled
griz´zly
groaned
groan´ing-ly
gro´cer
gro´cer-ies
gro´cery
grog´gery
grog´gi-ness
grog´gy

grog´ram
grog´shop
groin
grom´met
grooms´man
groove
groov´ing
grope
gro´per
grop´ing
gros´beak
gross´ly
gross´ness
gro-tesque´
gro-tesque´ly
gro-tes´que-rie´
grot´to
grouch´i-ness
grouch´y
ground crew
ground´er
ground floor
ground´hog
ground´less
ground´ling
ground plan
ground´work
grou´per
grouse
grous´er
grout´er
grov´el
grov´eled
grov´el-er
grov´el-ing
grow´er
grow´ing
growl´er
grown´—up
growth
grubbed
grub´bi-er
grub´bing
grub´by
grub´stake
grudge
grudg´ing
grudg´ing-ly
gru´el

gru´el-ing
grue´some
gruff´ly
grum´ble
grum´bler
grum´bling
gru´mose
grump´i-ness
grump´y
Grun´dy
grun´ion
grunt´er
grunt´ing
Gru-yère´
gry´phon
gua-ca-mo´le
Gua-dal-ca-nal´
Gua´de-loupe´
Guam
gua´na-mine
gua´nase
gua´ni-dine
gua-nif´er-ous
gua´nine
gua´no
guar´an-tee´
guar-an-tee´ing
guar´an-ties
guar´an-tor
guar´an-ty
guard´ed
guard´ed-ly
guard´house
guard´i-an
guard´i-an-ship
guard´room
guards´man
Gua-te-ma´la
gua´va
gu´ber-na-to´ri-al
gud´geon
Gud´run
Guelph
gue-non´
guer´don
Guern´sey
guer-ril´la
guess´ing
guess´work

guest
guest´ room
guf-faw´
Gui-an´a
guid´able
guid´ance
guide´book
guide´post
guid´ing
Gui´do
gui´don
guild
guil´der
guild´hall
guile´ful
guile´less
Guil´ford
guil´le-mot
guil´lo-tine
guilt
guilt´i-ly
guilt´i-ness
guilt´less
guilt´y
guin´ea
Guin´ea
Guin´e-vere
guise
gui-tar´
gul´let
gull-ibil´i-ty
gull´ible
gul´lies
Gul´li-ver
gul´ly
gu´lose
gu-los´i-ty
gulped
gum´bo
gum´drop
gum´ma
gummed
gum´mi-ness
gum-mo´sis
gum´mous
gum´my
gump´tion
gum´shoe
gun´boat

gun´fire
gun´flint
Gun´ite
gun´lock
gun´man
gun´met-al
gun´nel
gun´ner
gun´nery
gun´ning
gun´ny
gun´pow-der
gun´run-ner
gun´shot
gun´smith
gun´stock
Gun´ther
gun´wale
gup´py
gur-gi-ta´tion
gur´gle
gur´glet
gur´gling
gu-ru´
gush´er
gush´ing
gush´y
gus´set
gus-ta´tion
gus´ta-to-ry
Gus-ta´vus
gust´i-ly
gust-to
gust´y
Gu´ten-berg
gut´ta
gut´ted
gut´ter
gut´ter-snipe
gut´ting
gut´tur-al
gut-tur-al´i-ty
Guy-an´a
guy´ing
guz´zle
guz´zling
gym-na´si-arch
gym-na´si-ast
gym-na´si-um

gym´nast
gym-nas´tic
gym-nas´tics
gym-nos´o-phist
gym´no-sperm
gym´no-sper´mous
gym-no-stom´a-tous
gy-ne´co-crat
gy-ne-co-log´i-cal
gy-ne-col´o-gist
gy-ne-col´o-gy
gyn-i-at´rics
gyn´ics
gypped
gyp´ping
gyp´sum
gyp´sy
gy´rate
gy-ra´tion
gy´rat-ing
gy´ra-tor
gy´ra-to-ry
gyr´fal-con
gy´ro-com-pass
gy-rom´e-ter
gy´ro-plane
gy´ro-scope
gy-ro-scop´ic
gy-ro-sta˘bi-liz-er
gy-ro-stat´ics
gy´rus

H

ha´be-as
ha´be-as cor´pus
hab´er-dash-er
hab´er-dash-ery
hab´it
hab-it-abil´i-ty
hab´it-able
hab´i-tant
hab´i-tat
hab-i-ta´tion
ha-bit´u-al
ha-bit´u-al-ly
ha-bit´u-ate
ha-bit-u-a´tion
hab´i-tude

ha-bit´ué
ha-ci-en´da
hack´le
hack´ler
hack´ly
hack´man
hack´ney
hack´neyed
hack´saw
had´dock
Ha´des
Ha´dri-an
ha´fiz
Ha-ga´nah
Ha´gar
Ha´gen
hag´fish
hag-ga´da
hag´gard
hag´gis
hag´gle
hag´gling
Hague
Hai´fa
Hai´le Se-las´sie
hail´stone
hail´storm
hair˘breadth
hair˘brush
hair˘cloth
hair˘cut
hair˘dress-er
hair´i-ness
hair˘like
hair˘line
hair oil
hair˘pin
hair˘split-ter
hair˘split-ting
hair˘spring
hair ton˘ic
hair´y
Hai´ti
Ha-la´kah
ha-la´tion
hal´a-zone
hal˘berd
hal´cy-on
half

half˘back
half˘—baked´
half—breed
half˘heart-ed
half hour
half˘—mast´
half—moon´
half note
half˘pence
half˘pen-ny
half step
half ti˘tle
half˘tone
half—truth´
half˘way
half—wit´ted
hal´i-but
hal´ide
hal´i-dom
Hal´i-fax
hal´ite
hal-i-to´sis
hal´i-tus
hal´lan
hal-lel´
hal-le-lu´jah
Hal´ley
hal´ling
hall´mark
hal-loo´
hal˘low
hal´lowed
hal´lowed-ness
Hal´low-een´
hal-lu´ci-nate
hal-lu-ci-na´tion
hal-lu´ci-na-to-ry
hal-lu-ci-no´sis
hal´lux
hall´way
ha´lo
hal´o-gen
hal´o-gen-ate
hal-o-hy´drin
ha-lom´e-ter
hal´o-phyte
ha-lot´ri-chite
hal´ter
hal´tere

halt´ing
halt´ing-ly
halve
halves
halv´ing
hal´yard
Ham-ble-to´ni-an
Ham´burg
ham´burg-er
Ham´e-lin
Ham´il-ton
Ham´ite
ham´let
Ham´mar-skjöld
ham´mer
ham´mer-head
ham´mer-less
ham´mock
Ham´mond
Hamp´den
ham´per
Hamp´shire
Hamp´ton
ham´ster
ham´string
ham´strung
Ham´tramck
han´a-per
Han´cock
hand´bag
hand´ball
hand´bill
hand´book
hand´cart
hand´cuff
hand´ed
Han´del
hand´ful
hand´hold
hand´i-cap
hand´i-capped
hand´i-cap-ping
hand´i-craft
hand´i-crafts-man
hand´i-ly
hand´i-ness
hand´i-work
hand´ker-chief
han´dle

han´dle-bar
han´dler
hand´less
han´dling
hand´made´
hand´maid
hand´maid-en
hand´picked´
hand´rail
hand´saw
hand´shake
hand´some
hand´some-ly
hand´som-est
hand´spike
hand´spring
hand´work
hand´worked´
hand´writ-ing
hand´y
hand´y-man
han´gar
hang´dog
hang´er
hang´ing
hang´man
hang´nail
hang´out
hang´over
han´ker
han´ker-ing
Han´kow´
Han´na
Han´nah
Han´ni-bal
Ha-noi´
Han´o-ver
Han´sard
han´sel
han´som
Ha´nuk-kah
hap´haz´ard
hap´less
hap´ly
hap´pen
hap´pen-ing
hap´pi-ly
hap´pi-ness
hap´py

Haps´burg
hap´to-glo´bin
har´a-kir´i
ha-rangue´
ha-rangued´
ha-rangu´er
ha-rangu´ing
ha-rass´
ha-rassed´
ha-rass´ing
ha-rass´ment
har´bin-ger
har´bor
har´bor-age
hard´en
hard´en-er
hard´—eyed
hard´—faced
hard´—fist-ed
hard´hand-ed
hard´head
hard´head-ed
hard´—heart-ed
har´di-hood
har´di-ly
har´di-ness
Har´ding
hard´—look-ing
hard´ly
hard´ness
hard´ship
hard´tack
hard´top
hard´ware
hard´wood
har´dy
hare´bell
hare´lip
ha´rem
Har´lem
har´le-quin
har-le-quin-ade´
Har´ley
har´lot
harm´ful
harm´ful-ly
harm´less
harm´less-ly
harm´less-ness

har-mo´ni-al
har-mon´ic
har-mon´i-ca
har-mon´ics
har-mo´ni-ous
har´mo-nist
har-mo-ni-za´tion
har´mo-nize
har´mo-niz-ing
har´mo-ny
har´ness
Har´old
harp´er
harp´ing
harp´ist
har-poon´
harp´si-chord
har´py
har´que-bus
har´ri-dan
har´ri-er
Har´ri-et
Har´ris-burg
Har´ri-son
har´row
har´ry
harsh´ly
harsh´ness
har´te-beest
Hart´ford
Hart´ley
har´um—scar´um
Har´vard
har´vest
har´vester
Har´vey
ha´sen-pfef-fer
hash´ish
has´sle
has´sled
has´sock
has´tate
has´ten
hast´i-ly
hast´i-ness
hast´ing
Has´tings
hast´y
hat´band

hat´box
hat´brush
hatch´er
hatch´ery
hatch´et
hatch´ing
hatch´ment
hatch´way
hate´ful
hate´ful-ly
hat´er
hat´ing
hat´ rack
ha´tred
hat´stand
hat´ter
Hat´ter-as
haugh´ti-ly
haugh´ti-ness
haugh´ty
haul´age
haul´er
haunch
haunt´ed
haut´boy
Ha-va´na
have´lock
ha´ven
have´—not
Ha´ver-hill
hav´er-sack
hav´er-sine
hav´oc
hav´ocked
hav´ock-ing
Ha-wai´i
hawk´er
Haw´kins
haw´ser
haw´thorn
Haw´thorne
hay´cock
hay fe´ver
hay´field
hay´loft
hay´mak-er
Hay´mar-ket
hay´mow
hay´rack

hay´stack
hay´ward
hay´wire
haz´ard
haz´ard-ous
ha´zel
ha´zel-nut
ha´zi-ly
ha´zi-ness
haz´ing
ha´zy
head´ache
head´band
head´dress
head´ed
head´er
head´first´
head´gear
head´i-ness
head´ing
head´land
head´less
head´light
head´line
head´long
head´man
head´mas-ter
head´piece
head´quar-ters
head´room
head´ship
heads´man
head´spring
head´stone
head´strong
head´wait´er
head´wa-ters
head´way
head´work
head´y
heal´er
heal´ing
health´ful
health´ful-ness
health´i-er
health´i-est
health´i-ly
health´i-ness
health´y

| | | |
|---|---|---|
| heaped | heavy´heart-ed | hei´nous-ly |
| heard | heav´y-set | heir |
| hear´er | heav´y-weight | heir´ess |
| hear´ing | He-bra´ic | heir´loom |
| heark´en | He´bra-ism | Hei´sen-berg |
| hear´say | He´bra-ist | Hel´e-na |
| hearse | He´brew | he-li´a-cal |
| heart´ache | Heb´ri-des | he-li-an´thus |
| heart´beat | He´bron | hel´i-cal |
| heart´break | hec´a-tomb | hel´i-ces |
| heart´break-ing | heck´le | he-lic´i-ty |
| heart´bro-ken | heck´ler | hel´i-coi´dal |
| heart´burn | heck´ling | hel´i-con |
| heart´ed | hec´tare | hel´i-cop-ter |
| heart´en | hec´tic | he´lio-cen´tric |
| heart´felt | hec´ti-cal-ly | he´lio-graph |
| hearth | hec´to-graph | he-li-og´ra-phy |
| hearth´stone | hec´to-graph´ic | he-li-om´e-ter |
| heart´i-ly | hec´to-li-ter | He´li-os |
| heart´i-ness | hec´to-me-ter | he´lio-scope |
| heart´land | hec´tor | he´lio-trope |
| heart´less | Hec´u-ba | he-li-ot´ro-pism |
| heart´rend-ing | hed´er-in | he´lio-ty-pog´ra-phy |
| hearts´ease | hedge´hog | hel´i-port |
| heart´sick | hedg´er | he´li-um |
| heart´string | hedge´row | he´lix |
| heart´y | hedg´ing | Hel´las |
| heat´ed | he´dral | hell´-bent |
| heat´ed-ly | heed´ful | hell´cat |
| heat´er | heed´less | Hel´len |
| heath | heed´less-ness | Hel´lene |
| hea´then | hecl´er | Hel-len´ic |
| heath´er | heft´i-cr | Hel´le-nism |
| heath´y | heft´i-est | He´le-nis´tic |
| heaved | heft´y | Hel´les-pont |
| heav´en | He´gel | hell´fire |
| heav´en-ly | He-ge´li-an | hell´gram-mite |
| heav´en-ward | He-ge´li-an-ism | hel´lion |
| heav´er | heg´e-mon´ic | hell´ish |
| heav´i-er | he-gem´o-ny | hell´lo´ |
| heav´i-ly | He-gi´ra | hel´met |
| heav´i-ness | Hei´del-berg | hel´met-ed |
| heave-ing | heif´er | hel´minth |
| heav´y | Hei´fetz | hel-min´thic |
| heav´y—du´ty | height | helms´man |
| heav´y—eyed | height´en | He-lo-ise´ |
| heav´y—fist-ed | Heim´dall | hel´ot |
| heav´y—foot-ed | Hei´ne | help´er |
| heav´y—hand-ed | hei´nous | help´ful |

help´less
help´less-ly
help´less-ness
help´mate
help´meet
Hel´sin-ki
hel´ter—skel´ter
Hel-ve´tia
Hel-vet´ic
Hel-ve´tii
hel´vite
he´vol´ic
he-ma-fi´brite
he-mag-glu´ti-nin
he´mal
he-mal-bu´men
he´ma-tal
he-ma-te´in
he-mat´ic
hem´a-tite
hem´a-tit´ic
he´ma-toid
hem´a-to-lite
he-ma-tol´o-gy
he-ma-to´ma
he-ma-tom´e-ter
hem´a-to-por´phy-rin
hem´a-tose
he-ma-to´sis
he´mic
Hem´ing-way
hem´i-sphere
hem´i-spher´ic
hem´i-spher´i-cal
hem´i-spher´i-cal-ly
hem´i-sphe´roid
hem´i-stich
hem´i-stich´al
hem´lock
he´mo-glo-bin
he-mo-glo-bi-nom´e-
   ter
he´moid
he´mo-lymph
he-mol´y-sin
he-mol´y-sis
he´mo-lyt´ic
he-mom´e-ter
he-mo-phil´ia

he-mo-phil´i-ac
he-mop´ty-sis
hem´or-rhage
hem´or-rhag´ic
hem´or-rhoid
hem´or-rhoi´dal
hem´or-rhoids
he-mo-sid´er-in
he-mo-sid-er-o´sis
he-mo-stat´ic
hemp´en
hemp´seed
hem´stitch
hence´forth´
hence-for´ward
hench´man
hen´coop
Hen´der-son
hen´na
hen´nery
hen´peck
he´par
hep-a-ti´tis
hep-a-ti-za´tion
He-phaes´tus
hep-ta-dec´yl
hep´ta-gon
hep-tag´o-nal
hep-tam´e-ter
hep´tar-chy
He´ra
Her-a-cle´a
Her´a-cles
Her-a-cli´tus
her´ald
he-ral´dic
her´ald-ry
herb´age
herb´al
Her-bar´ti-an
Her´bert
her´bi-ci´dal
her´bi-cide
Her´cu-les
Her´der
herd´er
herds´man
here´abouts
here-af´ter

here´by
he-red-i-ta-bil´i-ty
he-red´i-ta-ble
her-e-dit´a-ment
he-red-i-tar´i-ly
he-red´i-tary
he-red´i-ty
Her´e-ford
here´in´
here´in-af´ter
here-in-be-fore´
here-of´
her´e-sy
her´e-tic
he-ret´i-cal
here´to-fore´
here´upon´
here-with´
her´i-ot
her´i-ta-ble
her´i-tage
her´i-tance
her´i-tor
Her´man
Her´mes
her-met´ic
her-met´i-cal
her-met´i-cal-ly
her´mit
her´mit-age
her´nia
her-ni-ar´in
he´ro
Her´od
He-ro´di-as
he´roes
he-ro´ic
he-ro´i-cal
her´o-in
her´o-ine
her´o-ism
her´on
He´ron
her´pes
her´ring
her´ring-bone
Her´schel
her-self´
Hert´ford

Hert´ford-shire
hes´i-tan-cy
hes´i-tant
hes´i-tant-ly
hes´i-tate
hes´i-tat-er
hes´i-tat-ing
hes´i-tat-ing-ly
hes-i-ta´tion
hes´i-ta-tive
Hes´per-is
Hes´per-us
Hes´se
Hes´sian
het´er-o-dox
het´er-o-doxy
het´ero-dyne
het´er-oe´cious
het-er-og´a-mous
het-er-o-ge-ne´i-ty
het-er-o-ge´neous
het-er-og´e-nous
het-er-og´e-ny
het-er-og´o-ny
het-er-og´ra-phy
het-ero-ki-ne´sis
het-er-ol´o-gy
het-er-ol´y-sis
het´er-om´er-ous
het-er-on´o-mous
het-er-on´y-mous
het-ero-ou´sia
het´er-o-pol´y
het-cr-os´co-py
het-ero-zy-go´sis
het-ero-zy´gote
het-ero-zy´gous
heu-ris´tic
hew´ing
hex´a-chlo´ro-eth´ane
hex-a-dec´ane
hex-a-em´er-on
hex´a-gon
hex-ag´o-nal
hey´day
Hez-e-ki´ah
hi-a´tus
Hi-a-wa´tha
hi-ber-nac´u-lum

hi-ber´nal
hi´ber-nate
hi´ber-nat-ing
hi-ber-na´tion
hi´ber-na-tor
Hi-ber´nia
Hi-ber´nian
hi-bis´cus
hic´cough
hic´cup
hick´o-ry
hi-dal´go
hid´den
hide´bound
hid´e-ous
hid´e-ous-ly
hid´e-ous-ness
hid´ing
hi-dro´sis
hi-drot´ic
hi´er-arch
hi´er-ar´chal
hi´er-ar´chi-cal
hi´er-ar-chy
hi´er-at´ic
hi´er-o-crat´i-cal
hi´er-o-dule
hi´er-o-glyph´ic
hi´er-o-glyph´i-cal
hi´er-o-glyph´i-cal-ly
hi´—fi
high´ball
high´born
high´boy
high´bred
high´brow
high chair
high-fa-lu´tin
high fi-del´i-ty
high´—flown´
high´—fre´quen-cy
high´—grade
high´—hand-ed
high´—hat´
high´land
High´land-er
high´lev´el
high´light
high´ly

high´—mind-ed
high´ness
high´road
high school
high seas
high´—spir´it-ed
high´—strung´
high´—ten´sion
high´—test´
high´way
high´way-man
hi´jack
hi´jack-er
hik´er
hik´ing
hi-lar´i-ous
hi-lar´i-ty
Hil´a-ry
Hil´de-brand
hill´bill´y
hill´i-ness
hill´ock
hill´ocked
hill´side
hill´top
hill´y
hi´lum
Him´a-lay´a
hi-mat´i-on
him-self´
Hin´den-burg
hin´dcr
hind´most
hind´quar-ter
hin´drance
hind´sight
Hin´du
Hin´du-stan´
hinge
hing´ing
hint´er
hin´ter-land
hint´ing-ly
hip´bone
hip´po-cras
Hfp-poc´ra-tes
Hip´po-crat´ic
hip´po-drome
Hip-pol´y-tus

hip-po-pot´a-mus
Hi´ram
hire´ling
hir´ing
Hi-ro-hi´to
Hir´o-shi´ma
hir´sute
His-pa´nia
His-pan´ic
His-pa-nio´la
hiss´ing
his´ta-mine
his´to-log´i-cal
his-tol´o-gy
his-tol´y-sis
his-to´ri-an
his-tor´ic
his-tor´i-cal
his-tor´i-cal-ly
his-to-ric´i-ty
his´to-ries
his-to-ri-og´ra-pher
his´to-ry
his-tri-on´ic
his-tri-on´i-cal
his-tri-on´ics
hitch´hike
hitch´hik-er
hith´er
hith´er-to´
Hit´ler
hit´ting
hoard
hoard´ing
hoar´frost
hoar´i-ness
hoarse
hoarse-ly
hoarse-ness
hoar´y
hoax
hoax´er
hob´ble
hob´bler
hob´bling
hob´by
hob´by-horse
hob´gob-lin
hob´nail

hob´nob
hob´nob-bing
ho´bo
ho´boes
Ho´bo-ken
hock´ey
ho´cus
ho´cus—po´cus
hodge´podge
Hodg´kin's
hod´o-graph
Hoff´mann
Ho´garth
hog´back
hog´ging
hog´gish
hogs´head
hog´tie
Ho´hen-stau-fen
Ho´hen-zol-lern
hoi pol-loi´
hoist´ed
hoist´er
ho´kum
Hol´bein
hold´back
hold´er
hold´fast
hold´ing
hold´over
hold´up
hol´i-day
ho´li-ness
ho´lism
Hol´land
hol´lan-daise´
Hol´land-er
hol´low
hol´low-ness
hol´ly
hol´ly-hock
Hol´ly-wood
hol´o-caust
hol´o-graph
hol´o-graph´ic
Hol´stein
hol´ster
ho´ly
Hol´yoke

hom´age
hom´ag-er
hom´bre
Hom´burg
home´bred´
home brew
home´land
home´less
home´like
home´li-ness
home´ly
home´made´
home´mak-er
ho´meo-path
ho´meo-path´ic
home´own-er
hom´er
Ho´mer
Ho-mer´ic
home´sick
home´sick-ness
home´spun
home´stead
home´stead-er
home town
home´ward
home´work
hom´ey
hom´i-ci-dal
hom´i-cide
hom´i-ly
hom´i-ny
Ho´mo
ho-mog´a-my
ho-mo-ge-ne´i-ty
ho-mo-ge´neous
ho-mog-e-ni-za´tion
ho-mog´e-nize
ho-mog´e-niz-er
ho-mog´e-niz-ing
ho-mog´e-nous
ho-mog´e-ny
ho-mog´o-ny
hom´o-graph
ho´mo-log
ho-mo-log´i-cal
ho-mol´o-gize
ho-mol´o-gous
ho´mo-logue

ho-mol´o-gy
ho-mol´y-sis
ho-mon´y-mous
hom´o-phone
ho-moph´o-nous
ho-moph´o-ny
ho-mop´ter-ous
Ho´mo sap´i-ens
ho-mo-sex´u-al
ho-mo-sex-u-al´i-ty
ho´mo-spor´ous
ho´mo-tax´is
ho´mo-thet´ic
Hon-du´ran
Hon-du´ras
honed
hon´est
hon´est-ly
hon´es-ty
hon´ey
hon´ey-bee
hon´ey-comb
hon´ey-dew
hon´eyed
hon´ey-moon
hon´ey-suck-le
hon´ing
Hon´i-ton
honk´y—tonk
Hon´o-lu´lu
hon´or
hon´or-able
hon´or-ably
hon-o-rar´i-um
hon´or-ary
Ho-no´ria
hon-or-if´ic
hood´ed
hood´lum
hoo´doo
hood´wink
hoof´beat
hoofed
hoof´print
hoo´kah
hook´er
hook´up
hook´worm
hook´y

hoo´li-gan
hoo-ray´
hoose´gow
Hoo´sier
Hoo´ver
hope´ful
hope´ful-ly
hope´ful-ness
hope´less
hope´less-ly
Ho´pi
Hop´kins
hop´lite
hop´per
hop´scotch
ho´ra
Hor´ace
Ho´rae
ho´ra-ry
Ho-ra´tian
Ho-ra´tio
Ho-ra´tius
horde
ho-ri´zon
hor´i-zon´tal
hor´i-zon´tal-ly
hor´mone
hor-mon´ic
horn´beam
horn´bill
horn´book
hor´net
horn´less
horn´pipe
horn´swog-gle
horn´y
hor´o-loge
ho-rol´o-ger
hor´o-log´ic
ho-rol´o-gist
ho-rol´o-gy
hor´o-scope
ho-ros´co-py
hor-ren´dous
hor´ri-ble
hor´ri-bly
hor´rid
hor-rif´ic
hor´ri-fied

hor´ri-fy
hor´ror
hor´ror—struck
hors d´oeuvre
horse
horse´back
horse´flesh
horse´fly
horse´hair
horse´hide
horse´laugh
horse´less
horse´man
horse´man-ship
horse op´era
horse pis´tol
horse´play
horse´pow-er
horse´rad-ish
horse sense
horse´shoe
horse´sho-er
horse´tail
horse´whip
horse´wom-an
hors´ey
hor´ta-to-ry
Hor´tense
hor-ti-cul´tur-al
hor´ti-cul-ture
hor´ti-cul´tur-ist
Ho´rus
ho-san´na
Ho-se´a
ho´sier
ho´siery
hos´pice
hos-pit´a-ble
hos-pit´a-bly
hos´pi-tal
hos´pi-tal-er
hos-pi-tal´i-ty
hos-pi-tal-iza´tion
hos´pi-tal-ize
hos-pi´ti-um
hos´po-dar
hos´tage
host´al
hos´tel

hos´tel-ry
host´ess
hos´tile
hos-til´i-ty
hos´tler
hot´bed
hot´box
hot dog
ho-tel´
hot´foot
hot´head
hot´head-ed
hot´house
hot´ly
hot´ness
hot´spur
hot´—tem´pered
Hou-di´ni
Hou´dry
hound
hour´glass
hou´ri
hour´ly
house´boat
house´break-ing
house´bro-ken
house´coat
house flag
house´fly
house´ful
house´hold
house´hold-er
house´keep-er
house´keep-ing
house´less
house´line
house´maid
house or´gan
house´room
house´top
house´warm-ing
house´wife
house´wife-ry
house´work
hous´ing
Hous´ton
hov´el
hov´er
hov´er-ing

How´ard
how-be´it
how´dah
how-ev´er
how´it-zer
howl´er
how´lite
how-so-ev´er
Hub´bard
hub´bub
Hu´bert
huck´le-ber-ry
huck´ster
hud´dle
hud´dling
Hud´son
huff´i-ly
huff´i-ness
huff´ish
huff´y
huge´ly
hugged
hug´ging
Hu´gue-not
hu´la
hu´la—hu´la
hulk´ing
hul´la-ba-loo
hu´man
hu-mane´
hu-mane´ly
hu´man-isin
hu´man-ist
hu´man-is´tic
hu-man-i-tar´i-an
hu-man-i-tar´i-an-ism
hu´man´i-ty
hu´man-ize
hu´man-kind
hu´man-ly
Hum´ber
Hum´bert
hum´ble
hum´ble-ness
hum´bling
hum´bly
Hum´boldt
hum´bug
hum´drum

hu´mer-al
hu´mer-us
hu´mic
hu´mid
hu-mid´i-fied
hu-mid´i-fy
hu-mid´i-ty
hu´mi-dor
hu-mi-fi-ca´tion
hu-mil´i-ate
hu-mil´i-at-ing
hu-mil-i-a´tion
hu-mil´i-ty
hu´mi-ture
hummed
hum´ming
hum´ming-bird
hum´mock
hu´mor
hu´mor-esque´
hu´mor-ist
hu´mor-ous
hu´mor-ous-ly
hu´mous
hump´back
hump´backed
Hum´phrey
hump´y
hu´mus
hunch´back
hunch´backed
hun´dred
hun´dred-fold
hun´dredth
hun´dred-weight
Hun´ga-ry
hun´ger
hun´ger-ing
hun´gri-er
hun´gri-ly
hun´gri-ness
hun´gry
hun´ker
hunt´er
hunt´ing
Hun´ting-don
Hun´ting-ton
hunt´ress
hunts´man

hur´dle
hur´dler
hur´dy—gur´dy
hurl´er
hur´ly—bur´ly
Hu´ron
hur-rah´
hur´ri-cane
hur´ried
hur´ried-ly
hur´ry
hur´ry—scur´ry
hurt´er
hurt´ful
hurt´ing
hur´tle
hur´tling
hus´band
hus´band-man
hus´band-ry
hush pup´py
husk´er
husk´i-ly
husk´i-ness
husk´ing
husk´y
hus-sar´
hus´sy
hus´ting
hus´tle
hus´tler
hus´tling
Hutch´ins
Hutch´in-son
Hux´ley
hy´a-cinth
hy´a-cin´thine
Hy-a-cin´thus
Hy´a-des
hy´a-line
hy-a-lin-iza´tion
hy-al´o-gen
hy-al´o-phane
hy-a-lu´ro-nate
hy´brid
hy´brid-iza´tion
hy´brid-ize
Hy´der-a-bad.
hy´dra

hy-drac´id
hy-drac´ry-late
hy-dra-cryl´ic
Hy´dra—Mat´ic
hy´dra-mine
hy-dran´gea
hy´drant
hy-dras´ti-nine
hy´drate
hy-dra´tion
hy´dra-tor
hy-drau´lic
hy´dra-zide
hy-draz´i-dine
hy´dra-zine
hy-dra-zo´ic
hy´dra-zone
hy´dride
hy-dri-od´ic
hy-dri´o-dide
hy-dro-acous´tic
hy´dro-car´bon
hy´dro-cele
hy-dro-ceph´a-lous
hy-dro-ceph´a-lus
hy-dro-chlo´ric
hy-dro-chlo´ride
hy-dro-cin-nam´ic
hy-dro-cor´ti-sone
hy-dro-cy-an´ic
hy-dro-dy-nam´ics
hy-dro-elec´tric
hy-dro-flu-or´ic
hy-dro-flu´or-ide
hy´dro-foil
hy-dro-form´ate
hy´dro-gen
hy´dro-gen-ate
hy-drog´e-nous
hy-drog´no-sy
hy-drog´ra-pher
hy´dro-graph´ic
hy-drog´ra-phy
hy´droid
hy´dro-lase
hy-drol´o-gy
hy-drol´y-sate
hy-drol´y-sis
hy´dro-lyt´ic

hy´dro-lyze
hy-dro-me-chan´i-cal
hy-drom´e-ter
hy´dro-met´ric
hy-drom´e-try
hy-dro´ni-um
hy-drop´a-thy
hy´dro-phane
hy´dro-pho´bia
hy´dro-pho´bic
hy´dro-phone
hy´dro-phyte
hy-drop´ic
hy´dro-plane
hy´dro-pon´ics
hy´dro-qui-none´
hy´dro-scope
hy´dro-scop´ic
hy´dro-some
hy´dro-sphere
hy´dro-stat
hy´dro-stat´ics
hy´dro-sul´fide
hy-dro-ther´a-py
hy´drous
hy-drox´ide
hy-drox-im´i-no
hy-drox´y-am´i-no
hy-drox´yl
hy-drox´y´amine´
hy-drox´yl-ate
hy-drox´y-my´cin
hy-drox´y-zine
hy-e´na
hy-e-tog´ra-phy
hy-e-tol´o-gy
hy-e-tom´e-ter
hy´ge-ist
hy´giene
hy´gi-en´ic
hy-gi-en´i-cal-ly
hy´gien´ist
hy-grom´e-ter
hy´gro-met´ric
hy-grom´e-try
hy-gro-my´cin
hy´gro-scope
hy´gro-scop´ic
hy´men

hymn
hym′nal
hym′no-dy
hym-nol′o-gy
hy′oid
hyp-al-ge′sia
hy′per-ac′id
hy-per-acid′i-ty
hy-per˝bo-la
hy-per˝bo-le
hy-per-bol′ic
hy-per-bol′i-cal
hy-per-bol′i-cal-ly
hy-per˝bo-lize
hy-per˝bo-loi′dal
hy′per-crit′i-cal
hy-per-du′lia
hy′per-e′mia
hy′per-gol
hy′per-go-lic′i-ty
hy-per′i-cin
hy′per-in
Hy-pe′ri-on
hy′per-on
hy-per-o′pia
hy′per-os-to′sis
hy-per-phys′i-cal
hy-per-pi-e′sia
hy-per-pla′sia
hy-per-pne′a
hy-per-sen′si-tive
hy-per-son′ic
hy′per-sthene
hy-per-ten′sion
hy-per-ten′sive
hy-per-thy′roid
hy-per′tro-phic
hy-per′tro-phy
hy′phen
hy′phen-ate
hy-phen-a′tion
hyp′noid
hyp-nol′o-gy
hyp-no′sis
hyp-not′ic
hyp-not′i-cal-ly
hyp′no-tism
hyp′no-tist
hyp′no-tize

hyp′no-tiz-ing
hy′po-caust
hy-po-chon′dria
hy-po-chon′dri-ac
hy′po-chon-dri′a-cal
hy-poc′ri-sy
hyp′o-crite
hyp-o-crit′i-cal
hyp-o-crit′i-cal-ly
hy′po-der′mal
hy′po-der′mic
hy-po-der′mi-cal-ly
hy-po-der′mis
hy′po-eu-tec′tic
hy-pog′a-my
hy-po-gas′tric
hyp′o-gene
hy-po-gen′ic
hy-pog′e-nous
hy-poph′y-sis
hy-po-pla′sia
hy-pos′ta-sis
hy′po-style
hy-po-sul′fite
hy-pot′e-nuse
hy-poth′ec
hy-poth′e-cary
hy-poth′e-cate
hy-poth-e-ca′tion
hy-poth′e-ca-tor
hy-poth′e-ses
hy-poth′e-sis
hy-poth′e-size
hy-po-thet′i-cal
hy-po-thet′i-cal-ly
hy-pox-e′mia
hy-pox′ia
hyp-sog′ra-phy
hyp-som′e-ter
hyp-som′e-try
hy′son
hys′sop
hys-taz′a-rin
hys-ter-ec′to-my
hys-ter-e′sis
hys-ter-et′ic
hys-te′ria
hys-ter′ic
hys-ter′i-cal

hys-ter′i-cal-ly
hys-ter′ics
hys-ter-or′rha-phy
hys-ter-os′co-py
hys-ter-ot′o-my
hy′ther-graph

# I

i′amb
iam˝bic
iam′bus
iat′ri-cal
Ibe′ria
Ibe′ri-an
i′bex
i′bis
Ib′sen
ice′ bag
ice˝berg
ice˝boat
ice˝box
ice′cap
ice cream
iced
Ice′land
ice′man
Ich′a-bod
ich-thy-o-log′i-cal
ich-thy-ol′o-gist
ich-thy-ol′o-gy
ich-thy-oph′a-gous
ich-thy-oph′a-gy
ich′thyo-saur
ich-thy-o′sis
ich′thy-ot′ic
ic′i-cle
ic′i-ly
ic′i-ness
ic′ing
i′con
icon′ic
icon′o-clasm
icon′o-clast
icon′o-clas′tic
ico-nom′e-ter
icon′o-scope
ic-ter′ic
ic′ter-us

ic´tus
ic´y
I´da-ho
ide´a
ide´al
ide´al-ism
ide´al-ist
ide´al-is´tic
ide´al-iza´tion
ide´al-ize
ide´al-ly
i´de-ate
ide-a´tion
i´dem
iden´tic
iden´ti-cal
iden-ti-fi-a-ble
iden-ti-fi-ca´tion
iden´ti-fied
iden´ti-fies
iden´ti-fy
iden´ti-ty
ide-oc´ra-cy
i´deo-graph
ide-og´ra-phy
ideo-log´i-cal
ide-ol´o-gist
ide-ol´o-gy
Ides
id-i-oc´ra-cy
id´i-o-cy
id´io-gram
id´i-o-lect
id´i-om
id´i-o-mat´ic
id-i-om´e-ter
id´i-o-path´ic
id-i-op´a-thy
id-i-o-syn´cra-sy
id´i-ot
id-i-ot´ic
id-i-ot´i-cal
id-i-ot´i-cal-ly
id´i-ot-ism
id´i-tol
i´dle
i´dled
i´dle-ness
i´dler

i´dling
i´dly
i´dol
idol´a-ter
idol´a-trize
idol´a-trous
idol´a-try
i´dol-ism
idol-i-za´tion
i´dol-ize
ido´ne-ous
i´dyll
idyl´lic
i´dyll-ist
ig´loo
Ig-na´tian
Ig-na´ti-us
ig´ne-ous
ig-nite´
ig-nit´er
Ig-nit´ing
ig-ni´tion
ig´ni-tron
ig-no-bil´i-ty
ig-no´ble
ig-no-min´i-ous
ig-no-min´i-ous-ly
ig´nomi-ny
ig-no-ra´mus
ig´no-rance
ig´no-rant
ig´no-rant-ly
ig-nore´
Ig-o-rot´
igua´na
igua´no-don
i´lex
il´i-ac
Il´i-ad
il´i-um
ilk
ill´—ad-vised´
il-lapse´
il-la´tion
il´la-tive
ill´—bred
il-le´gal
il-le-gal´i-ty
il-leg-i-bil´i-ty

il-leg´i-ble
il-le-git´i-ma-cy
il-le-git´i-mate
ill´—fat´ed
ill´—fa´vored
ill´—fit´ting
ill´—got´ten
ill´hu´mored
il-lib´er-al
il-lic´it
il-lim´it-able
il-lin´i-um
Il´li-nois´
il´lite
il-lit´er-a-cy
il-lit´er-ate
ill´—man´nered
ill´—na´tured
ill´ness
i´log´i-cal
ill´—o´mened
ill´—starred´
ill´—tem´pered
ill´—timed´
il-lu´mi-nant
il-lu´mi-nate
il-lu-mi-na´tion
il-lu´mi-nat-ing
il-lu-mi-na´tion
il-lu-mi-na-tive
Il-lu´mi-na-tor
il-lu´mine
il-lu´min-er
il-lu´min-ing
il-lu-mi-nom´e-ter
ill´—us´age
ill´—use´
il-lu´sion
il-lu´sive
il-lu´so-ri-ly
il-lu´so-ry
il´lus-trate
il´lus-trat-ing
il-lus-tra´tion
il-lus-tra-tive
il´lus-tra-tor
il-lus´tri-ous
il-lu´vi-al
il-lu´vi-ate

il-lu-vi-a´tion
Il-lyr´ia
im´age
im´ag-ery
imag´in-able
imag´i-nal
imag´i-nary
imag´i-na´tion
imag´i-na-tive
imag´ine
imag´in-ing
im´ag-ism
im´ag-ist
im´ag-is´tic
im-bal´ance
im´be-cile
tm-be-cil´i-ty
im-bed´
im-bibe´
im-bib´er
im-bi-bi´tion
im´bri-cate
im´bri-cat-ed
im-bri-ca´tion
im-bro´glio
imbrue´
im-bru´ing
im-bue´
im-bu´ing
im´i-do
imid´o-gen
im-i-ta-bil´i-ty
im´i-ta-ble
im´i-tate
im´i-ta´tion
im´i-ta-tive
im´i-ta-tor
im-mac´u-la-cy
im-mac´u-late
im´ma-nence
im´ma-nent
Im-man´u-el
im-mar´gin-ate
im-ma-te´ri-al
im-ma-te-ri-al´i-ty
im-ma-ture´
Im-ma-tur´i-ty
im-mea´sur-able
im-mea´sur-ably

im-me´di-a-cy
im-me´di-ate
im-me´di-ate-ly
im-med´i-ca-ble
Im´mel-mann
im-mem´o-ra-ble
im-me-mo´ri-al
im-mense´
im-mense´ly
im-men´si-ty
im-men´su-ra-ble
im-merge´
im-merse´
im-mersed´
im-mers´ible
im-mers´ing
im-mer´sion
im´mi-grant
im´mi-grate
im´mi-gra´tion
im´mi-nence
im´mi-nent
im-mit´i-ga-ble
im-mo´bile
im-mo-bil´i-ty
im-mo-bi-li-za´tion
im-mo´bi-lize
im-mod´er-a-cy
im-mod´er-ate
im-mod-er-a´tion
im-mod´est
im´mo-late
im-mo-la´tion
im-mor´al
im-mo-ral´i-ty
im-mor´al-ly
im-mor´tal
im-mor-tal´i-ty
im-mor-tal-iza´tion
im-mor´tal-ize
im-mo´tile
im-mov-a-bil´i-ty
im-mov´able
im-mov´ably
im-mune´
im-mu´ni-ty
im-mu-ni-za´tion
im´mu-nize
im-mu-nol´o-gy

im-mure´
im-mur´ing
im-mu-ta-bil´i-ty
im-mu´ta-ble
im´pact
im-pair´
im-pair´ment
im-pale´
im-pal´ing
im-pal´pa-ble
im-pan´el
im-pan´eled
im-par´i-ty
im-park´
im-par´lance
im-part´
im-par-ta´tion
im-par´tial
im-par-tial´i-ty
im-par´tial-ly
im-part´ible
im-pass-abil´i-ty
im-pass´able
im´passe
im-pas-si-bil´i-ty
im-pas´si-ble
im-pas´sion
im-pas´sion-ate
im-pas´sioned
im-pas-sive
im-pas´sive-ly
im-pas-siv´i-ty
im´pa-ter´nate
im-pa´tience
im-pa´tient
im-pa´tient-ly
im-pav´id
im-peach´
im-peach-abil´i-ty
im-peach´able
iin-peach´ment
im-pearl´
im-pec-ca-bil´i-ty
im-pec´ca-ble
im-ped´ance
im-pede´
im-ped´ible
im-pe´di-ent
im-ped´i-ment

im-ped-i-men´ta
im-ped-i-men´tal
im-ped-i-men´ta-ry
im-ped´ing
im-ped´i-tive
im-pe-dom´e-ter
im-pe´dor
im-pel´
im-pelled´
im-pel´lent
im-pel´ler
im-pel´ling
im-pend´
im-pend´ent
im-pend´ing
im-pen-e-tra-bil´i-ty
im-pen´e-tra-ble
im-pen´i-tence
im-pen´i-tent
im-pen´nate
im-per´a-tive
im-per´a-tive-ly
im-pe-ra´tor
im-per-a-to´ri-al
im-per-cep´ti-ble
im-per-cep´ti-bly
im-per´fect
im-per-fec´tion
im-per´fect-ly
im-per´fect-ness
im-per´fo-rate
im-per´fo-rat-ed
im-per-fo-ra´tion
im-pe´ri-al
im-pe´ri-al-ism
im-pe´ri-al-ist
im-pe´ri-al-is´tic
im-pe´ri-al-ly
im-per´il
im-per´iled
im-per´il-ing
im-pe´ri-ous
im-pe´ri-ous-ly
im-per´ish-able
im-pe´ri-um
im-per´ma-nence
im-per´ma-nent
im-per-me-abil-i-ty
im-per´me-able

im-per-scrip´ti-ble
im-per´son-al
im-per´son-al-ly
im-per´son-ate
im-per-son-a´tion
im-per´son-a-tor
im-per-sua´si-ble
im-per´ti-nence
im-per´ti-nen-cy
im-per´ti-nent
im-per-turb-abil´i-ty
im-per-turb´able
im-per-tur-ba´tion
im-per´vi-ous
im-pe-ti´go
im´pe-trate
im-pet-u-os´i-ty
im-pet´u-ous
im-pet´u-ous-ly
im´pe-tus
im-pi´e-ty
im-pinge´
im-pinge´ment
im-ping´er
im-ping´ing
imp´ish
im-placa-bil´i-ty
im-plac´a-ble
im-plant´
im-plan-ta´tion
im-plas-tic´i-ty
im-plau´si-ble
im´ple-ment
im-ple-men´tal
im´pli-cate
im-pli-ca´tion
im´plica-tive
im-plic´it
im-plic´it-ly
im-plied´
im-pli´ed-ly
im-plor´a-to-ry
im-plore´
im-plor´ing
im-plor´ing-ly
im-plo´sion
im-plo´sive
im-ply´
im-po-lite´

im-pol´i-tic
im-pon´der-able
im-port´
im-port´able
im-por´tance
im-por´tant
im-por´tant-ly
im-por-ta´tion
im-port´er
im-por´tu-na-cy
im-por´tu-nate
im´por-tune´
im´por-tun´ing
im-por-tu´ni-ty
im-pose´
im-pos´ing
im-po-si´tion
im-pos-si-bil´i-ty
im-pos´si-ble
im´post
im-pos´tor
im-pos´ture
im´po-tence
im´po-ten-cy
im´po-tent
im-pound´
im-pov´er-ish
im-pov´er-ish-ment
im-pow´er
im-prac-ti-ca-bil´i-ty
im-prac´ti-ca-ble
im-prac´ti-call
im-prac-ti-cal´i-ty
im´pre-cate
im-pre-ca´tion
im´pre-ca-tor
im´preca-to-ry
im-pre-cise´
im-preg-na-bil´i-ty
im-preg´na-ble
im-preg´nate
im-preg-na´tion
im-preg´na-tor
im´pre-sar´i-al
im-pre-sar´io
im-pre-scrip´ti-ble
im-press´
im-press´able
im-press´ibil´i-ty

im-press´ible
im-pres´sion
im-pres´sion-able
im-pres´sion-ism
im-pres-sion-is´tic
im-pres´sive
im-pres´sive-ly
im-press´ment
im-pri-ma´tur
im´print
im-pris´on
im-pris´on-ment
im-prob-a-bil´i-ty
im-prob´a-ble
im-pro´bi-ty
im-promp´tu
im-prop´er
im-prop´er-ly
im-pro´pri-ate
im-pro-pri´e-ty
im-prov´able
im-prove´
im-prove´ment
im-prov´er
im-prov´i-dence
im-prov´i-dent
im-prov´ing
im-provi-sa´tion
im-prov´i-sa-tor
im´pro-vise
im´pro-vis-ing
im-pru´dence
im-pru´dent
im-pru´dent-ly
im´pu-dence
im´pu-dent
im-pu-dic´i-ty
im-pugn´
im-pugn´able
im-pugna´tion
im-pugn´er
im-pu´is-sant
im´pulse
im-pul´sion
im-pul´sive
im-pul´sive-ly
im-pu´ni-ty
im-pure´
im-pu´ri-ty

im-put´able
im-pu-ta´tion
im-pu´ta-tive
im-pute´
im-put´ing
in-abil´i-ty
in ab-sen´tia
in-ac-ces-si-bil´i-ty
in-ac-ces´si-ble
in-ac´cu-ra-cy
in-ac´cu-rate
in-ac´tion
in-ac´ti-vate
in-ac-ti-va´tion
in-ac´tive
in-ac-tiv´i-ty
in-ad´e-qua-cy
in-ad´e-quate
in-ad-mis´si-ble
in-ad-ver´tence
in-ad-ver´tent
in-ad-ver´tent-ly
in-ad-vis´able
in-a´lien-able
in-al´ter-able
in-ane´
in-an´i-mate
in-an´i-ty
in-ap-peas´able
in-ap´pe-tence
in-ap´pli-ca-ble
in-ap´po-site
in-ap-pre´cia-ble
in-ap-pre´cia-tive
in-ap-proach´able
in-ap-pro´pri-ate
in-apt´
in-ap´ti-tude
in-ar-tic´u-late
in-ar-ti-fi´cial
in-ar-tis´tic
in-as-much´
in-at-ten´tion
in-at-ten´tive
in-au´di-ble
in-au´gu-ral
in-au´gu-rate
in-au´gu-rat-ing
in-au-gu-ra´tion

in-aus-pi´cious
in-aus-pi´cious-ly
in´board
in´born
in´bred
in´breed-ing
in´built
In´ca
in-cal´cu-la-ble
in-cal´cu-la-bly
in-ca-les´cent
in-can-desce´
in-can-des´cence
in-can-des´cent
in-can-ta´tion
in-ca-pa-bil´i-ty
in-ca´pa-ble
in-ca-pa´cious
in-ca-pac´i-tate
in-ca-pac-i-ta´tion
in-ca-pac´i-ty
in-car´cer-ate
in-car-cer-a´tion
in-car´di-nate
in-car´na-dine
in-car´nate
in-car-na´tion
in-case´
in-cau´tious
in-cen´di-a-rism
in-cen´di-ary
in´cense
in-cens´ing
in-cen´tive
in-cep´tion
in-cep´tive
in-cep´tor
in-cer´ti-tude
in-ces´san-cy
in-ces´sant
in-ces´sant-ly
in´cest
in-ces´tu-ous
in-cho´ate
in-cho´ate-ly
in-cho´a-tive
inch´worm
in´ci-dence
in-ci-dent

in-ci-den´tal
in-ci-den´tal-ly
in-cin´er-ate
in-cin-er-a´tion
in-cin´er-a-tor
in-cip´i-ence
in-cip´i-ent
in-cise´
in-ci´sion
in-ci´sive
in-ci´sor
in-cit´ant
in-ci-ta´tion
in-cite´
in-cite´ment
in-cit´er
in-cit´ing
in-ci´to-ry
in-ci-vil´i-ty
in-civ´ism
in-clem´en-cy
in-clem´ent
in-clin´able
in-cli-na´tion
in-cli´na-to-ry
in-cline´
in-clined´
in-clin´ing
in-cli-nom´e-ter
in-close´
in-clud´able
in-clude´
in-clud´ed
in-clud´ing
in-clu´sion
in-clu´sive
in-co-erc´i-ble
in-cog-ni´to
in-co-her´ence
in-co-her´ent
in-com-bus´ti-ble
in´come
in´com-ing
in-com-men´su-ra-ble
in-com-men´su-rate
in-com-mode´
in-com-mo´di-ous
in-com-mu´ni-ca-ble
in-com-mu-ni-ca´do

in-com´pa-ra-ble
in-com-pat-i-bil´i-ty
in-com-pat´i-ble
in-com´pe-tence
in-com´pe-ten-cy
in-com´pe-tent
in-com-plete´
in-com-plete´ly
in-com-pli´ant
in-com-pre-hen´si-ble
in-com-pre-hen´sion
in-com-press´i-ble
in-com-put´able
in-con-ceiv´able
in-con-ceiv´ably
in-con-clu´sive
in-con-cus´si-ble
in-con-dens´able
in-con-gru´i-ty
in-con´gru-ous
in-con-sec´u-tive
in-con´se-quence
in-con´se-quent
in-con-se-quen´tial
in-con-sid´er-a-ble
in-con-sid´er-ate
in-con-sid-er-a´tion
in-con-sist´en-cy
in-con-sist´ent
in-con-sol´a-ble
in-con´so-nance
in-con´so-nant
in-con-spic´u-ous
in-con´stan-cy
in-con´stant
in-con-test-abil´i-ty
in-con-test´able
in-con´ti-nence
in-con´ti-nent
in-con-tro-vert´i-ble
in-con-ve´nience
in-con-ve´nien-cy
in-con-ve´nient
in-con-vert´i-ble
in-con-vin´ci-ble
in-cor´po-ra-ble
in-cor´po-rate
in-cor´po-rat-ed
in-cor-po-ra´tion

in-cor´po-ra-tive
in-cor´po-ra-tor
in-cor-po´re-al
in-cor-po-re´i-ty
in-cor-rect´
in-cor-ri-gi-bil´i-ty
in-cor´ri-gi-ble
in´cor-rupt´
in-cor-rupt-i-bil´i-ty
in-cor-rupt´i-ble
in-creas´able
in-crease´
in-creas´er
in-creas´ing
in-cred-i-bil´i-ty
in-cred´i-ble
in-cred´i-bly
in-cre-du´li-ty
in-cred´u-lous
in-cred´u-lous-ly
in´cre-ment
in´cre-men´tal
in-cre´to-ry
in-crim´i-nate
in-crim-i-na´tion
in-crim´i-na-to-ry
in-crust´
in-crus-ta´tion
in´cu-bate
in´cu-ba´tion
in´cu-ba-tor
in´cu-bous
in´cu-bus
in-cul´cate
in-cul-ca´tion
in-cul´ca-tor
in-cul´pate
in-cul-pa´tion
in-cul´pa-to-ry
in-cum´ben-cy
in-cum´bent
in-cum´ber
in-cum´brance
in-cu-nab´u-la
in-cu-nab´u-lum
in-cur´
in-cur´a-ble
in-cu´ri-ous
in-cur´ra-ble

in-curred´
in-cur´rence
in-cur´ring
in-cur´sion
in-cur-sive
in´cur-vate
in´cur-va´tion
in-debt´ed
in-debt´ed-ness
in-de´cen-cy
in-de´cent
in-de-ci´pher-able
in-de-ci´sion
in-de-ci´sive
in-de-clin´able
in´de-com-pos´able
in-dec´or-ous
in-de-co´rum
in-deed´
in-de-fat-i-ga-bil´i-ty
in-de-fat´i-ga-ble
in´de-fea´si-ble
in-de-fen´si-ble
in-de-fin´a-ble
in-def´i-nite
in-def´i-nite-ly
in-de-lib´er-ate
in-del-i-bil´i-ty
in-del´i-ble
in-del´i-ca-cy
in-del´i-cate
in-dem-ni-fi-ca´tion
in-dem´ni-fied
in-dem´ni-fies
in-dem´ni-fy
in-dem´ni-tor
in-dem´ni-ty
in-dent´
in-den-ta´tion
in-dent´ed
in-dent´er
in-den´tion
in-den´ture
in-de-pen´dence
in-de-pen´den-cy
in-de-pen´dent
in-de-pen´dent-ly
in-de-scrib´able
in-de-struc-ti-bil´i-ty

in-de-struc´ti-ble
in-de-ter´min-able
in-de-ter´mi-nate
in-de-ter-mi-na´tion
in´dex
in´dex-er
in´dex-es
In´dia
In´di-an
In-di-an´a
In-di-an-ap´o-lis
in´di-cate
in-di-ca´tion
in-dic´a-tive
in´di-ca-tor
in-dic´a-to-ry
in´di-ces
in-di´cia
in-dic´o-lite
in-dict´
in-dict´able
in-dict´er
in-dic´tion
in-dict´ment
in-dict´or
In´dies
in-dif´fer-ence
in-dif´fer-ent
in-dif´fer-ent-ly
in´di-gen
in´di-gence
in-dig´e-nous
in´di-gent
in-di-gest´ible
in-di-ges´tion
in-dig´nant
in-dig´nant-ly
in-dig-na´tion
in-dig´ni-ty
in´di-go
in-dig´o-lite
In´di-go-sol
in-dig´o-tin
in-di-rect´
in-di-rec´tion
in-di-rect´ly
in-di-rect´ness
in-dis-cern´ible
in-dis-creet´

in´dis-crete´
in-dis-cre´tion
in-dis-crim´i-nate
in-dis-crim´i-nate-ly
in-dis-crim-i-na´tion
in-dis-pens´able
in-dis-pose´
in-dis-posed´
in-dis-po-si´tion
in-dis-put´able
in-dis-sol´u-ble
in-dis-tinct´
in-dis-tinc´tive
in-dis-tinct´ly
in-dis-tinct´ness
in-dis-tin´guish-able
in-dite´ment
in-di-vert´ible
in-di-vid´u-al
in-di-vid´u-al-ism
in-di-vid´u-al-ist
in-di-vid-u-al-is´tic
in-di-vid-u-al´i-ty
in-di-vid´u-al-ize
in-di-vid´u-al-ly
in-di-vis-i-bil´i-ty
in-di-vis´i-ble
In´do—Chi´na
in-doc´ile
in-doc´tri-nate
in-doc-tri-na´tion
in-doc´tri-na-tor
in´do-lence
in´do-lent
in´do-line
in-dom´i-ta-ble
In´do-ne´sia
in´door
in´doors´
in-dorse´
in-dors-ee´
in-dorse´ment
in-dors´er
in-dox´yl
in´drawn
in-du˘bi-ta-ble
in-duce´
in-duce´ment
in-duc´er

in-duc´ible
in-duc´ing
in-duct´
in-duc´tance
in-duct-ee´
in-duc´tile
in-duc-til´i-ty
in-duc´tion
in-duc´tive
in-duc-tiv´i-ty
in-duc-tom´e-ter
in-duc´tor
in-duc-to´ri-um
in-due´
indulge´
in-dul´gence
in-dul´gent
in-dul´gent-ly
in-dulg´er
in-dulg´ing
in´du-line
in-du´pli-cate
in´du-rate
in-du-ra´tion
in´du-ra-tive
In´dus
in-du´si-um
in-dus´tri-al
in-dus´tri-al-ism
in-dus´tri-al-ist
in-dus-tri-al-iza´tion
in-dus´tri-al-ize
in´dus-tries
in-dus´tri-ous
in-dus´tri-ous-ly
in´dus-try
in´dwell-ing
in-e´bri-ant
in-e´bri-ate
in-ebri-a´tion
in-ebri´ety
in-ed-i-bil´i-ty
in-ed´i-ble
in-ef-fa-bil´i-ty
in-ef´fa-ble
in-ef-face´able
in-ef-fec´tive
in-ef-fec´tive-ly
in-ef-fec´tu-al

in-ef-fec-tu-al´i-ty
in-ef-fi-ca´cious
in-ef´fi-ca-cy
in-ef-fi´cien-cy
in-ef-fi´cient
in-elas´tic
in-elas-tic´i-ty
in-el´e-gance
in-el´e-gant
in-el-i-gi-bil´i-ty
in-el´i-gi-ble
in-el´o-quent
in-eluc´ta-ble
in-elud´ible
in-ept´
in-ep´ti-tude
in-equal´i-ty
in-eq´ui-ta-ble
in-eq´ui-ty
in-erad´i-ca-ble
in-eras´able
in-err´able
in-er´rant
in-ert´
in-ert´ance
in-er´tia
in-er´tial
in-es-cap´a-ble
in-es-sen´tial
in-es´ti-ma-ble
in-ev-i-ta-bil´i-ty
in-ev´i-ta-ble
in-ev´i-ta-ble-ness
in-ev´i-ta-bly
in-ex-act´
in-ex-ac´ti-tude
in-ex-cus´able
in-ex-haust-i-bil´i-ty
in-ex-haust´ible
in-ex-is´tence
in-ex-is´tent
in-ex-o-ra-bil´i-ty
in-ex´o-ra-ble
in-ex´o-ra-bly
in-ex-pe´di-en-cy
in-ex-pe´di-ent
in-ex-pen´sive
in-ex-pe´ri-ence
in-ex-pe´ri-enced

in-ex´pert
in-ex´pi-a-ble
in-ex-plain´able
in-ex-plica-bil´i-ty
in-ex-plic´a-ble
in-ex-plic´it
in-ex-press´i-ble
in-ex-pres´sive
in-ex-pug´na-ble
in-ex-punng´-ible
in-ex-ten´si-ble
in-ex-tin´guish-able
in-ex´tir-pa-ble
in-ex-tre´mis
in-ex-trica-bil´i-ty
in-ex-tric´a-ble
in-ex-tric´a-bly
in-fal-li-bil´i-ty
in-fal´li-ble
in´fa-mous
in´fa-my
in´fan-cy
in´fant
in-fan´ti-cide
in´fan-tile
in´fan-ti-lism
in´fan-tine
in´fan-try
in´fan-try-man
in´farct
in-farc´tion
in-fat´u-ate
in-fat´u-at-ed
in-fat-u-a´tion
in-fect´
in-fect´ant
in-fect´ible
in-fec´tion
in-fec´tious
in-fec´tive
in-fec´tor
in-fe-lic´i-tous
in-fe-lic´i-ty
in-fer´
in-fer´able
in´fer-ence
in-fer-en´tial
in-fe´ri-or
in-fe-ri-or´i-ty

in-fer´nal
in-fer´no
in-ferred´
in-fer´ring
in-fer´tile
in-fer-til´i-ty
in-fest´
in-fcs´tant
in-fes-ta´tion
in-fest´er
in-feu-da´tion
in´fi-del
in-fi-del´i-ty
in´field
in-fil´trate
in´fil-tra´tion
in´fil-tra-tive
in´fil´tra-tor
in´fi-nite
in´fi-nite-ly
in-fin-i-tes´i-mal
in-fin´i-ti´val
in-fin´i-tive
in-fin´i-ty
in-firm´
in-fir´ma-ry
in-fir´mi-ty
in-flame´
in-flam´ing
in-flam-ma-bil´i-ty
in-flam´ma-ble
in-flam-ma´tion
in-flam´ma-to-ry
in-flat´able
in-flate´
in-flat´ed
in-flat´er
in-flat´ing
in-fla´tion
in-fla´tion-ary
in-fla´tion-ist
in-fla´tor
in-flect´
in-flect´ible
in-flec-tion
in-flec´tor
in-flex-i-bil´i-ty
in-flex´i-ble
in-flict´

in-flict´er
in-flic´tion
in-flo-res´cence
in-flo-res´cent
in´flow
in´fluence
in´flu-enc-er
in´flu-en´tial
in-flu-en´za
in´flux
in-fold´
in-form´
in-for´mal
in-for-mal´i-ty
in-for´ma-lize
in-for´mal-ly
in-for´mant
in-for-ma´tion
in-form´a-tive
in-form´er
in-fract´ible
in-frac´tion
in-fran´gi-ble
in´fra-red´
in-fra-son´ics
in´fra-sound
in´fra-struc-ture
in-fre´quen-cy
in-fre´quent
in-fre´quent-ly
in-fringe´
in-fringe´ment
in-fring´er
in-fring´ing
in-fu´ri-ate
in-fu´ri-at-ing
in-fu-ri-a´tion
in-fuse´
in-fu´si-ble
in-fu´sion
in-fu-so´ri-al
in-gen´er-ate
in-ge´nious
in-ge´nious-ly
in´ge-nue
in-ge-nu´i-ty
in-gen´u-ous
In´ger-soll
in-gest´

in-ges´tant
in-ges´tion
in´gle
in-glo´ri-ous
in´got
in-grained´
in´grate
in-gra´ti-ate
in-gra´ti-at-ing
in-gra-ti-a´tion
in-gra´tia-to-ry
in-grat´i-tude
in-gra-ves´cence
in´gra-ves´cent
in-grav´i-date
in-gre´di-ent
In´gres
in´gress
in-gres´sion
in´grown
in´growth
in´gui-nal
in-gur´gi-tate
in-hab´it
in-hab-it-abil´i-ty
in-hab´i-tant
in-hab-i-ta´tion
in-hab´it-er
in-hal´ant
in-ha-la´tion
in´ha-la-tor
in-hale´
in-hal´er
in-hal´ing
in-har-mon´ic
in-har-mo´ni-ous
in-here´
in-her´ence
in-her´ent
in-her´it
in-her´it-able
in-her´i-tance
in-her´i-tor
in-her´i-tress
in-he´sion
in-hib´it
in-hib´it-er
in-hi-bi´tion
in-hib´i-tor

in-hib´i-to-ry
in-hos-pit´a-ble
in-hos-pi-tal´i-ty
in-hu´man
in-hu-mane´
in-hu-man´i-ty
in-hu-ma´tion
in-im´i-cal
in-im´i-cal-ly
in-im´i-ta-ble
in-iq´ui-tous
in-iq´ui-ty
ini´tial
ini´tial-ly
ini´ti-ate
ini-ti-a´tion
ini´tia-tive
ini´tia-to-ry
in-ject´
in-jec´tion
in-jec´tor
in-ju-di´cious
in-junc´tion
in-junc´tive
in´jure
in´ju-ries
in´jur-ing
in-ju´ri-ous
in´ju-ry
in-jus´tice
ink bottle
ink´horn
ink´i-er
in´kle
in´kling
ink´stain
ink´stand
ink´well
ink´y
in´laid
in´land
in´—law
in´lay
in´let
in´ly
in´mate
in me-mo´ri-am
in´most
in-nas´ci-ble

in´nate´
in-nate´ly
in´nel-ite
in´ner
in´ner-most
in´ner´vate
in´ner-va´tion
in´ning
inn´keep-er
in´no-cence
in´no-cent
in´no-cent-ly
in-noc´u-ous
in-nom´i-nate
in´no-vate
in´no-va´tion
in´no-va-tor
in´no-va-to-ry
in-nox´ious
in-nu-en´do
in-nu-en´does
in-nu´mer-a-ble
in-nu-tri´tion
in-oc´u-la-ble
in-oc´u-late
in-oc´u-lat-ing
in-oc-u-la´tion
in-oc´u-la-tor
in-of-fen´sive
in-op´er-a-ble
in-op´er-a-tive
in-op-por-tune´
in-op-por-tune´ness
in-or´di-na-cy
in-or´di-nate
in-or´di-nate-ly
in-or-gan´ic
in-or-gan´i-cal-ly
in-os´cu-late
ino´si-tol
in´put
in´quest
in-qui´e-tude
in´qui-line
in-quire´
in-quir´er
in-quir´ies
in-quir´ing
in-quir´ing-ly

in´quiry
in-qui-si´tion
in-quis´i-tive
in-quis´i-tive-ly
in-quis´i-tive-ness
in-quis´i-tor
in´road
in-sane´
in-san´i-tary
in-san´i-ty
in-sa-tia-bil´i-ty
in-sa´tia-ble
in-sa´tiate
in-scrib´able
in-scribe´
in-scrib´er
in-scrib´ing
in-scrip´tion
in-scru´ta-ble
in´sect
in-sec-ti-ci´dal
in-sec´ti-cide
in´sec-ti´val
in-se-cure´
in-se-cur´i-ty
in-sem´i-nate
in-sem-i-na´tion
in-sen´sate
in-sen-si-bil´i-ty
in-sen´si-ble
in-sen´si-tive
in-sen´tient
in-sep´a-ra-ble
insert´
in-ser´tion
in-ser´tive
in´ses-so´ri-al
in´set
in-shore´
in-side´
in-sid´er
in-sid´i-ous
in-sid´i-ous-ly
in´sight
in-sig´ne
in-sig´nia
in-sig-nif´i-cance
in-sig-nif´i-cant
in-sin-cere´

in-sin-cere´ly
in-sin-cer´i-ty
in-sin´u-ate
in-sin-u-a´tion
in-sin´u-a-tor
in-sip´id
in-si-pid´i-ty
in-sip´i-ence
in-sist´
in-sis´tence
in-sis´tent
in-sis´tent-ly
in-sist´er
in-so-bri´e-ty
in´so-late
in-so-la´tion
in´sole
in´so-lence
in´so-lent
in-sol-u-bil´i-ty
in-sol´u-ble
in-solv´able
in-sol´ven-cy
in-sol´vent
in-som´nia
in´so-much´
in-spect´
in-spec´tion
in-spec´tor
in-spec´to-scope
in-spir´able
in-spi-ra´tion
in-spi-ra´tion-al
in-spir´a-tive
in-spir´a-to-ry
in-spire´
in-spir´er
in-spir´ing
in-spir´it
in-spis´sate
in-spis´sa-tor
in-sta-bil´i-ty
in-sta´ble
in-stall´
in-stal-la´tion
in-stalled´
in-stall´ing
in-stall´ment
in´stance

in´stan-cy
in´stant
in-stan-ta´neous
in-stan-ta´neous-ly
in-stan´ter
in´stant-ly
in´star
in-stau-ra´tion
in-stead´
in´step
in´sti-gate
in´sti-gat-ing
in-sti-ga´tion
in´sti-ga-tor
in-still´
in-stilled´
in-still´ing
in´stinct
in-stinc´tive
in-stinc´tive-ly
in´sti-tute
in-sti-tu´tion
in-sti-tu´tion-al
in´sti-tu-tor
in-struct´
in-struct´ed
in-struct´ible
in-struc´tion
in-struc´tion-al
in-struc´tive
in-struc´tor
in´stru-ment
in-stru-men´tal
in-stru-men-tal´i-ty
in-stru-men-ta´tion
in-sub-or´di-nate
in-sub-or-di-na´tion
in-sub-stan´tial
in-suf´fer-able
in-suf-fi´cien-cy
in-suf-fi´cient
in´suf-fla-tor
in´su-lar
in-su-lar´i-ty
in´su-late
in´su-la´tion
in´su-la-tor
in´su-lin
in´sult

in-sul-ta´tion
in-su´per-able
in-sup-port´able
in-sup-press´ible
in-sur´able
in-sur´ance
in-sure´
in-sured´
in-sur´er
in-sur´gence
in-sur´gen-cy
in-sur´gent
in-sur´ing
in-sur-mount´able
in-sur-rec´tion
in-sus-cep´ti-ble
in-tact´
in´take
in-tan-gi-bil´i-ty
in-tan´gi-ble
in-tar´sia
in´te-ger
in´te-gra-ble
in´te-gral
in´te-grate
in-te-gra´tion
in´te-gra-tive
in´te-gra-tor
in-teg´ri-ty
in´tel-lect
in-tel-lec´tu-al
in-tel-lec´tu-al-ism
in-tel-lec´tu-al-ly
in-tel´li-gence
in-tel´li-genc-er
in-tel´li-gent
in-tel-li-gen´tial
in-tel´li-gent-ly
in-tel-li-gi-bil´i-ty
in-tel´li-gi-ble
in-tem´er-ate
in-tem´per-ance
in-tem´per-ate
in-tend´
in-tend´ance
in-tend´an-cy
in-tend´ant
in-tense´
in-tense´ly

in-ten-si-fi-ca´tion
in-ten´si-fied
in-ten´si-fies
in-ten´si-fy
in-ten´sion
in-ten´si-ty
in-ten´sive
in-ten´sive-ly
in-tent´
in-ten´tion
in-ten´tion-al
in-ten´tion-al-ly
in-tent´ly
in-tent´ness
in-ter´
in-ter-act´
in-ter-ac´tion
in-ter´ca-late
in-ter-ca-la´tion
in-ter-cede´
in-ter-ced´ing
in-ter-cel´lu-lar
in´ter-cept
in-ter-cep´tion
in-ter-cep´tor
in-ter-ces´sion
in-ter-ces´sor
in-ter-ces´so-ry
in´ter-change
in-ter-change´able
in-ter-clav´i-cle
in-ter-col-le´giate
in-ter-co-lo´ni-al
in´ter-com
in-ter-com-mu´ni-
  cate
in-ter-com-mu-ni-
  ca´tion
in-ter-cos´tal
in´ter-course
in-ter-den´tal
in-ter-de-pen´dence
in-ter-de-pen´dent
in-ter-dict´
in-ter-dic´tion
in-ter-dic´tor
in´ter-est
in´ter-est-ed
in´ter-est-ing

in-ter-fere´
in-ter-fer´ence
in-ter-fe-ren´tial
in-ter-fer´ing
in-ter-fer-om´e-ter
in-ter-fer-om´e-try
in-ter-fer´on
in-ter-fuse´
in-ter-fu´sion
in-ter-gla´cial
in´ter-grade
in´ter-im
in-te´ri-or
in-ter-ject´
in-ter-jec´tion
in-ter-jec´tor
in-ter-jec´tur-al
in-ter-knit´
in-ter-lace´
in-ter-lam´i-nate
in-ter-lay´
in-ter-leave´
in-ter-lin´c-al
in-ter-lin´e-ar
In-ter-lin´gua
in´ter-lin-ing
in´ter-lock
in-ter-lo-cu´tion
in-ter-loc´u-tor
in-ter-loc´u-to-ry
in´ter-lop-er
in´ter-lude
in´ter-lu´nar
in´ter-mar´riage
in´ter-mar´ry
in-ter-med´dle
in-ter-med´dler
in-ter-me´di-ary
in-ter-me´di-ate
in-ter´ment
in-ter-mez´zo
in-ter´mi-na-ble
in-ter´mi-na-bly
in-ter-min´gle
in-ter-min´gling
in-ter-mis´sion
in´ter-mit´
in-ter-mit´tent
in-ter-mit´tent-ly

in-ter-mix´
in-ter-mix´ture
in-tern´
in-ter´nal
in-ter´nal-ly
in-ter-na´tion-al
in-ter-na´tion-al-ism
in-ter-na´tion-al-ist
in-ter-na´tion-al-ize
in-ter-na´tion-al-ly
in-ter-nec´ine
in-terned´
in-ter´nist
in´tern-ship
in´ter-o-cep´tive
in-ter-pel´late
in-ter-pel-la´tion
in-ter-pen´e-trate
in-ter-plan´e-tary
in´ter-play
in-ter-pose´
in-ter-pos´ing
in-ter-po-si´tion
in-ter´pret
in-ter´pret-able
in-ter´pre-ta´tion
in-ter´pre-ta-tive
in-ter´pret-er
in-ter´pre-tive
in-ter-ra´cial
in-ter-ra´di-al
in-terred´
in-ter-reg´num
in-ter-re-late´
in-ter-re-lat´ed
in-ter-re-la´tion
in-ter-re-la´tion-ship
in-ter´ring
in-ter´ro-gate
in-ter-ro-ga´tion
in-ter-rog´a-tive
in-ter´ro-ga-tor
in-ter-rog´a-to-ry
in-ter-rupt´
in-ter-rupt´ed
in-ter-rupt´er
in-ter-rupt´ible
in-ter-rupt´ing
in-ter-rup´tion

in-ter-sect´
in-ter-sec´tion
in´ter-space
in´ter-sperse´
in-ter-sper´sion
in´ter-state´
in-ter-stel´lar
in-ter´stice
in-ter´stic-es
in-ter-sti´tial
in´ter-twine
in´ter-twist
In´ter-type
in´ter-val
in-ter-vene´
in-ter-ven´er
in-ter-ve´nor
in-ter-ven´tion
in-ter-ven´tion-ist
in´ter-view
in´ter-view-er
in´ter-weave
in-ter-wo´ven
in-tes´tate
in-tes´ti-nal
in-tes´tine
in´ti-ma
in´ti-ma-cy
in´ti-mate
in´ti-mate-ly
in´ti-mat-er
in-ti-ma´tion
in-tim´i-date
in-tim-i-da´tion
in-tim´i-da-tor
in-tol´er-able
in-tol´er-ably
in-tol´er-ance
in-tol´er-ant
in-tone´
in-ton´ing
in-tox´i-cant
in-tox´i-cate
in-tox´i-cat-ing
in-tox-i-ca´tion
in-tox-im´e-ter
in-tra-cel´lu-lar
in-trac-ta-bil´i-ty
in-trac´ta-ble

in´tra-dos
in-tra-mo-lec´u-lar
in-tra-mu´ral
in-tran´si-gent
in-tran´si-tive
in-tra-state´
in-tra-tel-lu´ric
in-tra-ve´nous
in-treat´
in-trep´id
in-tre-pid´i-ty
in´tri-ca-cy
in´tri-cate
in´tri-gant´
in-trigue´
in-trigued´
in-trigu´er
in-trigu´ing
in-trigu´ing-ly
in-trin´sic
in-trin´si-cal
in-trin´si-cal-ly
in-tro-duce´
in-tro-duc´tion
in-tro-duc´to-ry
in-tro-jec´tion
in´tro-mit´tent
in´tro-spect´
in-tro-spec´tion
in-tro-spec´tive
in-tro-ver´si-ble
in-tro-ver´sion
in´tro-vert
in-trude´
in-trud´er
in-tru´sion
in-tru´sive
in-trust´
in-tu-i´tion
in-tu´i-tive
in-tu-mes´cence
in-tus-sus-cep´tion
in´un-date
in-un-da´tion
in´un-da-tor
in´un-da-to-ry
in-ure´
in-ur´ing
in-util´i-ty

in-vade´
in-vad´er
in-vad´ing
in-vag´i-nate
in-vag-i-na´tion
in-val´id
in-val´i-date
in-val-i-da´tion
in´va-lid-ism
in´va-lid´i-ty
in-val´u-able
in-var´i-able
in-var´i-ably
in-var´i-ant
in-va´sion
in-vec´tive
in-veigh´
in-vei´gle
in-vei´gling
in-vel´gling
in-vent´
in-vent´able
in-ven´tion
in-ven´tive
in-ven´tor
in-ven-to´ri-al
in´ven-to-ries
in´ven-to-ry
in-ve-rac´i-ty
In´ver-ness
in-verse´
in-ver´sion
in-vert´
in-vert´ase
in-ver´te-brate
in-vert´er
in-vert´ible
in-ver´tor
in-vest´
in-ves´ti-gate
in-ves-ti-ga´tion
in-ves´ti-ga-tor
in-ves´ti-ture
in-vest´ment
in-ves´tor
in-vet´er-ate
in-vig´i-late
in-vig´o-rate
in-vig´o-rat-ing
in-vig-o-ra´tion

in-vin-ci-bil´i-ty
in-vin´ci-ble
in-vi-o-la-bil´i-ty
in-vi´o-la-ble
in-vi´o-la-cy
in-vi´o-late
in-vis-i-bil´i-ty
in-vis´i-ble
in-vi-ta´tion
in-vi´ta-to-ry
in-vite´
in-vit´er
in-vit´ing
in-vit´ing-ly
in´vo-cate
in-vo-ca´tion
in-voc´a-tive
in´vo-ca-tor
in-voc´a-to-ry
in´voice
in´voic-ing
invoke´
in-vok´ing
in-vol-un-tar´i-ly
in-vol´un-tary
in´vo-lute
in´vo-lut-ed
in-vo-lu´tion
in-volve´
in-volve´ment
in-volv´ing
in-vul-ner-a-bil´i-ty
in-vul´ner-a-ble
in-vul-tu-a´tion
in´ward
in´ward-ly
in´weave´
in´wo-ven
in´wrought
i´o-date
iod´ic
i´o-dide
i´o-di-nate
i´o-dine
io´do-form
io-do-hy´drin
io-dom´e-try
io-do´ni-um
io-do-phthal´e-in

io-do-pyr´a-cet
io-dox´y-ben-zene´
iod´y-rite
i´on
Io´nia
Io´ni-an
Ion´ic
io´ni-um
ion-iza´tion
i´on-ize
io-nom´e-ter
ion´o-sphere
ion´o-spher´ic
io´ta
io´ta-cism
I´o-wa
ip´e-cac
ip-o-me´a
ip´so fac´to
Ips´wich
I´ra
ira´de
Iran´
Iraq´
iras-ci-bil´i-ty
iras´ci-ble
irate´
ire´ful
ire´ful-ly
Ire´land
Irene´
iren´ic
Iri-an´
iri-da´ceous
iri-dec´to-my
ir-i-des´cence
ir-i-des´cent
irid´ic
irid´i-um
iri-di-za´tion
i´ris
iris-a´tion
I´rish
I´rish-man
I´rish-wom-an
iri´tis
irk´some
Ir´ma
i´ron

i´ron-bound
i´ron-clad
i´ron gray´
iron´ic
iron´i-cal
iron´i-cal-ly
i´ron-ing
i´ron-mas-ter
i´ron-mon-ger
i´ron-side
I´ron-sides
i´ron-stone
i´ron-ware
i´ron-wood
i´ron-work
i´ro-ny
Ir´o-quois
ir-ra´di-ate
ir-ra-di-a´tion
ir-rad´i-ca-ble
ir-ra´tio-nal
Ir-ra-wad´dy
ir-re-claim´able
ir-rec´on-cil-able
ir-re-cov´er-able
ir-re-deem´able
ir-re-den´ta
ir-re-den´tist
ir-re-duc-ibil´i-ty
ir-re-duc´ible
ir-re-frag´a-ble
ir-re-fran´gi-ble
ir-re-fut-abil´i-ty
ir-re-fut´able
ir-reg´u-lar
ir-reg-u-lar´i-ty
ir-reg´u-lar-ly
ir-rel´e-vance
ir-rel´e-vant
ir-re-li´gion
ir-re-li´gious
ir-re´me-able
ir-re-me´di-able
ir-re-mov´able
ir-rep´a-ra-ble
ir-re-place´able
ir-re-press´ible
ir-re-proach´able
ir-re-sist´ible

ir-re-sist´ibly
ir-re-sol´u-ble
ir-res´o-lute
ir-res´o-lute-ly
ir-res-o-lu´tion
ir-re-solv´able
ir-re-spec´tive
ir-re-spon-si-bil´i-ty
ir-re-spon´si-ble
ir-re-triev´able
ir-rev´er-ence
ir-rev´er-ent
ir-re-vers-ibil´i-ty
ir-re-vers´ible
ir-rev-o-ca-bil´i-ty
ir-rev´o-ca-ble
ir-rev´o-ca-bly
ir´ri-ga-ble
ir´ri-gate
ir´ri-ga´tion
ir´ri-ga-tor
ir-rig´u-ous
ir-ri´sion
ir-ri-ta-bil´i-ty
ir´ri-ta-ble
ir´ri-ta-bly
ir´ri-tan-cy
ir´ri-tant
ir´ri-tate
ir´ri-tat-ing
ir´ri-ta´tion
ir-rup´tion
ir-rup´tive
Ir´ving
I´saac
Is´a-bel
is-acous´tic
Is-a-do´ra
Isa´iah
i´sa-tin
i´sa-tin´ic
Is-car´i-ot
is-che´mia
is´chi-al
is´chi-at´ic
is´chi-um
Ish´ma-el
Ish´tar
i´sin-glass

I´sis
Is-lam´
Is-lam´ic
is´land
is´land-er
is´let
i´so-bar
i´so-bath
iso-bath´y-therm
i´so-chro-mat´ic
isoch´ro-nal
i´so-chrone
isoch´ro-nism
isoch´ro-nous
iso-cla´site
iso-cli´nal
Isoc´ra-tes
iso-gon´ic
i´so-la-ble
i´so-lat-able
i´so-late
iso-la´tion
iso-la´tion-ist
Isolde´
iso-leu´cine
isol´o-gous
iso-mag-net´ic
i´so-mer
iso-mer´ic
isom´er-ism
isom´er-ize
iso-met´ric
iso-met´ri-cal´ly
iso-me-tro´pia
iso-mor´phic
iso-mor´phism
iso-ni´a-zid
ison´o-my
iso-oc´tane
iso-phthal´ic
iso-pi-es´tic
i´so-pod
iso-pol´i-ty
i´so-prene
iso-pre´noid
iso-pro´pa-nol
i´so-pro´pyl
isos´ce-les
iso-stat´ic

i´so-ther´al
i´so-there
i´so-therm
iso-ther´mal
i´so-ton´ic
iso-to-nic´i-ty
i´so-tope
i´so-top´ic
i´so-to-py
i´so-tron
iso-trop´ic
isot´ro-pous
isot´ro-py
i´so-zyme
Is´ra-el
Is´ra-el-ite
is´su-able
is´su-ance
is´sue
is´su-ing
Is´tan-bul´
isth´mi-an
isth´mus
is´tle
Is´tri-an
it´a-con´ic
Ital´ian
ital´ic
ital´i-cize
ital´i-ciz-ing
ital´ics
It´a-ly
itch´i-ness
itch´y
i´tem
i´tem-iza´tion
i´tem-ize
it´er-ance
it´er-ate
it-er-a´tion
it´er-a-tive
Ith´a-ca
itin´er-an-cy
itin´er-ant
itin´er-ary
itin´er-ate
its
it-self´
I´van

i´vied
i´vo-ry
i´vy
Iz-mir´

## J

jabbed
jab´ber
jab´bing
ja-bot´
jac-a-ran´da
ja´cinth
jack´al
jack´a-napes
jack´ass
jack´boot
jack´daw
jack´et
jack´knife
jack´—o'—lan-tern
jack plane
jack´pot
jack´rab-bit
Jack´son
Jack´son-ville
jack´straw
Ja´cob
jac´o-net
Jac´quard
Jac´que-line
jacque´mi-not
Jac-que-rie´
jac-ta´tion
jac-ti-ta´tion
jac´u-late
jad´ed
jade´ite
Jaf´fa
ja´ger
jag´ged
jag´gery
jag´uar
jai alai´
jail´bird
jail´break
jail´er
Jai-pur´
jal´ap

jal´a-pin
ja-lop´y
jal´ou-sie
Ja-mai´ca
jam-ba-lay´a
jam´bo-ree´
James´town
jam´ming
Jan´et
jan´gle
jan´gling
Jan´ice
jan´i-tor
Jan´sen
Jan´u-ary
Ja´nus
Ja-pan´
Jap´a-nese´
Ja´pheth
ja-ra´be
jar´di-niere´
Ja´red
jar´gon
jar´gon-ize
jar-goon´
jaro-vi-za´tion
jar´rah
jarred
jas´mine
Ja´son
jas´per
jaun´dice
jaun´ti-ly
jaun´ty
Jav´a
Jav´a-nese´
jav´e-lin
jaw´bone
jay´walk-er
jeal´ous
jeal´ous-ly
jeal´ou-sy
Jean-nette´
jeer´ing-ly
Jef´fer-son
Jef-fer-so´ni-an
Jef´frey
Je-ho´vah
je-ju´nal

je-june´
Jek´yll
jell
jel´lied
jel´li-fy
jel´ly
jel´ly-fish
Je-mi´mah
Jen´kins
Jen´ner
Jen´nie
Jen´ni-fer
jen´ny
jeop´ard
jeop´ar-dize
jeop´ar-diz-ing
jeop´ar-dy
Jer-e-mi´ah
Jer´i-cho
jerk´i-ly
jer´kin
jer´ky
Je-rome´
Jer´ry
jer´sey
Je-ru´sa-lem
Jes´se
Jes´sie
jest´er
jest´ing-ly
Jes´u-it
Je´sus
jet´lin-er
jet´sam
jet´ties
jet´ting
jet´ti-son
jet´ty
jew´el
jew´eled
jew´el-er
jew´el-ry
jew´fish
Jew´ish
Jew's harp
Jez´e-bel
jib´bing
jib´boom
jif´fy

jig´ger
jig´gle
jig´gling
jig´saw
jilt´ed
jim´mied
jim´my
jin´gle
jin´gling
jin´go
jin´goes
jit´ney
jit´ter-bug
jit´ters
jit´tery
Jo´ab
Job
job´ber
job´bery
job´bing
job´hold-er
job´less
jock´ey
jock´eys
joc´u-lar
joc-u-lar´i-ty
joc´und
jo-cun´di-ty
jodh´pur
Jo´el
jog´ging
jog´gle
jog´gling
Jo´hann
Jo-han´nes
Jo-han´nes-burg
Jo-han´nine
Jo-hans´son
john´ny-cake
John´son
John-so´ni-an
John´ston
Johns´town
join´der
join´er
join´ery
joint´ed
joint´er
joint´ly

joint´ress
joist
joked
jok´er
joke´ster
jok´ing
jok´ing-ly
Jo-li-et´
jol-li-fi-ca´tion
jol´li-fy
jol´li-ly
jol´li-ty
jol´ly
jol´ly-boat
Jo´nah
Jon´a-than
jon´quil
Jop´lin
Jop´pa
Jor´dan
Jo-se´
Jo´seph
jo´se-phine
Jo-se´phus
Josh´ua
Jo-si´ah
jos´tle
jos´tled
jos´tling
jot´ted
jot´ting
jounce
jounc´ing
jour´nal
jour´nal-ism
jour´nal-ist
jour-nal-is´tic
jour-nal-is´ti-cal-ly
jour´nal-ize
jour´ney
jour´neyed
jour´ney-man
jour´neys
joust
joust´er
jo´vial
jo-vial´i-ty
jo´vial-ly
Jo´vi-an

joy´ance
joy´ful
joy´ful-ly
joy´ous
joy´ous-ly
joy´ous-ness
joy´ride
Jua´rez
ju´ba
ju´bi-lance
ju´bi-lant
ju´bi-late
Ju-bi-la´te
ju-bi-la´tion
ju´bi-lee
Ju´dah
Ju-da´ic
Ju´da-ism
Ju´das
Ju-de´a
Ju-de´an
Judg´es
judge´ship
judg´ing
judg´ment
ju´di-ca-tive
ju´di-ca-to-ry
ju´di-ca-ture
ju-di´cial
ju-di´ciary
ju-di´cious
ju-di´cious-ly
Ju´dith
ju´do
Ju´dy
ju´gal
jug´ger-naut
jug´gle
jug´gler
jug´glery
jug´gling
ju´glone
Ju-go-slav´ia
jug´u-lar
jug´u-late
juic´i-ly
juic´i-ness
juic´y
ju-jit´su

ju´jube
juke˝box
ju´lep
Ju´lia
Ju´lian
Ju-li-an´a
ju-lienne´
Ju˝liet
Ju´lius
Ju-ly´
jum˝ble
jum˝bled
jum˝bling
jum˝bo
jump´er
jump´ing
jump´y
junc´tion
junc´tur-al
junc´ture
Ju´neau
Jung´frau
jun´gle
jun´gly
jun´ior
ju-nior´i-ty
ju´ni-per
Ju´nius
Jun˝ker
junk´er
jun˝ket
jun˝ke-teer´
junk´man
Ju´no
jun´ta
jun´to
Ju´pi-ter
Ju´ra
ju´ral
ju´rane
Ju-ras´sic
ju´rat
ju-rel´
ju-rid´i-cal
ju´ries
ju-ris-dic´tion
ju-ris-pru˝dence
ju´rist
ju-ris´tic

ju´ror
ju´ry
ju´ry-man
jus´tice
jus-ti˝cia-ble
jus-ti˝ci-ar
jus´ti-fi-able
jus-ti-fi-ca´tion
jus-tif´i-ca-to-ry
jus´ti-fied
jus´ti-fi-er
jus´ti-fy
Jus´tin
just´ly
just´ness
Jut˝land
jut˝ting
Ju´ve-nal
ju-ve-nes´cent
ju´ve-nile
jux´ta-pose
jux-ta-po-si´tion

### K

ka-bu˝ki
Ka-bul´
ka-chi´na
Kaf˝fir
kai´nos-ite
kai˝ser
ka˝ka
Kal-a-ma-zoo´
ka-lei´do-scope
ka-lei´do-scop´ic
Kal´i-spel´
Kal´muck
ka´long
ka´ma-la
Kam-chat˝ka
ka-mi-ka´ze
Kam-pa˝la
kan´ga-roo´
Kan˝san
Kan˝sas
kan-tar´
ka´olin
ka-olin´ic
ka´olin-ite

ka´pok
kap´pa
Ka-ra´chi
kar´at
Ka-ren´
kar´ma
Kar´nak
kar-rool
kar´yo-some
Kash˝mir
ka-tab´a-sis
kat´a-bat´ic
Ka-tan´ga
Kath´a-rine
ka´ty-did
kau´ri
ka´va
kay´ak
Ka-zan´
Kear´ney
Kear´ny
ked´dah
keel˝haul
keel˝son
keen´ly
keen˝mess
keep´er
keep´ing
keep´sake
Kel´ler
Kel˝logg
Kel´ly
ke´loid
kel´pie
Kel´vin
Ken´il-worth
Ken´ne-bec
Ken´ne-dy
ken´nel
Ken´sing-ton
Kent´ish
Ken-tuck´y
Ke´nya
Ken´yon
Ke´o-kuk
Kep´ler
ker´a-toid
Ker´a-tol
ker-a-tol´y-sis

ker-a-to´sis
ker´a-tot´ic
ker´chief
ker´chiefed
Ke-ren´sky
kerf
ker´mes
ker´mes-ite
ker´mis
kerned
ker´nel
ker´neled
ker´o-gen
ker´o-sene
Ker´ry
ker´sey
kes´trel
ke´ta-zine
ke´tene
ke´ti-mine
ke-to-gen´e-sis
ke-to-gen´ic
ke´tone
ke-ton´ic
ket´tle
ket´tle-drum
kev´el
key´board
keyed
key´hole
key´note
key´stone
khad´dar
khak´i
Khar´toum´
Khmer
Khy´ber
kib´itz
kib´itz-er
ki´bosh
kick´back
kick´off
kick´shaw
kid´ded
kid´ding
kid´nap
kid´naped
kid´nap-er
kid´nap-ing

kid´napped
kid´nap-per
kid´nap-ping
kid´ney
Kil-i-man-ja´ro
Kil-ken´ny
Kil-lar´ney
kill´er
kill´ing
kill´joy
kiln
ki´lo
kil´o-cy-cle
kil´o-gram
kil´o-li-ter
ki-lom´e-ter
kilo-met´ric
kil´o-ton
kil´o-watt
kil´o-watt—hour
Kil-pat´rick
kilt´ed
kil´ter
Kim´ber-ley
ki-mo´no
ki-mo´nos
kin´der-gar-ten
kin´der-gart-ner
kind´heart-ed
kin´dle
kind´less
kind´li-ness
kin´dling
kind´ly
kind´ness
kin´dred
kin-e-mat´ics
kin-e-mat´o-graph
kin´e-scope
ki-ne´sics
kin-e-sim´e-ter
ki-ne-si-ol´o-gy
kin-es-the´sia
kin-es-the´sis
kin´es-thet´ic
ki-net´ic
ki-ne´to-graph
ki-ne´to-graph´ic
ki-ne´to-phone

Ki-ne´to-scope
kin´folk
king´bird
king´dom
king´fish
king´fish-er
king´less
king´let
king´li-ness
king´ly
king´pin
king´ship
Kings´ley
Kings´ton
kin´ka-jou
kin´kled
kink´y
kin´ship
kins´man
kins´wom-an
ki´osk
Kip´ling
Ki´o-wa
kip´per
kir´tle
kis´met
kiss´able
kitch´en
kitch´en-ette´
kitch´en-maid
kitch´en-ware
kit´ten
kit´ten-ish
kit´ti-wake
kit´ty
ki´va
Ki-wa´nis
ki´wi
Klam´ath
Klee´nex
klep-to-ma´nia
klep-to-ma´ni-ac
Kling´sor
Klon´dike
knack´er
knag´gy
knap´sack
knav´ery
knav´ish

knead
knee´cap
kneed
knee´—deep´
knee´—high´
kneel´ing
knick´er-bock-er
knick´ers
knick´knack
knife
knight´hood
knight´li-ness
knight´ly
knit
knit´ter
knit´ting
knives
knobbed
knob´by
knob´ker-rie
knock´about
knock´down
knock´er
knock´out
knoll
knot´hole
knot´ted
knot´ter
knot´ting
knot´ty
know´able
know´—how
know´ing
know´ing-ly
knowl´edge
knowl´edge-able
Knox´ville
knuck´le
knuck´led
knuck´ling
knurl´y
ko-a´la
Ko´dak
Ko´di-ak
ko´la
ko-lin´sky
kol-khoz´
koo´doo
ko´peck

Ko-ran´
Ko-re´a
ko´ru-na
ko´sher
kow´tow
kra´ken
Kreis´ler
Krem´lin
kreu´zer
krim´mer
Krish´na
kro´na
kro´ne
kryp´ton
Ku´blai Khan
ku´du
kud´zu
Ku´fic
ku-lak´
kum´quat
Kur´di-stan´
ku´ru
ku-rus´
Ku-wait´
ky´ack
ky´a-nize
ky´mo-graph
ky-mog´ra-phy
kyn-uren´ine
ky-pho´sis
ky phot´ic

**L**

lab´a-rum
la´bel
la´beled
la´bel-er
la´bel-ing
la´bile
la-bil´i-ty
la´bi-lize
la´bio-den´tal
la´bi-um
la´bor
lab´o-ra-to-ry
la´bored
la´bor-er
la-bo´ri-ous

la-bo´ri-ous-ly
la´bor-ite
Lab´ra-dor
lab´ra-dor-ite
la´bret
la´broid
la´brum
La Bru-yère´
la-bur´num
lab´y-rinth
lab-y-rin´thi-an
lab-y-rin´thine
lac´co-lith
lac´er-ate
lac´er-at-ing
lac-er-a´tion
lac-er-til´i-an
lace´work
lach´es
lach´ry-mal
lach´ry-ma-to-ry
lach´ry-mose
lac´ing
lack-a-dai´si-cal
Lack-a-wan´na
lack´ey
lack´ing
lack´lus-ter
La-co´nia
la-con´ic
la-con´i-cal-ly
lac´o-nism
lac´quer
lac´ri-mal
lac´ri-ma-to-ry
la-crosse´
lac´ta-ry
lac´tase
lac´tate
lac´te-al
lac´te-ous
lac-tes´cence
lac-tes´cent
lac´tic
lac-tif´er-ous
lac´to-fla´vin
lac-tom´e-ter
lac-to-pro´tein
lac´tose

la-cu´na
lac´u-nary
la-cu´nu-lose
la-cus´trine
lac´y
lad´der
lad´die
lad´en
lad´en-ing
la´dies
lad´ing
la´dle
la´dle-ful
la´dy
la´dy-bird
la´dy-bug
la´dy-fin-ger
la´dy—kill-er
la´dy-like
la´dy-ship
la´dy's maid
la´dy's slip-per
La-fay-ette´
lag´an
la´ger
lag´gard
lag´ging
la-goon´
la-goon´al
La´gos
lais´sez—faire
lai´tance
la´i-ty
lake´side
lal-la´tion
la´ma
la´ma-ism
la´ma-sery
lam-baste´
lamb´da
lamb´doid
lam´ben-cy
lam´bent
lam´bert
Lam´beth
lamb´kin
lam´bre-quin
lamb´skin
la-mé´

la-mel´lar
lam´e´late
la-mel´lose
lame´ly
lame´ness
la-ment´
lam´en-ta-ble
lam´en-ta-bly
lam-en-ta´tion
la-ment´ed
lam´i-na
lam´i-na-graph
lam-i-nag´ra-phy
lam´i-nal
lam´i-nar
lam´i-nate
lam-i-na´tion
lam´i-na-tor
lam-i-ni´tis
lam´pad
lamp´black
lam´pi-on
lamp´light
lam-poon´
lamp´post
lam´prey
lamp´stand
la´nate
Lan´ca-shire
Lan´cas-ter
Lan´ce-lot
lan´ce-o-lar
lan´ce-o-late
lanc´er
lan´cet
lan´cet-ed
lance´wood
lan´ci-nate
lanc´ing
lan´dau
lan´dau-let´
land´ed
land´fall
land´grave
land´hold-er
land´ing
land´ing craft
land´ing field
land´ing gear

land´ing strip
land´la-dy
land´less
land´locked
land´lop-er
land´lord
land´lub-ber
land´mark
Lan´dor
land´own-er
land´—poor
land´scape
land´slide
land´slip
lands´man
Land´sturm
land´ward
Lang´shan
lang´spiel
lan´guage
lan´guid
lan´guid-ly
lan´guish
lan´guished
lan´guish-ing
lan´guor
lan´guor-ous
la´ni-ary
La-nier´
lank´i-er
lank´y
lan´o-lin
la´nose
Lan´sing
Lan´ston
lan-ta´na
lan´tern
lan´tha-nide
lan´yard
La-oc´o-on
Laos
lap´dog
la-pel´
lap´i-dary
lap-i-da´tion
la-pid´i-fy
la-pil´lus
lap´in
La-place´

Lap´land
lap´pet
lap´ping
lapsed
laps´ing
lap´wing
Lar´a-mie
lar´ce-nist
lar´ce-nous
lar´ce-ny
lar´der
large´ly
large´ness
larg´er
lar-gess´
larg´est
lar´go
lar´i-at
lar´ine
lark´spur
lar´rup
lar´va
lar´vae
lar´val
lar´vi-cid-al
lar´vi-cide
lar-vic´o-lous
lar-viv´o-rous
la-ryn´ges
lar´yn-git´ic
lar´yn-gi´tis
la-ryn´go-log´i-cal
lar-yn-gol´o-gist
lar-yn-gol´o-gy
la-ryn´go-scope
lar-yn-gos´co-py
la-ryn´go-spasm
lar´ynx
La Salle
la´ser
lash´ing
las´sie
las´si-tude
las´so
las´so-er
last´ing
last´ly
latch´et
latch´key

latch´string
la-teen´
late´ly
la´ten-cy
late´ness
la´tent
la´tent-ly
lat´er
lat´er-al
lat´er-al-ly
lat´er-ite
lat´er-i´tious
lat-er-i-za´tion
lat´est
la´tex
lath
lathe
lath´er
lath´er-ing
lath´ing
lath´work
lat´i-ces
lat-i-cif´er-ous
Lat´i-mer
Lat´in
Lat´in-ist
La-tin´i-ty
lat´ish
la´tite
lat´i-tude
lat-i-tu´di-nal
lat-i-tu-di-nar´i-an
lat-i-tu´di-nous
La´tium
La-to´na
la-tri´a
la-trine´
la´tron
lat´ter
lat´tice
lat´tice-work
lat´tic-ing
Lat´via
laud-abil´i-ty
laud´able
lau-dan´i-dine
lau´da-nine
lau-dan´o-sine
lau´da-num

lau-da´tion
laud´a-tive
lau´da-to-ry
Lau´der
Laud´ian
laugh´able
laugh´ing
laugh´ing-stock
laugh´ter
launched
launch´er
laun´der
laun´dress
laun´dries
Laun´dro-mat
laun´dry
laun´dry-man
Lau´ra
lau´rate
lau´re-ate
lau´rel
lau´reled
Lau´rence
Lau-ren´tian
Lau´ren-tide
lau´ric
Lau´ri-er
lau´ryl
Lau-sanne´
lau´ter
la´va
la-vage´
lav´a-liere´
la-va´tion
lav´a-to-ry
lav´en-der
la´ver
lav´ing
lav´ish
law´—abid´ing
law´break-er
law´ful
law´giv-er
law´less
law´less-ness
law´mak-er
law´mak-ing
Law´rence
law´suit

law´yer
lax-a´tion
lax´a-tive
lax´i-ty
lay´er
lay-ette´
lay´man
lay´off
lay´out
laz´ar
laz´a-ret´
laz-a-ret´to
Laz´a-rus
la´zi-er
la´zi-ly
la´zi-ness
la´zy
leach
lead´en
lead´er
lead´er-ship
lead´ing
leads´man
lead´y
leaf´age
leaf´less
leaf´let
leaf´y
league
lea´guer
leak´age
leak´proof
leak´y
lean
lean´ing
lean´ness
leap´frog
leap´ing
leap year
learned
learn´er
learn´ing
leased
lease´hold
leas´ing
leath´er
leath´er-ine´
leath´ern
Leath´er-neck

leath´er-work
leath´ery
leav´en
Leav´en-worth
leav´ing
Leb´a-nese´
Leb´a-non
lech´er-ous
lech´ery
lec´i-thin
lec´i-thin-ase
lec´tern
lec´tion
lec´tor
lec´ture
lee´tured
lec´tur-er
lec´tur-ing
ledg´er
lee´board
leech
leer´ing
leer´ing-ly
leer´y
lee´ward
lee´way
left—hand´ed
left´ist
left´over
leg´a-cies
leg´a-cy
le´gal
le´gal-is´tic
le-gal´i-ty
le-gal-iza´tion
le´gal-ize
le´gal-ly
leg´ate
leg´a-tee´
le-ga´tion
le-ga´to
leg´end
leg´end-ary
le-ger´i-ty
leg´ged
leg´gings
Leg´horn
leg-i-bil´i-ty
leg´i-ble

le´gion
le´gion-ary
le´gion-naire´
leg´is-late
leg-is-la´tion
leg´is-la-tive
leg´is-la-tor
leg-is-la-to´ri-al
leg´is-la-ture
le-git´i-ma-cy
le-git´i-mate
le-git´i-ma-tize
le-git´i-mist
le-git´i-mize
le-git´i-miz-ing
leg´man
leg´ume
le-gu´min
le-gu´mi-nous
Le´high
Leices´ter
Leip´zig
leis´ter
lei´sure
lei´sure-ly
lem´an
lem´ma
lem´ming
lem´on
lem´on-ade´
le´mur
Le´na
lend´er
lend´ing
length
length´en
length´i-er
length´wise
length´y
le´nience
le´nien-cy
le´nient
le´nient-ly
Len´in
Len´in-grad
Len´in-ism
len´i-tive
len´i-ty
Len´ox

len-ta-men´te
len-tan´do
Lent´en
len´ti-cel
len-tic´u-lar
len-tig´i-nous
len-ti´go
len´til
Leon´ard
le´o-nine
le´o-nite
leop´ard
Le´o-pold
le´o-tard
Le-pan´to
lep´er
lep´re-chaun
lep-rol´o-gy
lep-ro-sar´i-um
le-pro´sis
lep´ro-sy
lep-rot´ic
lep´rous
lep´ton
lep´tus
Ler-nae´an
Les´bi-an
Les´bos
le´sion
Le-so´tho
les-see´
less´en
less´er
les´son
les´sor
let´down
le´thal
le-thal´i-ty
le-thar´gic
le-thar´gi-cal-ly
leth´ar-gize
leth´ar-gy
Le-ti´tia
let´ter
let´ter box
let´ter car´ri-er
let´rered
let´ter-head
let´ter-ing

let´ter—per´fect
Lett´ish
let´tre de ca-chet´
let´tuce
let´up
leu´cine
leu´cite
leu-co´ma
leu´co-maine
leu´co-noid
leu-cop´te-rin
leu-cot´o-my
leu-cov´o-rin
leu-ke´mia
leu-ke´mic
leu´ker-gy
leu´ko-cyte
leu´ko-cyt´ic
leu´ko-cy-to´sis
leu-ko-pe´nia
leu-ko-poi-e´sis
leu´ko-poi-et´ic
leu-kor-rhe´a
leu-ko´sis
lev´an
Le-vant´
Le-vant´er
Lev´an-tine
le-va´tor
lev´ee
lev´el
lev´eled
lev´el-er
lev´el-ing
lev´el-ly
lev´er
lev´er-age
lev´er-et
Le´vi
lev´i-able
le-vi´a-than
lev´i-gate
lev´i-ga-tor
lev´i-rate
lev´i-rat´ic
lev´i-tate
lev´i-tat-ing
lev-i-ta´tion
Le´vite

le-vit´i-cal
Le-vit´i-cus
lev´i-ty
le´vo-gy´rate
le´vo-ro-ta´tion
le-vo-ro´ta-to-ry
lev´u-lose
lev´y
lev´y-ing
lewd´ness
Lew´is
Lew´i-sohn
lew´is-ite
lew´is-son
Lew´is-ton
Lew´is-town
lex´i-cal
lex-i-cog´ra-pher
lex´i-co-graph´ic
lex-i-co-graph´i-cal
lex-i-cog´ra-phy
lex´i-con
lex-ig´ra-phy
Lex´ing-ton
Ley´den
li-a-bil´i-ty
li´able
li´ai-son
li-a´na
li´ar
li-ba´tion
li´bel
li´bel-ant
li´beled
li´bel-ee´
li´bel-er
li´bel-ing
li´bel-lee´
li´bel-ous
lib´er-al
lib´er-al-ism
lib´er-al-is´tic
lib-er-al´i-ty
lib-er-al-iza´tion
lib´er-al-ize
lib´er-al-ly
lib´er-ate
lib-er-a´tion
lib´er-a-tor

Li-be´ria
lib-er-tar´i-an
li-ber´ti-cide
lib´er-tine
lib´er-ty
li-bid´i-nal
li-bid´i-nous
li-bi´do
Li´bra
li-brar´i-an
li´brary
li-bra´tion
li´bra-to-ry
li-bret´tist
li-bret´to
li-bret´tos
li´bri-form
Lib´ya
li´cens-able
li´cense
li´censed
li´cens-ee´
li´cens-er
li´cens-ing
li´censor
li-cen´ti-ate
li-cen´tious
li-cen´tious-ness
li´chen
li´chen-in
lic´it
lic´o-rice
lic´tor
lid´o-caine
Lieb´frau-milch
Liech´ten-stein
Lie´der-kranz
liege
lien
lien´or
li´en-tery
lieu-ten´an-cy
lieu-ten´ant
life
life belt
life´blood
life´boat
life buoy
life´guard

life´less
life´like
life´line
life´long
life net
life raft
life´sav-er
life´sav-ing
life´time
lift´er
lig´a-ment
lig´and
li´gate
li-ga´tion
lig´a-ture
li´geance
light´ed
light´en
light´ened
light´en-ing
light´er
light´er-age
light´—fin-gered
light´heart-ed
light´house
light´ing
light´ness
light´ning
light´proof
light´ship
light´tight
light´weight
light´—year
lig´ne-ous
lig-nes´cent
lig´ni-fy
lig´nite
lig´u-late
lig´ure
lik´able
like´li-hood
like´ly
lik´en
like-ness
like´wise
lik´ing
li´lac
Lil´i-an
Lil´ien-thal

lil´ies
Lil´ith
Lille
Lil´li-put
lil´y
Li´ma
lim´ber
lim´bo
Lim´burg-er
lim´bus
lime´ade
lime´kiln
lime´light
lim´er-ick
lime´stone
lime´wa-ter
li´min-al
lim´it
lim´i-tary
lim-i-ta´tion
lim´it-ed
lim´it-less
lim´ner
lim-nol´o-gy
lim´ou-sine
lim´pet
lim´pid
lim-pid´i-ty
lim´pid-ly
limp´ly
lim´y
lin´able
lin´age
lin-a-mar´in
linch´pin
Lin´coln
lin´dane
Lind´bergh
lin´den
lin´eage
lin´eal
lin´ea-ment
lin´ear
lin-ear´i-ty
lin´eate
lin-ea´tion
line´man
lin´en
lin´er

line´up
lin´ger
lin-ge-rie´
lin´go
lin´gua
lin´gual
lin´guist
lin-guis´tic
lin-guis´ti-cal-ly
lin-guis-ti´cian
lin-guis´tics
lin´guis-try
lin´gu-late
ling´y
lin´i-ment
li´nin
lin´ing
link´age
link´ing
lin´net
Li´no-type
lin´seed
lin´sey
lin´sey—wool´sey
lin´tel
lint´er
li´on
Li´o-nel
li´on-ess
li´on-heart-ed
li-on-iza´tion
li´on-ize
li´on-like
lip´ide
li-po´ic
lip´oid
lip-oi-do´sis
li-pol´y-sis
lip´o-lyt´ic
li-po´ma
li-po-ma-to´sis
lip-o-pro´tein
lip´stick
li´quate
li-qua´tion
liq´ue-fa´cient
liq-ue-fac´tion
liq´ue-fied
liq´ue-fy

liq´ue-fy-ing
li-ques´cence
li-ques´cent
li-queur´
liq´uid
liq´uid-am´bar
liq´ui-date
liq´ui-da´tion
liq´ui-da-tor
li-quid´i-ty
liq´ui-dus
li´quor
li´ra
Li´sa
Lis´bon
lis´e-ran
lisp´er
lisp´ing
lisp´ing-ly
lis´some
lis´tcn
lis´ten-er
Lis´ter
list´er
Lis-te´ria
Lis´ter-ize
list´less
list´less-ness
lit´a ny
li´tchi´
li´tcr
lit´er-a-cy
lit´er-al
lit´er-al-ly
lit´er-ary
lit´er-ate
lit-e-ra´ti
lit-e-ra´tim
lit´er-a-tor
lit´er-a-ture
lith´arge
lithe´some
lith´ia
lith´i-um
lith´o-cho´lic
lith´o-graph
li-thog´ra-pher
lith´o-graph´ic
li-thog´ra-phy

lith´oid
lith´o-log´ic
li-thol´o-gy
lith´o-mor´phic
lith´o-pone
lith´o-sol
lith´o-sphere
Lith´u-a´nia
lit´i-ga-ble
lit´i-gant
lit´i-gate
lit-i-ga´tion
lit´i-ga-tor
li-ti´gious
li-ti´gious-ly
lit´mus
li´to-tes
lit´ter
lit´tle
lit´to-ral
li-tur´gi-cal
li-tur´gi-cal-ly
lit´ur-gist
lit´ur-gy
liv´able
live´li-hood
live´li-ness
live´long
live´ly
liv´en
liv´er
liv´er-ied
Liv´er-pool
liv´er-wort
liv´er-wurst
liv´ery
liv´ery-man
live´stock
liv´id
li-vid´i-ty
liv´ing
liv´ing room
Liv´ing-ston
Li-vo´ni-an
li´vre
Liv´y
lix-iv´i-ate
liz´ard
lla´ma

lla´no
Llew-el´lyn
load´er
loaf
loaf´er
loam´y
loath
loathe
loath´er
loath´ing
loath´some
loaves
lo´bar
lo´bate
lo-ba´tion
lobbed
lob´bied
lob´bing
lob´by
lob´by-ing
lob´by-ist
lo-bec´to-my
lo-bot´o-my
lob´ster
lob´u-lar
lob´ule
lob´u-lose
lo´cal
lo-cale´
lo-cal´i-ty
lo-cal-iza´tion
lo´cal-ize
lo´cal-iz-er
lo´cal-ly
lo´cant
Lo-car´no
lo´cate
lo-cat´er
lo-cat´ing
lo-ca´tion
loc´a-tive
lo´ca-tor
lo-chet´ic
Loch´in-var
lock´age
lock´er
lock´et
lock´jaw
lock´out

lock´smith
lock´step
lock´stitch
lock´up
lo´co
lo-co-mo´tion
lo-co-mo´tive
lo-co-mo´tor
loc´u-lar
loc´u-late
lo´cust
lo-cu´tion
lode´star
lode´stone
lodg´er
lodg´ing
lodg´ment
loft´i-ly
loft´i-ness
loft´y
lo´gan-ber-ry
lo´ga-nin
log´a-rithm
log´a-rith´mic
log-a-rith´mi-cal
log-a-rith´mi-cal´ly
log´book
log´ger-head
log´gia
log´ging
lo´gia
log´ic
log´i-cal
log´i-cal-ly
lo-gi´cian
lo´gi-on
lo-gis´tic
lo-gis-ti´cian
lo-gis´tics
log´o-gram
log´o-gram-mat´ic
lo-gog´ra-phy
lo-gom´a-chy
log´o-pe´dic
log-or-rhe´a
Lo´gos
log´o-type
log´wood
Lo´hen-grin

loin´cloth
Lo´is
loi´ter
loi´ter-er
Lol´lard
loll´ing
lol´li-pop
Lom´bard
Lom´bar-dy
lo´ment
Lo´mond
Lon´don
Lon´don-der-ry
Lon´don-er
lone´li-ness
lone´ly
lone´some
long´boat
long—dis´tance
longe´ing
long´er
lon´ge-ron
long´est
lon-gev´i-ty
lon-ge´vous
Long´fel-low
long´—haired
long´hand
long´head-ed
long´horn
long´ing
lon´gi-tude
long´—lived´
long´—range´
long´shore-man
long´—suf´fer-ing
long´—term
long´—wind-ed
look´er
look´ing
look´ing glass
look´out
loo´ny
loop´hole
loop´y
loose´—leaf
loose´ly
loos´en
loot´er

Lo´pez
lop´per
lop´sid-ed
lo-qua´cious
lo-quac´i-ty
lo´ran
lord´li-ness
lord´ship
Lor´e-lei
Lo-ren´zo
Lo-ret´ta
lor´i-cate
lo´ris
Lorraine´
lor´ries
lor´ry
lo´ry
los´able
Los An´ge-les
los´cr
los´ing
Los´sen
loss´er
Lo-thar´io
lo´tion
lot´tery
lot´to
lo´tus
loud´ness
loud´speak-er
Lou´is
Lou-i´sa
Lou-ise´
Lou-i-si-an´a
Lou´is-ville
lounged
loung´er
loung´ing
louse
lous´i-ness
lous´y
lout´ish
lou´ver
Lou´vre
lov´able
lov´age
love´bird
love´less
love´li-er

love´li-ness
love´lorn
love´ly
lov´er
love´sick
low´boy
low´bred
low´brow
low´-cut´
low´down
Low´ell
low´er
low´er case
low´er-ing
low´-grade´
low´land
low´li-ness
low´ly
low´-pres-sure
low´-rate´
low´-spir-it-ed
lox
loy´al
loy´al-ist
loy´al-ly
loy´al-ty
Loy-o´la
loz´enge
Lu-an´da
lub´ber
Lub´bock
Lu´beck
lu´bri oant
lu´bri-cate
lu-bri-ca´tion
lu-bri-ca-tor
lu-bri´cious
lu-bric´i-ty
lu´bri-cous
lu´cen-cy
lu´cent
Lu-cerne´
Lu´cia
lu´cid
lu-cid´i-ty
lu´cid-ness
lu´ci-fer
lu-cif´er-ase
lu-cif´er-in

lu-cif´er-ous
Lu-cin´da
Lu´cite
Lu´cius
luck´i-er
luck´i-est
luck´i-ly
luck´less
luck´y
lu´cra-tive
lu´cre
Lu-cre´tia
Lu-cre´tius
lu´cu-brate
lu-cu-bra´tion
lu´cu-bra-tor
lu´cu-lent
Lu-cul´lan
Lu´cy
lu´di-crous
lu´di-crous-ness
lu-di-fi-ca´tion
Lud´low
Lud´wig
lu´es
lug´gage
lug´ger
lug´ging
lug´worm
luke´warm
lull´a-by
lum-ba´go
lum´bar
lum´ber
lum´ber-jack
lum´ber-man
lum´ber-yard
lum´bri-coid
lu-mi-naire´
lu´mi-nary
lu-mi-nesce´
lu-mi-nes´cence
lu-mi-nom´e-ter
lu´mi-nous
lum´mox
lump´i-er
lump´i-ly
lump´ish
lump´y

lu´na
lu´na-cy
lu´nar
lu´nate
lu´na-tic
lu-na´tion
lunch´eon
lunch´eon-ette´
lunch´room
lunged´
lung´er
lung´ing
lu-pet´i-dine
lu´pine
lu´pin-ine
lu´pu-lin
lu´pu-lone
lu´pus
lurch
lurched
lurch´ing
lured
lu´rid
lu´rid-ly
lur´ing
lurk´er
lurk´ing
lus´cious
lush´ly
Lu-si-ta´nia
lus´ter
lus´ter-ware
lust´ful
lust´i-er
lust´i-ly
lus´tral
lus´trate
lus-tra´tion
lus´tring
lus´trous
lus´trum
lust´y
lu´ta-nist
lu´te-in
lu´te-in-ize
lu´te-o-lin
lu´te-ous
lu-te´tium
Lu´ther

Lu´ther-an
lu´ti-din´ic
lut´ist
lux´ate
lux-a´tion
Lux´em-bourg
lux-u´ri-ance
lux-u´ri-ant
lux-u´ri-ate
lux-u´ri-at-ing
lux´u-ries
lux-u´ri-ous
lux´u-ry
Lu-zon´
ly´can-thrope
ly´can-throp´ic
ly-can´thro-py
ly-cée´
ly-ce´um
Ly-cur´gus
lydd´ite
Lyd´ia
Lyd´i-an
ly´ing
Lyl´y
lymph
lymph-ad-e-ni´tis
lymph-ad-e-nop´a-thy
lym-phan´gi-al
lym-phat´ic
lym´pho-cyte
lymph´oid
lym-pho-ma-to´sis
lym´pho-sar-co´ma
lynch
lynch´ing
lynx
ly´on-naise
Ly´ons
ly´rate
lyr´ic
lyr´i-cal
ly´ri-form
ly-ser´gic
Lys´i-as
ly-sim´e-ter
ly´sin
ly´sine
ly´so-gen´ic

Ly´sol
ly´so-some
lyt´ic

## M

ma-ca´bre
ma-ca´co
mac-ad´am
mac-ad-am-iza´tion
mac-ad´am-ize
Ma-ca´o
mac-a-ro´ni
mac´a-roon´
ma-cas´sar
ma-caw´
Mac-beth´
Mac-Dow´ell
ma´cé-doine´
Mac´e-don
Mac-e-do´nia
mac´er-al´
mac´er-ate
mac-er-a´tion
mac´er-a-tor
ma-chet´e
Ma-chia-vel´li
mach-i-na´tion
mach´i-na-tor
ma-chine´
ma-chine´ gun
ma-chin´ery
ma-chine´ shop
ma-chine´ tool
ma-chin´ist
ma-chree´
Mac-ken´zie
mack´er-el
Mack´i-nac
mack´i-naw
mack´in-tosh
Mac-Mil´lan
Ma´con
mac´ra-me´
mac´ro-cosm
mac´ro-cos´mic
mac´ro-cy´clic
mac-ro-cy-to´sis
mac-rog´ra-phy

mac´ro-mol´e-cule
ma´cron
mac´ro-phys´ics
mac-rop´sia
mac´u-la
mac-u-la´tion
mac´u-la-ture
mac´ule
Mad´a-gas´car
mad´am
ma-dame´
Ma-da-ria´ga
mad´cap
mad´den
mad´den-ing
mad´der
mad´dest
Ma-dei´ra
Mad´e-line
ma-de-moi-selle´
mad´house
Mad´i-son
mad´ly
mad´man
mad´ness
Ma-don´na
ma-dras´
mad´re-pore
Ma-drid´
mad´ri-gal
mael´strom
mae´stro
Maf´e-king
maf´fick
Ma´fia
maf´ic
mag´a-zine´
Mag´da-len
Mag´de-burg
Ma-gel´lan
Mag´el-lan´ic
ma-gen´ta
Mag-gio´re
mag´got
ma´gi
mag´ic
mag´i-cal
mag´i-cal-ly
ma-gi´cian

Ma´gi-not´
ma-gis´ter
mag-is-te´ri-al
mag´is-tery
mag´is-tra-cy
mag´is-trate
mag´is-tra-ture
mag´ma
Mag´na Car´ta
mag´na cum lau´de
Mag´na-flux
mag-na-nim´i-ty
mag-nan´i-mous
mag´nate
mag-ne´sia
mag-ne´sium
mag´net
mag-net´ic
mag-net´i-cal-ly
mag´net-ism
mag´net-ite
mag´net-iz-able
mag-net-iza´tion
mag´net-ize
mag-ne´to
mag´ne-to-graph
mag-ne-tom´e-ter
mag-ne-to-met´ric
mag-ne-tom´e-try
mag-ne´to-mo´tive
mag´ne-ton
mag-ne´tos
mag´ne-tron
Mag-nif´i-cat
mag-nif-i-ca´tion
mag-nif´i-cence
mag-nif´i-cent
mag-nif´i-co
mag´ni-fied
mag´ni-fi-er
mag´ni-fy
mag´ni-fy-ing
mag´ni-tude
mag-no´lia
mag´num
mag´pie
Mag´yar
Ma-ha´bha´ra-ta
Ma-han´

ma-ha-ra´ja
ma-ha-ra´ni
ma-hat´ma
Mah´—Jongg´
ma-hog´a-ny
Ma-hom´et
ma-hout´
Mah-rat´ta
maid´en
maid´en-hair
maid´en-head
maid´en-ly
maid´ser-vant
mail´able
mail´bag
mail´box
mail´er
mail-lot´
mail´man
Mai-mon´i-des
Maine
Main´er
main´land
main´ly
main´mast
main´sail
main´spring
main´stay
main-tain´
main´te-nance
maî´tre d'hô-tel´
maize
ma-jes´tic
ma-jes´ti-cal
ma-jes´ti-cal-ly
maj´es-ty
ma-jol´i-ca
ma´jor
Ma-jor´ca
ma-ior-do´mo
ma´jor gen´er-al
ma-jor´i-ties
ma-jor´i-ty
Ma-kas´sar
make´—be-lieve
make´fast
mak´er
make´shift
make´up

make´weight
mak´ing
Mal´a-bar
Ma-lac´ca
Mal´a-chi
mal´a-chite
mal´ad-just´ed
mal´ad-just´ment
mal´ad-min´is-ter
mal-ad-min-is-
  tra´tion
mal´a-droit´
mal´a-dy
Mal´a-ga
mala-gue´na
mal-aise´
ma-lar´ia
ma-lar´i-al
Ma-la´wi
Ma-lay´
Ma-lay´a
Ma-lay´an
Ma-lay´sia
Mal´colm
mal´con-tent
Mal´dives
mal-e-dic´tion
mal´e-fac´tion
mal´e-fac´tor
ma-lef´ic
ma-lef´i-cence
ma-lef´i-cent
ma-le´ic
ma-lev´o-lence
ma-lev´o-lent
mal-fea´sance
mal´for-ma´tion
mal´formed´
Ma´li
mal´ic
mal´ice
ma-li´cious
ma-li´cious-ly
ma-lif´er-ous
ma-lign´
ma-lig´nan-cy
ma-lig´nant
ma-lig´ni-ty
Ma-lines´

ma-lin´ger
ma-lin´ger-er
mal´lard
mal´lea-ble
mal´let
mal´low
mal-nu-tri´tion
mal´odor
mal-o´dor-ous
mal-o´dor-ous-ly
mal´prac-tice
Mal´ta
Mal-tese´
Mal´thus
malt´ose
mal´treat´
mal´treat´ment
malt´y
mal-va´ceous
mam´ba
mam´bo
mam´ma
mam´mal
mam-ma´li-an
mam-ma-lif´er-ous
mam-mal´o-gy
mam´ma-ry
mam-mif´er-ous
mam´mil-lary
mam´mil-late
mam´mon
mam´moth
man´a-cle
man´a-cling
man´age
man´age-abil´i-ty
man´age-able
man´age-ment
man´ag-er
man´a-ge´ri-al
man´ag-ing
Ma-na´gua
man´akin
ma-ña´na
Ma-nas´sas
Ma-nas´seh
man—at—arms
man´a-tee
Man´ches-ter

Man´chu´
Man´chu-kuo´
Man-chu´ria
Man´da-lay´
man´da-rin
man´date
man-da´tor
man´da-to-ry
man´del-ate
man-del´ic
Man´de-ville
man´do-lin´
man´do-lin´ist
man´drake
man´drel
man´drill
man´—eat-er
ma-nege´
ma´nes
Ma-net´
ma-neu´ver
ma-neu´ver-abil´i-ty
ma-neu´ver-er
man´ful
man´ful-ly
man´ga-nate
man´ga-nese
man-gan´ic
man-ga-nif´er-ous
man´ga-nite
man´ga-nous
man´ger
man´gi-er
nian´gi-ly
man´gi-ness
man´gle
man´gler
man´gling
man´go
man´goes
man´go-nel
man´grove
man´gy
man´han-dle
Man-hat´tan
man´hole
man´hood
man´—hour´
ma´nia

ma´ni-ac
ma-ni´a-cal
man´ic
man´ic—de-pres´sive
Man-i-che´an
man-i-co´ba
man´i-cure
man´i-cur-ist
man´i-fest
man-i-fes´tant
man-i-fes-ta´tion
man´i-fest-ly
man-i-fes´to
man-i-fes´tos
man´i-fold
man´i-fold-er
man´i-kin
Ma-nil´a
ma-nil´la
man´i-ple
ma-nip´u-late
ma-nip-u-la´tion
ma-nip´u-la-tive
ma-nip´u-la-tor
ma-nip´u-la-to-ry
Man-i-to´ba
man´i-tou
man´kind´
man´like
man´li-ness
man´ly
man´na
man´ne-quin
man´ner
man´ner-ism
man´ner-less
man´ner-ly
man´ni-kin
man´nose
man´nu-ron´ic
man—of—war
ma-nom´e-ter
man´o-met´ric
ma-nom´e-try
man´or
man´o-stat
man´pow-er
man´rope
man´sard

man´ser-vant
man´sion
man´slaugh-ter
man´slay-er
man´stop-per
man´sue-tude
man´ta
man-teau´
man´tel
man´tel-et
man´tel-piece
man´tel-shelf
man-til´la
man´tis
man´tle
man´tling
man´u-al
man´u-al-ly
man´u-duc´tive
Man´u-el
man-u-fac´to-ry
man-u-fac´ture
man-u-fac´tur-er
man-u-fac´tur-ing
man-u-mis´sion
ma-nure´
ma´nus
man´u-script
Manx
man-y
man-za-ni´ta
Mao´ri
ma´ple
ma-quette´
mar´a-bout
ma-ra-ca
Mar´a-cai´bo
mar-a-schi´no
Ma-ra´tha
mar´a-thon
ma-raud´
ma-raud´er
ma-raud´ing
mar´ble
mar´bled
Mar´ble-head
mar´ble-ize
mar´bling
marc

mar´ca-site
mar-cel´
march´er
mar´chio-ness
Mar´cia
Mar-co´ni
Mar´co Po´lo
Mar´di Gras
Ma-ren´go
mare´s nest
mare´s tail
mar´ga-rate
Mar´ga-ret
mar´ga-rine
mar´ga-rite
mar-ga-ro´san-ite
Mar´gery
mar´gin
mar´gin-al
mar-gi-na´lia
mar´gin-ate
Mar´got
mar´grave
mar´gue-rite´
Ma-ri´a
ma-ri-a´chi
Mar´i-an
Mar-i-co´pa
Ma-rie´
Mar-i-et´ta
mar´i-gold
mar-i-hua´na
mar-i-jua´na
ma-rim´ba
ma-ri´na
mar´i-nade´
mar´i-nate
mar´i-nat-ing
mar-i-na´tion
ma-rine´
mar´i-ner
Ma-ri´nist
ma-rin´ist
Mar´i-on
mar´i-o-nette´
mar´i-tal
mar´i-tal-ly
mar´i-time
Mar´i-us

mar´jo-ram
Mar´jo-ry
mark´ed-ly
mark´er
mar´ket
mar-ket-abil´i-ty
mar´ket-able
mar´ket-er
mar´ket-ing
mar´ket-place
Mark´ham
marks´man
marks´man-ship
Marl´bor-ough
mar´lin
mar´line
marl´ite
mar-lit´ic
Mar´lowe
mar´ma-lade
Mar´mi-on
mar-mo´re-al
mar´mo-set
mar´mot
ma-roon´
marque
mar-quee´
Mar-que´san
mar´quess
mar´quess-ate
mar´que-te-rie
mar´que-try
Mar-quette´
mar´quis
mar-quise´
mar´qui-sette´
mar´riage
mar´riage-able
mar´ried
mar-ron´ gla-cé´
mar´row
mar´row-bone
mar´ry
Mar-seil-laise´
Mar-seilles´
mar´shal
mar´shal-cy
mar´shaled
mar´shal-er

Mar´shall
marsh gas
marsh´i-ness
marsh´mal-low
marsh-y
mar-su´pi-al
Mar-tel´
Mar-tel´lo
mar´ten
mar´tens-ite
Mar´tha
mar´tial
mar´tial-ly
Mar´tian
mar´tin
Mar-ti-neau´
mar´ti-net´
mar´tin-gale
mar-ti´ni
Mar-ti-nique´
Mar´tin-mas
mar´tyr
mar´tyr-dom
mar´tyr-ize
mar´vel
mar´veled
mar´vel-ing
mar´vel-ous
mar´vel-ous-ly
Marx´ian
Marx´ism
Mar´y
Mar´y-land
mar´zi-pan
Ma-sa-ryk´
mas-car´a
mas´cle
mas´cot
mas´cu-line
mas-cu-lin´i-ty
ma´ser
mash´er
mash´ie
mask´er
mas´och-ism
mas´och-ist
mas´och-is´tic
ma´son
ma-son´ic

Ma´son-ite
ma´son-ry
Mas´o-rete
Mas´o-ret´ic
masqu´er
mas´quer-ade´
Mas´sa-chu´setts
mas´sa-cre
mas´sa-cred
mas´sa-crer
mas´sa-cring
mas-sage´
mas-sag´er
mas-sag´ing
mas´sa-sau´ga
mas-sé´
mas-se´ter
mas-seur´
mas-seuse´
mass´i-ness
mas´sive
mass meet-ing
mas´so-ther´a-py
mass´y
mas´ta-ba
mast´er
mas´ter—at—arms
mas´ter-dom
mas´ter-ful
mas´ter-ful-ly
mas´ter-ly
mas´ter-piece
mas´ter-ship
mas´ter-work
mas´tery
mast´head
mas´tic
mas´ti-cate
mas-ti-ca´tion
mas´ti-ca-tor
mas´ti-ca-to-ry
mas´tiff
mas-tit´ic
mas-ti´tis
mas´to-don
mas´toid
mas-toi´dal
mas-toid-i´tis
mat´a-dor

match´able
match´board
match´less
match´lock
match´mak-er
match´mak-ing
match´wood
ma´té
mate´lot
ma´ter
ma-te´ri-al
ma-te´ri-al-ism
ma-te´ri-al-ist
ma-te´ri-al-is´tic
ma-te´ri-al-is´ti-cal-ly
ma-te´ri-al-ism
ma-te´ri-al´i-ty
ma-te-ri-al-iza´tion
ma-te´ri-al-ly
ma-te-ri-el´
ma-ter´nal
ma-ter´nal-ly
ma-ter´ni-ty
math-e-mat´i-cal
math-e-mat´i-cal-ly
math-e-ma-ti´cian
math-e-mat´ics
ma-thet´ic
Ma-til´da
mat´in
mat´in al
mat´i-nee´
mat´ing
ma´tri-arch
ma´tri-ar´chal
ma´tri-arch-ate
ma´tri-ar-chy
ma´tri-ces
ma´tri-ci´dal
ma´tri-cide
ma-tric´u-late
ma-tric-u-la´tion
ma-tri-lin´eal
mat´ri-mo´ni-al
mat´ri-mo-ny
ma´trix
ma´tron
ma´tron-age
ma´tron-ize

ma´tron-li-ness
ma´tron-ly
mat´ted
mat´ter
Mat´ter-horn
mat´ter—of—fact´
Mat´thew
Mat-thi´as
mat´ting
mat´tock
mat´tress
mat´u-rate
mat-u-ra´tion
ma-ture´
ma-ture´ly
ma-ture´ness
ma-tur´i-ty
ma-tu´ti-nal
mat´zoth
Maugham
maul´er
maund´er
Maun´dy
Mau-pas-sant´
Mau-re-ta´nia
Mau-rice´
Mau-ri-ta´nia
Mau-ri´ti-us
Mau-rois´
Mau´ser
mau-so-le´um
mauve
mau´vine
mav´er-ick
ma´vis
mawk´ish
max-il´la
max´il-lary
max-il´lo—pal´a-tal
max´im
max´i-mal
max´i-mal-ist
Max-i-mil´ian
max´im-ite
max´i-mize
max´i-miz-er
max´i-mum
Max´well
Ma´ya

may´be
May Day
may´fish
May´flow-er
may´hap
may´hem
Mayo
may´on-naise
may´or
may´or-al-ty
may´pole
May´time
maz´a-rine´
maze
ma´zer
maz´i-ly
ma-zur´ka
ma-zut´
maz´y
maz´zard
McCar´thy
McClel´lan
McCor´mick
McKin´ley
me´a cul´pa
mead´ow
mead´owy
mea´ger
mea´ger-ly
meal´i-ness
meal´time
meal´worm
meal´y
meal´y-mouthed
mean
me-an´der
me-an´drous
mean´ing
mean´ing-ful
mean´ing-less
mean´ly
mean´ness
meant
mean´time
mean´while
mea´sles
mea´sly
mea-sur-abil´i-ty
mea´sur-able

mea´sure
mea´sured
mea´sure-ment
meat´y
Mec´ca
me-chan´ic
me-chan´i-cal
me-chan´i-cal-ly
mech-a-ni´cian
me-chan´ics
mech´a-nism
mech´a-nis´tic
mech-a-ni-za´tion
mech´a-nize
Mech´lin
Meck´len-burg
me-con´ic
med´al
med´aled
med´al-ist
me-dal´lic
me-dal´lion
med´dle
med´dler
med´dle-some
Me-de´a
me´dia
me´di-al
me´di-an
me-di-as-ti-ni´tis
me-di-as-ti´num
me´di-ate
me´di-ate-ly
me-di-a´tion
me´di-a-tive
me´di-a-tize
me´di-a-tor
me´di-a-to´ri-al
me´di-a-to-ry
med´ic
med´i-ca-ble
med´i-cal
med´i-cal-ly
me-dic´a-ment
med´i-cate
med-i-ca´tion
med´i-ca-tive
Med´i-ce´an
Med´i-ci

me-dic´i-na-ble
me-dic´i-nal
med´i-cine
med´i-cine bag
med´i-cine man
med´i-co
medie´val
medie´val-ist
Me-di´na
me´di-o´cre
medi-oc´ri-ty
med´i-tate
med-i-ta´tion
med´i-ta-tive
med´i-tat-or
Med´i-ter-ra´ne-an
me´di-um
me´di-um-is´tic
med´lar
med´ley
me-du´sa
meek´ly
meek´ness
meer´schaum
meet´ing
meet´ing-house
meet´ly
meg´a-cy-cle
meg´a-ga-mete´
meg´a-lith´ic
meg´a-lo-saur
meg´a-phone
meg´a-pod
meg´a-ton
mei´o-nite
mei-o´sis
mei-ot´ic
mei´ster
mel´a-mine
me´an-cho´lia
me´an-cho´li-ac
mel´an-chol´ic
mel´an-choly
Me-lanch´thon
Mel-a-ne´sia
me-lange´
me-lan´ger
me-lan´ic
mel´a-nin

mel´a-nism
mel´a-no
mel´a-noid
mel-a-no´ma
mel-a-no-stib´i-an
me-lan´ter-ite
mel-an-tha´ceous
Mel´bourne
Mel´chi-or
Mel-chiz´e-dek
meld´er
Mel-e-a´ger
me´lee
me-le´na
me-lez´i-tose
me-li-a´ceous
mel-i-bi´ose
mel´ic
Mel´i-cent
mel´i-lite
mel´i-lot
me´lio-rate
me-lio-ra´tion
me-lio-ra-tive
me´lio-rism
me´lio-rist
me-lior´i-ty
mel´is-mat´ic
Me-lis´sa
mel´i-tose
mel-lif´er-ous
mel-lif´lu-ence
mel-lif´lu-ent
mel´low
mel´low-ness
me-lo´de-on
me-lo´dia
me-lod´ic
me-lod´i-cal-ly
me-lo´di-on
me-lo´di-ous
me-lo´di-ous-ly
mel´o-dist
mel´o-dize
mel´o-dra-ma
mel´o-dra-mat´ic
mel´o-dram´a-tist
mel´o-dy
mel´oid

melo-ma´nia
mel´on
mel´o-nite
Mel´rose
melt-abil´i-ty
melt´able
melt´er
mel´ton
Mel´ville
mem´ber
mem´ber-ship
mem-bra-na´ceous
mem´bra-nate
mem´brane
mem´bra-nous
me-men´to
me-men´tos
Mem´non
mem´oir
mem-o-ra-bil´ia
mem-o-ra-bil´i-ty
mem´o-ra-ble
mem-o-ran´da
mem-o-ran´dum
me-mo´ri-al
me-mo´ri-al-ist
me-mo´ri-al-ize
me-mo´ri-al-iz-ing
me-mo´ri-um
mem´o-ries
mem-o-ri-za´tion
mem´o-rize
mem´o-riz-er
mem´o-riz-ing
mem´o-ry
Mem´phis
men´ace
men´ac-ing
men´ac-ing-ly
mé-nage´
me-nag´er-ie
me-naph´thone
Menc´ken
men-da´cious
men-da´cious-ly
men-dac´i-ty
Men´del
men-de-le´vi-um
Men´dels-sohn

mend´er
men´di-can-cy
men´di-cant
men-dic´i-ty
Men-e-la´us
men´folk
men-ha´den
men´hir
me´nial
Mé´ni-ère´
me-nin´ge-al
me-nin´ges
me-nin-gi-o´ma
men´in-git´ic
men-in-gi´tis
me-nin´go-cele
me-nin-go-coc´cus
Men´no-nite
Me-nom´i-nee
men-o-pau´sal
men´o-pause
Me-no´rah
men-or-rha´gia
men´ses
men´stru-al
men´stru-ate
men-stru-a´tion
men´stru-um
men-su-ra-bil´i-ty
men´su-ra-ble
men´su-ral
men-su-ra´tion
men´su-ra-tive
men´tal
men-tal´i-ty
men´tal-ly
men´thane
men´tha-nol
men´the-none
men´thol
men´tho-lat-ed
men´thyl
men´ti-cide
men´tion
men´tion-able
men´tion-er
men´tor
men´u
me-pro´ba-mate

mer´can-tile
mer´can-til-ism
mer-cap´tan
mer-cap´to
mer-cap-tom´er-in
mer´cap-tu´ric
Mer-ca´tor
mer´ce-nary
mer´cer
mer´cer-ize.
mer´cer-iz-ing
mer´cery
mer´chan-dise
mer´chan-dis-er
mer´chan-dis-ing
mer´chant
mer´chant-able
mer´chant-man
Mer´cia
mer´cies
mer´ci-ful
mer´ci-ful-ly
mer´ci-ful-ness
mer´ci-less
mer´cu-rate
mer-cu´ri-al
mer-cu´ri-al-ism
mer-cu-ri-al´i-ty
mer-cu´ric
mer-cu´ro-chrome
mer-cu´rous
mer´cu-ry
mer´cy
Mer´e-dith
mere´ly
me-re-ol´o-gy
mer´est
mer-e-tri´cious
mer-gan´ser
merge
mer´gence
Mer´gen-tha-ler
merg´er
Mer´i-den
me-rid´i-an
me-ringue´
me-ri´no
me-ri´nos
mer´ion

mer´ism
mer´i-stem
mer´i-ste-mat´ic
mer´it
mer´it-ed
mer-i-to´ri-ous
mer´lin
mer´maid
mer´man
mer-o-he´dral
mer´ri-ly
Mer´ri-mac
mer´ri-ment
mer´ri-ness
mer´ry
mer´ry—an´drew
mer´ry—go—round
mer´ry-mak-er
mer´ry-mak-ing
me´sa
mes´al-liance´
mes´ar-te-ri´tis
mes-cal´
mes´ca-line
mes-dames´
mesh´work
mesh´y
me´si-al
mes´ic
mes´i-dine
mes´i-tyl
me-sit´y-lene
mes´mer´ic
mes´mer-ism
mes-mer-iza´tion
mes´mer-ize
mes´mer-iz-ing
mes´nal-ty
mes´o-blast
meso-car´dia
mes´o-carp
mes´o-derm
mes´o-der´mal
mes´o-lite
mes´o-mer´ic
me-som´er-ism
mes´on
mes´o-neph´ric
mes´o-neph´ros

Mes-o-po-ta´mia
mes´o-sphere
mes´o-the´li-um
mes´o-tron
Mes´o-zo´ic
mes-quite´
mes´sage
mes´sa-line´
mes´sen-ger
Mes-si´ah
Mes´si-an´ic
mes-sieurs´
mess´i-ness
mess´mate
mess´y
mes-ti´zo
mes-ti´zos
me-tab´a-sis
meta-bi´o-sis
meta-bi-ot´ic
met´a-bol´ic
me-tab´o-lism
me-tab´o-lite
me-tab´o-liz-able
me-tab´o-lize
met´a-bo´rate
met´a-car´pus
met´age
met´a-ge-net´ic
me-tag´ra-phy
met´al
met-al´de-hyde
met´al-ing
met´al-ist
me-tal´lic
met-al-lif´er-ous
met´al-line
met´al-lize
me-tal´lo-graph´ic
met-al-log´ra-phy
met´al-loid
met´al-lur´gic
met´al-lur´gi-cal
met´al-lur-leist
met´al-lur-gy
met´al-ware
met´al-work
met´al-work-ing
met´a-mer

met´a-mer´ic
me-tam´er-ism
me-tam´er-ized
meta-mor´phic
meta-mor´phism
meta-mor´phose
meta-mor´pho-ses
meta-mor´pho-sis
met´a-phor
met-a-phor´i-cal
met´a-phrase
meta-phys´i-cal
meta-phy-si´cian
met´a-phys´ics
met´a-pro´tein
met´a-sta-ble
me-tas´ta-sis
met´a-stat´ic
met´a-tar´sal
meta-tar´sus
me-tath´e-sis
meta-thet´ic
meta-tho´rax
Meta-zo´a
met-en-ceph´a-lon
me´te-or
me-te-or´ic
me´te-or-ite
me-te-or-it´ics
me-te-or´o-graph
me-te-o-rog´ra-phy
me´te-or-oid
me-te-oro-log´i-cal
me-te-o-rol´o-gist
me-te-o-rol´o-gy
me-te-or-om´e-ter
me´te-or-o-scope
me-te-or-os´co-py
me´ter
meth-ac´ry-late
meth-acryl´ic
meth´a-done
meth-al´lyl
meth´ane
meth´a-nol
meth-a-nol´ic
meth-a-nol´y-sis
meth-a-nom´e-ter
meth-an´the-line

me-theg´lin
me-the´na-mine
meth´ene
meth´ide
meth´ion´ic
me-thi´o-nine
me´thi-um
meth´od
me-thod´i-cal
me-thod´i-cal-ly
Meth´od-ism
meth´od-ize
meth-od-ol´o-gy
me-tho´ni-um
Me-thu´se-lah
meth´yl
me-thyl´ic
me-thyl´i-dyne
meth´yl-naph´tha-
   lene
meth´yl-ol-ure´a
me-tic-u-los´i-ty
me-tic´u-lous
mé-tier´
me-ton´y-my
met´ope
met´o-pon
met´ric
met´ri-cal
me-tri´cian
met´ri-fy
me-tri´tis
me trol´o giot
me-trol´o-gy
met´ro-nome
met´ro-nom´ic
met´ro-pole
me-trop´o-lis
met´ro-pol´i-tan
met´tle
met´tled
met´tle-some
Mex´i-can
Mex´i-co
mez´za-nine´
mez´zo
mez´zo—so-pra´no
mez´zo-tint
mho´me-ter

Mi-am´i
mi-as´ma
mi´ca
Mi´cah
mi-cel´lar
mi-celle´
Mi´chael
Mich´ael-mas
Mi-chel-an´ge-lo
Mi-chele´
Mich´i-gan
mi´cro-anal´y-sis
mi´cro-an-a-lyt´ic
mi´crobe
mi-cro´bi-al
mi-cro´bic
mi-cro´bi-cide
mi´cro-bio-log´i-cal
mi´cro-bi-ol´o-gist
mi´cro-bi-ol´o-gy
mi´cro-blade
mi´cro-card
mi´cro-ceph´a-ly
mi´cro-chem´is-try
mi´cro-cir´cuit
mi´cro-copy
mi´cro-cosm
mi´cro-cos´mic
mi´cro-fiche
mi´cro-film
mi´cro-gram
mi´cro-graph
mi´cro graph´ic
mi-crog´ra-phy
mi´cro-groove
mi´cro-ma-chin´ing
mi-cro-me-rit´ics
mi-crom´e-ter
mi-cro-met´ri-cal
mi-rom´e-try
mi´cro-mod´ule
mi´cron
mi´cron-ize
mi-cro-or´ga-nism
ml´cro-phone
ml´cro-phon´ic
ml´cro-proc´es-sor
mi´cro-pro´gram
mi-cro-py-rom´e-ter

mi´cro-scope
mi´cro-scop´ic
mi-cros´co-py
mi´cro-seism
mi´cro-some
mi´cro-spore
mi´cro-tome
mi´cro-wave
mic´tu-rate
mic-tu-ri´tion
mid´af´ter-noon´
Mi´das
mid´brain
mid´day´
mid´den
mid´dle
mid´dle—aged´
mid´dle-man
mid´dle—of—the—
   road´
mid´dle weight
mid´dy
midg´et
mi-di´
Mid´i-an
mid´iron
mid´land
mid´most
mid´night
mid´rib
mid´riff
mid´ship-man
mid´ships
mid´stream´
mid´sum´mer
mid´way
mid-week´ly
mid´west´
mid´west´ern
Mid-west´ern-er
mid´wife
mid´wife-ry
mid´win´ter
mid´year´
mien
might
might´i-er
might´i-ly
might´i-ness

might´y
mi-gnon´
mi´gnon-ette´
mi´graine
mi´grant
mi´grate
mi´grat-ing
mi-gra´tion
mi´gra-to-ry
mi-ka´do
mi-la´dy
Mi-lan´
milch
mil´dew
mil´dew-proof
mil´dewy
mild´ly
mild´ness
Mil´dred
mile´age
mile´post
mile´stone
mil-i-a´ria
mil´i-ary
mi-lieu´
mil´i-tan-cy
mil´i-tant
mil´i-tant-ly
mil-i-tar´ily
mil´i-ta-rism
mil´i-ta-rist
mil´i-ta-ris´tic
mil-i-ta-ri-za´tion
mil´i-ta-rize
mil´i-ta-riz-ing
mil´i-tary
mil´i-tate
mil´i-tat-ing
mi-li´tia
mi-li´tia-man
mil´i-um
milk bar
milk´er
milk´—fed
milk´i-ness
milk´ leg
milk´—liv-ered
milk´man
milk run

milk shake
milk´weed
milk´y
Mi´lay´
mill´board
mill´dam
mil-le-nar´i-an
mil´le-nary
mil-len´ni-al
mil-len´ni-um
mil´le-pede
mill´er
mil-les´i-mal
mil´let
mil´li-am´me-ter
mil´li-am´pere
mil´liard
mil´li-ary
mil´li-gram
Mil´li-kan
mil´li-me-ter
mil´li-mi´cron
mil´li-ner
mil´li-nery
mill´ing
mil´lion
mil´lion-aire´
mil´lionth
mil´li-pede
mill´pond
mill´race
mill´stone
mill´stream
mill wheel
Milne
mi´lo
mi-lord´
Milque´toast
Mil-ton´ic
Mil-wau´kee
mim´e-o-graph
mim´er
mi-me´sis
mi-met´ic
mim´e-tite
mim´ic
mim´icked
mim´ick-er
mim´ick-ing

mim´ic-ry
mim´ing
mi-mo´sa
mi-mo´sine
min´able
min´a-to-ri-ly
min´a-to-ry
mince´meat
mince´ pie´
minc´er
minc´ing
Min-da-nao´
Min´del
mind´er
mind´ful
mind´less
mind read´ing
min´er
min-er-ag´ra-phy
min´er-al
min´er-al-ize
min´er-al-iz-er
min´er-al-og´i-cal
min´er-al´o-gist
min´er-al´o-gy
Mi-ner´va
min-e-stro´ne
min´gle
min´gling
min´i-a-ture
min´i-a-tur-ist
min´i-kin
min´im
min´i-mal
min-i-mi-za´tion
min´i-mize
min´i-miz-er
min´i-mum
min´ing
min´ion
min´is-ter
min´is-te´ri-al
min-is-te´ri-um
min´is-trant
min-is-tra´tion
min´is-tries
min´is-try
min´i-track
min´i-um

min´i-ver
Min-ne-ap´o-lis
min´ne-sing-er
Min-ne-so´ta
min´now
Mi-no´an
mi-nom´e-ter
mi´nor
Mi-nor´ca
mi-nor´i-ty
Mi´nos
Min´o-taur
min´ster
min´strel
min´strel-sy
mint´age
mint´er
min´u-end
min-u-et´
Min´u-it
mi´nus
mi-nus´cu-lar
min´us-cule
min´ute
min´ute hand
mi-nute´ly
min´ute-man
mi-nute´ness
mi-nu´tia
mi-nu´ti-ae
Mi´o-cene
mi-o´sis
mi-ot´ic
mir´a-belle´
mi-rab´i-lite
mir´a-cle
mi-rac´u-lous
mi-rac´u-lous-ly
mir´a-dor
mi-rage´
Mi-ran´da
mired
Mir´i-am
mir´ing
mir´ror
mirth´ful
mirth´less
mis-ad-ven´ture
mis-al-li´ance

mis´an-thrope
mis´an-throp´ic
mis´an-throp´i-cal-ly
mis-an´thro-pist
mis-an´thro-py
mis-ap-pli-ca´tion
mis´ap-plied´
mis´ap-ply´
mis´ap-pre-hend´
mis-ap-pre-hen´sion
mis-ap-pro´pri-ate
mis-ap-pro-pri-a´tion
mis-ar-range´ment
mis-be-com´ing
mis-be-got´ten
mis-be-have´
mis-be-hav´ing
mis-be-hav´ior
mis-be-lief´
mis-be-lieve´
mis-be-liev´er
mis-cal´cu-late
mis-cal-cu-la´tion
mis-call´
mis-car´riage
mis-car´ried
mis-car´ry
mis-car´ry-ing
mis´cege-na´tion
mis-cel-la-ne´i-ty
mis-cel-la´neous
mis´cel-la ny
mis-chance´
mis´chief
mis´chief—mak-er
mis´chie-vous
mis´chie-vous-ly
mis-con-ceive´
mis-con-cep´tion
mis-con´duct
mis-con-struc´tion
mis´con-strue´
mis´cre-ance
mis´cre-an-cy
mis´cre-ant
mis´cre-ate´
mis-cre-a´tion
mis-cue´
mis-deal´

mis-deed´
mis-de-mean´ant
mis´de-mean´or
mis-di-rect´
mis-di-rec´tion
mis-do´er
mis-do´ing
mi´ser
mis´er-a-ble
mis´er-a-bly
mi´ser-ly
mis´ery
mis-fea´sance
mis-fire´
mis´fit´
mis-for´tune
mis-gave´
mis-give´
mis-giv´ing
mis-gov´ern
mis-gov´ern-ment
mis-guid´ance
mis-guide´
mis-guid´ed
mis-han´dle
mis-han´dling
mis´hap
mis´hear´
mis´in-form´
mis´in-for-ma´tion
mis-in-ter´pret
mis´in-ter-pre-ta´tion
mis-judge´
mis-judg´ment
mis-laid´
mis-lay´
mis-lay´ing
mis-lead´
mis-lead´ing
mis-led´
mis-like´
mis-man´age
mis-man´age-ment
mis-match´
mis-mate´
mis-mat´ing
mis-name´
mis-no´mer
mi-sog´a-mist

mi-sog´a-my
mi-sog´y-nist
mi-sog´y-ny
mi-sol´o-gy
miso-ne´ism
mis-place´
mis-place´ment
mis´print
mis-pri´sion
mis´pro-nounce´
mis-pro-nounc´ing
mis-pro-nun-ci-a´tion
mis-quo-ta´tion
mis´quote´
mis´quot´ing
mis´read´
mis´rep-re-sent´
mis-rep-re-sen-ta´tion
mis-rule´
mis-rul´ing
mis´sal
mis-shape´
mis-shap´en
mis´sile
mis´sile-ry
miss´ing
mis´sion
mis´sion-ar-ies
mis´sion-ary
Mis-sis-sip´pi
mis´sive
Mis-sou´ri
mis-speak´
mis-spell´
mis-spelled´
mis-spell´ing
mis-spelt´
mis-spent´
mis-state´
mis-state´ment
mis-step´
mis-tak´able
mis-take´
mis-tak´en
mis-tak´en-ly
mis-tak´ing
mis´ter
mist´i-ness
mis´tle-toe

mis-took´
mis´tral
mis-treat´
mis-treat´ment
mis´tress
mis-tri´al
mis-trust´
mis-trust´ful
mist´y
mis-un-der-stand´
mis-un-der-stand´ing
mis-un-der-stood´
mis-us´age
mis-use´
mis-us´ing
Mitch´ell
mi´ter
mit´i-gate
mit´i-gat-ing
mit-i-ga´tion
mit´i-ga-tive
mit´i-ga-tor
mit´i-ga-to-ry
mi-to´sis
mi-tot´ic
mi´tral
mi´trate
mit´ten
mix´er
mix´ture
mix´—up
Miz´pah
miz´zen
miz´zen-mast
mo´a
Mo´ab-ite
moan´ing
mobbed
mob´bing
mo´bile
mo-bil´i-ty
mo-bi-li-za´tion
mo´bi-lize
moc´ca-sin
mo´cha
mo-chi´la
mock´er
mock´ery
mock´ing

mock´ing-bird
mock´ing-ly
mod´al
mod´al-ism
mo-dal´i-ty
mod´el
mod´eled
mod´el-ing
mod´er-ate
mod´er-ate-ly
mod´er-at-ing
mod-er-a´tion
mod´er-a-tor
mod´ern
mod´ern-ism
mod´ern-ist
mod´ern-is´tic
mo-der´ni-ty
mod-ern-iza´tion
mod´ern-ize
mod´ern-iz-ing
mod´ern-ly
mod´ern-ness
mod´est
mod´est-ly
mod´es-ty
mod´i-cum
mod´i-fi´able
mod-i-fi-ca´tion
mod´i-fi-ca-to-ry
mod´i-fied
mod´i-fi-er
mod´i-fy
mod´i-fy-ing
mod´ish
mo-diste´
mod-u-la-bil´i-ty
mod´u-lar
mod´u-late
mod-u-la´tion
mod´u-la-tor
mod´u-la-to-ry
mod´ule
mo´dus ope-ran´di
mo´dus vi-ven´di
mo´gul
mo´hair
Mo-ham´med
Mo-ham´med-an

Mo-ha´ve
Mo´hawk
Mo-hi´can
mo´hole
moi´e-ty
moil´ing
moi´ra
moi-ré´
moist´en
moist´en-er
moist´ly
moist´ness
mois´ture
mois´ture-proof
mo´lar
mo-lar´i-ty
mo´la-ry
mo-las´ses
mold
mold´able
mold´board
mold´er
mold´i-ness
mold´ing
mold´y
mo-lec´u-lar
mol´e-cule
mole´hill
mole´skin
mo-lest´
mo-les-ta´tion
mo-lest´er
Mo-li´na
mol-les´cent
mol-li-fi-ca´tion
mol´li-fied
mol´li-fy
mol´li-fy-ing
mol´li-sol
mol´lusk
Mol´ly
mol´ly-cod-dle
Mo-lo-kai´
Mo´lo-tov
mol´ten
molt´er
Mo-luc´ca
mo-lyb´date
mo-lyb´de-nite

mo-lyb´de-num
mo-lyb´dic
mo´ment
mo´men-tar´i-ly
mo´men-tary
mo´ment-ly
mo-men´tous
mo-men´tum
Mon´a-can
mon´a-chal
mon´a-chism
Mo´na-co
mo´nad
mo-nad´ic
mo-nad-is´tic
mo-nad´nock
mon´arch
mo-nar´chal
mo-nar´chi-al
mo-nar´chi-an-ism
mo-nar´chic
mo-nar´chi-cal
mon´ar-chism
mon´ar-chist
mon´ar-chy
mon´as-te´ri-al
mon´as-tery
mo-nas´tic
mo-nas´ti-cism
mon´atom´ic
mon-ax´i-al
mon´a-zite
Mon´day
Mo-net´
mon-e-tar´i-ly
mon´e-tary
mon´e-tite
mon-e-ti-za´tion
mon´e-tize
mon´ey
mon´ey-bags
mon´eyed
mon´ey-mak-er
mon´ey-mak-ing
mon´ey or-der
mon´eys
mon´ey-wort
mon´ger
Mon´gol

Mon-go´lia
Mon´gol-oid
mon´goose
mon´grel
Mon´i-ca
mon´i-ker
mo-ni´tion
mon´i-tor
mon´i-to´ri-al
mon´key
mon´key-ish
mon´keys
mon´key-shine
monk´hood
monk´ish
monks´hood
Mon´mouth
mon´o-ac´id
mon´o-acid´ic
mon´o-am´ide
mon´o-aminc´
mon´o-ba´sic
mon´o-chord
mon´o-chro-mat´ic
mono-chro´ma-tor
mon´o-chrome
mon´o-chro´mous
mo-noch´ro-nous
mon´o clc
mo-noc´u-lar
mo-nod´ic
mo-nod´i-cal-ly
mon´o-dra´ma
mon´o-dy
mo-noe´cious
mon´o-gam´ic
mo-nog´a-mist
mo-nog´a-mous
mo-nog´a-my
mon´o-ge-net´ic
mon´o-gen´ic
mo-nog´e-nism
mo-nog´e-ny
mo-nog´o-ny
mon´o-gram
mon´o-gram-mat´ic
mon´o-grammed
mon´o-graph
mo-nog´ra-pher

mon´o-graph´ic
mo-nog´y-ny
mo-nol´a-try
mon´o-lith
mon´o-lith´ic
mon´o-log
mo-nol´o-gist
mon´o-logue
mon´o-ma´nia
mon´o-ma´ni-ac
mon´o-ma-ni´a-cal
mon´o-mer
mo-nom´er-ous
mon´o-me-tal´lic
mon´o-met´al-lism
mo-nom´e-ter
mo-no´mi-al
Mo-non-ga-he´la
mon´o-nu-cle-o´sis
mon´o-plane
mo-nop´o-list
mo-nop´o-lis´tic
mo-nop-o-li-za´tion
mo-nop´o-lize
mo-nop´o-ly
mo-nop´so-ny
mon´o-rail
mon´o-spor´ous
mon´o-stome
mon´o-strophe
mon´o-syl-lab´ic
mon´o-syl´la-ble
mon´o-the-ism
mon´o-the-ist
mon´o-the-is´tic
mon´o-tone
mo-not´o-nous
mo-not´o-ny
mon´o-treme
mo-not´ri-chous
mo-not´ro-py
Mon´o-type
mon´o-typ´ic
mon´o-va´lent
mon-ox´ide
Mon-roe´ Doc´trine
Mon-ro´via
mon-sei-gneur´
mon-sieur´

mon-si´gnor
mon-soon´
mon´ster
mon´strance
mon-stros´i-ty
mon´strous
mon-tage´
Mon-taigne´
Mon-tan´a
Mon´te Car´lo
Mon´te-ne-´grin
Mon´te-ne´gro
Mon´te-rey
Mon´ter-rey´
Mon´tes-quieu´
Mon´tes-so´ri
Mon-te-vi-de´o
Mon-te-zu´ma
Mont-gol-fier´
Mont-gom´ery
month´ly
Mon-ti-cel´lo
mon-tic´u-late
mon´ti-cule
Mont-mar´tre
Mont-pe´lier
Mon´tre-al´
mon´u-ment
mon-u-men´tal
mood´i-ly
mood´i-ness
mood´y
mooed
moo´ing
moon´beam
moon´eye
moon´fish
moon´less
moon´light
moon´lit
moon´rise
moon´shine
moon´shin-er
moon´stone
moon´struck
moor´age
moor´hen
moor´ing
Moor´ish

moor´land
moped
mop´ing
mop´pet
mop´ping
mo-quette´
mor´al
mo-rale´
mor´al ism
mor´al-ist
mor´al-is´tic
mo-ral´i-ty
mor-al-iza´tion
mor´al-ize
mor´al-ly
mo-rass´
mor-a-to´ri-um
mor´a-tory
Mo-ra´vi-an
mo-ra´vite
mo-ray´
mor´bid
mor-bid´i-ty
mor´bid-ly
mor-bose´
mor-da´cious
mor-dac´i-ty
mor´dan-cy
mor´dant
Mor´de-cai
mor´dent
mo-reen´
more-o-ver
mo´res
Mor´gan
mor´ga-nat´ic
Mor´gan-ton
Mor´gan-town
Mor´gen-thau
morgue
mor´i-bund
mor-i-bun´di-ty
mo-rin´done
mo´rin-ite
mo´ri-on
Mor´ley
Mor´mon
Mor´mon-ism
Mor´mon-ite

morn´ing
morn´ing glo´ry
morn´ing star
Mo´ro
Mo-roc´can
Mo-roc´co
mo´ron
mo-ron´ic
mo-rose´
mo-rose´ly
mo-rose´ness
mo-ros´i-ty
mor´pheme
mor-phe´mics
Mor´pheus
mor´phine
mor-phog´ra-phy
mor´pho-line
mor´pho-log´ic
mor´pho-log´i-cal
mor-phol´o-gist
mor-phol´o-gy
mor-phom´e-try
mor´ris
mor´row
mor´sal
mor´sel
mor´tal
mor tal´i ty
mor´tal-ly
mor´tar
mor´tar-board
mort´gage
mort´ga-gee´
mort´gag-ing
mort´ga-gor´
mor-ti´cian
mor-ti-fi-ca´tion
mor´ti-fied
mor´ti-fy
mor´ti-fy-ing
Mor´ti-mer
mor´tise
mor´tis-er
mor´tis-ing
Mor´ton
mor´tu-ary
mor´u-la
mo-sa´ic

mo-sa´i-cism
Mos´cow
Mo-selle´
Mo´ses
Mos´lem
mosque
mos-qui´to
mos-qui´toes
moss´back
moss´—grown
moss´i-er
moss´i-ness
moss´y
most´ly
mo-tel´
mo-tet´
moth´—eat-en
moth´er
moth´er-hood
moth´er—in—law
moth´er-land
moth´er-less
moth´er-li-ness
moth´er-ly
moth´proof
mo-tif´
mo´tile
mo-til´i-ty
mo-tion
mo´tion-less
mo´ti-vate
mo´ti-vat-ing
mo-ti-va´tion
mo-tive
mo´tive-less
mo-tiv´i-ty
mot´ley
mo´tor
mo´tor-bus
mo´tor-cade
mo´tor-car
mo´tor-cy-cle
mo´tor-cy-clist
mo´tor-ist
mo-tor-iza´tion
mo´tor-ize
mo´tor-man
mot´tle
mot´tled

mot´tling
mot´to
mot´toes
mouf´lon
mou-lage´
mou-lin´
mount´able
moun´tain
moun´tain-eer´
moun´tain-ous
moun´te-bank
mount´ed
mount´er
mount´ing
Mount Ver´non
mourn´er
mourn´ful
mourn´ing
mous´er
mouse´tail
mouse´trap
mousse-line´
Mous-sorg´sky
mous´tache
mous´y
mouth´ful
mouth´piece
mou´ton
mov-a-bil´i-ty
mov´able
move´ment
mov´er
mov´ie
mov´ies
mov´ing
mowed
mow´er
mow´ing
mown
Mo-zam-bique´
Mo´zart
mu-ced´i-nous
mu´cic
mu´cid
mu-cif´er-ous
mu´ci-lage
mu´ci-lag´i-nous
muck´rake
muck´y

mu´coid
mu´cous
mu´cus
mud´dle
mud´dled
mud´dy
mud´fish
mud´guard
mu-ez´zin
muf´fin
muf´fin-eer´
muf´fle
muf´fler
muf´fling
muf´ti
mug´ger
mug´gi-ness
mug´ging
mug´gy
mug´wump
Mu-ham´mad
mu-lat´to
mu-lat´toes
mul´ber-ry
mulch´er
mulct
mul´ish
mul´lah
mull´er
mul´let
mul´li-gan
mul-li-ga-taw´ny
mul´lion
mul´ti-cel´lu-lar
mul´ti-col´ored
mul´ti-di-men´sion-al
mul´ti-di-rec´tion-al
mul´ti-dis´ci-pli-nary
mul´ti—eth´nic
mul´ti-fam´i-ly
mul´ti-far´i-ous
mul´ti-fid
mul´ti-form
mul´ti-fu´el
mul´ti-lat´er-al
mul´ti-lay-er
mul-ti-lev´el
mul´ti-lin´gual
mul´ti-me´dia

mul-ti-mil´lion-aire´
mul´ti-na´tion-al
mul´ti-pack
mul´ti-ped
mul´ti-ple
mul´ti-plex
mul´ti-pli-able
mul´ti-plic´a-ble
mul-ti-pli-cand´
mul-ti-pli-ca´tion
mul´ti-pli-ca´tive
mul-ti-plic´i-ty
mul´ti-plied
mul´ti-pli-er
mul´ti-ply
mul´ti-ply-ing
mul´ti-tude
mul-ti-tu´di-nous
mul´ti-va´lent
mum´ble
mum´bling
mum´mer
mum´mery
mum´mi-fy
mum´my
Mun´chau-sen
mun´dane´
mun´go
Mu´nich
mu-nic´i-pal
mu-nic-i-pal´i-ty
mu-nic´i-pal-ize
mu-nif´i-cence
mu-ni´tion
mu´ral
mu-rar´i-um
mur´der
mur´der-er
mur´der-ess
mur´der-ous
mu´ri-at´ic
Mu-ril´lo
mu´rine
mu´ri-um
murk´i-er
murk´i-ly
murk´y
mur´mur
mur´mur-ing

mur´mur-ous
Mur´phy
mur´rain
mu-sa´ceous
mus´ca-dine
mus´ca-rine
mus´cat
mus´ca-tel´
mus´cle
mus´cle—bound
Mus´co-vite
Mus´co-vy
mus´cu-lar
mus-cu-lar´i-ty
mus´cu-la-ture
mused
mu-se-og´ra-phy
mu-se-ol´o-gy
mus´er
mu-sette´
mu-se´um
mush´room
mush´y
mu´sic
mu´si-cal
mu´si-cale´
mu´si-cal-ly
mu-si´cian
mu-si-col´o-gy
mus´ing
musk deer
Mus-ke´gon
mus´ket
mus-ke-teer´
mus´ket-ry
musk´mel-on
Mus-ko´gee
musk´—ox
musk´—ox-en
musk´rat
musk´y
mus´lin
mus´sel
Mus-so-li´ni
muss´y
mus´tache
mus´tang
mus´tard
mus´te-line

mus´ter
must´i-ness
must´y
mu-ta-bil´i-ty
mu´ta-ble
mu´ta-gen´ic
mu´tant
mu´tase
mu´tate
mu´tat-ing
mu-ta´tion
mu´ta-tive
mut´ed
mute´ly
mute´ness
mu´ti-late
mu-ti-la´tion
mu´ti-la-tor
mu´ti-neer´
mut´ing
mu´ti-nied
mu´ti-nous
mu´tiny
mu´ti-ny-ing
mut´ism
mu´ton
mut´ter
mut´ter-ing
mut´ton
mut´ton-head
mu´tu-al
mu´tu-al-ism
mu-tu-al´i-ty
mu´tu-al-iza´tion
mu´tu-al-ly
mu´tu-el
mu´tule
mu-zhik´
muz´zle
muz´zle—load-er
muz´zling
my-al´gia
my-ce´li-oid
my-ce´li-um
My-ce´nae
my-ce-to´ma
my-col´o-gist
my-col´o-gy
my-co-my´cin

my-co´sis
my´e-lo-cyte
my´e-loid
my-e-lo-ma-to´sis
my´e-lom´a-tous
my-e-lop´a-thy
my-e-lo´sis
my´na
my-o-car-di´tis
my-o´ma
my-op´a-thy
my-o´pia
my-op´ic
my´o-sin
my-o-si´tis
my-os´mine
my-ot´o-my
myr´i-ad
myr´i-am-e-ter
myr´i-a-pod
myr´i-cyl
myr-in-gi´tis
my-ris´tate
my-ris´tic
My´ron
myrrh
myrrh´ic
myr´tle
my-self´
mys´ter-ies
mys-te´ri-ous
mys-te´ri-ous-ly
mys´tery
mys´tic
mys´ti-cal
mys´ti-cism
mys´ti-fi-ca´tion
mys´ti-fied
mys´ti-fy
mys´ti-fy-ing
mys´ti-fy-ing-ly
mys-tique´
myth´ic
myth´i-cal
myth´i-cal-ly
myth´i-cist
myth´i-cize
my-thog´ra-pher
myth-o-log´i-cal

my-thol´o-gist
my-thol´o-gy
myth-o-ma´nia
myx-ede´ma
myx´o-bac-te´ri-al
myx-o-ma-to´sis

# N

nab´bing
na´bob
na´cre
na´cre-ous
na´crite
na´dir
na-ga´na
Na´ga-sa´ki
nag´ging
Na-go´ya
nah´co-lite
Na´hum
na´iad
nail´er
nail´wort
nain´sook
Nai-ro´bi
na-ive´
na-ive-té´
na´ked
na´ked-ness
nam´by—pam´by
name´able
name´less
name´ly
nam´er
name´sake
nam´ing
Na-mur´
Na-nai´mo
Nan´cy
nan-keen´
Nan´king´
na´no-gram
na´noid
Nan´sen
Nantes
Nan-tuck´et
na-ol´o-gy
Na-o´mi

na´palm
nape
na-phaz´o-line
naph´tha
naph´tha-lene
naph´tha-len´ic
naph-thal´ic
naph´thene
naph´the-nic
naph´thi-o-nate
naph´thi-on´ic
naph´thyl
naph´thy-lene
Na´pi-er
nap´kin
Na´ples
Na-po´leon
nap´per
nap´ping
nar´ce-ine
nar´cis-sism
nar´cis-sist
nar-cis´sus
nar´co-lep-sy
nar-co-lep´tic
nar-co´ma
nar-co´sis
nar-cot´ic
nar´co-tism
nar´co-tize
nard
nar´es
nar´gi-leh
nar-in-gen´in
na-rin´gin
nar´is
Nar-ra-gan´sett
nar´rate
nar-ra´tion
nar´ra-tive
nar´ra-tor
nar´row
nar´row—gage´
nar´row-ly
nar´row—mind´ed
nar´row-ness
Nar-va´ez
na´sal
na-sa´lis

na-sal´i-ty
na´sal-ize
na´sal-ly
Nash´ville
na´si-on
na´so-scope
Nas´sau
nas´tic
nas´ti-ly
nas´ti-ness
nas´ty
na´tal
Na-tal´
na´tant
na-ta´tion
na-ta-to´ri-al
na-ta-to´ri-um
na´ta-to-ry
Natch´ez
Na´than
Na-than´iel
na´tion
na´tion-al
na´tion-al-ism
na´tion-al-ist
na´tion-al-is´tic
na-tion-al´i-ty
na-tion-al-iza´tion
na´tion-al-ize
na´tion-al-ly
na´tion-wide´
na´tive
na´tive—born´
na´tive-ly
na´tive-ness
na´tiv-ism
na´tiv-is´tic
na-tiv´i-ty
na´tri-um
na´tro-lite
na´tron
nat´ti-ly
nat´ty
nat´u-ral
nat´u-ral-ism
nat´u-ral-ist
nat´u-ral-is´tic
nat-u-ral-iza´tion
nat´u-ral-ize

nat´u-ral-ly
nat´u-ral-ness
na´ture
na´tur-o-path
na-tur-op´a-thy
naught
naugh´ti-ly
naugh´ti-ness
naugh´ty
nau´pli-us
Na-u´ru
nau´sea
nau´se-ate
nau´se-at-ed
nau´seous
nau´ti-cal
nau´ti-cal-ly
nau´ti-lus
Nav´a-ho, Nav´a-jo
na´val
Na-varre´
na´vel
na-vic´u-lar
na´vies
nav-i-ga-bil´i-ty
nav´i-ga-ble
nav´i-gate
nav-i-ga´tion
nav´i-ga-tor
na´vy
na´vy yard
Naz´a-rene
Naz´a-reth
Na´zi
na´zi-ism
na´zism
Ne-an´der-thal
Ne-a-pol´i-tan
neap tide
near´by´
Ne-arc´tic
near´est
near´ly
near´ness
near´sight-ed
neat´ly
neat´ness
Ne´bo
Ne-bras´ka

neb´ris
Neb-u-chad-nez´zar
neb´u-la
neb´u-lae
neb´u-lar
ne-bu´li-um
neb-u-los´i-ty
neb´u-lous
nec´es-sar´i-ly
nec´es-sary
ne-ces´si-tar´i-an
ne-ces´si-tate
ne-ces´si-ties
ne-ces´si-tous
ne-ces´si-tous-ly
ne-ces´si-ty
Neck´er
neck´er-chief
neck´ing
neck´lace
neck´line
neck´piece
neck´tie
neck´wear
nec´ro-bi-o´sis
nec´ro-log´i-cal
ne-crol´o-gist
ne-crol´o-gy
nec´ro-man-cer
nec´ro-man-cy
ne´crop-sy
ne-cro´sis
ne-crot´ic
nec´ro-tize
ne-crot´o-my
nec´tar
nec-tar´e-ous
nec´tar-ine´
nec´ta-ry
need´ful
need´i-er
need´i-est
need´i-ness
nee´dle
nee´dle-fish
nee´dle-ful
nee´dle-like
nee´dle-point
nee´dler

need´less
need´less-ly
need´less-ness
nee´dle-wom-an
nee´dle-work
need´y
ne´er´—do—well
ne-far´i-ous
ne-gate´
ne-ga´tion
neg´a-tive
neg´a-tive-ly
neg´a-tiv-ism
neg´a-tiv-is´tic
neg-a-tiv´i-ty
neg´a-to-ry
neg´a-tron
ne-glect´
ne-glect´er
ne-glect´ful
neg-li-gee´
neg´li-gence
neg´li-gent
neg´li-gent-ly
neg-li-gi-bil´i-ty
neg´li-gi-ble
ne-go-tia-bil´i-ty
ne-go´tia-ble
ne-go´ti-ate
ne-go´ti-at-ing
ne-go´ti-a´tion
ne-go´ti-a-tor
Ne´gro
ne´gus
Ne-he-mi´ah
Neh´ru
neigh
neigh´bor
neigh´bor-hood
neigh´bor-ing
neigh´bor-li-ness
neigh´bor-ly
nei´ther
Nel´son
Nem´bu-tal
ne-mes´ic
nem´e-sis
nem´o-ral
Ne´o-Ant-er´gan

ne´o-blast
Ne´o-cene
ne´o-clas´si-cal
neo-dym´i-um
ne-og´a-my
Ne´o-lith´ic
ne´o-log´i-cal
ne-ol´o-gism
ne-ol´o-gist
ne-ol´o-gy
ne´o-my´cin
ne´on
ne´o-phyte
ne-o-pla´sia
ne´o-plasm
ne´o-prene
Neo-sy-neph´rine
ne´o-ter´ic
ne-ot´er-ism
ne-ot´o-cite
Ne-pal´
Nep´a-lese´
ne-pen´the
ne-pen´the-an
neph´e-line
neph´e-lin-ite
neph´e-lite
neph´ew
ne-phol´o-gy
neph´o-scope
neph´ric
neph´rite
ne-phrit´ic
ne-phri´tis
ne-phrol´o-gy
nep´o-tism
Nep´tune
Ne´re-id
ne-rit´ic
Ne´ro
ner´o-li
ne-rol´i-dol
Ne-ro´ni-an
ner-ter-ol´o-gy
ner´vate
ner-va´tion
nerve´less
ner´vine
nerv´ing

ner-vos´i-ty
ner´vous
ner´vous-ly
ner´vous-ness
nerv´y
nest´er
nes´tle
nes´tling
Nes´tor
neth´er
Neth´er-lands
neth´er-most
net´ting
net´tle
net´tled
net´work
neu´ral
neu-ral´gia
neu-ral´gic
neu´rine
neu-rit´ic
neu-ri´tis
neu´ro-gen´ic
neu-rog´lia
neu-rog´ra-phy
neu´roid
neu-ro-log´i-cal
neu-rol´o-gist
neu-rol´o-gy
neu-rol´y-sis
neu-ro´ma
neu´ron
neu´ro-nal
neu-ron´ic
neu´ro-path´ic
neu-rop´a-thy
neu-rop´ter-ous
neu-ro´ses
neu-ro´sis
neu-rot´ic
neu-rot´i-cism
neu-rot´o-my
neu´ro-trop´ic
neu-rot´ro-pism
neu´ter
neu´tral
neu´tral-ism
neu-tral´i-ty
neu-tral-i-za´tion

neu´tral-ize
neu´tral-iz-er
neu´tral-ly
neu-tri´no
neu´tron
Ne-vad´a
nev´er
nev´er-more´
nev´er-the-less´
ne´vus
New´ark
new´born
New´burgh
New´cas-tle
new´com-er
new´el
new´fan´gled
New´found-land
New Guin´ea
New Hamp´shire
New Ha´ven
New Jer´sey
new´ly
New´man
New´market
New Mex´i-co
new´ness
New Or´leans
New´port
news´boy
news´cast
news´cast-er
news´ deal-er
news´let-ter
news´man
news´pa-per
news´pa-per-man
news´print
news´reel
news´room
news´stand
news´y
New´ton
New Zea´land
nex´us
ni´a-cin
ni-a-cin´a-mide
Ni-ag´a-ra
nib´ble

nib´bling
nib´lick
Nic´a-ra´gua
nice´ly
Ni´cene
nice´ness
nic´est
ni´ce-ty
niche
Nich´o-las
nick´el
nick-el-if´er-ous
nick´el-ine´
nick-el-o´de-on
nick´el—plate
nick´el-type
nick´er
nick´name
nic-o-tin´amide
nic-o-tin´ate
nic´o-tine
nic´o-tin´ic
nic´o-tin-ism
nic-o-ti´no-yl
nic´o-tin-u´ric
nic´ti-tate
nic-ti-ta´tion
ni´dor
ni´dus
Nie´buhr
niece
Nietz-sche
nif´ty
Ni´ger
Ni-ge´ria
ni´ger-ite
nig´gard
nig´gard-ly
night´cap
night´club
night´fall
night´gown
night´hawk
night´in-gale
night´long
night´ly
night´mare
night´shirt
night´time

ni-gres´cence
ni-gres´cent
ni´grous
ni´hi-lism
ni´hi-list
ni´hi-lis´tic
ni-hil´i-ty
Ni´ke
nim´ble
nim´ble-ness
nim´bly
nim´bo-stra´tus
nim´bus
ni-mi´e-ty
Nim´rod
nin´com-poop
nine´fold
nine´pins
nine´teen´
nine´teenth´
ninc´ti-eth
nine´ty
Nin´e-veh
nin´ny
ninth
ninth´ly
Ni´o-be
ni-o´bic
ni-o´bi-um
ni´pa
nip´e-cot´ic
nip´per
nip´ping
nip´ple
Nip´pon
nip´py
Ni-sei´
Nis´sen
ni´sus
ni´ter
nit´id
ni-tid´i-ty
ni-tra-mine´
ni´trate
ni´tra-tor
ni´tric
ni´tride
ni´trid-ize
ni-tri-fi-ca´tion

ni´tri-fy
ni´trile
ni´trite
ni-tro-an´i-line
ni´tro-gen
ni´tro-gen-ate
ni-tro´gen-ize
ni-trog´en-ous
ni-tro-glyc´er-in
ni-tro´lic
ni-trom´e-ter
ni-tro´ni-um
ni-tros-amine´
ni´tro-sate
ni-tro´so
ni´trous
nit´wit
Nix´on
No´ah
No-bel´
no-bel´i-um
no-bil´i-ary
no-bil´i-ty
no´ble
no´ble-man
no´ble-ness
no´ble-wom-an
no´bly
no´body
no-car-di-o´sis
no´cent
noc-ti-lu´ca
noc-tiv´a-gant
noc´to-vi-sion
noc-tur´nal
noc´turne
noc´u-ous
nod´al
no-dal´i-ty
nod´ding
nod´dle
nod´dy
nod´i-cal
nod´u-lar
nod´ule
No-el´
nog´gin
no´how
noise´less

noise´less-ly
nois´i-ly
nois´i-ness
nois´ing
noi´some
nois´y
No-ko´mis
no´lo con-ten´de-re
no´mad
no-mad´ic
no-mad´i-cal
no´mad-ism
nom´arch
nom´archy
nom de plume
no´men-cla-tor
no´men-cla-ture
nom´ic
nom´i-nal
nom´i-nal-ly
nom´i-nal-ism
nom´i-nal-ist
nom´i-nal-ize
nom´i-nate
nom´i-nat-ed
nom-i-na´tion
nom´i-na-tive
nom´i-na-tor
nom´i-nee´
no-moc´ra-cy
nom´o-gram
nom´o-graph´ic
no mog´ra phy
no-mol´o-gy
nom-o-thet´ic
non-ac-cept´ance
non-a-co´sane
non-a-dec´ane
non´age
nona-ge-nar´i-an
non-ag-gres´sion
non´a-gon
non-ap-pear´ance
non´cha-lance´
non´cha-lant´
non´cha-lant-ly
non-com-bat´ant
non-com-mis´sioned
non-com-mit´tal

non com´pos men´tis
non-con-duc´tor
non-con-form´ist
non-con-form´i-ty
non-co-op-er-a´tion
non´de-script
no´nene
non-en´ti-ty
non-es-sen´tial
none´such
non-ex-is´tence
non-ex-is´tent
non-fea´sance
non´fic´tion
non-ful-fill´ment
non-in-ter-ven´tion
non-join´der
non-me-tal´lic
non-ni-trog´e-nous
non´pa-reil´
non´parous
non-par-tic´i-pat-ing
non-par´ti-san
non´pay´ment
non´plus´
non-plussed´
non-plus´sing
non-pro-duc´tive
non-prof´it
non pro-se´qui-tur
non-res´i-dence
non-res´i-dent
non-sec-tar´i-an
non´sense
non-sen´si-cal
non se´qui-tur
non´skid´
non´stop´
non´suit´
non´sup-port´
non-un´ion
noo´dle
no-ol´o-gy
noon´day
noon´tide
noon´time
no´pal
no´pi-nene
No´ra

Nor´dic
Nor´folk
no´ria
nor´mal
nor´mal-cy
nor-mal´i-ty
nor´mal-ize
nor´mal-iz-er
nor´mal-ly
Nor´man
Nor´man-dy
nor´ma-tive
Nor´ris
Norse´man
North Amer´i-ca
North-amp´ton
North Car-o-li´na
North Da-ko´ta
north´east´
north-east´er
north-east´er-ly
north-east´ern
north-east´ward
north´er
north´er-ly
north´ern
north´ern-er
north´ern-most
north´land
North-um´ber-land
North-um´bri-an
north´ward
north´ward-ly
north´west´
north´west´er-ly
north-west´ern
Nor´way
Nor´wich
nose bag
nose´band
nose´bleed
nose´—dive
nose´gay
no´se-lite
nose´piece
nos´ing
no-sog´ra-phy
nos-o-log´i-cal
no-sol´o-gist

no-sol´o-gy
nos-tal´gia
nos-tal´gic
nos-tol´o-gy
nos´tril
nos´trum
nos´y
no´ta-ble
no´ta-ble-ness
no´ta-bly
no´tam
no-tar´i-al
no´ta-ries
no´ta-rize
no´ta-ry
no´ta-ry pub´lic
no-ta´tion
notched
notch´er
note´book
not´ed
note´less
note´pa-per
note´wor-thi-ly
note´wor-thi-ness
note´wor-thy
noth´ing
noth´ing-ness
no´tice
no´tice-able
no´tice-ably
no´tic-ing
no´ti-fi-ca´tion
no´ti-fied
no´ti-fi-er
no´ti-fy
no´ti-fy-ing
not´ing
no´tion
no´tion-al
No-to-gae´an
no-to-ri´e-ty
no-to´ri-ous
no-to´ri-ous-ly
no-to-un´gu-late
Not´ting-ham
not-with-stand´ing
nou´gat
nour´ish

nour´ish-ing
nour´ish-ment
nou-veau´ riche
No´va Sco´tia
no-va´tion
nov´el
nov´e´ette´
nov´el-ist
nov-el-is´tic
nov´el-ize
no-vel´la
nov´el-ties
nov´el-ty
No-vem´ber
no-ve´na
nov´ice
no-vi´tiate
No´vo-cain
now´a-days
no´way
no´ways
no´where
no´wise
nox´ious
noz´zle
nu´ance
nub´bin
nu´chal
nu´ci-form
nu´cle-ar
nu´cle-ate
nu-cle-a´tion
nu´cle-a-tor
nu´clei
nu-cle´ic
nu´cle-us
nu´clide
nu-clid´ic
nude´ness
nudged
nudg´er
nudg´ing
nud´ism
nud´ist
nu´di-ty
nu´ga-to-ry
nug´get
nui´sance
nul-li-fi-ca´tion

nul´li-fied
nul´li-fi-er
nul´li-fy
nul´li-fy-ing
nul´li-ty
num´ber
num´bered
num´ber-er
num´ber-less
numb´fish
numb´ing
num´bles
numb´ly
numb´ness
nu´men
nu-mer-a-ble
nu´mer-al
nu´mer-ary
nu´mer-ate
nu-mer-a´tion
nu´mer-a-tive
nu´mer-a-tor
nu-mer´i-cal
nu-mer´i-cal-ly
nu-mer-ol´o-gy
nu´mer-ous
nu´mi-nous
nu-mis-mat´ics
nu-mis´ma-tist
num´skull
nun´ci-a-ture
nun´cio
nun´cu-pa-tive
nun´like
nun´nery
nup´tial
nup-ti-al´i-ty
Nur´em-berg
nurse´maid
nurse-er
nur´sery
nur´sery-man
nurs´ing
nurs´ling
nur´tur-al
nur´ture
nur´tur-ing
nut´crack-er
nut´hatch

nut´meg
nu´tria
nu´tri-ent
nu´tri-lite
nu´tri-ment
nu-tri´tion
nu-tri´tion-al
nu-tri´tion-ist
nu-tri´tious
nu´tri-tive
nut´shell
nut´ter
nut´ti-er
nut´ti-ness
nut´ting
nut´ty
nuz´zle
Ny-an´za
ny´lon
nymph
nym´pha
nym-phae-a´ceous
nymph´al
nymph´a-lid
nym-pho-ma´nia

O

Oa´hu
oak´en
Oak´land
oa´kum
oar´fish
oar´lock
oars´man
oars´man-ship
oa´ses
oa´sis
oat´cake
oat´en
oat´meal
O´be-ah
obe´di-ence
obe´di-ent
obe´di-ent-ly
obei´sance
obei´sant
obe´li-al
ob´e-lisk

ob´e-lus
Ober-am´mer-gau
O´ber-lin
O´ber-on
obese´
obe´si-ty
obey´
obey´ing
ob-fus´cate
ob-fus-ca´tion
ob-fus´ca-tor
ob-fus´ca-to-ry
obit´u-ar-ies
obit´u-ary
ob´ject
ob-jec-tee´
ob-jec-ti-fi-ca´tion
ob-jec´ti-fy
ob-ject´ing
ob-jec´tion
ob-jec´tion-able
ob-jec´tive
ob-jec´tive-ly
ob-jec´tive-ness
ob-jec´tiv-ism
ob-jec-tiv´i-ty
ob-jec´tor
ob´jet d'art
ob-ju-ra´tion
ob´jur-gate
ob-jur-ga´tion
ob´jur-ga-tor
ob´last
ob´late
ob-la´tion
ob´la-to-ry
ob´li-gate
ob´li-gat-ing
ob-li-ga´tion
ob-li-ga-tor
oblig´a-to-ry
oblige´
ob´li-gee´
oblig´er
oblig´ing
oblig´ing-ly
ob´li-gor´
oblique´
oblique´ly

oblique´ness
ob-liq´ui-tous
ob-liq´ui-ty
ob-lit´er-ate
ob-lit-er-a´tion
ob-lit´er-a-tive
ob-lit´er-a-tor
ob-li-ves´cence
ob-liv´i-on
ob-liv´i-ous
ob´long
ob´long´at-ed
ob´lo-quy
ob-mu-tes´cence
ob-nox´ious
ob-nu-bi-la´tion
o´boe
o´bo-ist
ob´o-lus
ob-scene´
ob-scene´ly
ob-scen´i-ty
ob-scu´rant
ob-scu´ran-tism
ob-scu-ra´tion
ob-scure´
ob-scure´ly
ob-scure´ness
ob-scur´ing
ob-scu´ri-ty
ob-se-cra´tion
ob´se-quies
ob-se´qui-ous
ob-se´qui-ous-ness
ob-seq´ui-ty
ob´se-quy
ob-serv´able
ob-serv´ance
ob-serv´ant
ob-ser-va´tion
ob-serv´a-tive
ob-serv´a-to-ry
ob-serve´
ob-serv´er
ob-serv´ing
ob-sess´
ob-ses´sion
ob-ses´sive
ob-ses´sor

ob-sid´i-an
ob-so-les´cence
ob-so-les´cent
ob´so-lete´
ob´so-lete´ness
ob´sta-cle
ob-stet´ri-cal
ob-ste-tri´cian
ob-stet´rics
ob´sti-na-cy
ob´sti-nance
ob´sti-nate
ob´sti-nate-ly
ob-strep´er-ous
ob-struct´
ob-struct´er
ob-struc´tion
ob-struc´tion-ism
ob-struc´tion-ist
ob-struc´tive
ob-struc´tor
ob-tain´
ob-tain´able
ob-tain´ment
ob-test´
ob-tes-ta´tion
ob-trude´
ob-trud´er
ob-trud´ing
ob-tru´sion
ob-tru´sive
ob-tru´sive-ly
ob-tund´
ob-tund´ent
ob´tu-rate
ob´tu-ra´tion
ob´tu-ra-tor
ob-tuse´
ob-tu´si-ty
ob-verse´
ob-verse´ly
ob-ver´sion
ob´ver-tend
ob´vi-ate
ob´vi-at-ing
ob-vi-a´tion
ob´vi-a-tor
ob´vi-ous
ob´vi-ous-ly

ob´vi-ous-ness
ob´vo-lute
oc-a-ri´na
oc-ca´sion
oc-ca´sion-al
oc-ca´sion-al-ism
oc-ca´sion-al-ly
oc´ci-den´tal
oc-ci-den´ta´ize
oc-clude´
oc-clud´ent
oc-clud´ing
oc-clu´sal
oc-clu´sion
oc-clu´sive
oc-cult´
oc-cul-ta´tion
oc-cult´ism
oc-cult´ist
oc´cupan-cy
oc´cu-pant
oc-cu-pa´tion
oc-cu-pa´tion-al
oc´cu-pa-tive
oc´cu-pied
oc´cu-pi-er
oc´cu-py
oc´cu-py-ing
oc-cur´
oc-curred´
oc-cur´rence
oc-cur´rent
oc-cur´ring
o´cean
ocea-nar´i-um
Oce-an´ia
oce-an´ic
ocean-og´ra-pher
ocean-o-graph´ic
ocean-og´ra-phy
ocel´late
o´ce-lot
o´cher
o´cher-ous
o'clock´
oc´ta-gon
oc-tag´o-nal
oc-ta-he´dral
oc-ta-he´dron

oc´tal
oc´ta-mer
oc-tam´er-ous
oc-tam´e-ter
oc´tane
oc-tan´gu-lar
oc-ta-no´ate
oc´ta-nol
oc´ta-no´yl
oc´tant
oc-tan´tal
oc-ta´val
oc´ta-va´lent
oc´tave
Oc-ta´vi-us
oc-ta´vo
oc-ta´vos
oc-ten´ni-al
oc-tet´
Oc-to´ber
oc-to-ge-nar´i-an
oc-tog´e-nary
oc-to´ic
oc´to-nary
Oc-top´o-da
oc´to-pus
oc´to-roon´
oc´u-lar
oc´u-list
odd´i-ty
odd´ly
odd´ment
odd´ness
Odes´sa
od´ic
odif´er-ous
O´din
odi-om´e-ter
o´di-ous
od´ist
o´di-um
o´do-graph
odom´e-ter
odon-tal´gia
odon-ti´tis
odon´to-gen´ic
odon-tol´o-gy
odon-tom´e-ter
o´dor

o´dor-ant
odor-if´er-ous
o´dor-ize
o´dor-less
odor-om´e-ter
o´dor-ous
Odys´seus
Od´ys-sey
oed´i-pal
Oed´i-pus
of´fal
off´beat
off´cast
off´—cen´ter
off´—col´or
of-fend´
of-fend´er
of-fend´ing
of-fense´
of-fen´sive
of-fen´sive-ness
of´fer
of´fer-ing
of´fer-to´ri-al
of´fer-to-ry
off´hand´ed
of´fice
of´fice-hold-er
of´fi-cer
of-fi´cial
of-fi´cial-dom
of-fi´cial-ese´
of-fi´cial-ly
of-fi´ci-ant
of-fi´ci-ary
of-fi´ci-ate
of-fi-ci-a´tion
of-fi´ci-a-tor
of-fic´i-nal
of-fi´cious
of-fi´cious-ly
off´ing
off´ish
off´set
off-set´ting
off´shoot
off-shore´
off´side´
off´spring

off´stage´
of´ten
of´ten-times
Og´den
o´gee´
o´give
o´gle
O´gle-thorpe
o´gling
o´gre
o´gre-ish
o´gress
Ohi´o
ohm
ohm´age
ohm´ic
ohm´me-ter
oil cake
oil´cloth
oil´er
oil field
oil´i-ness
oil´man
oil paint´ing
oil´skin
oil slick
oil´stone
oil well
oil´y
oint´ment
Ojib´way, Ojib´wa
oka´pi
okay´
o´ken-ite
O´ki-na´wa
Okla-ho´ma
ok´o-nite
o´kra
O´laf
old´en
old—fash´ioned
old´ish
old´ness
old´ster
old´—time´
old—tim´er
old´—world´
o´le-a´ceous
ole-ag´i-nous

ole-an´der
ole-an´drin
o´le-ate
olec´ra-non
o´le-fin
o´le-fin´ic
ole´ic
o´le-in
o´leo
o´le-o-graph
o-le-og´ra-phy
o´le-o-mar´ga-rine
ole-om´e-ter
ole-o-res´in
ole´o-yl
ol-fac´tion
ol-fac´tive
ol-fac-tom´e-ter
ol-fac´to-ry
ol´i-garch
ol´i-gar´chic
ol´i-gar-chy
ol-i-ge´mia
ol-i-gop´o-ly
ol-i-gop´so-ny
ol´i-va´ceous
ol´i-vary
ol´ive
oliv´en-ite
Ol´i-ver
ol-i-ves´cent
Ol´i-vet
Oliv´ia
ol´i-vine
ol´la
olym´pi-ad
Olym´pi-an
Olym´pic
Olym´pus
O´ma-ha
Oman´
O´mar Khay-yam´
omeg´a
om´e-let
o´men
omen-ol´o-gy
omen´tum
o´mer
om´i-cron

om´i-nous
om´i-nous-ly
omis´si-ble
omis´sion
omis´sive
omit´
omit´ted
omit´ting
om´ni-bus
om´ni-far´i-ous
om-nif´ic
om-nif´i-cence
om-nif´i-cent
om-nim´e-ter
om-nip´o-tence
om-nip´o-tent
om-ni-pres´ence
om-ni-pres´ent
om´ni-range
om-ni´science
om-ni´scient
om-niv´o-rous
omo-pho´ri-on
on´a-ger
o´nan-ism
o´nan-ist
once—o´ver
on-com´e-ter
on´com-ing
on-cot´o-my
on´do-graph
on-dom´e-ter
on´du-le´
one´—armed´
one´—celled´
one´—eyed
one´—horse´
Onei´da
onei´ric
one´—leg´ged
one´ness
one´—piece´
on´er-ous
one-self´
one´—sid´ed
one´—step
one´time
one´—track´
one´—way´

one´—world´er
on´ion
on´ion-skin
on´look-er
on´ly
On-on-da´ga
on´rush
on´set
on´shore´
on´slaught
On-tar´io
on´to
on-tog´e-ny
on´to-log´i-cal
on-tol´o-gist
on-tol´o-gy
o´nus
on´ward
on´yx
o´o-lite
oo-lit´ic
ool´o-gy
oo´long
oom´e-ter
oozed
ooz´ing
ooz´y
opa-cim´e-ter
opac´i-ty
o´pal
opal-esce´
opal-es´cence
opal-es´cent
o´pal-ine
o´pal-oid
opaque´
opaque´ly
opaqu´er
opaqu´ing
o´pen
o´pen—air´
o´pen—door´
o´pen-er
o´pen—eyed´
o´pen—faced
o´pen-hand´ed
o´pen-heart-ed
o´pen—hearth
open house´

o´pen-ing
o´pen-ly
o´pen—mind´ed
o´pen-mouthed´
o´pen-ness
o´pen-work
op´era
op´er-a-ble
op´era glass
op´er-and´
op´er-at-able
op´er-ate
op-er-at´ic
op-er-at´i-cal-ly
op-er-a´tion
op-er-a´tion-al
op´er-a-tive
op´er-a-tor
oper´cu-lar
oper´cu-lum
op-er-et´ta
op´er-on
op´er-ose
Ophe´lia
oph´i-cleide
ophid´i-an
ophi-ol´a-try
ophi-ol´o-gy
O´phir
ophit´ic
oph-thal´mia
oph-thal´mic
oph-thal-mi´tis
oph-thal´mo-log´ic
oph-thal´mo-log´i-cal
oph-thal-mol´o-gist
oph-thal-mol´o-gy
oph-thal-mom´e-ter
oph-thal´mo-met´ric
oph-thal´mo-scope
oph-thal-mos´co-py
opine
opin´ion
opin´ion-at-ed
opin´ion-a-tive
o´pi-um
opos´sum
op´pi-dan
op-pi-la´tion

op-po´nent
op´por-tune´
op´por-tune´ly
op-por-tune´ness
op-por-tun´ism
op-por-tun´ist
op-por-tun-is´tic
op-por-tu´ni-ty
op-pos-abil´i-ty
op-pos´able
op-pose´
op-pos´ing
op´po-site
op-po-si´tion
op-press´
op-press´ible
op-pres´sion
op-pres´sive
op-pres´sor
op-pro´bri-ate
op-pro´bri-ous
op´so-nin
op´ta-tive
op´tic
op´ti-cal
op-ti´cian
op´tics
op´ti-mal
op´ti-mal-ize
op´ti-me
op-tim´e-ter
op´ti-mism
op´ti-mist
op´ti-mis´tic
op-ti-mis´ti-cal-ly
op´ti-mum
op´tion
op´tion-al
op-tom´e-ter
op´to-met´ric
op-tom´e-trist
op-tom´e-try
op´u-lence
op´u-len-cy
op´u-lent
o´pus
or´a-cle
orac´u-lar
orac-u-lar´i-ty

o´ral
o´ral-ly
Oran´
or´ange
or´ange-ade´
or´ange-wood
orang´utan
orate´
ora´tion
or´a-tor
or-a-tor´i-cal
or-a-tor´i-cal-ly
or-a-to´rio
or´a-to-ry
or-bic´u-lar
or´bit
or´bit-al
or´bit-ed
or´bit-er
or´bit-ing
or´chard
or´chard-ist
or´ches-tra
or-ches´tral
or´ches-trate
or-ches-tra´tion
or´chid
or-dain´
or´deal
or´der
or´dered
or´der-li-ness
or´der-ly
or´di-nal
or´di-nance
or-di-nar´i-ly
or´di-nary
or´di-nate
or-di-na´tion
ord´nance
or´dure
orec´tic
oreg´a-no
Or´e-gon
Ores´tes
or´gan
or´gan-dy
or-gan´ic
or-gan´i-cal-ly

or-gan´i-cism
or-gan´i-cist
or´ga-nism
or´gan-ist
or´ga-niz´able
or-ga-ni-za´tion
or´ga-nize
or´ga-niz-er
or´ga-niz-ing
or´gasm
or-gas´tic
or´gi-ast
or´gi-as´tic
or´gies
or´gone
or´gu-lous
or´gy
o´ri-el
o´ri-ent
ori-en´tal
Ori-en´tal-ism
Ori-en´tal-ist
o´ri-en-tate
ori-en-ta´tion
o´ri-en-ta´tor
or´i-fice
or´i-fi´cial
or´i-gin
orig´i-nal
orig-i-nal´i-ty
orig´i-nal-ly
orig´i-nate
orig´i-nat-ing
orig-i-na´tion
orig´i-na-tive
orig´i-na-tor
O´ri-no´co
o´ri-ole
Ori´on
Or-lan´do
Or´leans
Or´lon
or´mo-lu
or´na-ment
or´na-men´tal
or-na-men-ta´tion
or´nate´
or-nate´ness
or´nery

or-nith´ic
or´ni-thine
or-nith´o-log´i-cal
or-ni-thol´o-gist
or-ni-thol´o-gy
or´ni-thop-ter
or-ni-tho´sis
or-ni-thot´o-my
or´nith-u´ric
or´o-graph´ic
orog´ra-phy
o´ro-ide
orol´o-gy
orom´e-ter
or´o-met´ric
o´ro-tund
oro-tun´di-ty
or´phan
or´phan-age
or´phan-hood
Or´phe-um
Or´pheus
or´phic
or´phism
or´phrey
or´pi-ment
or´pine
or´rery
or´ris
or´ris-root
Or´sat
or´thi-con
or-tho-don´tia
or-tho-don´tic
or-tho-don´tist
or´tho-dox
or´tho-doxy
or-tho-ep´ic
or-tho-ep´i-cal-ly
or-tho´epist
or-tho´epy
or-tho-for´mic
or-tho-gen´e-sis
or-thog´na-thous
or-thog´o-nal
or-thog´ra-pher
or-tho-graph´ic
or-thog´ra-phy
or-thom´e-try

or´tho-pe´dic
or´tho-pe´dist
or-thop´nea
or-thop´ter-al
or-thop´tics
or´tho-scop´ic
or-tho´sis
or-thos´ti-chy
or-thot´ro-pism
or´tho-typ´ic
or´to-lan
o´ryx
O´sage´
Osa´ka
o´sa-zone
Os´car
Os-ce-o´la
os´cil-late
os´cil-la´tion
os´cil-la-tor
os´cil-la-to-ry
os-cil´lo-graph
os-cil-lom´e-ter
os-cil´lo-scope
os´cu-lar
os´cu-late
os-cu-la´tion
os´cu-la-to-ry
Osh´kosh
Osi´ris
Os´lo
os-mi-rid´i-um
os´mi-um
os-mo´sis
os-mot´ic
os-phre´sis
os´prey
Os´sa
os´se-ous
os´si-cle
os-sic´u-lar
os-si-cu-lec´to-my
os-si-fi-ca´tion
os-sif´i-ca-to-ry
os´si-fied
os´si-fy
os´si-fy-ing
Os´si-ning
os´su-ary

os´te-al
os-te-ec´to-my
os´te-it´ic
os-te-i´tis
os-tend´
os-ten´si-ble
os-ten´si-bly
os-ten´sive
os-ten´sive-ly
os-ten-ta´tion
os-ten-ta´tious
os-ten-ta´tious-ly
os-te-o-chon-dro´sis
os-te-oc´la-sis
os-te-ol´o-gist
os-te-ol´o-gy
os-te-ol´y-sis
os-te-o´ma
os´te-o´ma-tous
os-te-om´e-try
os´teo-my-e-li´tis
os´te-o-path
os´te-o-path´ic
os-te-op´a-thy
os´te-o-plas-ty
os-te-ot´o-my
os´ti-ary
os´ti-ole
os-to´sis
os´tra-cism
os´tra-cize
os´tra-ciz-ing
os´trich
Os´wald
Os-we´go
otal´gia
Othel´lo
oth´er
oth´er-wise
o´ti-ose
oti-os´i-ty
oti´tis
oti´tis me´dia
o´to-log´ic
otol´o-gy
otos´co-py
oto´sis
Otran´to
ot-ta´va

Ot´ta-wa
ot´ter
Ot´to
ot´to-man
ought
Oui´da
Oui´ja
ounce
ou´ri-cu-ry´
our-self´
our-selves´
oust´er
out-bal´ance
out-bid´
out´board
out´bound´
out´break
out´build
out´build-ing
out´burst
out´cast
out´class´
out´come
out´crop
out´crop-ping
out´cry
out´curve
out´did
out´dis´tance
out-do´
out-done´
out´door´
out-doors´
out´er
out´er-most
out´face´
out´field
out´field-er
out´fit
out´fit-ter
out´flank
out´flow
out-gen´er-al
out´go
out´go´ing
out´grew´
out´grow´
out´growth
out´house

out-ing
out´land
out´land-er
out-land´ish
out´last´
out´law
out´law-ry
out´lay
out´let
out´line
out-live´
out´look
out´ly-ing
out-ma-neu´ver
out´mod´ed
out-num´ber
out—of—date
out—of—doors
out—of—the—way
out´pa-tient
out´play´
out´point´
out´post
out´pour
out´pour-ing
out´put
out´rage
out-ra´geous
out-ra´geous-ly
out´rag-er
out´ran´
ou-trance´
out´rank´
ou-tré´
out´reach
out´rid-er
out´rig-ger
out´right
out´root´
out´run´
out´run-ner
out-sell´
out´set
out´shine
out´shone
out-side´
out-sid´er
out´sit´
out´size

out´skirts
out-smart´
out´soar´
out´speak´
out´spo´ken
out´spread´
out-stand´
out-stand´ing
out´stay´
out´stretch´
out-stretched´
out´strip´
out-stripped´
out´ward
out´ward-ly
out-wear´
out-weigh´
out´wit´
out´wit´ted
out´work´
out-worn´
o´val
oval´i-form
oval´i-ty
ovar´i-an
ovari-ec´to-my
ovar´i-ole
ovar-i-ot´o-my
ova-ri´tis
o´va-ry
o´vate
ova´tion
ov´en
ov´en-bird
ov´en-ware
o´ver
o´ver-act´
o´ver-ac-tiv´i-ty
o´ver-all
o´ver-arm´
over-awe´
over-bal´ance
o´ver-bear´
over-bear´ing
o´ver-bid´
o´ver-blown´
o´ver-board
o´ver-bold´
o´ver-bore

o´ver-borne´
o´ver-build´
o´ver-bur´den
over-came´
over-cap´i-tal-ize
o´ver-cast
over-charge´
over-cloud´
o´ver-coat
over-come´
o´ver-crowd´
over-did´
over-do´
over-done´
o´ver-dose
o´ver-draft
over-draw´
over-drawn´
over-dress´
o´ver-drive´
o´ver-due´
o´ver-eat
over-es´ti-mate
over-fed´
o´ver-feed´
o´ver-flow
over-grown´
o´ver-growth
o´ver-hand
o´ver-hang´
o´ver-haul´
o´ver-head
over-hear´
o´ver-hung
o´ver-joy´
o´ver-joyed
o´ver-laid
o´ver-land
o´ver-land-er
o´ver-lap´
over-lap´ping
o´ver-lay
o´ver-load´
o´ver-look´
o´ver-lord
o´ver-ly
o´ver-match´
o´ver-much´
over-night´

o´ver-pass
over-pay´
over-play´
over-pop-u-la´tion
over-pow´er
over-pro-duc´tion
over-ran´
over-rate´
over-reach´
over-ride´
over-rule´
over-run´
over-seas´
over-see´
o´ver-seer
o´ver-set´
over-shad´ow
o´ver-shoot´
over-shot´
o´ver-sight´
o´ver-size´
over-sleep´
over-slept´
over-state´
over-stay´
over-step´
over-stock´
o´ver-stuffed
o´ver-sup-ply´
overt´
over-take´
over-tak´en
over-tax´
over-threw´
over-throw´
over-thrown´
o´ver-time
o´ver-tired´
overt´ly
o´ver-tone
over-took´
o´ver-ture
over-turn´
o´ver-wear
o´ver-wea´ry
over-ween´ing
o´ver-weight
over-whelm´
over-whelm´ing

over-whelm´ing-ly
over-work´
over-worked´
o´ver-wrought´
Ov´id
o´vi-duct
o´vi-form
ovig´er-ous
ovi-na´tion
o´vine
o´void
o´vo-vi-vip´a-rous
o´vu-lar
o´vu-late
ovu-la´tion
o´vu-la-to-ry
o´vule
o´vum
Ow´en
Ow´ens-boro
ow´ing
owl´et
owl´ish
own´er
own´er-ship
ox´bow
ox´cart
ox´en
Ox´ford
ox´heart
ox´i-dant
ox´i-dase
ox´i-da´tion
ox´i-da-tive
ox´ide
ox´i-diz-able
ox-i-di-za´tion
ox´i-dize
ox´i-diz-er
ox-id´u-lat-ed
ox-im´e-ter
ox´i-met´ric
ox-in-dole
ox´tail
ox´tongue
oxy-acan´thine
oxy-acet´y-lene
ox´y-bi´o-tin
ox´y-gen

ox´y-gen-ate
ox-y-gen-a´tion
ox´y-gen´ic
ox´y-gen-ize
oxy-sul´fide
oxy-tet-ra-cy´cline
oys´ter
oys´ter bed
oys´ter-man
Oz´a-lid
O´zark
o´zone
o´zon-ide
o´zon-if´er-ous
o´zon-iz-er
ozo´no-sphere

P

pab´u-lum
paced
pace´mak-er
pac´er
pach´y-derm
pachy-san´dra
pach´y-tene
pac´i-fi-able
pa-cif´ic
pa-cif´i-cal-ly
pa-cif´i-cate
pac-i-fi-ca´tion
pac´i-fi-ca-tor
pa-cif´i-ca-to-ry
pac´i-fied
pac´i-fi-er
pac´i-fism
pac´i-fist
pac´i-fis´tic
pac´i-fy
pac´i-fy-ing
pac´ing
pack´age
pack´ag-er
pack´ag-ing
Pack´ard
pack´er
pack´et
pack´ing
pack´ing-house

pack´man
pack rat
pack´sack
pack´sad-dle
pack´thread
pac´tion
pad´ding
pad´dle
pad´dle-fish
pad´dler
pad´dle wheel
pad´dling
pad´dock
pad´dy
pad´lock
pa´dre
pa-dro´ne
Pad´ua
Pa-du´cah
pae´an
pae´on
pa´gan
pa´gan-ism
pa´gan-ize
pag´eant
pag´eant-ry
paged
pag´er
Pag´et
pag´i-nal
pag´i-nate
pag-i-na´tion
pag´ing
pa-go´da
pa-gu´ri-an
pail´ful
pain´ful
pain´ful´ly
pain´less
pain´less-ly
pains´tak-ing
pains´tak-ing-ly
paint box
paint´brush
paint´er
paint´ing
paint´work
pai-sa´no
Pais´ley

pa-ja´ma
Pak´i-stan
pal´ace
pa-la´ceous
pal´a-din
pal-at-abil´i-ty
pal´at-able
pal´a-tal
pal´ate
pa-la´tial
pa-lat´i-nate
pal´a-tine
pal-a-ti´tis
pa-lav´er
pa´lea
pale´face
pale´ness
pa´leo-graph´ic
pa-le-og´ra-phy
Pa´leo-lith´ic
pa-le-ol´o-gy
pa-le-on-tol´o-gist
pa-le-on-tol´o-gy
Pa´leo-zo´ic
Pa-ler´mo
Pal´es-tine
pal´ette
pal´frey
pal´in-drome
pal´ing
pal-in-gen´e-sis
pal-i-sade´
Pal-la´di-an
pal-la´di-um
pall´bear-er
pal´let
pal´let-ize
pal-lette´
pal´li-ate
pal´li-at-ing
pal-li-a´tion
pal´lia-tive
pal´li-a-tor
pal´lia-to-ry
pal´lid
pal´li-um
pall´—mall´
pal´lor
palmar´i-an

pal´mate
palma´tion
palm´er
pal´met´to
palm´ist
palm´is-try
pal´mi-tate
pal´mi-tin
palm leaf
palm´y
pal-o-mi´no
Pa´los
pal-pa-bil´i-ty
pal´pa-ble
pal´pa-bly
pal´pate
pal-pa´tion
pal´pebral
pal´pi-tant
pal´pi-tate
pal´pi-tat-ing
pa´pi-ta´tion
pal´sy
pal´ter
pal´tri-ness
pal´try
pal-y-nol´o-gy
Pam´e-la
pam´pa
pam´per
pamph´let
pam´phlet-ize
pan-a-ce´a
pa-nache´
Pan´a-ma
Pan—Amer´i-can
pan´a-ry
pan-a-tel´a
pan´cake
pan-chro-mat´ic
pan´cre-as
pan´cre-at´ic
pan´cre-a-tin
pan-cre-a-ti´tis
pan´da
pan-dem´ic
pan-de-mo´ni-um
pan´der
Pan-do´ra

pan-dow´dy
pan´du-rate
pan´el
pan´el-board
pan´eled
pan´el-ing
pan´el-ist
pan´han-dle
pan´han-dling.
pan´ic
pan´icked
pan´ick-ing
pan´icky
pan´i-cle
pan´ic—strick-en
pan´nier
pan´ning
pan´o-ply
pan-o-ram´a
pan´o-ram´ic
pan-soph´ic
pan´so-phism
pan´sies
pan´sy
pan-ta-loon´
pan-te-the´ine
pan´the-ism
pan´the-ist
pan´the-is´tic
pan´the-lism
pan´the-on
pan´the-on´ic
pan´ther
pant´ing
pan´to-graph
pan-tog´ra-pher
pan-tol´o-gy
pan-tom´e-ter
pan´to-mime
pan´to-mim´ic
pan´to-mimist
pan´to-then´ic
pan´tries
pan´try
pan´zer
pa´pa-cy
pa-pa´in
pa´pal
pa-paw´

pa-pay´a
pa´per
pa´per-back
pa´per-board
pa´per boy
pa´per chase
pa´per cut-ter
pa´per-hang-er
pa´per knife
pa´per-like
pa´per—thin´
pa´per-weight
pa´per work
pa´pery
pa-pier—mâ-ché´
pa-pil´la
pap´il-lary
pap-il-lo´ma
pap-il-lo´ma-to´sis
pap´il-lom´a-tous
pap´il-lose
pap-il-los´i-ty
pa-poose´
pa-pri´ka
Pap´ua
papy´rus
par´a-ble
pa-rab´o-la
par´a-bol´ic
par´a-bol´i-cal
pa-rab´o-lize
pa-rab´o-loid
pa-rab´o-loi´dal
par´a-chute
par´a-chut-ist
Par´a-clete
pa-rade´
pa-rad´er
pa-rad´ing
par´a-digm
par´a-di-sa´ic
par´a-dise
par´a-di-si´a-cal
par´a-dox
par´a-dox´i-cal
par´af-fin
par´af-fin´ic
para-gen´e-sis
par´a-gon

pa-rag´o-nite
par´a-graph
par´a-graph-er
par´a-graph´i-cal-ly
Par´a-guay
par´a-keet
par´al-lax
par´al-lel
par´al-leled
par´al-lel-ing
par´al-lel-ism
par-al-lel´o-gram
par-al-lel-om´e-ter
pa-ral´o-gism
pa-ral´o-gize
pa-ral´y-sis
par´a-lyt´ic
par-a-ly-za´tion
par´a-lyze
par´a-lyzed
par´a-lyz-ing
Par-a-mar´i-bo
par-a-me´cium
pa-ram´e-ter
par´a-mount
par´amour
par-a-noi´a
par´a-noi´ac
par´a-noid
par´ant-he´li-on
par´a-pet
par´a-pet-ed
par´aph
par´a-pha´sia
par-a-pher-na´lia
par´a-phrase
par´a-phras-er
par´a-phras-ing
pa-raph´ra-sis
par´a-phrast
par´a-phras´tic
pa-raph´y-sis
para-ple´gia
par´a-ple´gic
pa-rap´sis
par´a-se-le´ne
par´a-site
par-a-sit-e´mia
par´a-sit´ic

par´a-sit´i-cal
par-a-sit´i-ci´dal
par-a-sit´i-cide
par´a-sit-ism
par´a-si-tize
par-a-sito´sis
par´a-sol
para-syn´the-sis
para-tax´is
para-thi´on
par´a-thy´roid
par´a-troop-er
pa-rat´ro-phy
par´a-vane
par´boil
par´cel
par´celed
par´cel-ing
par´cel post
par´ce-nary
parch´ment
par´don
par´don-able
par´don-er
pared
par´ent
par´ent-age
pa-ren´tal
par-en´ter-al
pa-ren´the-ses
pa-ren´the-sis
pa-ren´the-size
par´en-thet´ic
par´en-thet´i-cal
par´en-thet´i-cal-ly
par´ent-hood
pa-ret´ic
par ex-cel-lence´
par-fait´
par-he´lion
pa-ri´ah
Par´i-an
pa-ri´e-tal
pari-mu´tu-el
par´i-nar´ic
par´ing
Par´is
par´ish
pa-rish´io-ner

par´i-son
par´i-ty
par´ka
park´er
Par´kin-son
park´way
par´lance
par´lay
par´ley
par´lia-ment
par-lia-men-tar´i-an
par´lia-men´ta-ry
par´lor
par´lor car
par´lous
Par´ma
Par´me-san
Par-nas´sus
Par-nell´
pa-ro´chial
par´o-died
par´o-dist
par´o-dis´tic
par´o-dy
par´o-dy-ing
pa-role´
pa-roled´
pa-rol-ee´
pa-rol´ing
par´o-nym
pa-ron´y-mous
pa-ro´tic
pa-rot´id
par´ous
par´ox-ysm
par´ox-ys´mal
par-quet´
par´que-try
par´ri-ci´dal
par´ri-cide
par´ried
par´rot
par´ry
par´ry-ing
parse
pars´ley
pars´nip
par´son
par´son-age

par-tage´
par-take´
par-tak´en
par-tak´er
part´ed
part´er
par´the-no-gen´e-sis
par´the-no-ge-net´ic
Par´the-non
par´tial
par-tial´i-ty
par´tial-ly
par-ti-bil´i-ty
par-tic´i-pant
par-tic´i-pate
par-tic-i-pa´tion
par-tic´i-pa-tor
par-ti-cip´i-al
par´ti-ci-ple
par´ti—col-ored
par-tic´u-lar
par-tic-u-lar´i-ty
par-tic´u-lar-ize
par-tic´u-lar-ly
par-tic´u-late
par´ties
part´ing
par´ti-san
par´ti-san-ship
par-ti´tion
par-ti´tion-er
par-ti´tion-ing
par´ti-tive
part´ly
part´ner
part´ner-ship
par-took´
par´tridge
part´—time´
par´ty
par´ve-nu
par´vo-line
Pas´a-de´na
pas´chal
pa-sha
pass´able
pass´ably
pas´sage
pas´sage-way

Pas-sa´ic
pass˘book
pas-sé´
passe-men´terie
pas´sen-ger
pass´er
pass´er-by
pas´si-ble
pas´sim
pas-sim´e-ter
pass´ing
pas´sion
pas´sion-ate
pas´sion-ate-ly
pas´sion-less
pas´sive
pas´sive-ly
pas´sive-ness
pas´siv-ism
pas´siv-ist
pas-siv´i-ty
pass´key
Pass˘over
pass´port
pass´word
paste˘board
past´ed
pas-tel´
past´er
pas´tern
Pas-teur´
pas-teur-iza´tion
pas´teur-ize
pas-tille´
pas´time
past´i-ness
past´ing
pas´tor
pas´tor-age
pas´to-ral
pas-to-rale´
pas´to-ral-ism
pas´to-ral-ist
pas´to-ral-ize
pas´tor-ate
pas-to´ri-um
pas´torship
pas-tra´mi
pas´tries

pas´try
pas´try-cook
pas´tur-able
pas´tur-age
pas´ty
pa-ta´gi-um
Pat-a-go´nia
Pa-taps´co
patch´er
patch´ery
patch´i-ness
patch´work
patch´y
pâ-té´ de foie gras´
pa-tel´la
pat´ent
pat-ent-abil´i-ty
pat´ent-able
pat´en-tee´
pat´ent-ly
pat´en-tor
pa´ter
pa-ter´nal
pa-ter´nal-ism
pa-ter´nal-is´tic
pa-ter´nal-ly
pa-ter´ni-ty
Pat´er-son
pa-thet´ic
pa-thet´i-cal-ly
path´find-er
path´less
path-o-ge-nic´i-ty
pa-thog´e-ny
path´o-log´i-cal
pa-thol´o-gist
pa-thol´o-gy
pa-thom´e-ter
pa´thos
pa-tho´sis
path´way
pat´i-ble
pa´tience
pa´tient
pa´tient-ly
pat´i-na
pat-i-na´tion
pat´io
pa´tois

pa´tri-arch
pa´tri-ar´chal
pa´tri-arch-ate
pa´tri-archy
Pa-tri´cia
pa-tri´cian
pa-tri´ci-ate
pat´ri-cid´al
pat´ri-cide
Pat´rick
pat´ri-mo´ni-al
pat´ri-mo-ny
pa´tri-ot
pa´tri-ot´ic
pa´tri-ot´i-cal-ly
pa´tri-ot-ism
pat´ri-pas´si-an
pa-trol´
pa-trolled´
pa-trol´ler
pa-trol´ling
pa-trol´man
pa´tron
pa´tron-age
pa´tron-ess
pat´ro-nite
pa´tron-ize
pa´tron-iz-ing
pat-ro-nym´ic
pat-ro-nym´i-cal-ly
pat´ter
pat´tern
pat´terned
pat´tern-mak-er
Pat´ter-son
pat´ting
pat´ty
pat´u-lous
pau´ci-ty
Pau´li
Pau-li´na
Pau-line´
Paul´ist
paunch´i-ness
paunch´y
pau´per
pau´per-ism
pau´per-ize
paus´al

paus´ing
pave´ment
pav´er
pa-vil´ion
pav´ing
Pav´lov
pawn´bro-ker
pawn´brok-ing
Paw-nee´
pawn-ee´
pawn´er
pawn´shop
Paw-tuck´et
pay´able
pay´day
pay-ee´
pay´er
pay´ing
pay´mas-ter
pay´ment
pay-o´la
pay´roll
Pea´body
peace´able
peace´ably
peace´ful
peace´ful-ly
peace´ful-ness
peace´mak-er
peace of´fer-ing
peace pipe
peace´time
peach´blos´som
peach´blow
peach´y
pea´cock
pea´hen
pea jack´et
peaked
pea´nut
pearl ash
pearl´er
pearl´i-ness
pearl´ite
pearl´y
pear´—shaped
Pear´son
Pea´ry
peas´ant

peas´ant-ry
peat´y
pea´vey
peb´ble
peb´bled
peb´bling
peb´bly
pe-can´
pec´ca-ble
pec-ca-dil´lo
pec-ca-dil´loes
peck´er
peck´ing
pec´tase
pec´tate
pec´ten
pec´tic
pec´tin
pec´tin-ase
pec´ti-nate
pec-tin´ic
pec´to-ral
pec´tous
pec´tus
pec´u-late
pec´u-lat-ing
pec-u-la´tion
pec´u-la-tor
pe-cu´liar
pe-cu´liar´i-ty
pe-cu´liar-ly
pe-cu´li-um
pe-cu´niar´i-ly
pe-cu´niary
ped´a-gog´ic
ped´a-gog´i-cal
ped´a-gogue
ped´a-gogy
ped´al
ped´aled
pe-dal´fer
ped´al-ine
ped´ant
pe-dan´tic
pe-dan´ti-cal-ly
pe-dan´ti-cism
ped´ant-ry
ped´ate
ped´dle

ped´dler
ped´dlery
ped´dling
ped´er-ast
ped´er-as-ty
Pe´der-sen
ped´es-tal
pe-des´tri-an
pe-des´tri-an-ism
pe´di-at´ric
pe-di-a-tri´cian
pe-di-at´rics
ped´i-cel
ped´i-cle
pe-dic´u-lar
pe-dic-u-lo´sis
pe-dic´u-lous
ped´i-cure
ped´i-form
ped´i-gree
ped´i-ment
ped´i-men´tal
ped-i-men-ta´tion
ped´o-cal
pe-dol´o-gy
pe-dom´e-ter
Pe´dro
peel´er
peel´ing
peep´er
peep´hole
peer´age
peer´ess
peer´less
pee´vish
pee´vish-ness
Peg´a-sus
peg´ging
Pei´ping
pei-ram´e-ter
pej´o-ra-tive
Pe´kin-ese´
Pe´king´
pe´koe
pel´age
Pe-la´gian
Pel´ham
pel´i-can
Pe´li-on

pel-la´gra
pel-la´grous
pel´let
pel´let-er
pel´let-ize
pel´li-cle
pel-lic´u-lar
pell´—mell´
pelt´er
pel´try
pel´vic
pel´vis
pe´nal
pe-nal-iza´tion
pe´nal-ize
pe´nal-iz-ing
pen´al-ties
pen´al-ty
pen´ance
pe-na´tes
pench´ant
pen´cil
pen´ciled
pen´cil-ing
pen´cil-ler
pen´dant
pen-de-loque´
pen´dency
pen´dent
pen-den´tive
pend´ing
pen-drag´on
pen´du-lous
pen´du-lum
Pe-nel´o-pe
pe´ne-plain´
pe-ne-pla-na´tion
pen-e-tra-bil´i-ty
pen´e-tra-ble
pen-e-tra´lia
pen-e-tram´e-ter
pen´e-trance
pen´e-trate
pen´e-trat-ing
pen-e-tra´tion
pen´e-tra-tive
pen´e-tra-tor
pen-e-trom´e-ter
pen´guin

pen´hold-er
pen-i-cil´lin
pen-i-cil´lin-ase
pen-i-cil-li-o´sis
pen-i-cil´li-um
pe-nin´su-la
pe-nin´su-lar
pe´nis
pen´i-tence
pen´i-tent
pen-i-ten´tial
pen-i-ten´tia-ry
pen´i-tent-ly
pen´knife
pen´man
pen´man-ship
pen name
pen´nant
pen´nate
pen´nies
pen´ni-less
pen´ning
pen´ni-nite
pen´non
Penn-syl-va´nia
pen´ny
pen´ny-roy´al
pen´ny-weight
pen´ny—wise´
pen´ny-worth
Pc-nob´scot
pe´no-log´i-cal
pe-nol´o-gist
pe-nol´o-gy
pen point
Pen-sa-co´la
pen´sion
pen´sion-ary
pen´sion-er
pen´sive
pen´sive-ly
pen´stock
pen´ta-cle
pen´ta-gon
pen-tag´o-nal
pen-tag´o-nal-ly
pen´ta-he´dral
pen-ta-hy´drite
pen´ta-mer

pen-tam´er-al
pen-tam´er-ous
pen-tam´e-ter
Pen´ta-teuch
pen-tath´lon
Pen´te-cost
pent´house
pen´to-bar´bi-tal
Pen´to-thal
pent´—up´
pe-nu´che
pe´nult
pe-nul´ti-mate
pe-num´bra
pe-nu´ri-ous
pen´ury
pen´writ-ten
Pen-zance´
pe´on
pe´on-age
pe´o-nies
pe´o-ny
peo´ple
peo´pling
Pe-o´ria
pep´per
pep´per-box
pep´per-corn
pep´per-mint
pep´pery
pep´py
pep´sin
pep´sin if´cr-ous
pep´tic
pep´ti-dase
pep´to-nate
pep´tone
pep-to-niz-a´tion
pep´to-nize
per´ad-ven´ture
per-am´bu-late
per-am´bu-lat-ing
per-am-bu-la´tion
per-am´bu-la-tor
per-am´bu-la-to-ry
per an´num
per-bo´rate
Per´bu´nan
per-cale´

per´ca-line
per cap´i-ta
per-ceiv´able
per-ceiv´ably
per-ceive´
per-ceiv´er
per-cent´
per-cent´age
per-cent´ile
per´cept
per-cep-ti-bil´i-ty
per-cep´ti-ble
per-cep´ti-bly
per-cep´tion
per-cep´tive
per-cep´tu-al
per-chance´
perch´er
per´co-late
per-co-la´tion
per´co-la-tor
per cu´ri-am
per-cuss´
per-cus´sion
per-cus´sive
Per´cy
per di´em
per-di´tion
per´e-grine
pe-rei´ra
pe-rei´rine
pe-remp´tive
pe-remp´to-ri-ly
pe-remp´to-ri-ness
pe-remp´to-ry
pe-ren´nial
per´fect
per-fect´er
per-fect´ibil´i-ty
per-fect´ible
per-fec´tion
per-fec´tion-ism
per-fec´tive
per´fect-ly
per-fec´to
per-fec´tor
per-fec´tos
per-fer´vid
per-fid´i-ous

per-fid´i-ous-ly
per-fid´i-ous-ness
per´fi-dy
per´fo-rate
per´fo-rat-ed
per-fo-ra´tion
per´fo-ra-tive
per´fo-ra-tor
per-force´
per-form´
per-form´able
per-form´ance
per-form´er
per´fume
per-fum´er
per-fum´ery
per-func´to-ri-ly
per-func´to-ry
per-fu´sion
per-fu´sive
per´go-la
per-haps´
pe´ri
per´i-clase
Per´i-cles
per´i-gee
per´i-he´lion
per´il
per´iled
per´il-ing
per´il-ous
per´il-ous-ly
pe-rim´e-ter
per´i-met´ric
per´i-met´ri-cal
pe-rim´e-try
pe´ri-od
pe´ri-od´ic
pe-ri-od´i-cal
pe-ri-od´i-cal-ly
pe-ri-o-dic´i-ty
peri-pa-tet´ic
peri-pe-tei´a
pe-rip´e-ty
pe-riph´er-al
pe-riph´er-al-ly
pe-riph´ery
per´i-phrase
pe-riph´ra-sis

per´i-phras´tic
per´i-scope
per´i-scop´ic
per´ish
per´ish-able
pe-ris´sad
peri-to-ni´tis
peri-vis´cer-al
per´i-win-kle
per´jure
per´jur-er
per´jur-ing
per-ju´ri-ous
per´jury
perk´i-ness
Per´kins
perk´y
per´ma-nence
per´ma-nen-cy
per´ma-nent
per´ma-nent-ly
per-man´ga-nate
per-me-abil´i-ty
per´me-able
per´meame-ter
per´me-ance
per´me-ant
per´me-ate
per-me-a´tion
per´me-ative
Per´mi-an
per-mis-si-bil´i-ty
per-mis´si-ble
per-mis´sion
per-mis´sive
per-mit´
per-mit´ted
per-mit-tee´
per-mit´ting
per-mit-tiv´i-ty
per-mut´able
per-mu-ta´tion
per´mu-ta-tor
per-mute´
per-ni´cious
per-nick´e-ty
per-ni-o´sis
Pe-ron´
per´o-ne´al

per´orate´
per-ora´tion
pe-ro´sis
per-ox´i-dase
per-ox´ide
per-ox´y-di-sul´fate
per-pen-dic´u-lar
per´pe-trate
per´pe-tra´tion
per´pe-tra-tor
per-pet´u-al
per-pet´u-al-ly
per-pet´u-ate
per-pet-u-a´tion
per-pet´u-a-tor
per-pe-tu´ity
per-plex´
per-plexed´
per-plexed´ness
per-plex´ing
per-plex´i-ty
per´qui-site
per´ron
per´ry
per´se-cute
per´se-cu´tion
per´se-cu-tor
per´se-cu-to-ry
per-se-ver´ance
per-sev´er-a-tive
per´se-vere´
per´se-ver´ing
Per´shing
Per´sia
per´si-flage
per-sim´mon
per-sist´
per-sist´ence
per-sist´en-cy
per-sist´ent
per-sist´ent-ly
per-sist´er
per-snick´e-ty
per´son
per-so´na
per´son-able
per´son-age
per´son-al
per-son-al´i-ty

per´son-al-ize
per´son-al-ly
per´son-al-ty
per-so´na non gra´ta
per´son-ate
per-son-a´tion
per-son-i-fi-ca´tion
per-son´i-fi-er
per-son´i-fy
per-son´i-fy-ing
per´son-nel´
per-spec´tive
per-spi-ca´cious
per-spi-cac´i-ty
per-spi-cu´ity
per-spic´u-ous
per-spir´able
per-spi-ra´tion
per-spi´ra-tive
per-spir´a-to-ry
per-spire´
per-spir´ing
per-suad´able
per-suade´
per-suad´er
per-suad´ing
per-sua´si-ble
per-sua´sion
per-sua´sive
per-sua´sive-ly
per-tain´
per´ti-na´cious
per´ti-na´cious-ly
per-ti-nac´i-ty
per´ti-nence
per´ti-nen-cy
per´ti-nent
pert´ly
per-turb´
per-turb´able
per-tur-ba´tion
per-turb´ed-ly
per-turb´er
per-tus´sal
per-tus´sis
Pe-ru´
pe-ruke´
pe-rus´able
pe-rus´al

pe-ruse´
pe-rus´er
pe-rus´ing
per-vade´
per-vad´ing
per-va´sion
per-va´sive
per-va´sive-ly
per-verse´
per-verse´ly
per-verse´ness
per-ver´sion
per-ver´sity
per-ver´sive
per-vert´
per-vert´ed
per-vert´er
per-vert´i-ble
per-vi-ca´cious
per-vi-cac´i-ty
per´vi-ous
per´y-lene
pe-se´ta
Pe-sha´war
pes´ky
pe´so
pes´sa-ry
pes´si-mism
pes´si mist
pes-si-mis´tic
pes-si-mis´ti-cal-ly
pes´ter
pes´tered
pest´house
pes´ti-ci´dal
pes-tif´er-ous
pes´ti-lence
pes´ti-lent
pes´ti-len´tial
pes´tle
pes-tol´o-gy
pet´al
pet´aled
pet´al-ism
pet´al-ite
pet´a-lo-dy
pet´al-ous
pet´cock
Pe´ter

pe´tered
Pe´ters-burg
pe-tit´
pe-tite´
pe-ti´tion
pe-ti´tion-ary
pe-ti´tion-er
pe-tits´ fours
Pe´trarch
pe´trel
pe-tres´cent
Pe´tri
pet-ri-fac´tion
pet´ri-fac´tive
pet´ri-fi-ca´tion
pet´ri-fied
pet´ri-fy
pe´tro-chem´i-cal
Pet´ro-grad
pet´rol
pet´ro-lage
pet-ro-la´tum
pet´ro-lene
pe-tro´leum
pe-trol´ic
pet´ro-lif´er-ous
pet´ro-lize
pet´ro-log´ic
pet-ro-log´i-cal
pet-ro-log´i-cal-ly
pe-trol´o-gist
pe-trol´o-gy
pe-tro´sal
pet´rous
pe-trox´o-lin
pet´ti-coat
pet´ti-fog
pet´ti-fog´ger
pet´ti-fog-gery
pet´ti-ly
pet´ti-ness
pet´tish
pet´tish-ness
pet´ty
pet´u-lance
pet´u-lan-cy
pet´u-lant
pe-tu´nia
pe´wit

pew´ter
pew´ter-er
pfef´fer-nuss
pfen´nig
pha-com´e-ter
pha´e-ton
pha´lanx
phal´a-rope
phal´lic
phal´lus
phan-er-os´co-py
phan´tasm
phan-tas-ma-go´ria
phan-tas-ma-gor´ic
phan-tas´ma-gor´i-cal
phan-tas´mal
phan´tom
phan´to-scope
phar´aoh
Phar´i-sa´ic
Phar´i-sa-ism
Phar´i-see
phar´ma-ceu´ti-cal
phar-ma-ceu´tics
phar-ma-ceu´tist
phar´ma-cist
phar-ma-cog´no-sy
phar-mac´o-lite
phar´ma-co-log´i-cal
phar-ma-col´o-gist
phar-ma-col´o-gy
phar-ma-co-pe´ia
phar-ma-co-poe´ia
phar´ma-cy
Pha´ros
pha-ryn´ge-al
phar-yn-gi´tis
pha-ryn´go-log´i-cal
phar-yn-gol´o-gy
pha-ryn´go-scope
phar-yn-gos´co-py
phar-yn-got´o-my
phar´ynx
phase
phase´me-ter
pha-se´o-lin
phas´er
pha´sic
pha´si-tron

pha´sor
pheas´ant
phen´a-cite
phe´no-bar´bi-tal
phe´no-cop´y
phe´nol
phe-no´lic
phe-nol´o-gist
phe-nol´o-gy
phe´nol-phthal´ein
phe-nom´e-na
phe-nom´e-nal
phe-nom´e-nal-ism
phe-nom´e-no-log´i-
  cal
phe-nom-e-nol´o-gy
phe-nom´e-non
phe´no-plast
phe´no-type
phen-ox´ide
phe-nox´y-ace´tic
phen´yl
phi´al
Phi Be´ta Kap´pa
Phil-a-del´phia
phi-lan´der
phi-lan´der-er
phil´an-throp´ic
phi-lan´thro-pist
phi-lan´thro-py
phil´a-tel´ic
phi-lat´e-list
phi-lat´e-ly
phil´har-mon´ic
phil´hel-len´ic
phil´i-a-ter
Phil´ip
Phi-lip´pi-ans
Phil´ippine
Phil´is-tine
Phi´lo
phil-o-den´dron
phil´o-graph
phi-log´y-ny
phil´o-log´i-cal
phi-lol´o-gist
phi-lol´o-gy
phil´o-mel
phil-o-pe´na

phil´o-pro-gen´i-tive
phi-los´o-pher
phil´o-soph´ic
phil´o-soph´i-cal
phil´o-soph´i-cal-ly
phi-los´o-phism
phi-los´o-phize
phi-los´o-phiz-er
phi-los´o-phy
phil´ter
phle-bit´ic
phle-bi´tis
phleb´o-graph´ic
phle-bog´ra-phy
phle-bot´o-my
phlegm
phleg-mat´ic
pho´bia
pho´bic
phoe´be
Phoe´bus
Phoc-ni´cia
Phoe´nix
phon-au´to-graph
pho´ne-mat´ic
pho-net´ic
pho-net´i-cal-ly
pho-ne-ti´cian
pho-net´i-cize
pho´nc-tism
pho´ne-tist
Phone´vi-sion
phon´ic
pho´no-gen´ic
pho´no-gram
pho´no-graph
pho´no-graph´ic
pho-nog´ra-phy
pho´no-lite
pho´no-log´i-cal
pho-nol´o-gist
pho-nol´o-gize
pho-nol´o-gy
pho-nom´e-ter
pho-nom´e-try
pho´no-phore
pho-noph´o-rous
pho´no-typy
pho´ny

pho-re´sis
phor´e-sy
pho-ret´ic
pho-rom´e-ter
pho-rom´e-try
phos´phate
phos´phat´ic
phos´pha-tize
phos´phide
phos´phi-nate
phos´phine
phos´phite
phos´pho-nate
phos´phor
phos´pho-rate
phos-pho´re-al
phos´pho-resce´
phos-pho-res´cence
phos´pho-res´cent
phos´phor´ic
phos´pho-rism
phos-phor´o-gen
phos´pho-ro-gen´ic
phos-pho-rol´y-sis
phos´pho-rous
phos´pho-rus
phos´pho-ryl-ase
pho´tics
pho´to
pho´to-chem´is-try
pho´to-chro-my
pho´to-elec´tric
pho´to-en-grav´ing
pho´to-flash
pho´to-gene
pho´to-gen´ic
pho´to-gram´me-try
pho´to-graph
pho-tog´ra-pher
pho´to-graph´ic
pho-tog´ra-phy
pho´to-gra-vure´
pho´to-ki-ne´sis
pho´to-lith´o-graph
pho´to-li-thog´ra-phy
pho-tol´y-sis
pho´to-lyt´ic
pho-tom´e-ter
pho´to-met´ric

pho-tom´e-try
pho´ton
pho´to-nas´tic
pho-top´a-thy
pho-to-pho-re´sis
pho´to-play
phot-op-tom´e-ter
pho´to-re-cep´tor
pho´to-sen´si-tive
pho´to-stat
pho´to-stat-ed
pho-to-syn´the-sis
pho-tot´o-nus
pho´to-tran-sis´tor
pho´to-troph´ic
pho-to-trop´ic
pho-tot´ro-pism
pho´to-typy
Pho-tron´ic
phras´able
phras´al
phrase
phra´se-o-gram
phra-se-og´ra-phy
phra-se-ol´o-gy
phrase-er
phras´ing
phre-net´ic
phren´ic
phren-i-cot´o-my
phre-ni´tis
phren-o-log´i-cal
phre-nol´o gist
phre-nol´o-gy
phren´o-sin
Phryg´i-an
phyl´lo-por´phy-rin
phy´lo-ge-net´ic
phy-log´e-ny
phy´lum
phys-i-at´rics
phys´ic
phys´i-cal
phys´i-cal-ly
phy-si´cian
phys´i-cist
phys´icked
phys´ick-ing
phys´ics

phys-i-og´no-my
phys-i-og´ra-pher
phys´io-graph´ic
phys-i-og´ra-phy
phys-i-ol´a-ter
phys´i-o-log´i-cal
phys-i-ol´o-gist
phys-i-ol´o-gy
phys-l-om´e-try
phys-i-os´o-phy
phys´io-ther´a-py
phy-sique´
pi´a-nis´si-mo
pi-an´ist
pi-a-niste´
pi-a-nis´tic
pi-an´o
pi-an´o-forte
pi-an´os
pi-as-sa´va
pi-as´ter
pi-az´za
pi´ca
pic´a-dor
Pic´ar-dy
pic´a-resque´
pic´a-roon´
Pi-cas´so
pic-a-yune´
Pic´ca-dil´ly
pic´ca-lil´li
pic´co-lo
pic´co-lo-ist
pic´e-in
pi´cene
pic´e-ous
pick´a-back
pick´a-nin-ny
pick´ax
pick´er
pick´er-el
pick´et
pick´et-er
pick´et-ing
Pick´ett
pick´ing
pick´le
pick´led
pick´ling

pick´lock
pick´pock-et
pick´up
Pick´wick
pic´nic
pic´nicked
pic´nick-er
pic´nick-ing
pic´to-graph
pic´to-graph´ic
pic-to-graph´i-cal-ly
pic-tog´ra-phy
pic-to´ri-al
pic´tur-able
pic´ture
pic-tur-esque´
pic´tur-esque´ness
pic´tur-ing
pid´dle
pid´dler
pid´dling
pid´gin
pie´bald
pieced
pièce de ré´sis-tance´
piece goods
piece´meal
piec´er
piece rate
piece´work
pie chart
piec´ing
pie´crust
Pied´mont
pie´man
pie´plant
pierced
pierc´er
pierc´ing
pier´head
Pi-e´ri-an
pi-er´i-dine
Pier´rot
pi´etism
pi-etis´tic
pi´e-ty
pif´fle
pi´geon
pi´geon-eer´

pi´geon-hole
pi´geon—toed
pi´geon-wing
pig´fish
pig´gery
pig-gish
pig´head-ed
pig iron
pig´ment
pig´men-tary
pig-men-ta´tion
pi´gnon
pig´nut
pig´pen
pig´skin
pig´stick-ing
pig´sty
pig´tail
pig´weed
pike´man
pike perch
pik´er
pike´staff
pi-laf´
pi-las´ter
Pi´late
pil´chard
pi´le-ate
pi´le-at-ed
pi-le´o-lus
pi´le-ous
pil´er
pil´fer
pil´fer-age
pil´grim
pil´grim-age
pi-lif´er-ous
pil´ing
pil´lage
pil´lag-er
pil´lar
pil´lared
pill´box
pil´lion
pil´lo-ried
pil´lor-ize
pil´lo-ry
pil´low
pil´low-case

pil´low-slip
pil´lowy
pi´lot
pi´lot-age
pi´lot-house
Pil´sner
pil´u-lar
pi-men´to
pi-mien´to
pim´per-nel
pim´ple
pim´pled
pim´ply
pi´na
pi-na´ceous
pin´a-coid
pin´a-coi´dal
pin´a-col
pi-nac´o-late
pi-nac´o-lone
pin´a-fore
pi´nane
pi-nas´ter
pin´ball
pince´—nez´
pin´cers
pinch´beck
pinch´er
pinch´—hit
pin´cushion
Pin´dar
Pin-dar´ic
pin´e-al
pine´ap-ple
Pi-ne´ro
pin´ery
pi-ne´tum
pi´ney
pin´feath-er
pin´fold
Ping´—Pong
pin´head
pin´hole
pin´ion
pink´er
pink´eye
pink´ish
pink´root
pin´ky

pin mon-ey
pin´na
pin´nace
pin´na-cle
pin´mate
pin´ning
pi-no-cam´phe-ol
pi´noch-le
pin´point
pin´tle
pin´to
pin´up
pin´weed
pin´wheel
pin´worm
pin´y
pi´nyl
pi´o-neer´
pi´o-neered´
pi-os´i-ty
pi´ous
pi´ous-ly
pip´age
pipe dream
pipe´ful
pipe´line
pipe or´gan
pip´er
piper´a-zine
pi-per´ic
pi-per´i-dine
pip´er-ine
pipe´stem
pipe´stone
pip´ing
pip´kin
pip´pin
pi´quan-cy
pi´quant
pi-qué´
pique
piqued
pi-quet´
piqu´ing
pi´ra-cy
Pi-rae´us
pi-ra´nha
pi´rate
pi-rat´i-cal

pi´rogue
pir´ou-ette´
pir´ou-ett´ed
pir´ou-ett´ing
Pi´sa
Pis´ces
pis´mire
pis-tach´io
pis´til
pis´til-late
pis´tol
pis´ton
pitch´blende
pitch´er
pitch´fork
pitch´ing
pitch´stone
pitch´y
pit´e-ous
pit´e-ous-ly
pit´fall
pith´i-ly
pith´i-ness
pith´y
pit´i-able
pit´ied
pit´i-er
pit´ies
pit´i-ful
pit´i-ful-ly
pit´i-less
pit´man
pit saw
pit´tance
pit´ted
pit´ter—pat´ter
pit´ting
Pitts´burg
Pitts´burgh
pi-tu´i-tary
pi-tu´i-tous
pit´y
pit´y-ing
Pi´us
pi-val´ic
piv´ot
piv´ot-al
piv´ot-er
pix´ie

pix´i-lat-ed
pix´y
Pi-zar´ro
piz-ze-ri´a
piz´zi-ca´to
placa-bil´i-ty
plac´a-ble
plac´ard
pla´cate
pla´cat-er
pla´cat-ing
pla-ca´tion
pla´ca-tive
pla´ca-to-ry
place´able
pla-ce´bo
place´—kick
place´ment
pla-cen´ta
plac´en-tary
pla-cen´tate
plac-en-ta´tion
plac-en-ti´tis
plac´er
pla´cet
plac´id
pla-cid´i-ty
plac´id-ly
plac´ing
plack´et
plac´oid
pla´gia-rism
pla´gia-rist
pla´gia-ris´tic
pla´gia-rize
pla´gia-riz-ing
pla´gia-ry
plague
plagu´ed
plagu´ing
pla´guy
plaid
plain´—laid´
plain´ly
plain´ness
plains´man
plain´tiff
plain´tive
plain´tive-ly

plait
plait´er
pla´nar
pla-nar´ia
pla-nar´i-an
pla-nar´i-ty
pla-na´tion
plan´chet
plan-chette´
plan´er
plan´et
plan-e-tar´i-um
plan´e-tary
plan-e-tes´i-mal
plan´et-oid
plan´et-oi´dal
plan-et-o-log´ic
plan-et-ol´o-gy
plan´gen-cy
plan´gent
plank´ing
plank´—sheer
plank´ton
planned
plan´ner
plan´ning
plan´o-graph
pla-nog´ra-phy
pla-nom´e-ter
plan´o-sol
plan´tain
plan-ta´tion
plant´er
plan´ti-grade
plant´ing
plant louse
pla´num
plaque
pla-quette´
plash´y
plas´ma
plas´mic
plas-min´o-gen
plas-mo-di´a-sis
plas-mo´di-um
plas´ter
plas´tered
plas´ter-er
plas´ter-ing

plas´ter-work
plas´tic
plas´ti-ca-tor
plas-ti-cim´e-ter
plas-tic´i-ty
plas´ti-cize
plas´ti-ciz-er
pla-teau´
plat´ed
plate´ful
plate glass
plat´en
plat´er
plat´form
pla-ti´na
plat´ing
plat´i-nize
plat´i-num
plat´i-tude
plat-i-tu´di-nize
plat´i-tu´di-nous
Pla´to
pla-ton´ic
pla-toon´
plat´ter
plat´y-pus
plau´dit
plau-si-bil´i-ty
plau´si-ble
plau´sive
play´able
play´back
play´bill
play´boy
play´er
play´fel-low
play´ful
play´ful-ly
play´ful-ness
play´go-er
play´ground
play´house
play´ing card
play´mate
play´—off
play´room
play´script
play´thing
play´time

play´wright
plaz´a
plea
plead´able
plead´er
plead´ing
plead´ing-ly
pleas´ance
pleas´ant
pleas´ant-ly
pleas´ant-ness
pleas´ant-ry
pleas´ing
plea´sur-able
plea´sure
pleat
pleat´ed
pleat´er
plebe
ple-be´ian
pleb´i-scite
pledged
pledg-ee´
pledg´er
pled´get
pledg´ing
pled´gor
ple´nar-ty
ple´na-ry
plen´i-po-ten´tia-ry
plen´i-tude
plen´te-ous
plen´ti-ful
plen´ti-ful-ly
plen´ty
pleth´o-ra
pleth´o-ric
pleu´ra
pleu´ral
pleu´ri-sy
pleu-rit´ic
Plex´i-glas
plex-im´e-ter
plex´us
pli-a-bil´i-ty
pli´a-ble
pli´an-cy
pli´ant
pli´cate

pli-ca´tion
plied
pli´ers
plight
plinth
plod´ded
plod´der
plod´ding
plot´less
plot´ter
plot´ting
plov´er
plow
plow´boy
plow´er
plow´—hand
plow´ing
plow´man
plow´share
pluck´er
pluck´i-er
pluck´y
plug´board
plug´ging
plug´—ug-ly
plum
plu´mage
plu´mate
plumb
plum-ba´gin
plum-ba´go
plum´bate
plumb bob
plumb´er
plum´bif´er-ous
plumb´ing
plumb´ite
plumb line
plumb´ous
plum´ing
plum´met
plump´er
plump´ness
plu´mule
plum´y
plun´der
plun´der-er
plun´der-ous
plung´er

plung´ing
plu-per´fect
plu´ral
plu´ral-ism
plu-ral´i-ty
plu´ral-ize
plu´ral-ly
plu´ri-va´lent
plush´y
Plu´tarch
plu´tar-chy
Plu´to
plu-toc´ra-cy
plu´to-crat
plu´to-crat´ic
plu-to´ni-an
plu-ton´ic
plu´to-nism
plu-to´ni-um
plu´vi-al
plu´vi-ous
ply´ing
Plym´outh
ply´wood
pneu-drau´lic
pneu-mat´ic
pneu-mat´i-cal-ly
pneu-ma-tic´i-ty
pneu-ma-tol´o-gy
pneu-ma-tol´y-sis
pneu-ma-tom´e-ter
pneu-ma-to´sis
pneu-mec´to-my
pneu-mo-coc´cus
pneu-mol´o-gy
pneu-mo´nia
pneu-mon´ic
pneu-mo-ni´tis
poach´er
Po-ca-hon´tas
pock´et
pock´et-book
pock´et-ful
pock´et-knife
pock´mark
pod´ding
po´de-sta´
podg´i-ness
podg´y

po-di´a-trist
po-di´a-try
po´di-um
po´do-lite
po´em
po´e-sy
po´et
po´et-as-ter
po´et-ess
po-et´ic
po-et´i-cal
po-et´i-cal-ly
po-et´ics
po´et-ize
po´et-ry
po-grom´
poi´gnan-cy
poi´gnant
poin-ci-an´a
poin-set´tia
point´—blank´
point´—de-vice´
point´ed
point´ed-ly
point´er
poin´til-lism
point´less
Poi-ret´
poised
pois´er
pois´ing
poi´son
poi´son-er
poi´son i´vy
poi´son-ous
Poi-tiers´
pok´er
pok´ing
pok´y
Po´land
po´lar
po-lar-im´e-ter
po-lar´i-met´ric
Po-lar´is
po-lar´i-scope
po-lar´i-ty
po-lar-iza´tion
po´lar-ize
po´lar-iz-er

po´lar-iz-ing
po-lar´o-graph´ic
po-lar-og´ra-phy
Po´lar-oid
po´lar-on
pol´der
pole´ax
pole´cat
po-lem´i-cal
po-lem´i-cal-ly
po-lem´i-cist
pol´e-mize
po-len´ta
pol´er
pole´star
pole´—vault
po´li-a-nite
po-lice´
po-lice´man
pol´i-cies
po-lic´ing
pol´i-clin´ic
pol´i-cy
pol´i-cy-hold-er
Po´lio
po´lio-my-e-li´tis
po-li-o´sis
pol´ish
Pol´ish
pol´ish-er
pol´it-bu-ro
po-lite´
po-lite´ly
po-lite´ness
pol´i-tic
po-lit´i-cal
po-lit´i-cal-ly
pol-i-ti´cian
po-lit´i-cize
pol´i-tic-ly
pol´i-tics
pol´i-ty
Po-litz´er
pol´ka
pol´ka—dot
pol´kaed
pol´lack
pol´lard
pol´len

pol´len-izc
pol´len-iz-er
poll´er
pol´li-nate
pol´li-nat-ing
po´li-na´tion
pol´li-nif´er-ous
pol-lin´i-um
pol-li-no´sis
pol´li-wog
poll´ster
poll tax
pol-lu´cite
pol-lu´tant
pol-lute´
pol-lut´er
pol-lut´ing
pol-lu´tion
Pol´lux
po´lo
po´lo-ist
pol´o-naise´
pol´y-acryl´ic
pol´y-am´ide
pol´y-an´drous
pol´y-an-dry
poly-an´thus
poly-ar´gy-rite
poly-ba´sic
poly-ba´site
pol´y-chro-ism
poly-chro-mat´ic
pol´y-chrome
pol´y-chro-my
pol´y-clin´ic
pol´y-crase
poly-cy-the´mia
po-lyd´y-mite
pol´y-ene
pol´y-es-ter
poly-eth´yl-ene
po-lyg´a-la
pol´y-gam´ic
po-lyg´a-mist
po-lyg´a-mous
po-lyg´a-my
po-lyg´e-ny
pol´y-glot
pol´y-gon

po-lyg´o-nal
pol´y-graph
pol´y-graph´ic
po-lyg´ra-phy
po-lyg´y-ny
pol´y-he´dral
pol´y-he´dron
pol´y-hi-dro´sis
pol´y-i´so-bu´tyl-ene
pol´y-i´so-top´ic
pol´y-kar´y-on
pol´y-math
po-lym´a-thy
pol´y-mer
pol´y-mer´ic
po-lym´er-ism
po-lym-er-i-za´tion
po-lym´er-ize
po-lym´er-iz-er
po-lym´er-ous
pol´y-me-ter
pol´ym-nite
pol´y-mor´phic
pol´y-mor´phism
pol´y-mor´phous
Pol´y-ne´sia
Pol´y-ne´sian
pol´y-no´mi-al
poly-nu-cle-o´sis
pol´yp
pol´yp-ec´to-my
poly-pep´tide
poly-pha´gia
po-lyph´a-gous
pol´y-phase
Pol´y-phe´mus
pol´y-ploid
pol´y-ploi-dy
pol´yp-tych
pol´y-se´mous
poly-sty´rene
pol´y-syl-lab´ic
pol´y-syl´la-ble
pol´y-tech´nic
pol´y-tech´ni-cal
pol´y-the-ism
pol´y-the-ist
pol´y-the-is´tic
poly-ton´al-ism

pol´y-to-nal´i-ty
pol´y-trop´ic
poly-u´re-thane
poly-va´lent
poly-vi´nyl
pom´ace
po-ma´ceous
po-made´
po-ma´tum
pome´gran-ate
Pom-er-a´nia
pom´mel
pom´meled
pom´pa-dour
pom´pa-no
Pom-peii´
Pom´pey
pom´—pom
pom´pon
pom-pos´i-ty
pomp´ous
Pon´ce
Pon´ce de Le-ón´
pon´cho
pon´chos
pond´age
pon´der
pon´der-abil´i-ty
pon´der-able
pon-der-o´sa
pon-der-os´i-ty
pon´der-ous
po´nies
pon´tage
Pon´ti-ac
pon´tiff
pon-tif´i-cal
pon-tif´i-cate
pon-tif´i-ca-tor
pon´tine
Pon´tius
pon-toon´
po´ny
poo´dle
pool´room
poor farm
poor´house
poor´ly
poor´ness

pop´corn
pope´dom
pop´e-line´
pop´ery
pop´gun
pop´in-jay
pop´ish
pop´lar
pop´lin
pop-lit´e-al
Po-po-ca-te´petl
pop´over
pop´per
pop´pies
pop´ping
pop´py
pop´py-cock
pop´u-lace
pop´u-lar
pop-u-lar´i-ty
pop-u-lar-iza´tion
pop´u-lar-ize
pop´u-lar-ly
pop´u-late
pop-u-la´tion
pop´u-list
pop´u-lous
pop´u-lous-ness
por´ce-lain
por´cine
por´cu-pine
pore
por´gy
po-rif´er-ous
pork´er
pork´y
por-nog´ra-pher
por-no-graph´ic
por-nog´ra-phy
po-rom´e-ter
po´ro-scope
po-ros´co-py
po´rose
po-ros´i-ty
po-rot´ic
po´rous
por´phin
por´phy-rit´ic
por´phyr-ox´ine

por´poise
por´ridge
por-ta-bil´i-ty
por´ta-ble
por´tage
por´tal
Port—au—Prince
por-tend´
por´tent
por-ten´tous
por´ter
por´ter-age
por´ter-house
port-fo´lio
port´hole
Por´tia
por´ti-co
por´ti-coes
por´tion
Port´land
port´li-er
port´li-ness
port´ly
por´trait
por´trai-ture
por-tray´
por-tray´al
por´tress
Ports´mouth
Por´tu-gal
Por´tu-guese´
por-tu-lac´a
posed
Po-sei´don
pos´er
pos´ing
pos´it
po-si´tion
po-si´tion-er
pos´i-ti´val
pos´i-tive
pos´i-tive-ly
pos´i-tiv-ism
pos´i-tiv-is´tic
pos-i-tri´no
pos´i-tron
pos-i-tro´ni-um
po-sol´o-gy
pos´se

pos-sess´
pos-sessed´
pos-sess´es
pos-ses´sion
pos-ses´sive
pos-ses´sive-ly
pos-ses´sive-ness
pos-ses´sor
pos-ses´so-ry
pos´set
pos-si-bil´i-ty
pos´si-ble
pos´si-bly
pos´sum
post´age
post´al
post-ax´i-al
post´boy
post´card
post´date´
post´er
pos-te´ri-or
pos-ter´i-ty
pos´tern
post-gla´cial
post-grad´u-ate
post´haste´
post´hu-mous
post´hu-mous-ly
post-hyp-not´ic
post´man
post´mark
post´mas-ter
post-me-rid´i-an
post-mil-len´ni-al
post´mis-tress
post´—mor´tem
post of fire
post-or´bit-al
post´paid´
post-pone´
post-pone´ment
post-pran´di-al
post´script
pos´tu-lant
pos´tu-late
pos´tu-lat-ing
pos-tu-la´tion
pos´tu-la-tor

pos´tur-al
pos´ture
pos´tur-ing
post´war´
pos´y
po-ta-bil´i-ty
po´ta-ble
po-tage´
po-tam´ic
pot´ash
po-tas´si-um
po-ta´tion
po-ta´to
po-ta´toes
Pot-a-wat´o-mi
pot´bel-lied
pot´bel-ly
pot´boil-er
pot´boy
Po-tem´kin
po´ten-cy
po´tent
po´ten-tate
po-ten´tial
po-ten-ti-al´i-ty
po-ten´tial-ly
po´tent-ly
poth´er
pot´hole
pot´hook
pot´house
po-tion
pot´luck´
Po-to´mac
pot´pie
pot´pour-ri´
Pots´dam
pot´shot
pot´tage
pot´ted
pot´ter
pot´ter-ies
pot´tery
pot´tle
Pough-keep´sie
poul´ter-er
poul´tice
poul´try
pounc´er

pounc´ing
pound´age
pound´al
pound cake
pound´er
pound´—fool´ish
pour
poured
pour´er
pour´ing
pout´er
pout´ing
pout´ing-ly
pout´y
pov´er-ty
pov´er-ty—strick´en
pow´der
pow´dered
pow´dery
pow´er
pow´ered
pow´er-ful
pow´er-ful-ly
pow´er-house
pow´cr-less
Pow´ha-tan´
pow´wow
prac-ti-ca-bil´i-ty
prac´ti-ca-ble
prac´ti-cal
prac-ti-cal´i-ty
prac´ti-cal-ly
prac´ti-cal-ness
prac´tice
prac´ticed
prac´tic-er
prac´tic-ing
prac-ti´tion-er
prae´ci-pe
prae´di-al
prae-mu-ni´re
prae´tor
prag-mat´ic
prag-mat´i-cal-ly
prag´ma-tism
prag´ma-tist
Prague
prai´rie
prais´er

praise´wor-thy
prais´ing
pra´line
pranced
pranc´er
pranc´ing
prank´ish
prank´ster
prase
prat´er
prat´ing
pra-tique´
prat´tle
prat´tler
prax-e-ol´o-gy
Prax-it´e-les
prayed
prayer
prayer book
prayer´ful
preachcd
preach´er
preach´ing
preach´ment
preach´y
pre´am-ble
pre´ar-range´
pre-ar-range´ment
pre-ax´i-al
pre-car´i-ous
pre-car´i-ous-ness
prec´a-to-ry
pre-cau´tion
prc-cau´tion-ary
pre-cau´tious
pre-ced´able
pre-cede´
prec´e-dence
prec´e-den-cy
prec´e-dent
prec-e-den´tial
pre-ced´ing
pre-cen´tor
pre´cept
pre-cep´tive
pre-cep´tor
pre-cep-to´ri-al
pre-cep´to-ry
pre-cep´tress

pre-ces´sion
pre-ces´sion-al
pre´cinct
pre-ci-os´i-ty
pre´cious
prec´i-pice
pre-cip´i-tance
pre-cip´i-tan-cy
pre-cip´i-tant
pre-cip´i-tate
pre-cip´i-tate-ly
pre-cip´i-tate-ness
pre-cip-i-ta´tion
pre-cip´i-ta-tive
pre-cip´i-ta-tor
pre-cip´i-tin
pre-cip-i-tin´o-gen
pre-cip´i-tous
pre-cip´i-tous-ly
pré-cis´
pre-cise´
pre-cise´ly
pre-cise´ness
pre-ci´sian
pré-ci´sion
pre-ci´sive
pre-clin´i-cal
pre-clude´
pre-clud´ing
pre-clu´sion
pre-clu´sive
pre-co´cious
prc-coc´i-ty
pre´con-ceive´
pre´con-ceiv´ing
pre-con-cep´tion
pre-con-cert´
pre-con-cert´ed
prec´o-nize
pre-cor´di-um
pre-cur´sive
pre-cur´sor
pre-cur´so-ry
pre-da´cious
pre-dac´i-ty
pre-da´tion
pred´a-tor
pred´a-to´ri-ly
pred´a-to-ry

pre-de-cease´
pred´e-ces-sor
pre-den´ta-ry
pre´des-ti-nar´i-an
pre-des´ti-nate
pre-des-ti-na´tion
pre-des´tine
pre-de-ter´mi-nate
pre-de-ter-mi-na´tion
pre-de-ter´mine
pre-de-ter´min-ing
pred-i-ca-bil´i-ty
pred´i-ca-ble
pre-dic´a-ment
pred´i-cant
pred´i-cate
pred´i-cat-ing
pred-i-ca´tion
pred´i-ca-tive
pred´i-ca-to-ry
pre-dict´
pre-dict´able
pre-dic´tion
pre-dic´tive
pre-dic´tor
pre´di-gest´
pred´i-lec´tion
pre´dis-pose´
pre-dis-pos´ing
pre-dis-po-si´tion
pred-nis´o-lone
pre-dom´i-nance
pre-dom´i-nant
pre-dom´i-nate
pre-dom-i-na´tion
pre-em´i-nence
pre-em´i-nent
pre-em´i-nent-ly
pre-empt´
pre-emp´tion
pre-emp´tive
pre-emp´tor
pre-emp´to-ry
preened
pre´ex-ist´
pre-ex-is´tent
pre-fab´ri-cate
pre-fab´ri-ca-tor
pref´ace

pref´ac-ing
pref´a-to´ri-ly
pref´a-to-ry
pre´fect
pre-fec-to´ri-al
pre-fec-ture
pre-fer´
pref´er-a-bil´i-ty
pref´er-a-ble
pref´er-a-bly
pref´er-ence
pref´er-en´tial
pre-fer´ment
pre-ferred´
pre-fer´ring
pre-fig-u-ra´tion
pre-fig´u-ra-tive
pre-fig´ure
pre´fix
pre-for-ma´tion
pre-fron´tal
preg-na-bil´i-ty
preg´na-ble
preg´nan-cy
preg´nant
pre-hen´si-ble
pre-hen´sile
pre-hen-sil´i-ty
pre-hen´sion
pre´his-tor´ic
pre´his-tor´i-cal-ly
pre´judge´
pre-judg´ment
prej´u-dice
prej´u-di´cial
pre´—ju-di´cial
prel´ate
pre-lim´i-nary
prel´ude
pre-lu´di-al
pre´ma-ture´
pre´ma-ture´ly
pre-ma-tur´i-ty
pre-med´i-cal
pre-med´i-tate
pre-med-i-ta´tion
pre-med´i-ta-tive
pre-med´i-ta-tor
pre-mier´

pre-miere´
pre-mier´ship
pre´mil-le-nar´i-an
pre-mil-len´i-al-ism
prem´ise
pre´mi-um
pre´mo´lar
pre-mon´ish
pre-mo-ni´tion
pre-mon´i-to-ry
pre-na´tal
pren´tice
pre-oc´cu-pan-cy
pre-oc-cu-pa´tion
pre-oc´cu-pied
pre-oc´cu-py
pre-or-dain´
pre-or-di-na´tion
pre-paid´
prep-a-ra´tion
pre-par´a-tive
pre-par´a-to-ry
pre-pare´
pre-pared´
pre-par´ed-ness
pre-par´er
pre-pay´
pre-pay´ment
pre-pon´der-ance
pre-pon´der-ant
pre-pon´der-ate
pre-pon´der-at-ing
pre-pose´
prep-o-si´tion
prep-o-si´tion-al
pre-pos-sess´
pre-pos-sess´ing
pre-pos-ses´sion
pre-pos´ter-ous
pre-pos´ter-ous-ly
pre-po´ten-cy
pre-po´tent
pre´puce
pre-req´ui-site
pre-rog´a-tive
pres´age
pres´age-ful
pres´by-ter
pres-byt´er-ate

pres-by-te´ri-al
Pres-by-te´ri-an
pre´school´
pre´science
pre-scind´
pre-scis´sion
Pres´cott
pre-scribe´
pre-scrib´er
pre-scrib´ing
pre´script
pre-scrip´ti-ble
pre-scrip´tion
pre-scrip´tive
pres´ence
pres´ent
pre-sent´able
pre-sen-ta´tion
pre-sen´ta-tive
pres´ent—day´
pres´en-tee´
pre-sent´er
pre-sen´ti-ment
pres´en-tist
pres´ent-ly
pre-sent´ment
pre-serv´able
pres-er-va´tion
pre-serv´a-tive
pre-serve´
pre-serv´er
pre-side´
pres´i-den-cy
pres´i-dent
pres´i-dent—elect´
pres´i-den´tial
pre-sid´er
pre-sid´i-al
pre-sid´ing
pre-sid´io
pre-sid´i-um
press agent
press´board
press´er
press´—gang
press´ing
press´man
press´mark
pres´sor

press´room
pres´sure
pres´sur-ize
press´work
pres-ti-dig-i-ta´tion
pres-ti-dig´i-ta-tor
pres-tige´
pres-tig´i-ous
pres´to
Pres´ton
Pres´tone
pre-sum´able
pre-sum´ably
pre-sume´
pre-sumed´
pre-sum´er
pre-sump´tion
pre-sump´tive
pre-sump´tu-ous
pre-sup-pose´
pre-sup-po-si´tion
pre-tend´
pre-tend´ed
pre-tend´er
pre-tense´
pre-ten´sion
pre-ten´tious
pre-ten´tious-ness
pret´er-ist
pret´er-it
pre-ter´i-tal
pret-er-i´tion
pre-ter´i-tive
pre-ter-mit´
pre´ter-nat´u-ral
pre´text
Pre-to´ria
pret´ti-fied
pret´ti-fy
pret´ti-ly
pret´ti-ness
pret´ty
pre-typ´i-fy
pret´zel
pre-vail´
pre-vail´ing
prev´a-lence
prev´a-lent
pre-var´i-cate

pre-var-i-ca´tion
pre-var´i-ca-tor
pré-ve-nance´
pre-ven´ience
pre-ven´ient
pre-vent´
pre-vent´able
pre-vent´ative
pre-vent´er
pre-ven´tion
pre-ven´tive
pre´view
pre´vi-ous
pre´vi-ous-ly
pre-vi´sion
pre-war´
prey
Pri´am
pri´a-pism
Pri-a´pus
Prib´i-lov
price´less
pric´er
pric´ing
prick´er
prick´ing
prick´le
prick´ling
prick´ly
pride´ful
prid´ing
priest´craft
priest´ess
priest´hood
Priest´ley
priest´ly
pri´ma-cy
pri´ma don´na
pri´ma fa´cie
pri´mage
pri´mal
pri´ma-quine
pri-mar´i-ly
pri´mary
pri´mate
pri-ma´tial
pri-ma-tol´o-gy
pri´ma-ve´ral
prime´ly

prime´ness
prim´er
pri-me´val
prim´ing
prim´i-tive
prim´i-tiv-ism
prim´ness
pri-mo-gen´i-tary
pri-mo-gen´i-tor
pri´mo-gen´i-ture
pri´mor´di-al
prim´rose
prim´u-line
pri´mus
prince´dom
prince´li-ness
prince-ly
prin´ceps
prin´cess
Prince´ton
prin´ci-pal
prin-ci-pal´i-ty
prin´ci-pal-ly
prin´ci-pal-ship
prin´ci-pate
prin´ci-ple
print´able
print´er
print´ery
print´ing
print´less
pri´on
pri´or
pri´or-ate
pri´or-ess
pri-or´i-ty
pri´or-ship
pri´o-ry
Pris-cil´la
prism
pris-mat´ic
pri-som´e-ter
pris´on
pris´on-er
pris´sy
pris´tine
pri´va-cy
pri´vate
pri´va-teer´

pri´va-teers´man
pri´vate-ly
pri´vate-ness
pri-va´tion
priv´a-tive
pri´vat-ize
priv´et
priv´i-lege
priv´i-leged
priv´i-ly
priv´i-ty
priv´y
priz´able
prize´fight
prize ring
priz´ing
prob´a-bi-lism
prob-a-bil´i-ty
prob´a-ble
prob´a-bly
pro´bate
pro´bat-ing
pro-ba´tion
pro-ba´tion-al
pro-ba´tion-ary
pro-ba´tion-er
pro´ba-tive
pro´ba-to-ry
prob´ing
pro´bi-ty
prob´lem
prob´lem-at´ic
prob´lem-at´i-cal
prob´lem-at´i-cal-ly
prob´o-la
pro-bos´cis
pro-bos´cis-es
pro´caine
pro´ca-the´dral
pro-ce´dur-al
pro-ce´dure
pro-ceed´
pro-ceed´ing
pro-ce-phal´ic
proc´ess
proc´ess-ing
pro-ces´sion
pro-ces´sion-al
pro-ces´sion-ary

proc´es-sor
pro-claim´
proc-la-ma´tion
pro-clam´a-to-ry
pro-clit´ic
pro-cliv´i-ty
pro-cli´vous
pro-con´sul
pro-con´sul-ate
pro-cras´ti-nate
pro-cras´ti-na´tion
pro-cras´ti-na-tor
pro´cre-ant
pro´cre-ate
pro´cre-a´tion
pro´cre-ative
pro´cre-a-tor
pro-crus´te-an
proc-ti´tis
proc-tol´o-gy
proc´tor
proc-to´ri-al
proc´tor-ship
proc´to-scop´ic
proc-tos´co-py
pro-cum´bent
pro-cur´able
proc´u-ra-cy
proc-u-ra´tion
proc´u-ra-tor
proc´u-ra-to-ry
pro-cure´
pro-cured´
pro-cure´ment
pro-cur´er
pro-cur´ess
pro-cur´ing
prod´ding
prod´i-gal
pro-dig-i-o´sin
pro-di´gious
prod´i-gy
pro-duce´
pro-duc´er
pro-duc´ible
pro-duc´ing
prod´uct
pro-duct-ibil´i-ty
pro-duc´tion

pro-duc´tive
pro-duc´tive-ness
pro-duc-tiv´i-ty
pro´em
prof-a-na´tion
pro-fan´a-to-ry
pro-fane´
pro-fane´ly
pro-fan´er
pro-fan´ing
pro-fan´i-ty
pro´fert
pro-fess´
pro-fess´ant
pro-fessed´
pro-fess´ed-ly
pro-fes´sion
pro-fes´sion-al
pro-fes´sion-al-ism
pro-fes´sion-al-ly
pro-fes´sor
pro´fes-so´ri-al
pro´fes-so´ri-at
pro-fes´sor-ship
prof´fer
prof´fered
pro-fi´cien-cy
pro-fi´cient
pro´file
prof´it
prof´it-able
prof´it-ably
prof´i-teer´
prof´it-er
prof´it-less
prof´li-ga-cy
prof´li-gate
prof´lu-ence
prof´lu-ent
pro-found´
pro-found´ly
pro-fun´di-ty
pro-fuse´
pro-fuse´ly
pro-fu´sion
pro-fu´sive
pro-gen´i-tor
pro-gen´i-to´ri-al
pro-gen´i-ture

prog´e-ny
pro-ges´ter-one
prog´na-thous
prog-no´sis
prog-nos´tic
prog-nos´ti-cate
prog-nos-ti-ca´tion
prog-nos´ti-ca-tor
pro´gram
pro´gramed
pro´gram-mat´ic
pro´gram-mer
pro´gram-ming
prog´ress
pro-gres´sion
pro-gres´sion-al
pro-gres´sion-ist
prog´ress-ist
pro-gres´sive
pro-gres´sive-ly
pro-gres´siv-ism
pro-hib´it
pro-hib´it-er
pro-hi-bi´tion
pro-hi-bi´tion-ist
pro-hib´i-tive
pro-hib´i-to-ry
proj´ect
pro-ject´ed
pro-jec´tile
pro-jec´tion
pro-jec´tive
pro-jec´tor
pro-lapse´
pro-late´
pro-la´tive
pro-le-tar´i-an
pro-le-tar´i-an-ism
pro-le-tar´i-at
pro-lif´er-ate
pro-lif´er-a-tive
pro-lif´er-ous
pro-lif´ic
pro-lif´i-ca-cy
pro-lif´i-cal-ly
pro-lif-i-ca´tion
pro-li-fic´i-ty
pro-lig´er-ous
pro´line

pro-lix´
pro-lix´i-ty
pro-loc´u-tor
pro´log
pro´log-ize
pro´rogue
pro-long´
pro-lon´gate
pro-lon-ga´tion
pro-longed´
pro-lu´sion
pro-lu´so-ry
pro´ma-zine
prom´e-nade´
prom´e-nad´er
prom´i-nence
prom´i-nent
prom´i-nent-ly
prom-is-cu´i-ty
pro-mis´cu-ous
prom´ise
prom´is-ee´
prom´is-er
prom´is-ing
prom´i-sor
prom´is-so-ry
prom´on-to-ry
pro-mote´
pro-mot´er
pro-mot´ing
pro-mo´tion
pro-mo´tion-al
pro-mo´tive
prompt
prompt´er
promp´ti-tude
prompt´ly
prompt´ness
prom´ul-gate
promul-ga´tion
prom´ul-ga-tor
pro´nate
prone´ness
prong´horn
pro-nom´i-nal
pro-no´tus
pro´noun
pro-nounce´
pro-nounce´able

pro-nounced´
pro-nounce´ment
pro-nounc´ing
pro-nun-cia-men´to
pro-nun-ci-a´tion
proof´er
proof´read
proof´read-er
prop´a-ga-ble
prop-a-gan´da
prop-a-gan´dist
prop-a-gan´dize
prop´a-gate
prop´a-ga´tion
prop´a-ga-tive
prop´a-ga-tor
pro-pam´i-dine
pro´pane
pro´pa-nol
pro-par´gyl
pro-pel´
pro-pel´lant
pro-pelled´
pro-pel´lent
pro-pel´ler
pro-pel´ling
pro-pense´
pro-pen´si-ty
pro´pe-nyl
prop´er
pro´per-din
prop´er-ly
prop´er-tied
prop´er-ties
prop´er-ty
proph´e-cies
proph´e-cy
proph´e-sied
proph´e-si-er
proph´e-sy
proph´et
proph´et-ess
pro-phet´ic
pro-phet´i-cal
pro´phy-lac´tic
pro-phy-lax´is
pro´pi-o-late
pro-pi-ol´ic
pro´pi-o-nate

pro-pi-on´ic
pro´pi-o-nyl
pro-pi-on´y-late
pro-pi´ti-ate
pro-pi-ti-a´tion
pro-pi´ti-a-tor
pro-pi´ti-a-to-ry
pro-pi´tious
pro-po´de-um
pro-po´nent
pro-por´tion
pro-por´tion-able
pro-por´tion-al
pro-por´tion-ate
pro-por´tion-ate-ly
pro-por´tioned
pro-pos´al
pro-pose´
pro-pos´er
pro-pos´ing
prop-o-si´tion
prop-o-si´tion-al
pro-pound´
pro-pound´er
pro-pri´e-tary
pro-pri´e-tor
pro-pri´e-tor-ship
pro-pri´e-to-ry
pro-pri´e-tress
pro-pri´e-ty
pro-pul´sion
pro-pul´sive
pro-pul´so-ry
pro´pyl-ene
pro-pyl´ic
prop´y-lite
pro-ra´ta
pro-rat´able
pro-rate´
pro-rat´er
pro-ra´tion
pro-ro-ga´tion
pro-rogue´
pro-sa´ic
pro-sa´i-cal-ly
pro-sce´ni-um
pro-sciut´to
pro-scribe´
pro-scrip´tion

pro-scrip´tive
pro-scrip´tive-ly
prose
pros´e-cute
pros-e-cu´tion
pros´e-cu-tor
pros´e-cu-to-ry
pros-e-cu´trix
pros´e-lyte
pros´e-lyt-ism
pros´e-lyt-ize
pros´e-lyt-iz-er
pros´er
pros´i-er
pro´sit
pro-slav´ery
pros´o-pite
pros-o-pla´sia
pros´pect
pro-spec´tive
pro-spec´tive-ly
pros´pec-tor
pro-spec´tus
pros´per
pros-per´i-ty
pros´per-ous
pros´per-ous-ly
pros´tate
pros-tat´ic
pros-ta-ti´tis
pros-ter-na´tion
pros-then´ic
pros´the-sis
pros-thet´ic
pros´the-tist
pros-tho-don´tics
pros´ti-tute
pros-ti-tu´tion
pros´trate
pros´trat-ing
pros-tra´tion
pros´tra-tor
pros´y
pro´ta-gon
pro-tag´o-nist
prot´amine´
pro´te-ase
pro-tect´
pro-tect´ant

pro-tect´ing
pro-tect´ing-ly
pro-tec´tion
pro-tec´tion-ism
pro-tec´tion-ist
pro-tec´tive
pro-tec´tive-ly
pro-tec´tor
pro-tec´tor-ate
pro-tec´to-ry
pro-tec´tress
pro´té-gé´
pro´té-gée´
pro´te-ide
pro´tein
pro-tem´po-re
pro-te-ol´y-sin
pro-te-ol´y-sis
pro´teo-lyt´ic
Prot´ero-zo´ic
pro´test
Prot´es-tant
Prot´es-tant-ism
prot´es-ta´tion
pro-test´er
pro-test´ing
Pro´teus
proth´e-sis
pro-thon´o-tary
pro-tho´rax
pro-throm´bin
pro´tide
pro´to-blast
pro´to-clas´tic
pro´to-col
pro´to-gen
pro-tog´y-ny
pro´ton
pro´ton-ate
pro´to-plasm
pro´to-plas´mal
pro´to-plas´mic
pro´to-plast
pro´to-stele
pro´to-trop´ic
pro-tot´ro-py
pro´to-typ´al
pro´to-type
pro´to-typ´i-cal

prot-ox´ide
pro-to-zo´a
pro´to-zo´al
pro´to-zo´an
pro-tract´
pro-tract´ed
pro-tract´i-ble
pro-trac´tile
pro-trac´tion
pro-trac´tive
pro-trac´tor
pro-trude´
pro-tru´si-ble
pro-tru´sion
pro-tru´sive
pro-tru´sive-ly
pro-tu´ber-ance
pro-tu´ber-ant
pro-tu´ber-ate
proud´ly
proust´ite
prov´able
proved
prov´en
prov´e-nance
Pro-ven-cal´
Prov´ence
prov´en-der
pro-ve´nience
prov´er
prov´erb
pro-ver´bi-al
pro-vide´
pro-vid´ed
prov´i-dence
prov´i-dent
prov´i-den´tial
pro-vid´er
pro-vid´ing
prov´ince
Prov´ince-town
pro-vin´cial
pro-vin´cial-ism
pro-vin-ci-al´i-ty
pro-vin´cial-ly
prov´ing
pro-vi´sion
pro-vi´sion-al
pro-vi´sion-al-ly

pro-vi´sion-ary
pro-vi´sion-er
pro-vi´so
pro´vi-so-ri-ly
pro-vi´so-ry
pro-vi´sos
prov-o-ca´tion
pro-voc´a-tive
pro-voc´a-to-ry
pro-voke´
pro-vok´ing
pro-vo-lo´ne
pro´vost
prov´ost-al
pro´vost mar´shal
prow´ess
prowl´er
prox´ies
prox´i-mal
prox´i-mate
prox´i-mate-ly
prox-im´i-ty
prox´i-mo
prox´y
prude
pru´dence
pru´dent
pru-den´tial
prud´ery
Prud´hoe
prud´ish
pru-nel´la
prun´er
pru´ne-tin
prun´ing
pru-ri´tus
Prus´sia
prus´si-ate
pried
pry´ing
psalm
psalm´ist
psal´tery
pseud´an-dry
pseud-ar-thro´sis
pseu´do
pseu´do-aquat´ic
pseu´do-carp
pseu´do-cu´mi-dine

pseu´do-nym
pseu-don´y-mous
pseu´do-pod
pseu´do-po´di-um
pseu-dos´co-py
pseu-dos´to-ma
psil-an´thro-py
psi-lo-mel´ane
psi-lo´sis
psi-lot´ic
psit´ta-cine
psit-ta-co´sis
psit´ta-cot´ic
pso´as
pso-phom´e-ter
pso-ri´a-sis
pso´ri-at´ic
pso-ro´sis
psy´cha-gog´ic
psy´cha-gogy
psych´as-the´nia
psy´che
psy-che-om´e-try
psy-chi-at´ric
psy-chi´a-trist
psy-chi´a-try
psy´chic
psy´chi-cal
psy´chi-cal-ly
psy-cho-anal´y-sis
psy´cho-an´a-lyst
psy´cho-an-a-lyt´ic
psy-cho-an-a-lyt´i-cal
psy´cho-an´a-lyze
psy´cho-gen´ic
psy-cho-ge-nic´i-ty
psy-chog-no´sis
psy´cho-graph´ic
psy-chog´ra-phy
psy´cho-lep-sy
psy´cho-lep´tyc
psy´cho-log´i-cal
psy-cho-log´i-cal-ly
psy-chol´o-gist
psy-chol´o-gize
psy-chol´o-gy
psy-chom´a-chy
psy-chom´e-ter
psy´cho-met´ric

psy-chom-e-tri´cian
psy-chom´e-try
psy-cho-neu-ro´sis
psy-cho-neu-rot´ic
psy-cho-nom´ics
psy´cho-path
psy´cho-path´ic
psy-chop´a-thist
psy-chop´a-thy
psy-cho´sis
psy-cho-so-mat´ic
psy-cho-ther´a-py
psy-chot´ic
psy´cho-trine
psy-chrom´e-ter
psy-chrom´e-try
psyl´li-um
pter´o-dac´tyl
pte-ro´ic
pter´o-pod
pter´o-yl
pte-ryg´i-um
pter´y-goid
pti-san´
Ptol´e-ma´ic
Ptol´e-my
pto-maine´
pto´sis
pty´a-lin
pty´a-lism
pu´ber-ty
pu-ber´u-lent
pu-ber´u-lon´ic
pu-bes´cence
pu-bes´cent
pu´bic
pu-bi-ot´o-my
pub´lic
pub´li-can
pub-li-ca´tion
pub´lic house
pub´li-cist
pub-lic´i-ty
pub´li-cize
pub´lic-ly
pub´lic—spir´it-ed
pub´lish
pub´lish-able
pub´lish-er

Pub´li-us
Puc-ci´ni
puck´er
puck´ered
puck´ery
puck´ish
pud´ding
pud´dle
pud´dler
pud´dling
pudg´i-ness
pudg´y
pueb´lo
pueb´los
pu´er-ile
pu-er-il´i-ty
pu-er´per-al
pu-er-pe´ri-um
Puer´to Ri´co
puff´er
puf´fin
puff´i-ness
puff´y
Pu´get
pu´gi-lism
pu´gi-list
pu´gi-lis´tic
pug-na´cious
pug-na´cious-ly
pug-nac´i-ty
pug nose
pug´—nosed
Pu-las´ki
pul´chri-tude
pul-chri-tu´di-nous
pu´le-gone
pu´li-cide
pul´ing
Pul´itz-er
pull´er
pul´let
pul´ley
pull´ing
Pull´man
pull´over
pul´lu-late
pul-lu-la´tion
pul-mom´e-ter
pul´mo-nary

pul-mon´ic
Pul´mo-tor
pulp´er
pulp´i-ness
pul´pit
pul´pi-teer´
pulp´ous
pulp´wood
pulp´y
pul´sate
pul´sa-tile
pul´sa´tion
pul´sa-tive
pul´sa´tor
pul´sa-to-ry
pulsed
puls´er
pul-sim´e-ter
puls´ing
pul-som´e-ter
pul´ver-iz-able
pu´ver-i-za´tion
pul´ver-ize
pul´ver-iz-er
pu´ver´u-lent
pu´ma
pu´mi-cate
pum´ice
pum´mel
pump´age
pump´er
pum´per nick-el
pump´kin
punch´er
pun-chi-nel´lo
punc´tate
punc´tat-ed
punc-ta´tion
punc´ti-form
punc-til´io
punc-til´i-ous
punc´tu-al
punc-tu-al´i-ty
punc´tu-al-ly
punc´tu-ate
punc-tu-a´tion
punc´tu-a-tor
punc´tur-able
punc´ture

punc´tured
punc´tur-ing
pun´dit
pun´gen-cy
pun´gent
Pu´nic
pu-nic´ic
pu´ni-ness
pun´ish
pun´ish-able
pun´ish-er
pun´ish-ment
pu´ni-tive
Pun´jab
punned
pun´ning
pun´ster
punt´er
pun´ty
pu´ny
pu´pa
pu´pal
pu´pil
pu-pil-lar´i-ty
pu´pil-lary
pu´pil-late
pu-pil-lom´e-ter
Pu-pin´
pup´pet
pup´pe-teer´
pup´pet-ry
pup´py
Pur´cell
pur´chas-able
pur´chase
pur´chased
pur´chas-er
pur´chas-ing
Pur-due´
pu-ree´
pure´ly
pure´ness
pur-ga´tion
pur´gative
pur´ga-to´ri-al
pur-ga-to´ri-an
pur´ga-to-ry
purge
purg´er

purg´ing
pu-ri-fi-ca´tion
pu-rif´i-ca-to-ry
pu´ri-fi-er
pu´ri-fy
Pu´rim
pu´rine
pur´ism
pur´ist
pu-ris´tic
pu´ri-tan
pu-ri-tan´i-cal
pu´ri-tan-ism
pu´ri-ty
pur´lin
pur-loin´
pu´ro-my´cin
pur´ple
pur-port´
pur´pose
pur´pose-ful
pur´pose-ful-ly
pur´pose-less
pur´pose-ly
pur´pos-ive
purr´ing
purse—proud
purs´er
purs´ing
pur-su´al
pur-su´ance
pur-su´ant
pur-su´ant-ly
pur-sue´
pur-sued´
pur-su´er
pur-su´ing
pur-suit´
pur´sy
pur´te-nance
pu´ru-lence
pu´ru-lent
pur-vey´
pur-vey´ance
pur-vey´or
pur´view
push´ball
push but´ton
push´cart

push´er
push´ing
push´over
push´pin
push´—pull´
pu´sil-lan´i-mous
puss´y
puss´y-foot
puss´y wil´low
pus´tu-lant
pus´tu-lar
pus´tu-late
pus-tu-la´tion
pus´tule
pus´tu-lous
pu-ta´men
pu´ta-tive
pu´tre-fied
pu´tre-fy
pu´tre-fy-ing
pu-tres´cence
pu´trid
pu-trid´i-ty
put-tee´
putt´er
put´ty
puz´zle
puz´zle-ment
puz´zler
puz´zling
Pyg-ma´lion
pyg´my
py´lon
py-lo-rec´to-my
py-lor´ic
py-lo´ro-plas-ty
py-lo´rus
py-or-rhe´a
pyr´a-cene
pyr´a-mid
py-ram´i-dal
pyr´a-mid-er
pyr´a-mid´i-cal
Pyr´a-mus
pyre
py´rene
Pyr´e-nees
pyre-tol´o-gy
Py´rex

py-rex´ia
py-rex´in
pyr´i-bole
py-rid´ic
pyr´i-dine
pyr-i-din´i-um
pyr-i-dox´ine
py´rite
py-rit´es
py-rit´ic
py´ro-graph´ic
py-rog´ra-phy
py´ro-lig´ne-ous
py-rol´o-gy
py-ro-lu´site
py-rol´y-sis
py´ro-lyze
py-ro-ma´nia
py-ro-ma´ni-ac
py-rom´e-ter
py´rone
py-ro´sis
py´ro-sphere
py´ro-tech´nic
py-ro-tech´ni-cal
py-rox´ene
py-rox´e-nite
py-rox´y-lin
pyr´rhic
Pyr´rhus
Py-thag´o-ras
Pyth´i-an
Pyth´i-as
py´thon
py-thon´ic

## Q

Qa´tar
quack´ery
quad´ra-ges´i-mal
quad´ran-gle
quad-ran´gu-lar
quad´rant
qua-dran´tal
quad´rate
qua-drat´ic
quad´ra-ture
qua-dra´tus

qua-dren´ni-al
qua-dren´ni-al-ly
qua-dren´ni-um
quad´ric
quad´ri-lat´er-al
quad´ri-lin´gual
qua-drille´
qua-dril´lion
quad-ri-ple´gic
quad´ri-va´lent
qua-driv´i-um
qua-droon´
qua-drum´vi-rate
quad´ru-ped
quad´ru-pe-dal
quad-ru´ple
quad-rup´let
quad´ru-plex
qua-dru´pli-cate
quad-ru´pling
quaff
quaffed
quag´mire
qua´hog
quaint´ly
quaked
Quake-er
quak´ing
qual-i-fi-ca´tion
qual´i-fied
qual´i-fy
qual´i-fy-ing
qua-lim´e-ter
qual´i-ta-tive
qual´i-ta-tive-ly
qual´i-ty
qualm
qualm´ish
quan´da-ry
quan´tile
quan´ti-ta-tive
quan´ti-ta-tive-ly
quan´ti-ty
quan´tum
quar´an-tine
quar´an-tin-er
quar´rel
quar´reled
quar´rel-ing

quar´rel-some
quar´ry
quar´tan
quar´ter
quar´ter-back
quar´ter-deck
quar´tered
quar´ter-ing
quar´ter-ly
quar´ter-mas-ter
quar´tern
quar-tet´
quar´tile
quar´to
quar´tos
quarts
quartz
quartz-if´er-ous
quartz´ite
quartz-it´ic
quartz´ose
qua´si
quat´er-nary
qua´train
qua´tre
qua´ver
qua´vered
qua´ver-ing
quay
quea´si-ly
quea´si-ness
quea´sy
Que-bec´
queen´li-ness
queen´ly
Queens´ber-ry
Queens´land
queer´ly
quelled
quell´er
Que-moy´
quenched
quench´er
quench´less
Quen´tin
quer´ce-tin
que´ried
que´rist
quer´u-lous

que´ry
que´ry-ing
ques´tion
ques´tion-able
ques´tion-er
ques´tion-ing
ques´tion-ing-ly
ques´tion mark
ques´tion-naire´
quet-zal´
queue
queu´er
queu´ing
quib´ble
quib´bled
quib´bler
quib´bling
quick´en
quick´en-ing
quick´—fire´
quick´lime
quick´ly
quick´ness
quick´sand
quick´set
quick´—set´ting
quick´sil-ver
quick´step
quick´—tem´pered
quick´—wit´ted
qui-es´cence
qui-es´cent
qui´et
qui´et-ism
qui´et-ly
qui´et-ness
qui´e-tude
qui-e´tus
quilt´ed
quilt´ing
quin´a-crine
quin´a-mine
qui´na-ry
quin-az´o-line
quin-cun´cial
Quin´cy
qui-nel´la
quin´i-dine
qui-nie´la

qui´nine
Quin-qua-ges´i-ma
quin-quen´ni-al
quin´sy
quin´tal
quin´tant
quin-ter´ni-on
quin-tes´sence
quin-tes-sen´tial
quin-tet´
quin´tic
quint-tile
quin-tu´ple
quin-tup´let
quin-tu´pling
quipped
quip´ping
quip´ster
quire
Quir´i-nal
quir´i-tar´i-an
Quis´ling
quit´claim
quit´rent
quit´tance
quit´ted
quit´ter
quit´ting
quit´tor
quiv´er
quiv´ered
quiv´er-ing
qui vive
quix-ot´ic
quix-ot´i-cal-ly
quix´o-tism
quiz
quizzed
quiz´zi-cal
quiz´zing
quoin
quoit
quon´dam
Quon´set
quo´rum
quo´ta
quot-abil´i-ty
quot´able
quo-ta´tion

quote
quot´ed
quot´er
quo-tid´i-an
quo´tient
quot´ing

**R**

rab´at
Ra-bat´
ra-ba´to
rab´bet
rab´bet-ed
rab´bi
rab´bin-ate
rab-bin´ic
rab-bin´i-cal
rab´bit
rab´bit-ry
rab´ble
rab´bler
Rab´e-lais´
rab´id
ra-bid´i-ty
ra´bies
rac-coon´
race´course
race´horse
rac´e-mate
ra-ceme´
rac´er
race´track
race´way
Ra´chel
ra-chel´
Rach-man´i-noff
ra´cial
ra´cial-ism
ra´cial-ly
ra-ci-a´tion
rac´i-ly
Ra-cine´
rac´ing
rac´ism
rac´ist
rack´er
rack´et
rack´e-teer´

rack´ety
rack rail
ra´con
rac´on-teur
rac´y
ra´dar
ra´dar-scope
Rad´cliffe
ra´di-ac
ra´di-al
ra´di-an
ra´di-ance
ra´di-an-cy
ra´di-ant
ra´di-ant-ly
ra´di-ate
ra-di-a´tion
ra-di-a-tive
ra´di-a-tor
rad´i-cal
rad´i-cal-ism
rad´i-cal-ly
rad´i-cand
rad´i-cate
rad-i-ca´tion
rad´i-cle
ra´dii
ra´dio
ra´dio-ac´tive
ra´dio-ac-tiv´i-ty
ra´dio—fre´quen-cy
ra´dio-gram
ra´dio-graph
ra-di-og´ra-pher
ra´dio-graph´ic
ra-di-og´ra-phy
ra´dio-i´so-tope
ra´dio-lar´i-an
ra-di-o-log´i-cal
ra-di-ol´o-gist
ra-di-ol´o-gy
ra-di-ol´y-sis
ra-di-om´e-ter
ra-dio-met´ric
ra´di-on´ic
ra´dio-nu´clide
ra´dio-phone
ra´di-os
ra-di-os´co-py

ra´dio-sonde
ra´dio-tel´e-gram
ra´dio-tel´e-graph
ra-dio-tel´e-phone
ra´dio-te-leph´o-ny
ra´dio-ther´a-py
ra´dio-tho´ri-um
rad´ish
ra´di-um
ra´di-us
ra´dix
ra´dome
ra´don
rad´u-la
raf´fia
raff´ish
raff´ish-ly
raf´fle
raf´fled
raf´fling
raf´ter
rafts´man
rag´a-muf-fin
rag´ged
rag´ged-ness
rag´ing
rag´lan
rag´man
ra-gout´
rag´pick-er
rag´time
rair´weed
raid´er
rail´er
rail´head
rail´ing
rail´lery
rail´road
rail´road-ing
rail´way
rain´band
rain´bow
rain cloud
rain´coat
rain´drop
rain´fall
rain gage
rain´i-er
Rai-nier´

rain´less
rain´mak-er
rain pipe
rain´proof
rain´storm
rain´tight
rain´wa´ter
rain´y
rais´er
rai´sin
rais´ing
rai-son´
ra´ja, ra´jah
Raj´put
raked
rake´hell
rake´—off
rak´er
rak´ing
rak´ish
Ra´leigh
ral´lied
ral´ly
ral´ston-ite
Ram´a-dan
Ra´man
ram´ble
ram´bler
ram´bling
ram-bunc´tious
Ram´e-ses
ram-i-fi-ca´tion
ram´i-fied
ram´i-fy
ram´i-fy-ing
ram´jet
rammed
ram´ming
Ra-mo´na
ram´page
ram-pa´geous
ram´pag-er
ram´pag-ing
ram´pant
ram´part
ram´pi-on
ram´rod
ram´shack-le
ram´u-lose

ranch´er
ran-che´ro
ranch´man
ran´cho
ran´cid
ran-cid´i-ty
ran´cor
ran´corous
Ran´dolph
ran´dom
ran´dom-ize
ranged
rang´er
rang-ette´
rang´ing
Ran-goon´
rang´y
ra-ni´
ra´nine
rank´er
ran´kle
ran´kled
ran´kling
rank´ness
ran´sack
ran´som
ran´som-er
rant´er
rant´ing
ra-pa´cious
ra-pa´cious-ness
Raph´a-el
rap´id
rap´id—fire
ra-pid´i-ty
rap´id-ly
ra´pier
rap´ine
rap´ist
rap-pa-ree´
rapped
rap´ping
rap-port´
rap-proche-ment´
rap-scal´lion
rapt´ly
rap-to´ri-al
rap´ture
rap´tur-ous

rare´bit
rar´e-fac´tion
rar´e-fied
rar´e-fy
rare´ly
rare´ness
rar´i-ty
ras´cal
ras-cal´i-ty
ras´cal-ly
rash´er
rash´ly
rash´ness
rasp´ber-ry
rasp´er
rasp´ing
Ras-pu´tin
ras´ter
ra´sure
ratch´et
ra´tel
rate´pay-er
rat´er
rath´er
raths´kel-ler
rat-i-fi-ca´tion
rat´i-fied
rat´i-fy
rat´i-fy-ing
rat´ing
ra´tion
ra´tio-nal
ra´tio-nale´
ra´tio-nal-ism
ra´tio-nal-ist
ra-tio-nal-is´tic
ra-tio-nal´i-ty
ra-tio-nal-iza´tion
ra´tio-nal-ize
ra´tio-nal-ly
rat´ite
rat´line
ra-toon´
rat´proof
rat-tan´
rat´tle
rat´tler
rat´tle-snake
rat´tle-trap

rau´cous
rau´vite
rav´age
rav´ag-er
rav´ag-ing
rav´el
Ra-vel´
rav´eled
rave´lin
rav´el-ing
ra´ven
rav´en-ing
Ra-ven´na
rav´en-ous
rav´in
ra-vine´
rav´ing
rav-i-o´li
rav´ish
rav´ish-er
rav´ish-ing
rav´ish-ment
raw´boned´
raw´hide
ra´win-sonde
Ray´mond
ray´on
ra´zon
ra´zor
ra´zor-back
raz´zle—daz-zle
re-act´
re-ac´tance
re-ac´tion
re-ac´tion-ary
re-ac´tive
re-ac´tor
read-abil´i-ty
read´able
re-ad-dress´
read´er
read´i-ly
read´i-ness
read´ing
Read´ing
read´ing room
re-ad-just´
re-ad-just´ment
read´y

read´y—made
re-af-firm´
re-a´gent
re´al
re-al´gar
re´al-ism
re´al-ist
re´al-is´tic
re-al-is´ti-cal-ly
rc-al´i ty
re-al-iza´tion
re´al-ize
re´al-ly
realm
re´al-tor
re´al-ty
ream´er
re-an´i-mate
reap´er
re-ap-pear´
re-ap-pear´ance
re-ap-point´
rear ad´mi-ral
rear guard
re-arm´
re-ar´ma-ment
re-ar-range´
re-ar-range´ment
re-ar-rang´ing
rear´ward
re-as-cend´
rea´son
rea´son-able
rea´son-able-ness
rea´son-ably
rea´son-er
rea´son-ing
re-as-sem´ble
re-as-sert´
re-as-sume´
re-as-sur´ance
re´as-sure´
re´as-sur´ing
reav´er
re-awak´en
re´bate
re´bat-er
re´bec
Re-bec´ca

reb´el
re-belled´
re-bel´ling
re-bel´lion
re-bel´lious
re-bel´lious-ly
re´birth´
re´born´
re-bound´
re-buff´
re-build´
re-built´
re-buke´
re-buk´ing
re´bus
re-but´
re-but´ta-ble
re-but´tal
re-but´ted
re-but´ting
re-cal´ci-trance
re-cal´ci-trant
re-ca-les´cence
re-ca-les´cent
re-call´
re-cant´
re-can-ta´tion
re´cap´
re-ca-pit´u-late
re-ca-pit´u-la´tion
re-ca-pit´u-la-to-ry
re´capped´
re´cap´ping
re-cap´ture
re-cast´
re-cede´
re-ced´ed
re-ced´ence
re-ced´er
re-ced´ing
re-ceipt´
re-ceipt´or
re-ceiv´able
re-ceive´
re-ceiv´er
re-ceiv´er-ship
re-ceiv´ing
re´cen-cy
re-cen´sion

re´cent
re´cent-ly
re-cep´ta-cle
re-cep´ti-ble
re-cep´tion
re-cep´tion-ist
re-cep´tive
re-cep-tiv´i-ty
re-cep´tor
re´cess
re´cess´er
re-ces´sion
re-ces´sion-al
re-ces´sive
re-charge´
rec´i-pe
re-cip´i-ence
re-cip´i-ent
re-cip´ro-ca-ble
re-cip´ro-cal
re-cip´ro-cal-ly
re-cip´ro-cate
re-cip´ro-ca´tion
rec-i-proc´i-ty
re-ci´sion
re-cit´al
rec-i-ta´tion
rec´i-ta-tive´
re-cite´
re-cit´er
re-cit´ing
reck´less
reck´less-ly
reck´less-ness
reck´on
reck´on-ing
re-claim
re-claim´able
rec-la-ma´tion
rec-li-na´tion
re-clin´able
rec-li-na´tion
re-cline´
re-clin´er
re-clin´ing
rec´luse
re-clu´sive
rec-og-ni´tion
rec´og-niz-able
re-cog´ni-zance

rec´og-nize
re-cog´ni-zee´
rec´og-niz-er
rec´og-niz-or´
re-coil´
re—coil´
rec-ol-lect´
re—col-lect´
rec-ol-lec´tion
re-com-bi-na´tion
re´com-bine´
re-com-mence´
rec-om-mend´
rec-om-men-da´tion
rec-om-mend´a-to-ry
re-com-mit´
re-com-mit´tal
re-com-mit´ment
rec´om-pense
rec´om-pens-er
rec´om-pens-ing
re-con´cen-trate
rec´on-cil-able
rec´on-cile
rec´on-cile-ment
rec´on-cil-er
rec-on-cil-i-a´tion
rec´on-cil´ia-to-ry
rec´on-dite
re-con-di´tion
re-con´nais-sance
recon-noi´ter
re-con´quer
re-con´se-crate
re-con-sid´er
re-con-sid´er-a´tion
re-con´sti-tute
re-con-struct´
re-con-struc´tion
re-cord´
re-cord´able
rec-or-da´tion
re-cord´er
re-count´
re-coup´
re´course
re-cov´er
re-cov´er-able
re-cov´ery

rec´re-ant
rec´re-ate
re—cre-ate´
rec-re-a´tion
re—cre-a´tive
rec´re-a-tive
rec´re-ment
rec´re-men´tal
rec´re-men-ti´tious
re-crim´i-nate
re-crim´i-nat-ing
re-crim´i-na´tion
re-crim´i-na-to-ry
re-cru-des´cence
re-cru-des´cent
re-cruit´
re-cruit´er
re-cruit´ment
rec´tal
rec´tan-gle
rec-tan´gu-lar
rec´ti-fi-able
rec-ti-fi-ca´tion
rec´ti-fied
rec´ti-fi-er
rec´ti-fy
rec´ti-tude
rec´tor
rec´tor-ate
rec´tor-ship
rec´to-ry
rec´tum
rec´tus
re-cum´ben-cy
re-cum´bent
re-cu´per-ate
re-cu-per-a´tion
re-cu´per-a-tive
re-cur´
re-curred´
re-cur´rence
re-cur´rent
re-cur´ring
re-cur´sive
re-cur´vate
re-dact´
re-dac´tion
re-dac´tor
re-dan´

red´bird
red´—blood´ed
red´breast
red´bud
red´cap
red´coat
red´den
red´dish
re-dec´o-rate
re-deem´
re-deem´able
re-deem´er
re-demp´ti-ble
re-demp´tion
re-demp´tive
re-demp´tor
re-demp´to-ry
re-de-ploy´
re-de-ploy´ment
red´—faced
red´—hand´ed
red´head
red´head-ed
red her´ring
red´—hot´
re-di-rect´
re-dis´count
re-dis-cov´er
re-dis-cov´ery
re-dis-trib´ute
re-dis-tri-bu´tion
re-dis´trict
red lead
red´—lead´
red´—let´ter
red´ness
red´o-lence
re-dou´ble
re-dou´bling
re-doubt´
re-doubt´able
re-dound´
re-draw´
re-dress´
re-dress´able
re-dress´er
red´skin
red tape
re-duce´

re-duc´er
re-duc´ible
re-duc´ing
re-duc´tase
re-duc´tion
re-duc´tive
re-duc´tone
re-dun´dan-cy
re-dun´dant
re-du´pli-cate
re-du-pli-ca´tion
red´wing
red´wood
re-ech´o
reed´y
reef´er
re-elect´
re-elec´tion
reel´er
re-em-bark´
re-en-act´
re-en-force´
re-en-force´ment
re-en-gage´
re´en-list´
re-en´ter
re-en´trant
re-en´try
re-es-tab´lish
re-es-tab´lish-ment
re-ex-am-i-na´tion
re-ex-am´ine
re-fas´ten
re-fec´tion
re-fec´to-ry
re-fer´
ref´er-able
ref´er-ee´
ref´er-ence
ref-er-en´dum
refer´ent
ref´er-en´tial
re-ferred´
re-fer´ring
re-fill´
re-fill´able
re-fine´
re-fined´
re-fine-ment

re-fin´er
re-fin´ery
re-fin´ing
re-fit´
re-flect´
re-flec´tance
re-flect´ible
re-flec´tion
re-flec´tive
re-flec-tom´e-ter
re-flec-tom´e-try
re-flec´tor
re-flec´tor-ize
re´flex
re-flex´ive
re-flex-iv´i-ty
ref´lu-ent
re´flux
re-for´est
re-for-est-a´tion
re-form´
re-form´able
ref-or-ma´tion
re-for´ma-tive
re-for´ma-to-ry
re-form´er
re-fract´
re-frac´tion
re-frac´tive
re-frac-tom´e-ter
re-frac´to-met´ric
re-frac-tom´e-try
re-frac´tor
re-frac´to-ri-ness
re-frac´to-ry
re-frain´
re-fran´gi-ble
ref-re-na´tion
re-fresh´
re-fresh´ing
re-fresh´ment
re-frig´er-ant
re-frig´er-ate
re-frig´er-at-ing
re-frig-er-a´tion
re-frig´er-a-tor
re-frin´gent
re-fu´el
ref´uge

ref´u-gee
re-ful´gence
re-ful´gent
re´fund
re-fur´bish
re-fur´nish
re-fus´al
re-fyse´
re—fuse´
re-fus´ing
re-fut´able
re-fut´ably
re-fut´al
ref-u-ta´tion
re-fute´
re-fut´er
re-fut´ing
re-gain´
re´gal
re-gale´
re-ga´lia
re-gal´ing
re-gal´i-ty
re´gal-ly
re-gard´
re-gard´ing
re-gard´less
re-gat´ta
re´ge-late
re´ge-la´tion
re´gen-cy
re-gen´er-a-cy
re-gen´er-ate
re-gen-er-a´tion
re-gen´er-a-tive
re-gen´er-a-tor
re´gent
re-gime´
reg´i-men
reg´i-ment
reg´i-men´tal
reg-i-men´ta-ry
reg-i-men-ta´tion
Re-gi´na
Reg´i-nald
re´gion
re´gion-al
reg´is-ter
reg´is-tered

reg´is-tra-ble
reg´is-trar
reg´is-trate
reg-is-tra´tion
reg´is-try
reg´let
reg´nant
Re-gnault´
reg´o-sol
re-gress´
re-gres´sion
re-gres´sive
re-gres´sor
re-gret´
re-gret´ful
re-gret´ful-ly
re-gret´ta-ble
re-gret´ta-bly
re-gret´ted
re-gret´ting
reg´u-lar
reg-u-lar´i-ty
reg´u-lar-ize
reg´u-lar-ly
reg´u-lat-able
reg´u-late
reg-u-la´tion
reg´u-la-tive
reg´u-la-tor
reg´u-la-to-ry
reg´u-lus
re-gur´gi-tate
re-gur-gi-ta´tion
re-ha-bil´i-tate
re-ha-bi´i-ta´tion
re-ha-bil´i-ta-tive
re´hash´
re-hears´al
re-hearse´
re-hears´er
re-hears´ing
re-heat´
Re´ho-both
Reichs´tag
re´ify
reign
re-im-burs´able
re-im-burse´
re-im-burse´ment

re-im-port´
re-im-por-ta´tion
rein
re-in-car´nate
re-in-car-na´tion
rein´deer
Rei´necke
re-in-force´
re-in-forced´
re-in-force´ment
re-in-sert´
re-in-stall´
re-in-stal-la´tion
re-in-state´
re-in-state´ment
re-in-sure´
re-in-te-gra´tion
re-in-vest´
re-in-vig´o-rate
re-is´sue
re-it´er-ate
re-it-er-a´tion
re-it´er-a-tive
re-ject´
re-ject´able
re-ject´er
re-jec´tion
re-jec´tor
re-joice´
re-joic´ing
re-join´
re-join´der
re-ju´ve-nate
re-ju-ve-na´tion
re-ju´ve-na-tor
re-kin´dle
re-lapse´
re-lapsed´
re-laps´er
re-laps´ing
re-late´
re-lat´ed
re-lat´er
re-lat´ing
re-la´tion
re-la´tion-ship
rel´a-tive
rel´a-tive-ly
rel´a-tiv-ism

rel´a-tiv´i-ty
re-la´tor
re-lax´
re-lax-a´tion
re-lax´ed-ly
re-lax-om´e-ter
re´lay
re´layed
re-lease´
re-leased´
re-leas´er
re-leas´ing
rel´e-ga-ble
rel´e-gate
rel´e-gat-ed
rel-e-ga´tion
re-lent´
re-lent´ing
re-lent´ing-ly
re-lent´less
rel´e-vance
rel´e-van-cy
rel´e-vant
re-li-abil´i-ty
re-li´able
re-li´ably
re-li´ance
re-li´ant
rel´ic
rel´ict
re-lied´
re-lief´
re-lief´er
re-liev´able
re-lieve´
re-lieved´
re-liev´er
re-liev´ing
re-li´gion
re-li-gi-os´i-ty
re-li´gious
re-li´gious-ly
re-lin´quish
rel´i-quary
rel´ish
rel´ish-able
rel´ish-ing
re-load´
re´lo-cate´

re-lu´cence
re-luc´tance
re-luc´tant
re-luc´tant-ly
rel-uc-tiv´i-ty
re-lume´
re-lu´mine
re-ly´
re-ly´ing
re-made´
re-main´
re-main´der
re-main´ing
re-mand´
re-mand´ment
rem´a-nence
rem´a-nent
re-mark´
re-mark´able
re-mark´ably
Re-marque´
re-marque´
re-mar´riage
re-mar´ry
Rem´brandt
re-me´di-able
re-me´di-al
rem´e-died
rem´e-dies
rem´e-di-less
rem´e-dy
re-mem´ber
re-mem´brance
re-mind´
re-mind´er
Rem´ing-ton
rem-i-nisce´
rem-i-nis´cence
rem-i-nis´cent
rem-i-nis´cent-ly
rem-i-nis´cer
rem-i-nis´cing
re-miss´
re-miss-ibil´i-ty
re-miss´ible
re-mis´sion
re-mis´sive
re-miss´ness
re-mit´

re-mit´tance
re-mit´ted
re-mit´tee´
re-mit´tent
re-mit´ter
re-mit´ting
rem´nant
re-mod´el
re-mod´eled
re-mon-e-ti-za´tion
re-mon´e-tize
re-mon´strance
re-mon´strant
re-mon´strate
re-mon´stra´tion
re-mon´stra-tive
re-mon´stra-tor
rem´on-toir´
re-morse´
re-morse´ful
re-morse´less
re-mote´
re-mote´ly
re-mote´ness
re-mot´est
re-mount´
re-mov-abil´i-ty
re-mov´able
re-mov´al
re-move´
re-moved´
re-mov´er
re-mov´ing
re-mu´ner-a-ble
re-mu´ner-ate
re-mu-ner-a´tion
re-mu´ner-a-tive
Re´mus
ren´ais-sance´
Ren´ais-sant´
re-name´
Re-nan´
re-nas´cence
re-nas´cent
ren-coun´ter
ren´der
ren´der-able
ren´dez-vous
rend´ible

rend´ing
ren-di´tion
Re-né´
ren´e-gade
re-nege´
re-neg´er
re-neg´ing
re-new´
re-new´able
re-new´al
re-newed´
re-new´ed-ly
ren´net
ren´nin
Re´no
Re-noir´
re-nom´i-nate
re-nom-i-na´tion
re-nounce´
re-nounce´ment
re-nounc´ing
ren´o-vate
ren´o-vat-ing
ren´o-va´tion
ren´o-va-tor
re-nown´
re-nowned´
rent´able
rent´al
rent´er
rent´ing
re-nun-ci-a´tion
re-nun´ci-a-to-ry
re-oc´cu-py
re-o´pen
re-or-ga-ni-za´tion
re-or´ga-nize
re-paid´
re-paint´
re-pair´
re-pair´able
re-pair´er
re-pair´man
rep´a-ra-ble
rep-a-ra´tion
re-par´a-tive
re-par´a-to-ry
rep´ar-tee´
re-par-ti´tion

re-past´
re-pa´tri-ate
re-patri-a´tion
re-pay´
re-pay´ing
re-pay´ment
re-peal´
re-peal´able
re-peal´er
re-peat´
re-peat´able
re-peat´ed
re-peat´ed-ly
re-peat´er
re-pel´
re-pelled´
re-pel´len-cy
re-pel´lent
re-pel´ling
re-pent´
re-pent´ance
re-pent´ant
re-peo´ple
reper-cus´sion
reper-cus´sive
rep´er-toire
rep´er-to-ry
rep´e-tend
rep-e-ti´tion
rep´e-ti´tious
rep e-ti´tious-ly
re-pet´i-tive
re-pine´
re-place´
re-place´able
re-place´ment
re-plac´ing
re-plant´
re-plen´ish
re-plen´ish-er
re-plen´ish-ment
re-plete´
re-ple´tion
re-ple´tive
re-plev´in
rep´li-ca
rep´li-cate
rep-li-ca´tion
re-plied´

re-ply´
re-ply´ing
re-port´
re-port´er
re-pose´
re-pose´ful
re-pos´ing
re´po-si´tion
re-pos´i-to-ry
re´pos-sess´
re-pos-ses´sion
re-pous-sé´
Rep´plier
rep-re-hend´
rep-re-hen-si-bil´i-ty
rep-re-hen´si-ble
rep-re-hen´sion
rep-re-hen´sive
rep-re-sent´
rep-re-sent´a-ble
rep-re-sen-ta´tion
rep-re-sent´a-tive
rep-re-sent´er
re-press´
re-press´er
re-press´ible
re-pres´sion
re-pres´sive
re-pres´sor
re-prieve´
rep ri-mand
re-print´
re-pri´sal
re-prise´
re-proach´
re-proach´ful
re-proach´ful-ly
re-proach´ing
rep´ro-ba-cy
rep´ro-bate
rep-ro-ba´tion
re´pro-duce´
re´pro-duc´er
re´pro-duc´ible
re´pro-duc´ing
re-pro-duc´tion
re-pro-duc´tive
re-pro-duc-tiv´i-ty
re-proof´

re-prove´
re-prov´ing
re-prov´ing-ly
rep´tile
rep-til´ian
re-pub´lic
re-pub´li-can
re-pub´li-can-ism
re-pub-li-ca´tion
re-pub´lish
re-pu´di-ate
re-pu-di-a´tion
re-pu´di-a-tor
re-pug´nance
re-pug´nan-cy
re-pug´nant
re-pulse´
re-puls´ing
re-pul´sion
re-pul´sive
re-pur´chase
rep´u-ta-ble
rep´u-ta-bly
rep-u-ta´tion
re-pute´
re-put´ed
re-put´ing
re-quest´
re-quest´er
req´ui-em
re-qui-es´cat
re-quire´
re-quire´ment
re-quir´er
re-quir´ing
req´ui-site
req-ui-si´tion
re-quit´al
re-quite´
re-quit´ed
re-quit´ing
re-read´
rer´e-dos
re-sal´able
re´sale
re-scind´
re-scind´able
re-scind´ment
re-scis´si-ble

re-scis´sion
re´script
re-scrip´tive
res´cu-able
res´cue
rea´cued
res´cu-er
res´cu-ing
re´search´
re-search´er
re-seat´
re-sect´able
re-sec´tion
re-sell´
re-sem´blance
re-sem´ble
re-sem´bler
re-sem´bling
res´ene
re-sent´
re-sent´ful
re-sent´ful-ly
re-sent´ment
res-er-va´tion
re-serve´
re-served
re-serv´ed-ly
re-serv´ist
res´er-voir
re-set´
re-set´ting
re-set´tle-ment
re-ship´
re-side´
res´i-dence
res´i-den-cy
res´i-dent
res´i-den´tial
res-i-den´ti-ary
re-sid´ing
re-sid´u-al
re-sid´u-ary
res´i-due
re-sid´u-um
re-sign´
res-ig-na´tion
re-signed´
re-sign´ed-ly
re-sil´ience

re-sil´ien-cy
re-sil´ient
re-sil´ient-ly
re-sil-i-om´e-ter
res´in
res´in-a´ceous
res´in-ate
res´in-ous
resist´
re-sist´ance
re-sist´ant
re-sist´er
re-sist-ibil´i-ty
re-sist´ible
re-sis-tiv´i-ty
re-sist´less
re-sis´tor
re-sold´
re-sol´u-ble
res´o-lute
res´o-lute-ly
res-o-lu´tion
res-o-lu´tion-er
re-sol´u-tive
re-solv´able
re-solve´
re-solved´
re-solv´ed-ly
re-solv´ent
re-solv´er
re-solv´ing
res´o-nance
res´o-nant
res´o-nate
res´o-na-tor
res-or´cin-ol
res´or-cyl´ic
re-sorp´tive
re-sort´
re-sound´
re-sound´ed
re-sound´ing
re-sound´ing-ly
re´source
re-source´ful
re-source´ful-ly
re-source´ful-ness
re-spect´
re-spect-abil´i-ty

re-spect´able
re-spect´ably
re-spect´er
re-spect´ful
re-spect´ful-ly
re-spect´ing
re-spec´tive
re-spec´tive-ly
res´pi-ra-ble
res-pi-ra´tion
res´pi-ra-tor
res´pi-ra-to-ry
re-spire´
re-spir´ing
res´pite
re-splen´dence
re-splen´den-cy
re-splen´dent
re-spond´
re-spon´dence
re-spon´den-cy
re-spon´dent
re-spond´er
re-sponse´
re-spons´er
re-spon-si-bil´i-ty
re-spon´si-ble
re-spon´si-bly
re-spon´sive
re-spon´sive-ly
re-spon´sive-ness
re-spon´sor
re-spon´so-ry
re´state´
res´tau-rant
res´tau-ra-teur´
rest´ful
res´ti-form
res-ti-tu´tion
res´tive
rest´less
rest´less-ly
rest´less-ness
re´stock´
res-to-ra´tion
re-stor´ative
re-store´
re-stor´er
re-stor´ing

re-strain´
re-strained´
re-straint´
re-strict´
re-strict´ed
re-stric´tion
re-stric´tive
re-sult´
re-sult´ant
re-sume´
ré´su-mé´
re-sum´ing
re-sump´tion
re-sump´tive
re-sur´gence
re-sur´gent
res´ur-rect´
res´ur-rec´tion
res´ur-rec´tor
re-sus´ci-ta-ble
re-sus´ci-tate
rc-sus-ci-ta´tion
re-sus´ci-ta-tor
re´tail
re´tail-er
re-tain´
re-tain´er
re-tain´ing
re-take´
rc tal´i-atc
re-tal-i-a´tion
re-tal´i-a-tive
re-tal´ia-to-ry
re-tard´
re-tard´ant
rc-tar-da´tion
re-tard´a-to-ry
re-tard´ed
retch
re-tell´
re-tent´
re-ten´tion
re-ten´tive
re-ten-tiv´i-ty
re-ten´tor
ret´i-cence
ret´i-cent
ret´i-cle
re-tic´u-lar

re-tic´u-late
re-tic-u-la´tion
ret´i-cule
re-tic´u-lin
re-tic´u-li´tis
ret´i-na
ret´i-nal
re-tin´a-lite
ret´i-nene
ret-i-ni´tis
ret´i-nol
ret´i-nue
re-tir´al
re-tire´
re-tired´
re-tir´ee´
re-tire´ment
re-tir´ing
re-told´
re-tort´
re-tort´er
re-tor´tion
re-touch´
re-trace´
re-trace´able
re-trac´ing
re-tract´
re-tract´able
re-trac-til´i-ty
re-trac´tion
rc-trac´tive
re-trac´tor
re´tral
re´tread´
re-treat´
re-trench´
re-trench´ment
ret-ri-bu´tion
re-trib´u-tive
re-trib´u-to-ry
re-triev´able
re-triev´al
re-trieve´
re-triev´er
re-triev´ing
ret´ro-ac´tive
ret-ro-ces´sion
ret´ro-gra´da-to-ry
ret´ro-grade

ret´ro-gress
ret-ro-gres´sion
ret´ro-gres´sive
ret´ro-spect
ret-ro-spec´tion
ret´ro-spec´tive
ret´ro-vert´ed
re-turn´
re-turn´able
re-turn-ee´
Reu´ben
re-un´ion
re-unite´
re-unit´ing
re-val´u-ate
re-val-u-a´tion
re-vamp´
re-veal´
rev´eil-le
rev´el
rev-e-la´tion
rev´e-la-tor
re-vel´a-to-ry
rev´eled
rev´el-er
rev´el-ing
rev´el-ry
rev´e-nant
re-venge´
re-venge´ful
re-venge´ful-ness
re-veng´er
re-veng´ing
rev´e-nue
re-ver´able
re-ver˝ber-ant
re-ver˝ber-ate
re-ver-ber-a´tion
re-ver˝ber-a-tor
re-vere´
rev´er-ence
rev´er-end
rev´er-ent
rev´er-en´tial
rev´er-ent-ly
rev´er-ie
re-ver´ing
re-ver´sal
re-verse´

re-vers´er
re-vers-ibil´i-ty
re-vers´ible
re-vers´ing
re-ver´sion
re-ver´sion-ary
re-vert´
re-vert´er
re-vert´ible
re-view´
re-view´able
re-view´er
re-vile´
re-vile´ment
re-vil´er
re-vil´ing
re-vise´
re-vised´
re-vis´er
re-vi´sion
re-vis´it
re-vis-i-ta´tion
re-vi´so-ry
re-vi´tal-ize
re-viv´al
re-viv´al-ist
re-vive´
re-viv´i-fy
re-viv´ing
rev-i-vis´cence
rev-i-vis´cent
re-vi´vor
rev-o-ca-bil´i-ty
rev´o-ca-ble
rev-o-ca´tion
rev´o-ca-to-ry
re-vok´able
re-voke´
re-vok´er
re-vok´ing
re-volt´
re-volt´er
re-volt´ing
re-volt´ing-ly
rev´o-lu-ble
rev-o-lu´tion
rev´o-lu´tion-ary
rev-o-lu´tion-ist
rev-o-lu´tion-ize

re-volv´able
re-volve´
re-volv´er
re-volv´ing
re-vue´
re-vul´sion
re-vul´sive
re-ward´
re-ward´able
re´write´
Rey˝kja-vik
Rey´nard´
Reyn´olds
rhap-sod´ic
rhap-sod´i-cal
rhap´so-dist
rhap´so-dize
rhap´so-diz-ing
rhap´so-dy
rhe´a
rhe´a-dine
rhe-mat´ic
Rhenish
rhe´ni-um
rhe-om´e-ter
rhe´o-stat
rhe´o-stat´ic
rhe´tor
rhet´o-ric
rhe-tor´i-cal
rhet-o-ri´cian
rheum
rheu-mat´ic
rheu´ma-tism
rheu´ma-toid
rhine´stone
rhi-noc´er-os
rhi´zome
Rhode Is´land
Rho-de´sia
Rho´di-an
rho´dic
rho´di-um
rho´di-zon´ic
rho-do-chro´site
rho-do-den´dron
rho-do´ra
rhom´bic
rhom´bo-clase

rhom´bus
Rhon´da
rhu´barb
rhyme
rhyme´ster
rhym´ing
rhythm
rhyth´mic
rhyth´mi-cal
rhyth´mi-cal-ly
Ri-al´to
rib´ald
rib´al-dry
ribbed
rib´bing
rib´bon
rib´boned
ri-bo-fla´vin
ri´bo-nu-cle´ic
Ri-car´do
rice field
ric´er
Rich´ard
Riche´lieu´
rich´es
rich´ly
Rich´mond
rich´ness
Rich´ter
rick´ets
rick-ett´si-al
rick´ety
rick sha
ric´o-chet
ric´o-cheted
rid´able
rid´dance
rid´den
rid´der
rid´ding
rid´dle
rid´dled
ride´able
ri´dent
rid´er
rid´er-less
ridge
ridge´pole
ridg´ing

ridg´y
rid´i-cule
ri-dic´u-lous
ri-dic´u-lous-ly
rid´ing
rif´fle
rif´fling
riff´raff
ri´fle
ri´fle-man
ri´fle pit
ri´fling
rig-a-to´ni
rigged
rig´ger
rig´ging
right
right´—an´gled
righ´teous
righ´teous-ness
right´er
right´ful
right´ful-ly
right´—hand-ed
right´ist
right´ly
right´—mind-ed
right´ness
right´—of—way
rig´id
ri-gid´i-ty
rig´id-ly
rig´or mor´tis
rig´ma-role
rig´or
rig´or-ous
rig´or-ous-ly
Ri´ley
rime
rim´less
rimmed
rim´ming
rin´der-pest
ring´bolt
ring´bone
ring´dove
ringed
ring´er
ring´ing

ring´lead-er
ring´let
ring´mas-ter
ring´side
ring´ster
ring´worm
rins´able
rinsed
rins´er
rins´ing
Ri´o de Ja-nei´ro
Ri´o Grande
ri´ot
ri´ot-er
ri´ot-ous
ri´ot-ous-ly
ri-par´i-an
rip´en
ripe´ness
rip´ping
rip´ple
rip´pled
rip´pling
rip´rap
rip´saw
ris´en
ris´er
ris-i-bil´i-ty
ris´i-ble
ris´ing
risk´i-ness
risk´y
ris-qué´
ris-sole´
rite
rit´u-al
rit´u-al-is´tic
ri´val
ri´valed
ri´valing
ri´val-ry
riv´er
Ri-ve´ra
riv´er-ain
riv´er-bank
riv´er-side
riv´et
riv´et-er
riv´et-ing

Riv-i-er´a
riv´u-let
Ri-yadh´
ri-yal´
road´bed
road´house
road´side
road´stead
road´ster
road´way
roam´er
Ro´a-noke
roast´ed
roast´er
robbed
rob´ber
rob´bery
rob´bing
Rob´ert
Robes´pierre
rob´in
rob´ing
Rob´in-son Cru´soe
ro´ble
ro´bot
ro-bust´
ro-bus´tious
ro-bust´ness
Ro-cham-beau´
Ro-chelle´
Roch´es-ter
rock´bound
Rock´e-fel-ler
rock´er
rock´et
rock´e-teer´
rock´et-er
rock´et-ry
Rock´ford
Rock´ies
rock´ing
rock´ing chair
rock-oon´
rock´—ribbed´
rock salt
rock´work
rock´y
ro´dent
ro´deo

Rod´er-ick
Ro-din´
roe´buck
roent´gen
roent´gen-o-graph
roent-gen-og´ra-phy
Rog´er
ro-gnon´
rogue
rogu´ery
rogu´ish
rogu´ish-ness
rois´ter
rois´ter-er
rois´ter-ous
Ro´land
roll´back
roll call
rolled
roll´er
roll´er skate
rol´lick-ing
rol´lick-some
roll´ing
roll´ing mill
roll´ing pin
roll top
Röl´vaag
ro´ly—po´ly
Ro-ma´gna
ro-maine´
Ro´man
ro-man´
ro-mance´
ro-manc´er
ro-manc´ing
Ro´man-esque´
Ro-man´ic
Ro´man-ism
Ro´man-ist
ro-ma´ni-um
Ro´man-ize
Ro´ma-nov
ro-man´tic
ro-man´ti-cal-ly
ro-man´ti-cism
ro-man´ti-cist
Ro´meo
Rom´ish

romp´er
romp´ish
Rom´u-lus
roof´er
roof gar´den
roof´ing
roof´less
roof´tree
rook´ery
rook´ie
room´er
room-ette´
room´ful
room´mate
room´y
Roo´se-velt
roost´er
root´ed
root´er
root´less
root´let
root´stock
roped
rop´er
rope´walk-er
rop´ing
Roque´fort
Ror´schach
ro-sa´lia
Ros´a-lind
Ros´a-mond
Ro-sa´rio
ro´sa-ry
Ros´coe
ro´se-ate
rose´bud
rose´bush
rose cold
rose´—col-ored
rose fe-ver
rose´mary
ro-se´o-la
Ro-set´ta
ro-sette´
rose wa´ter
rose´wood
Rosh Ha-sha´nah
ro´sier
ros´i-ly

ros´in
ros´in-ate
ros´i-ness
Ros-set´ti
Ros-si´ni
ros´ter
ros´trum
ros´y
Ro-tar´i-an
ro´ta-ry
ro´tat-able
ro´tate
ro-ta´tion
ro´ta-tive
ro´ta-tor
ro´ta-to-ry
rote
ro´te-noid
ro´te-none
Roth´schild
ro-tis´ser-ie
ro´to-graph
ro´to-gra-vure´
ro´tor
rot´ten
rot´ten-ness
Rot´ter-dam
rot´ting
ro-tund´
ro-tun´da
ro-tun´di-ty
ro-tund´ly
roué´
Rou´en´
rouged
rough´age
rough´cast
rough´dry
rough´en
rough´er
rough´hew
rough´house
rough´ly
rough´neck
rough´ness
rough´rid-er
rough´shod
rou-lade´
rou-lette´

Rou-ma´nian
round´about
round´er
Round´head
round´house
round´ish
round´ly
round´ness
round´—shoul-dered
round´up
round´worm
roused
rous´ing
rous´ing-ly
Rous-seau´
roust´about
route
rout´ed
rout´er
rou-tine´
rout´ing
rov´er
rov´ing
row´an
row´boat
row´dies
row´di-ness
row´dy
row´dy-ish
row´dy-ism
Row-e´na
row´er
row´lock
roy´al
roy´al-ist
roy´al-ly
roy´al-ty
Ru-bai-yat´
rubbed
rub´ber
rub´ber-ize
rub´bing
rub´bish
rub´ble
rub´down
Ru´bens
ru-be´o-la
Ru´bi-con
ru´bi-cund

ru-bi-cun´di-ty
ru-bid´i-um
ru-big´i-nous
Ru´bin-stein
ru´ble
ru´brene
ru´bric
ru´by
ruck´us
rud´der
rud´di-ness
rud´dy
rude´ly
rude´ness
rud´est
ru´di-ment
ru´di-men´ta-ry
Ru´dolf
Ru´dolph
rue´ful
rue´ful-ly
ruffed
ruf´fi-an
ruf´fle
ruf´fled
ruf´fler
ruf´fling
Ru´fus
Rug´by
rug´ged
Ruhr
ru´in
ru´in-ate
ru-in-a´tion
ru´ined
ru´in-ing
ru´in-ous
rul´able
ruled
rul´er
rul´ing
Ru-ma´nia
rum´ba
rum´ble
rum´bler
rum´bling
ru´mi-nant
ru´mi-nate
ru-mi-na´tion

rum´mage
rum´mag-er
rum´mag-ing
rum´my
ru´mor
rump´er
rum´ple
rum´pled
rum´pling
rum´pus
run´about
run´a-gate
run´around
run´away
run´down
run´ner
run´ner—up´
run´ning
runt´y
run´way
ru-pee´
Ru´pert
rup´tur-able
rup´ture
rup´tured
rup´tur-ing
ru´ral
ru´ral-ly
rush´ing
rush´light
rush´y
Rus´kin
Rus´sell
rus´set
Rus´sia
Rus´sian
rus´tic
rus´ti-cate
rus-ti-ca´tion
rus´ti-ca-tor
rus-tic´i-ty
rust´i-ly
rust´i-ness
rus´tle
rus´tler
rust-tling
rust´proof
rust´y
ru´ta-ba´ga

Ru-the´ni-an
ru-then´ic
ru-the´ni-ous
ru-the´ni-um
Ruth´er-ford
ruth´less
ruth´less-ly
ruth´less-ness
Rut´land
rut´ted
rut´ty
Rwan´da
Ryu´kyu

S

Sab´a-oth
Sab´a-ti´ni
Sab´bath
sab-bat´i-cal
sa´ber
sa´ble
sabot´
sab´o-tage
sab´o-teur´
sa´bra
sac
sac´cha-rate
sac-char´ic
sac´cha-ride
sac´cha-rin
sac´cha-rin-ate
sac´cha-rine
sac-cha-rin´ic
sac´cu-lat-ed
sa-chet´
sack
sack´cloth
sack´ful
sack´ing
sac´ra-ment
sac´ra-men´tal
sac-ra-men´ta-ry
Sac´ra-men´to
sa´cred
sac´ri-fice
sac´ri-fi´cial
sac´ri-fic-ing
sac´ri-lege

sac´ri-le´gious
sac´ro-il´i-ac
sac´ro-sanct
sac´ro-sanc´ti-ty
sac´ro-sci-at´ic
sac´rum
sad´den
sad´der
sad´dle
sad´dle-bag
sad´dle-bow
sad´dler
sad´dlery
Sad´du-cee
sa´dism
sa´dist
sa-dis´tic
sa-dis´ti-cal-ly
sad´ly
sad´ness
sa-fa´ri
safe—con´duct
safe´guard
safe´keep-ing
safe´ly
saf´est
safe´ty
safe´ty match
safe´ty pin
safe´ty valve
saf´flor-ite
saf´fron
sa´ga
sa-ga´cious
sa-gac´i-ty
sag´a-more
sage´brush
sage´ly
sagged
sag´ging
Sag´i-naw
sag´it-tal
Sag-it-tar´i-us
sag´it-tate
Sag-ue-nay´
Sa-ha´ra
sa´hib
Sai-gon´
sail´boat

sail´cloth
sailed
sail´fish
sail´or
saint´ed
saint´hood
saint´li-ness
saint´ly
Sai-pan´
sa˝ke
Sa-kha-lin´
sa-laam´
sal-abil´i-ty
sal´able
sa-la´cious
sa-la´cious-ly
sa-lac´i-ty
sal´ad
Sal-a-man´ca
sal´a-man-der
sa-la˝mi
sal´a-ried
sal´a-ry
Sa˝lem
Sa-ler´no
sales´girl
sales´man
sales´man-ship
sales´per-son
sales´room
sales´wom-an
sa˝lience
sal´i-fy
sa-lim´e-ter
sa-li˝na
sal-i-na´tion
sa˝line
sa-lin´i-ty
Salis-bury
sa-li´va
sal´i-vary
sal´i-vate
sal-i-va´tion
sal´lied
sal´low
sal´ly
sal´ly-ing
sal´ly port

salm´on
Sal-mo-nel´la
Sa-lo˝me
sa-lon´
Sa-lon´i-ka
sa-loon´
sa-loon´keep-er
sal´si-fy
sal-ta´tion
salt´cel-lar
salt´ed
salt´ery
salt´i-er
sal´tire
salt marsh
salt´ness
salt-pe´ter
salt´y
sa-lu˝bri-ous
sa-lu˝bri-ty
Sa-lu˝ki
sal-u-tar´i-ly
sal´u-tary
sal-u-ta´tion
sa-lu-ta-to´ri-an
sa-lu´ta-to-ry
sa-lute´
sa-lut´ing
sal´va-ble
Sal´va-dor
sal´vage
sal´vage-able
sal´vag-er
sal-va´tion
salved
sal´ver
sal´via
salv´ing
sal´vo
sal´vor
Salz´burg
Sa-mar´ia
sa-mar´i-um
Sam´ar-kand
sam˝ba
sam-bu-ni´grin
same´ness
Sa-mo´a
Sa´mos

sam´o-var
sam´pan
sam´ple
sam´pler
sam´pling
Sam´son
Sam´u-el
sa´mu-rai
San An-to´nio
san-a-to´ri-um
San´cho
sanc-ti-fi-ca´tion
sanc´ti-fied
sanc´ti-fy
sanc´ti-fy-ing
sanc´ti-mo´ni-ous
sanc´ti-mo-ny
sanc´tion
sanc´tion-er
sanc´ti-ty
sanc´tu-ary
sanc´tum
san´dal
san´daled
san´dal-wood
sand´bag
sand´bank
sand´blast
sand´box
sand´er
sand´glass
sand´hog
San Di-e´go
sand´l-er
sand´i-ness
sand´man
San Do-min´go
sand´pa-per
sand´pip-er
sand´stone
sand´storm
San-dus´ky
sand´wich
sand´y
san-er
sane´ly
san´for-ize
San Fran-cis´co
sang-froid´

| | | |
|---|---|---|
| san´gui-nar´i-ly | Sar´ah | sat´iny |
| san-guin´a-rine | Sa´ra-je-vo | sat´ire |
| san´gui-nary | Sa-ran´ | sa-tir´ic |
| san´guine | Sar-a-to´ga | sa-tir´i-cal |
| san-guin´e-ous | Sa-ra´tov | sat´i-rist |
| san-guin´o-lent | Sa-ra´wak | sat´i-rize |
| San-he´drin | sar´casm | sat´i-riz-ing |
| san´i-dine | sar-cas´tic | sat-is-fac´tion |
| sa´ni-ous | sar-cas´ti-cal-ly | sat´is-fac´to-ri-ly |
| san-i-tar´i-an | sar-co´ma | sat´is-fac´to-ry |
| san´i-tar´i-ly | sar-co´ma-toid | sat´is-fied |
| san´i-tar´ium | sar-co-ma-to´sis | sat´is-fy |
| san´i-tary | sar-com´a-tous | sat-u-ra-bil´i-ty |
| san-i-ta´tion | sar-coph´a-gi | sat´u-ra-ble |
| san´i-tiz-er | sar-coph´a-gus | sat´u-rate |
| san´i-ty | sar-cop´side | sat´u-rat-ed |
| San Joa-quin´ | sar-dine´ | sat´u-rat-er |
| San Ma-ri´no | Sar-din´ia | sat´u-rat-ing |
| San Sal´va-dor | sar-don´ic | sat-u-ra´tion |
| San Se-bas´tian | sar-don´i-cal-ly | sat´u-ra-tor |
| San´skrit | sar-don´yx | Sat´ur-day |
| San´ta Bar´ba-ra | sar-gas´so | Sat´urn |
| San´ta Claus | sa´ri | sat-ur-na´lia |
| San´ta Fe | sa-rong´ | Sat-ur-na´lian |
| San´ta Ma-ri´a | sar-sa-pa-ril´la | Sa-tur´ni-an |
| San-ta-ya´na | sar-to´ri-al | sat´ur-nine |
| San´ti-a´go | sar-to´ri-us | sat-ur-nin´i-ty |
| San´to Do-min´go | sa-shay´ | sa´tyr |
| São To-mé´ and | Sas-katch´e-wan | sa-tyr´ic |
| Prín´ci-pe | sas´sa-fras | sauce´pan |
| sap´id | Sa´tan | sau´cer |
| sa-pid´i-ty | sa-tan´ic | sau´ci-ly |
| sap´i-ence | sa-tan´i-cal | sau´ci-ness |
| sap´i-ent | sa-tan´i-cal-ly | sau´cy |
| sap´i-en´tial | satch´el | Sau´di |
| sap´less | sat´ed | sau´er-bra-ten |
| sap´ling | sa-teen´ | sau´er-kraut |
| sa-pon-i-fi-ca´tion | sat´el-lite | Sault Sainte Ma-rie´ |
| sa-pon´i-fy | sat´el-lit-ed | sau´na |
| sap´per | sat´el-lit-oid | saun´ter |
| sap´phire | sat-el-lit-o´sis | saun´ter-ing |
| sap´ping | sat´el-loid | sau´sage |
| sap´py | sa-tia-bil´i-ty | sau-té´ |
| sap´suck-er | sa´tia-ble | sau-téd´ |
| sap´wood | sa´ti-ate | sau-téed´ |
| sar´a-band | sa-ti-a´tion | sau-té´ing |
| Sar´a-cen | sa-ti´e-ty | sau-terne´ |
| Sar-a-cen´ic | sat´in | sav´able |
| Sar´a-gos´sa | sat´in-et´ | sav´age |

sav´age-ly
sav´age-ry
sa-van´na
Sa-van´nah
sa-vant´
sa-vate´
saved
sav´er
sav´in
sav´ing
sav´ior
sa´voir faire´
sa´vor
sa´vor-ous
sa´vory
Sa-voy´
sav´vy
saw´buck
saw´dust
saw´horse
saw´mill
saw´yer
Sax´on
Sax´o-ny
sax´o-phone
sax´o-phon-ist
say´ing
scab
scab´bard
scabbed
scab´bing
scab´bler
scab´by
sca´bies
scaf´fold
scaf´fold-ing
sca´lar
scal´a-wag
scald´ed
scald´er
scaled
sca-lene´
scal´er
scal´ing
scal´lion
scal´lop
scal´loped
scal´pel
scalp´er

scal´y
scam´per
scan´dal
scan-da´iza´tion
scan´dal-ize
scan´dal-monger
scan´dal-ous
scan´dia
Scan-di-na´via
scanned
scan´ner
scan´ning
scan´sion
scant´i-ly
scant´i-ness
scant´ly
scant´y
scape´goat
scape´grace
scap´u-la
scap´u-lar
scar´ab
scarce
scarce´ly
scar´city
scare´crow
scared
scarf´er
scar-i-fi-ca´tion
scar´i-fi-ca-tor
scar´i-fied
scar´i-fy
scar´i-ly
scar´ing
scar´let
scarred
scar´ring
scary
scathe
scathed
scathe´less
scath´ing
scat-o-log´ic
scat-o-log´i-cal
sca-tol´o-gy
scat´ter
scat´ter-brain
scat´tered
scav´eng-er

scav´eng-ing
sce-nar´io
sce-nar´ist
sce´nery
sce´nic
scent
scent´ed
scent´er
scent´less
scep´ter
scep´tic
scep´ti-cal
scep´ti-cism
sche´di-asm
sched´ule
sched´uled
sched´ul-ing
Sche-her-a-zade´
sche´ma
sche-mat´ic
sche´ma-tism
sche´ma-list
scheme
schem´er
schem´ing
Sche-nec´ta-dy
scher´zo
Schia-pa-rel´li
schism
schis-mat´ic
schist
schist´oid
schist´ose
schis´to-some
schiz´oid
schiz-o-phre´nia
schiz´o-phren´ic
schle-miel´
schnap´per
Schnau´zer
Schnitz´ler
schol´ar
schol´ar-ly
schol´ar-ship
scho-las´tic
scho-las´ti-cal
scho-las´ti-cal-ly
scho-las´ti-cism
school bell

school board
school´book
school´boy
school bus
school´child
school´girl
school´house
school´ing
school´man
school´mas-ter
school´mate
school´mis-tress
school´room
school´teach-er
school´work
school´yard
schoo´ner
Scho´pen-hauer
Schu´bert
Schu´mann
Schuy´ler
Schuyl´kill
Schweit´zer
Schwei´zer
sci-at´ic
sci-at´i-ca
sci´ence
sci-en´tial
sci-en-tif´ic
sci-en-tif´i-cal-ly
sci´en-tist
scim´i-tar
scin-til´la
scin´til-late
scin´til-lat-ing
scin-til-la´tion
scin´til-la-tor
scin-til-lom´e-ter
sci-o-graph´ic
sci´on
scis´sors
sclar´e-ol
scle-ri´a-sis
scle-ri´tis
scle-rot´ic
scle-ro-ti´tis
scle´rous
scoff´er
scold´er

scold´ing
scold´ing-ly
sconce
scone
scoop´er
scoop´ful
scoot´er
scope
scorch´ing
scored
scor´ing
scorn´er
scorn´ful
scorn´ful-ly
Scor´pio
scor´pi-on
Scotch´—I´rish
Scotch´man
scot´—free´
Scot´land
Scots´man
Scot´tish
scoun´drel
scourge
scourg´er
scourg´ing
scout´ing
scout´mas-ter
scowl´er
scowi´ing-ly
scrab´ble
scrab´bler
scrab´bling
scrag´gly
scrag´gy
scram´ble
scram´bling
Scran´ton
scrap´book
scraped
scrap´er
scrap´ing
scrapped
scrap´ping
scrap´ple
scrap´py
scratch
scratch´er
scratch´i-ness

scratch´proof
scratch´y
scrawl´er
scrawl´y
scrawn´i-ness
scrawn´y
scream´er
scream´ing
screech
screech´y
screen
screen´er
screw´driv-er
scrib´ble
scrib´bler
scrib´bling
scribe
scrib´er
scrim´mage
scrim´mag-er
scrimp´i-ly
scrimp´y
scrip
script
scrip-to´ri-um
scrip´tur-al
scrip´ture
scriv´en-er
scroll
scroll´work
scro´tum
scrounge
scroung´ing
scrub
scrub´bing
scrub´by
scrump´tious
scru´ple
scru-pu-los´i-ty
scru´pu-lous
scru´pu-lous-ly
scru´ti-nize
scru´ti-ny
scud´ded
scuf´fle
scuf´fling
scull
scul´lery
sculp´tor

sculp´tur-al
sculp´ture
scum´bled
scum´my
scur-ril´i-ty
scur´ri-lous
scur´ried
scur´ry
scur´ry-ing
scur´vi-ly
scur´vy
scut´ter
scut´tle
scut´tle-butt
scut´tling
Scyl´la
scythe
scyth´ing
Sea´bee
sea´board
sea´coast
sea´drome
sea´far-er
sea´far-ing
sea fight
sea´food
sea´fowl
sea´girt
sea´go-ing
sea´—green
sea gull
sea horse
seal´able
seal´ant
sea legs
seal´er
seal´ery
sea lev´el
seal-ine´
seal´ing wax
sea li´on
sea lord
seal ring
seal´skin
Sea´ly-ham
sea´man
sea´manship
sea´men
seam´i-ness

seam´less
seam´stress
seam´y
sé´ance
sea´plane
sea´port
search´able
search´er
search´ing
search´light
search war´rant
sea rov´er
sea ser´pent
sea´shore
sea´sick
sea´sick-ness
sea´side
sea´son
sea´son-able
sea´son-al
sea´son-ing
seat´ed
seat´er
seat´ing
Se-at´tle
sea ur´chin
sea´wall
sea´ward
sea´way
sea´weed
sea´wor-thy
seb´a-cate
se-ba´ceous
Se-bas´tian
se-cede´
se-ced´ed
se-ced´er
se-ced´ing
se-ces´sion
se-ces´sion-ist
se-clude´
se-clud´ed
se-clud´ed-ly
se-clud´ing
se-clu´sion
se-clu´sive
Sec´o-nal
sec´ond
sec´ond-ar´i-ly

sec´ond-ary
sec´ond—class
sec´ond-er
sec´ond-hand´
sec´ond-ly
sec´ond—rate´
se´cre-cy
se´cret
sec´re-tar´i-al
sec-re-tar´i-at
sec´re-tary
se-crete´
se-cret´ed
se-cre´tin
se-cre´tion
se´cre-tive
se´cret-ly
se-cre´to-ry
sect
sec-tar´i-an
sec-tar´i-an-ism
sec´ta-ry
sec´tion
sec´tion-al
sec´tion-al-ism
sec´tion-al-ly
sec´tion-al-ize
sec´tor
sec´tor-al
sec to´ri-al
sec´u-lar
sec´u-lar-ism
sec´u-lar-ist
sec-u-lar´i-ty
sec-u-lar-iza´tion
sec´u-lar-ize
se-cure´
se-cure´ly
se-cur´ity
se-dan´
se-date´
se-date´ly
se-date´ness
sed´a-tive
sed´en-tar´i-ly
sed´en-tary
sedge
sedg´y
sed´i-ment

sed´i-men-tar´i-ly
sed´i-men´ta-ry
sed-i-men-ta´tion
se-di´tion
se-di´tion-ary
se-di´tious
se-duce´
se-duce´ment
se-duc´er
se-duc´i-ble
se-duc´ing
se-duc´tion
se-duc´tive
se-du´li-ty
sed´u-lous
seed´er
seed´ing
seed´less
seed´ling
seeds´man
seed´time
seed´y
see´ing
seek´er
seem´ing
seem´ing-ly
seem´ly
seep´age
seer´suck-er
see´saw
seethe
seethed
seeth´ing
seg´ment
seg-men´tal
seg-men´tal-ly
seg´men-tary
seg-men-ta´tion
seg´re-ga-ble
seg´re-gate
seg-re-ga´tion
seg-re-ga´tion-ist
sei´gneur´
seine
seis´mic
seis-mic´i-ty
seis´mism
seis´mo-graph
seis-mog´ra-pher

seis´mo-graph´ic
seis-mog´ra-phy
seis-mo-log´ic
seis-mo-log´i-cal
seis-mol´o-gist
seis-mol´o-gy
seis-mom´e-ter
seis´mo-met´ric
seiz´able
seize
seiz´er
seiz´ing
sei´zor
sei´zure
sel´dom
se-lect´
se-lect´ance
se-lect´ee´
se-lec´tion
se-lec´tive
se-lec-tiv´i-ty
se-lect´man
se-lec´tor
sel´e-nate
se-le´ni-um
self—as-sur´ance
self—cen´tered
self—com-mand´
self—con´fi-dence
self—con´fi-dent
self—con´scious
self—con´scious-ness
self—con-tained´
self—con-tra-dic´tion
self—con-trol´
self—de-fense´
self—de-ni´al
self—de-ter-mi-
    na´tion
self—dis´ci-pline
self—es-teem´
self—ev´i-dent
self—gov´ern-ment
self—help´
self—im-por´tance
self—im-por´tant
self—im-posed´
self´ish
self´ish-ly

self´ish-ness
self´less
self—made´
self—pit´y
self—pos-sessed´
self—pos-ses´sion
self—pres-er-va´tion
self—pro-tec´tion
self—re-gard´
self—re-li´ance
self—re-li´ant
self—re-spect´
self—re-spect´ing
self—sac´ri-fice
self´same
self—sat´is-fied
self—seek´ing
self´—start-er
self—suf-fi´cien-cy
self—suf-fi´cient
self—sup-port´ing
self—willed´
sell´er
sell´ing
selt´zer
sel´vage
selves
se-man´tic
se-man´ti-cist
se-man´tics
sem´a-phore
sem´a-phor´ic
sem´a-phor-ist
se-masi-ol´o-gy
sem´blance
se-mei-ol´o-gy
se´mei-ot´ic
se´men
se-mes´ter
se-mes´tral
sem´i-an´nu-al
sem´i-ar´id
sem´i-cir-cle
sem´i-cir´cu-lar
sem´i-co-lon
sem´i-con´scious
sem´i-de-tached´
sem´i-dine
sem´i-fi-nal

sem´i-lu´nar
sem´i-month´ly
sem´i-nal
sem´i-nar
sem´i-nary
sem´i-na´tion
Sem´i-nole
sem´i-pre´cious
Sem´ite
Se-mit´ic
Sem´i-tism
sem-o-li´na
se´na-ry
sen´ate
sen´a-tor
sen-a-to´ri-al
send´er
send´ing
send´—off
Sen´e-ca
se-ne´cic
sen´e-ga
Sen´e-gal
se´nile
se-nil´i-ty
sen´ior
se-nior´i-ty
sen´na
Sen-nach´er-ib
se-nor´
se-no´ra
se-ño-ri´ta
sen-sa´tion
sen-sa´tion-al
sen-sa´tion-al-ism
sensed
sense´less
sen-si-bil´i-ty
sen´si-ble
sen´si-bly
sen´sile
sens´ing
sen´si-tive
sen´si-tive-ness
sen-si-tiv´i-ty
sen-si-tiza´tion
sen´si-tize
sen´si-tiz-er
sen-si-tom´e-ter

sen-so´ri-al
sen-so´ri-um
sen´so-ry
sen´su-al
sen´su-al-ist
sen-su-al-is´tic
sen-su-al´i-ty
sen´su-ous
sen´su-ous-ly
sen´tence
sen-ten´tial
sen-ten´tious
sen´tience
sen´tient
sen´ti-ment
sen-ti-men´tal
sen-ti-men´tal-ism
sen-ti-men´tal-ist
sen-ti-men-tal´i-ty
sen-ti-men´tal-ize
sen-ti-men´tal-ly
sen´ti-nel
sen´ti-neled
sen´try
se´pal
se´paled
sep-a-ra-bil´i-ty
sep´a-ra-ble
sep´a-rate
sep´a-ra-tee´
sep´a-rate-ly
sep´a-ra´tion
sep´a-rat-ist
sep´a-ra-tor
se pia
Sep-tem´ber
sep-ten´ary
sep-ten´ni-al
sep-tet´
sep´tic
sep-ti-ce´mia
sep-tic´i-ty
sep-tif´ra-gal
sep-til´lion
sep´ti-mal
sep´tu´age-nar´i-an
Sep-tu´a-gint
sep´tum
sep´tu-ple

sep-tup´let
sep-tu´pli-cate
sep´ul-cher
se-qua´cious
se-quac´i-ty
se´quel
se-que´la
se´quence
se´quent
se-quen´tial
se-quen´tial-ly
se-ques´ter
se-ques´tered
seques´trate
seques-tra´tion
se´quin
se´quined
se-quoi´a
se-ra´glio
ser´al
se-ra´pe
ser´aph
se-raph´ic
ser´a-phim
Ser´bia
Ser-bo´ni-an
ser´e-nade´
ser´e-nad´er
ser´e-nad´ing
ser-en-dip´i-ty
se-rene´
se-rene´ly
se-ren´i-ty
serf´dom
serge
ser´geant
ser´geant at arms
se´ri-al
se´ri-al-ly
se-ri-a´tim
se-ri´ceous
ser´i-cin
se´ries
ser´if
se´ri-ous
se´ri-ous-ly
se´ri-ous-ness
ser´mon
ser-mon´ic

ser´mon-ize
se´ro-log´ic
se´ro-log´i-cal
se-rol´o-gist
se-rol´o-gy
se-ro-si´tis
se-ros´i-ty
se´rous
ser´pent
ser´pen-tine
ser´pen-tin-ite
ser-pi´go
ser´rate
ser´rat-ed
ser-ra´tion
ser´ried
ser´ru-late
ser´ry
se´rum
ser´vant
served
serv´er
serv´ice
serv´ice-able
ser´vile
ser-vil´i-ty
serv´ing
ser´vi-tor
ser´vi-tude
ser´vo-mech´a-nism
ser´vo-mo´tor
ses´a-me
ses´qui-cen-ten´ni-al
ses´sion
se-ta´ceous
set´back
se´ti-ger
se´ton
set-tee´
set´ter
set´ting
set´tle
set´tle-ment
set´tler
set´tling
set´—to
set´up
sev´en
sev´en-fold

sev´en-teen´
sev´en-teenth´
sev´enth
sev´en-ti-eth
sev´en-ty
sev´en-ty—six´
sev´er
sev´er-able
sev´er-al
sev´cr-al-ly
sev´er-ance
se-vere´
sev´ered
se-vere´ly
se-ver´i-ty
Se-ville´
sew
sew´age
Sew´ard
sew´er
sew´er-age
sew´ing
sex-a-ge-nar´i-an
sex-ag´e-nary
sex´tant
sex-tet´
sex-tette´
sex´ton
sex-tu´ple
sex-tup´let
sex-tu´pli-cate
sex´u-al
sex-u-al´i-ty
shab´bi-ness
shab´by
shack´le
shack´led
shack´ling
shade
shad´ed
shad´er
shad´i-er
shad´ing
shad´ow
shad´owy
shad´y
shag´bark
shagged
shag´ging

shag´gy
shah
shake
shake´down
shak´en
shak´er
Shake´speare
Shake-spear´ean
shak´i-ly
shak´ing
shak´y
shale
shal-lot´
shal´low
sham
sha´man
sha´man-ism
sham´ble
sham´bles
shame
shamed
shame´faced
shame´ful
shame´ful-ly
shame´less
shame´less-ly
sham´ing
shammed
sham´mer
sham´ming
sham-poo´
sham-pooed´
sham´rock
Shang´hai´
Shan´gri—La´
shank´er
Shan´non
shan-tung´
shan´ty
shaped
shape´less
shape´li-ness
shape´ly
shap´er
shap´ing
shar´able
share´crop-per
share´hold-er
shar´er

sha-rif´
shar´ing
shark´skin
Shar´on
sharp´en
sharp´en-er
sharp´en-ing
sharp´er
sharp´ly
sharp´ness
sharp´shoot-er
sharp´—sight-ed
Shas´ta
shat´ter
shat´tered
shaved
shave´ling
shave´tail
shav´en
shav´er
shav´ing
shawl
Shaw-nee´
sheaf
shear
shear´er
shear´ing
sheath
sheathe
sheathed
sheath´er
sheath´ing
sheath knife
sheaves
She´ba
shed´ding
sheen
sheep
sheep´cote
sheep dog
sheep´fold
sheep´herd-er
sheep´ish
sheep´skin
sheep´walk
sheer
sheer´ness
sheet´age
sheet an´chor

sheet´ing
sheet iron
Shef´field
sheik
shek´el
shelf
shel-lac´
shel-lacked´
she´lack´ing
shell´er
shell´fish
shell´proof
shell shock
shel´ter
shel´tered
shel´ter-ing
shelve
shelves
shelv´ing
Shen-an-do´ah
she-nan´i-gan
shep´herd
shep´herd-ess
Sher´a-ton
sher´bet
Sher´i-dan
sher´iff
Sher´lock
Sher´man
sher´ry
Sher´wood
Shet´land
shib´bo-leth
shield
shield´er
shift´er
shift´i-er
shift´i-ly
shift´ing
shift´less
shift´less-ness
shift´y
shi´le´lagh
shil´ling
Shi´loh
shim´mer
shim´mery
shim´ming
shim´my

shin´bone
shin´dig
shine
shin´er
shin´gle
shin´gled
shin´i-er
shin´ing
shin´ny
shin´plas-ter
shin´y
ship´board
ship´build-er
ship´build-ing
ship´load
ship´mas-ter
ship´mate
ship´ment
ship´own-er
shipped
ship´per
ship´ping
ship´ping room
ship´shape
ship´worm
ship´wreck
ship´wright
ship´yard
shirk
shirk´er
shirr
shirred
shirr´ing
shirt´ing
shirt´sleeve
shirt´waist
shiv´er
shiv´ered
shiv´ery
shoal
shoat
shock´er
shock´ing
shock´proof
shod´di-ness
shod´dy
shoe
shoe box
shoe brush

shoe´horn
shoe´ing
shoe´lace
shoe´mak-er
shoe pol´ish
shoe store
shoe´string
sho´gun
shoot´er
shoot´ing
shoot´ing star
shop´keep-er
shop´lift
shop´lift-er
shopped
shop´per
shop´ping
shop´talk
shop´walk-er
shop´worn
shore´line
shore´ward
shor´ing
shorn
short´age
short´cake
short cir´cuit
short´com-ing
short´en
short´en-ing
short´hand
short´hand´ed
short´horn
short´—lived´
short´ly
short´ness
short´sight-ed
short´stop
short—term´
short´wave´
short´—wind´ed
Sho-sho´ne
shot´gun
should
shoul´der
shoul´der blade
shoul´dered
shout´ed
shoved

shov´el
shov´eled
shov´el-er
shov´el-ful
shov´el-ing
shov´er
shov´ing
show´boat
show´case
show´down
showed
show´er
show´er bath
show´ery
show´i-ly
show´ing
show´man
show´man-ship
shown
show´room
show´y
shrap´nel
shred´ded
shred´ding
Shreve´port
shrewd
shrewd´ly
shrewd´ness
shrew´ish
Shrews´bury
shriek
shrieked
shriek´ing
shrill´ness
shril´ly
shrimp
shrined
shrin´er
shrink´able
shrink´age
shrink´er
shriv´el
shriv´eled
shriv´el-ing
shriv´en
shriv´ing
Shrop´shire
shroud´ed
Shrove´tide

shrub´bery
shrub´bi-ness
shrub´by
shrugged
shrug´ging
shrunk´en
shuck´ing
shud´der
shuf´fle
shuf´fle-board
shuf´fled
shunned
shun´ning
shunt´ing
shut´down
shut´—in
shut´off
shut´out
shut´ter
shut´ting
shut´tle
shut´tle-cock
Shy´lock
shy´ly
shy´ness
shy´ster
Si-am´
Si´a-mese´
Si-be´lius
Si-be´ria
sib´i-lance
sib´i-lant
sib´i-la-to-ry
sib´ling
Sic´i-ly
sick´en
sick´en-ing
sick´en-ing-ly
sick´ish
sick´le
sick´led
sick´li-er
sick´li-ness
sick´ly
sick´ness
sick´room
side arm
side´board
side´burns

sid´ed
side´long
side´sad-dle
side step
side´swipe
side´track
side´walk
side´ways
sid´ing
si´dle
si´dled
si´dling
siege
Sieg´fried
sieg´ing
Si-en´a
si-en´na
si-er´o-zem
si-er´ra
Si-er´ra Le-one´
Si-er´ra Ma´dre´
si-es´ta
sieve
siev´er
sift´er
sigh´ing
sight´ed
sight´er
sight´less
sight´ly
sight´see-ing
sight´seer
sig´ma
sig´ma-tism
sig´moid
sig-moid-ec´to-my
sig-moid-os´to-my
sig´nal
sig´naled
sig´nal-ing
sig´nal-ize
sig´nal-ly
sig´na-ry
sig´na-to-ry
sig´na-ture
sign´board
sig´net
sig-nif´i-cance
sig-nif´i-cant

sig-nif´i-cant-ly
sig-ni-fi-ca´tion
sig-nif´i-ca-tive
sig´ni-fied
sig´ni-fy
sig´ni-fy-ing
sign´post
si´lage
si´lence
si´lenc-er
si´lenc-ing
si´lent
si´lent-ly
Si-le´sia
Si-le´sian
sil-hou-ette´
sil-hou-et´ted
sil´i-ca
sil´i-cate
sil-i-ca-ti-za´tion
sil´i-ca-tor
sil´i-con
sil´i-cone
sil-i-co´sis
sil-i-cot´ic
silk´en
silk´i-er
silk´i-ness
silk—stock´ing
silk´weed
silk´worm
silk´y
sil´li-ness
sil´ly
si´lo
si´los
si-lox´ane
si´ta´tion
sil´va
sil´van
sil´ver
sil´ver gray
sil´ver—plat´ed
sil´ver-smith
sil´ver-ware
sil´ver-work
sil´very
Sim´e-on
sim´i-an

sim´i-lar
sim-i-lar´i-ty
sim´i-lar-ly
sim´i-le
si-mil´i-tude
sim´mer
si´mo-nize
si´mon—pure´
sim-pat´i-co
sim´per
sim´pered
sim´per-er
sim´per-ing
sim´ple
sim´ple-heart-ed
sim´pler
sim´plest
sim´ple-ton
sim´plex
sim-plic´i-ty
sim-pli-fi-ca´tion
sim´pli-fied
sim´pli-fy
sim´pli-fy-ing
sim´ply
sim´u-lant
sim´u-late
sim´u-lat-ing
sim-u-la´tion
sim´u-la-tive
sim´u-la-tor
si´mul-cast
si´mul-ta´neous
si´mul-ta´neous-ly
Si´nai
Sin´bad
sin-cere´
sin-cere´ly
sin-cer´est
sin-cer´i-ty
sine
sin´e-cure
sin´e-cur-ist
sin´ew
sin´ewy
sin´ful
Sing´a-pore
singe
singed

singe´ing
sing´er
sing´ing
sin´gle
sin´gle—hand´ed
sin´gle—mind´ed
sin´gle-ness
sin´gle-stick
sin´glet
sin´gle-ton
sin´gle-tree
sin´gling
sin´gly
sing´song
sin´gu-lar
sin-gu-lar´i-ty
sin´gu-lar-ly
sin´is-ter
sin´is-tral
sink´age
sink´er
sink´hole
sink´ing
sink´ing fund
sin´less
sinned
sin´ner
sin´ning
sin-u-os´i-ty
sin´u-ous
si´nus
si-nus-i´tis
si´nus-oi´dal
Sioux
Sioux Cit´y
si´phon
si´phon-age
si-pid´i-ty
sipped
sip´ping
sired
si´ren
sir´ing
sir´loin
si-roc´co
sir´up
sis´sy
sis´ter
sis´ter-hood

sis´ter—in—law
sis´ter-ly
Sis´tine
site
Sit´ka
sit´ter
sit´ting
sit´ting room
sit´u-ate
sit´u-at-ed
sit-u-a´tion
six´fold
six´—foot´
six´pence
six´—shoot-er
six´teen´
six´teenth´
sixth
six´ti-eth
six´ty
siz´able
siz´able-ness
siz´ar
sized
siz´ing
siz´zle
siz´zled
siz´zling
siz´zling-ly
skald
skat´ed
skat´er
skat´ing
skeet´er
skein
skel´e-tal
skel´e-ton
skel´e-ton-ize
skep´tic
skep´ti-cal
skep´ti-cism
sketch
sketch´book
sketched
sketch´i-est
sketch´i-ly
sketch´y
skew´er
ski

skid´ded
skid´ding
skied
skies
ski´ing
skilled
skil´let
skill´ful
skill´ful-ly
skill´ful-ness
skimmed
skim´mer
skim´ming
skimp´i-est
skimp´i-ly
skimp´ing
skimp´y
skin´—deep´
skin´flint
skinned
skin´ner
skin´ni-est
skin´ni-ness
skin´ning
skin´ny
skin´tight´
skip´per
skip´ping
skir´mish
skir´mish-er
skirt´er
skirt´ing
skit´ter
skit´tish
skit´tles
skiv´er
sku´dug´gery
skulk
skulk´er
skulk´ing
skull
skull´cap
skunk
sky´—blue´
sky´lark
sky´light
sky´line
sky´rock-et
sky´scrap-er

sky´ward
sky´writ-ing
slack´en
slack´ened
slack´er
slack´ness
slag´gy
slain
slake
slaked
slak´er
slak´ing
slam´—bang´
slammed
slam´ming
slan´der
slan´der-er
slan´der-ous
slang´i-ly
slang´y
slant´ing
slant´wise
slapped
slap´ping
slap´stick
slash´ing
slate
slat´ed
slath´er
slat´ing
slat´ted
slat´tern
slat´ting
slaugh´ter
slaugh´ter-house
slav´er
slav´ery
Slav´ic
slav´ish
slay´er
slay´ing
slea´zi-er
slea´zy
sled´ding
sledge
sledge´ham-mer
sleek´ly
sleep´er
sleep´i-ly

sleep´i-ness
sleep´ing
sleep´ing car
sleep´less
sleep´walk-er
sleep´walk-ing
sleep´y
sleet´i-ness
sleet´y
sleeve´less
sleigh
sleigh´ing
sleight
slen´der
slen´der-ize
slen´der-ness
slept
sleuth
slew
sliced
slic´er
slic´ing
slick´en-side
slick´er
slick´ness
slide
slide rule
slid´ing
sli´er
slight
slight´ing
slight´ly
slime
slim´i-er
slim´i-ness
slim´ness
slim´y
sling´er
sling´shot
slink´ing
slipped
slip´per
slip´pered
slip´per-i-ness
slip´per-y
slip´ping
slip´shod
slith´er
slith´ery

slit´ting
sliv´er
sli´ver
slob´ber
slob´ber-ing
sloe
sloe´berry
sloe gin
slo´gan
slog´ging
sloop
slope
sloped
slop´ing
slopped
slop´pi-ly
slop´ping
slop´py
slosh´y
sloth´ful
slot´ted
slouch
slouch´i-ly
slouch´ing
slouch´y
slough
Slo´vak
Slo-vak´ia
slov´en
slov´en-li-ness
slov´en-ly
slow´ly
slow´ness
sludge
sludg´er
sludg´y
slug´gard
slug´gish
sluice
sluice´way
sluic´ing
slum´ber
slum´ber-ous
slum´ming
slurred
slur´ring
slush
slush´i-ness
slush´y

slut´tish
sly´ly
sly´ness
smack´ing
small´ish
small´ness
small´pox
small´—time´
smart´en
smart´ly
smart´ness
smashed
smash´up
smat´ter
smat´ter-ing
smeared
smell´er
smell´ing
smell´y
smelt
smelt´er
smiled
smil´ing
smil´ing-ly
smirch
smirk´ing
smite
smith-er-eens´
Smith-so´ni-an
smith´y
smit´ten
smock´ing
smoke´house
smoke´less
smok´er
smoke´stack
smok´i-er
smok´ing
smok´y
smol´der
smol´dered
smol´der-ing
smooth
smooth´bore
smooth´en
smooth´ly
smooth´ness
smor´gas-bord
smoth´er

smoth´ered
smudge
smudg´er
smudg´i-ly
smudg´ing
smudg´y
smug´gle
smug´gler
smug´ly
smut´ti-ness
smut´ty
Smyr´na
snaf´fle
sna´fu´
snagged
snag´ging
snake´root
snak´i-ly
snak´y
snap´drag-on
snap´per
snap´pi-ly
snap´pish
snap´py
snap´shot
snared
snare drum
snar´ing
snarled
snarl´ing
snarl´ing-ly
snarl´ish
snatch´er
snatch´y
sneaked
sneak´er
sneak´i-ly
sneak´i-ness
sneak´ing
sneak´y
sneer´ing
sneeze
sneezed
sneez´er
sneez´ing
snick´er
snick´er-ing
sniff´er
sniff´ing

snif´fle
snif´ter
snip´er
snip´ing
snipped
snip´pet
snip´pi-er
snip´ping
snip´py
sniv´el
sniv´el-er
sniv´el-ing
snob´bery
snob´bish
snook´er
snoop´er
snoop´ery
snored
snor´er
snor´ing
snor´kel
snort´er
snort´ing
snout
snow´ball
snow´bank
snow´bird
snow´—blind
snow´bound
snow´drift
snow´drop
snow´fall
snow´flake
snow´i-er
snow line
snow´plow
snow´shed
snow´shoe
snow´storm
snow—white
snow´y
snubbed
snub´ber
snub´bing
snub´by
snub´—nosed
snuff´box
snuff´er
snuf´fle

snuf´fled
snug´gle
snug´gled
snug´gling
snug´gly
snug´ly
snug´ness
soak´age
soak´ing
soap´box
soap´er
soap´i-er
soap´i-ness
soap op´era
soap´stone
soap´suds
soap´y
soar
soar´ing
sob´bing
so´ber
so´ber-ly
so´ber—mind-ed
so-bri´e-ty
so´bri-quet
so—called
soc´cer
so-cia-bil´i-ty
so´cia-ble
so´cial
so´cial-ism
so´cial-ist
so-cial-is´tic
so´cial ite
so-ci-al´i-ty
so-cial-iza´tion
so´cial-ize
so´cial-ly
so-ci´a-try
so-ci´e-tal
so-ci´e-ty
so-ci-oc´ra-cy
so´ci-o-log´ic
so´ci-o-log´i-cal
so´ci-o-log´i-cal-ly
so-ci-ol´o-gist
so-ci-ol´o-gy
sock´et
Soc´ra-tes

so´da
so´da-lite
so-dal´i-ty
so´da wa´ter
sod´den
sod´ding
so´di-um
Sod´om
sod´omy
so´fa
so´far
So´fi´a
soft—boiled
soft´en
soft´en-er
soft´en-ing
soft´heart-ed
soft´ly
soft´ness
soft´—shell
soft´—soap
soft´y
sog´gi-ly
sog´gi-ness
sog´gy
soil´age
soiled
soi-rée´
Sois-sons´
so´journ
so´journ-er
sol´ace
sol´aced
sol´ac er
sol´ac-ing
so´lar
so´lar-ism
so-lar´i-um
so-lar-iza´tion
so-las´o-nine
sol´der
sol´dered
sol´dier
sol´dier-ly
sol´diery
sol´e-cism
sol´e-cist
sol´e-cis´tic
sole´ly

sol´emn
so-lem´ni-ty
sol-em-ni-za´tion
sol´em-nize
sol´emn-ly
so´le-noid
so-lic´it
so-lic-i-ta´tion
so-lic´i-tor
so-lic´i-tous
so-lic´i-tude
so-lic´i-tu´di-nous
sol´id
sol´i-dar´ic
sol´i-da-ris´tic
so´i-dar´i-ty
so-lid-i-fi-ca´tion
so-lid´i-fied
so-lid´i-fy
so-lid´i-ty
sol´id-ly
sol´id-ness
so-lil´o-quist
so-lil´o-quize
so-lil´o-quy
sol´i-taire
sol´i-tar-i-ly
sol´i-tary
sol´i-tude
sol´lar
so´lo
so´lo ist
Sol´o-mon
So´lon
sol´stice
sol-u-bil´i-ty
sol´u-bi-liz-er
sol´u-ble
sol´ute
so-lu´tion
sol´u-tizer
solv-abil´i-ty
solv´able
solved
sol´ven-cy
sol´vent
solv´ing
So-ma´li
So-ma´lia

so-mat´ic
so-mat´i-cal-ly
so-ma-ti-za´tion
so´ma-to-gen´ic
so-ma-tol´o-gy
som´ber
som´ber-ness
som-bre´ro
som-bre´ros
some´body
some´day
some´how
some´one
som´er-sault
Som´er-set
Som´er-ville
some´thing
some´time
some´times
some´what
some´where
som-nam´bu-late
som-nam´bu-la-tor
som-nam´bu-lism
som-nam´bu-list
som-nam´bu-lis´tic
som´no-lence
som´no-lent
som´no-lent-ly
so´nar
so-na´ta
son-a-ti´na
song´bird
song´ster
song´stress
son´ic
son—in—law
son´net
son´ne-teer´
son´ny
so-nom´e-ter
So-no´ra
son-o-res´cent
son´o-rif´er-ous
so-nor´i-ty
sono´rous
sono´rous-ly
soon´er
soon´est

sooth
soothe
soothed
sooth´er
sooth´ing
sooth´ing-ly
sooth´say-er
soot´i-ness
soot´y
So-phi´a
soph´ism
soph´ist
soph´is-ter
so-phis´tic
so-phis´ti-cate
so-phis´ti-cat-ed
so-phis-ti-ca´tion
soph´is-try
Soph´o-cles
soph´o-more
soph´o-mor´ic
sop´o-rif´ic
sop´ping
sop´py
so-pra´no
Sor-bonne´
sor´cer-er
sor´cer-ess
sor´cery
sor´did
sor´did-ly
sore´ly
sore´ness
sor´ghum
so-ror´i-ty
sor´rel
sor´ri-ness
sor´row
sor´row-ful
sor´row-ful-ly
sor´ry
sort´able
sor´ter
sor´tie
sor´ti-lege
sot´tish
sot´to vo´ce
souf-flé´
sought

soul´ful
soul´ful-ly
soul´less
soun´der
sound´ing
sound´less
sound´ly
sound´ness
sound´proof
soup´i-er
soup´y
source
sour´ly
sour´ness
South-amp´ton
South Car-o-li´na
South Da-ko´ta
south´east´
south-east´er-ly
south-east´ern
south´er-ly
south´ern
south´ern-er
south´ern-most
south´land
south´ward
South´wark
south´west´
south-west´er-ly
south-west´ern
sou-ve-nir´
sov´er-eign
sov´er-eign-ty
so´vi-et
soy
soy´a
soy´bean
Space´ Age
space´craft
spaced
space´man
space´men
space´ship
space´walk
spac´ing
spa´cious
spa´cious-ness
spack´le
spack´led

spack´ling
spade
spad´ed
spad´er
spade´ful
spade´work
spad´ing
spa-ghet´ti
span´gle
span´gled
span´gly
Span´iard
span´iel
Span´ish
spank´er
spank´ing
spanned
span´ner
span´ning
spared
spare´ness
spare´rib
spar´ing
spar´ing-ly
spar´kle
spar´kler
spark´let
spar´kling
spar´kling-ly
sparred
spar´ring
spar´row
sparse´ly
spar´si-ty
Spar´ta
Spar´tan
Spar´tan-burg
spasm
spas-mod´ic
spas-mod´i-cal-ly
spas-mol´y-sis
spas-mo-lyt´ic
spas´tic
spas´ti-cal-ly
spas-tic´i-ty
spa´tial
spa-ti-al´i-ty
spa´tial-ly
spa-ti-og´ra-phy

spat´ter
spat´ting
spat´u-la
spawned
spawn´er
speak´able
speak´easy
speak´er
speak´ing
spear´fish
spear´head
spear´man
spear´mint
spe´cial
spe´cial-ist
spe-ci-al´i-ty
spe-cial-iza´tion
spe´cial-ize
spe´cial-ly
spe´cial-ty
spe´cie
spe´cies
spec´i-fi-able
spe-cif´ic
spe-cif´i-cal-ly
spec-i-fi-ca´tion
spec-i-fic´i-ty
spec´i-fied
spec´i-fi-er
spec´i-fy
spec´i-fy-ing
spec´i-men
spe-ci-os´i-ty
spe´cious
speck´le
speck´led
speck´ling
spec´ta-cle
spec´ta-cled
spec-tac´u-lar
spec-tac-u-lar´i-ty
spec-tac´u-lar-ly
spec´ta-tor
spec´ta-to´ri-al
spec´ter
spec´tral
spec-trog´ra-phy
spec´tro-scope
spec´tro-scop´ic

spec´tro-scop´i-cal
spec-tros´co-pist
spec-tros´co-py
spec´trum
spec´u-late
spec´u-lat-ing
spec-u-la´tion
spec´u-la-tive
spec´u-la-tor
sped
speech
speech´i-fy
speech´less
speed´boat
speed´er
speed´i-ly
speed´ing
speed lim´it
speed-om´e-ter
speed´ster
speed´way
speed´well
speed´y
spe´le-ol´o-gist
spe´le-ol´o-gy
spell´bind-er
spell´bound
spell´er
spell´ing
spe-lunk´er
spend´er
spend´ing
spend´thrift
spent
sper-ma-ce´ti
sper-mat´ic
sper´ma-tin
sper-ma-ti-za´tion
sper´ma-to-zo´ic
sper´ma-to-zo´id
sper´ma-to-zo´on
spher´al
sphere
spher´i-cal
spheri-cal´i-ty
sphe-ric´i-ty
sphe´roid
sphe-roi´dal
sphe-roi´dal-ly

spheroid-ic´i-ty
sphinc´ter
sphinc-ter-ot´o-my
sphin-gom´e-ter
sphinx
spice´bush
spiced
spic´i-ly
spic´i-ness
spic´ing
spic´u-la
spic´u-lar
spic´ule
spic´y
spi´der
spi´der web
spi´dery
spiel´er
spig´ot
spiked
spike´let
spike´nard
spik´i-ness
spik´ing
spik´y
spill´age
spilled
spill´er
spill´ing
spill´way
spin´ach
spi´nal
spin´dle
spin´dler
spin´dling
spin´dly
spin´drift
spine´less
spin´et
spin´na-ker
spin´ner
spin´ning
spin´ning wheel
spi´nose
spi-nos´i-ty
spi´nous
Spi-no´za
spin´ster
spin´ster-hood

spi´nule
spi´nu-les´cent
spin´y
spir´a-cle
spi-rac´u-lar
spi´ral
spi-ral´e
spi´raled
spi´ral-ing
spi´ral-ly
spi´rant
spir´it
spir´it-ed
spir´it-ism
spir´it-is´tic
spir´it-less
spir´i-tu-al
spir´i-tu-al-ism
spir´i-tu-al-ist
spir´i-tu-al-is´tic
spir-i-tu-al´i-ty
spir´i-tu-al-ize
spir´i-tu-al-ly
spir´i-tu-el´
spir-i-tu-os´i-ty
spir´i-tu-ous
spi´ro-graph
spi´roid
spir´y
spite
spit´ed
spite´ful
spit´fire
spit´ing
spit´ting
spit´tle
spit-toon´
splash´ing
splash´y
splat´ter
spleen´ish
splen´dent
splen´did
splen´did-ly
splen-dif´er-ous
splen´dor
splen´dor-ous
sple´nic
sple-ni´tis

sple´ni-um
spliced
splic´er
splic´ing
splin´ter
splin´tered
split´—lev´el
split´ting
splotch´y
splurge
splurged
splut´ter
spoil´age
spoiled
spoil´er
spoil´ing
spoils´man
Spo-kane´
spo´ken
spokes´man
sponge
sponged
spong´er
spong´i-ness
spong´ing
spong´y
spon´sor
spon-so´ri-al
spon´sor-ship
spon-ta-ne´i-ty
spon-ta´ne-ous
spook´ish
spook´y
spoon´er-ism
spoon´ful
spo-rad´ic
spo-rad´i-cal-ly
spo-ran´gia
spo-ran´gi-um
spore
sport´i-er
sport´i-est
sport´i-ly
sport´i-ness
sport´ing
spor´tive
sports´cast-er
sports´man
sports´man-like

| | | |
|---|---|---|
| sports´man-ly | spruce | squat´ted |
| sports´man-ship | spruced | squat´ter |
| sports´men | spruce´ly | squat´ting |
| sports´wear | spruc´ing | squat´ty |
| sports´wom-an | spry´ly | squaw |
| sports´women | spu´mous | squawk |
| sports´writ-er | spum´y | squawked |
| sport´y | spunk´i-ness | squawk´er |
| spot | spunk´y | squeak |
| spot´less | spurge | squeak´i-ly |
| spot´less-ly | spu´ri-ous | squeak´ing |
| spot´less-ness | spu´ri-ous-ly | squeak´y |
| spot´light | spurn´ing | squeal´er |
| spot´ted | spurred | squeal´ing |
| spot´ter | spur´ring | squea´mish |
| spot´ti-er | spurt´ed | squea´gee |
| spot´ti-est | spur´tive | squeezed |
| spot´ti-ly | sput´nik | squeez´er |
| spot´ting | sput´ter | squeez´ing |
| spot´ty | sput´ter-ing | squelched |
| spous´al | spu´tum | squid |
| spouse | spy´glass | squil´la |
| spout´er | spy´ing | squint´ed |
| sprained | squab´ble | squint´er |
| sprawl´er | squab´bled | squint´ing |
| sprawl´ing | squab´bling | squire |
| sprayed | squad | squir´ing |
| spray´er | squad´ron | squirm´y |
| spread´er | squa´lene | squir´rel |
| spread´ing | squal´id | squirt |
| sprig´gy | squa-lid´i-ty | squirt´ed |
| spright´li-ness | squall | squirt´ing |
| spright´ly | squall´cr | stabbed |
| spring´board | squall´y | stab´bing |
| spring´bok | squal´or | sta´bile |
| spring´er | squan´der | stab-i-lim´e-ter |
| Spring´field | squan´dered | sta-bil´i-ty |
| spring´i-ness | squan´der-ing | sta-bi-li-za´tion |
| spring´ing | square | sta´bil-i-za´tor |
| spring´time | squared | sta´bi-lize |
| spring´y | square dance | sta´bi-liz-er |
| sprin´kle | square´ly | sta´ble |
| sprin´kler | squar´er | sta´bled |
| sprin´kling | square root | sta´ble-mate |
| sprint´er | squar´ing | sta´bling |
| sprite | squash | stac-ca´to |
| sprit´sail | squash´i-ness | stach´y-drine |
| sprock´et | squash´ing | stacked |
| sprout | squash´y | stack´er |

stac´te
sta´di-um
staffed
staff´er
Staf´ford
stage´coach
stage´craft
staged
stage´hand
stag´er
stag´ger
stag´ger-ing
stag´hound
stag´ing
stag-mom´e-ter
stag´nan-cy
stag´nant
stag´nate
stag´nat-ing
stag-na´tion
stag´y
staid
stain´er
stain´ing
stain´less
stair´case
stair´way
staked
stak´ing
stalac´tite
stal´ac-tit´ic
sta´lag
stalag´mite
stal´ag-mit´ic
stale´mate
stale´ness
stal´er
Sta´lin
Sta´lin-grad
stalk´er
stalk´ing
stal´lion
stal´wart
sta´men
Stam´ford
stam´i-na
stam´mer
stam´mer-er
stam´mer-ing

stamped
stam-pede´
stamp´er
stance
stanch
stan´chion
stan´dard
stan´dard—bear-er
stan´dard-iza´tion
stan´dard-ize
stand´by
stand´ee´
stand´ing
Stan´dish
stand´ish
stand´off
stand´pipe
stand´point
stand´still
Stan´ford
sta´nine
Stan´ton
stan´za
sta´pes
staph-y-lo-coc´cus
staph-y-lot´o-my
sta´ple
sta´pled
sta´pler
sta´pling
star´board
starch´er
starch´i-ness
starch´y
stared
star´er
star´fish
star´gaz-er
star´ing
stark´ly
star´less
star´let
star´light
star´like
star´ling
star´lit
star´lite
starred
star´ring

star´ry
star´ry—eyed
star´—shaped
star shell
star´—span´gled
start´er
star´tle
star´tling
star-va´tion
starve
starved
starv´er
starv´ing
sta´sis
state´craft
stat´ed
state´hood
state´house
state´li-ness
state´ly
state´ment
Stat´en Is´land
stat´er
state´room
states´man
states´man-ship
state´wide
stat´ic
stat´i-cal-ly
stat´i-ce
sta´tion
sta´tion-ary
sta´tio-ner
sta´tio-nery
sta´tion-mas-ter
stat´ism
stat´ist
sta-tis´tic
sta-tis´ti-cal
sta-tis´ti-cal-ly
stat-is-ti´cian
sta-tis´tics
sta´tor
stat´u-ary
stat´ue
stat´u-esque´
stat´u-ette´
stat´ure
sta´tus

stat´ut-able
stat´ute
stat´u-to-ry
staunch
staunch´ly
stay´ing
stead´fast
stead´i-ly
stead´i-ness
stead´y
steal
steal´age
stealth
stealth´i-ly
stealth´i-ness
stealth´y
steam´boat
steam boil´er
steam en´gine
steam´er
steam´fit-ter
steam´roll-er
steam´ship
steam shov´el
steam ta´ble
steam´tight
steam´y
steel
steel´works
steel´y
steep´en
steep´er
stee´ple
stee´ple-chase
stee´ple-jack
steep´ly
steep´ness
steer´age
stego-sau´rus
stel´lar
Stel´lite
stel´lu-lar
stem´less
stemmed
stem´ming
sten´cil
sten´ciled
sten´cil-ing
ste-nog´ra-pher

sten´o-graph´ic
sten´o-graph´i-cal-ly
ste-nog´ra-phy
sten´o-type
sten´o-typ-ist
sten-to´ri-an
step´child
step´daugh-ter
step´fa-ther
step—in
step´lad-der
step´moth-er
steppe
step´per
step´ping
step´ping—stone
step´son
stere-og-no´sis
ste´reo-graph
stere-og´ra-pher
ste´reo-graph´ic
stere-om´e-ter
stereo-met´ric
stere-om´e-try
ste´reo-phon´ic
stere-oph´o-ny
stere-op´sis
stere-op´ti-con
ste´re-op´tics
ste´reo scope
ste´reo-scop´ic
stere-os´co pist
stere-os´co-py
stere-ot´o-my
stere-ot´ro-pism
ste´reo-type
ste´reo-typ-er
ste´reo-typ-ing
ste´reo-typy
ster´ic
ster´i-cal-ly
ster´ile
ste-ril´i-ty
ster-i-liza´tion
ster´i-lize
ster´i-liz-er
ster´let
ster´ling
stern´ly

stern´ness
ster´num
ster´oid
ste-roi´dal
steth´o-scope
steth´o-scop´ic
ste-thos´co-py
stet´ted
Steu´ben
Steu´ben-ville
ste´ve-dore
Ste´vens
Ste´ven-son
stew´ard
stew´ard-ess
stew´ard-ship
Stew´art
stew´pan
stick´er
stick´ful
stick´i-er
stick´i-ness
stick´ing
stick´le
stick´le-back
stick´y
stiff´en
stiff´en-er
stiff´en-ing
stiff´ly
stiff—necked
stiff´ness
sti´fle
sti´fling
stig´ma
stig-mat´ic
stig-mat´i-cal
stig´ma-tism
stig´ma tist
stig-ma-ti-za´tion
stig´ma-tize
sti-let´to
still´born
still´—hunt
still´ness
stilt´ed
stim´u-lant
stim´u-late
stim-u-la´tion

stim´u-la-tive
stim´u-la-tor
stim´u-li
stim´u-lus
sting´er
stin´gi-er
stin´gi-ness
sting´ing
stin´gy
stink´er
stink´ing
stink´weed
stint´ing
sti´pend
stip´ple
stip´pled
stip´pling
stip´u-late
stip´u-lat-ing
stip-u-la´tion
stip´u-la-tor
stip´u-la-to-ry
stir
stirred
stir´ring
stir´rup
stitch´er
stitch´ing
stoc-ca´do
stock-ade´
stock´bro-ker
stock dove
stock´hold-er
Stock´holm
stock´ing
stock´job-ber
stock´man
stock mar´ket
stock´pile
Stock´ton
stock´y
stock´yard
stodg´i-ness
stodg´y
sto´gie
sto´ic
sto´i-cal
sto´i-cism
stoked

stok´er
stok´ing
sto´len
stol´id
sto-lid´i-ty
stol´id-ly
sto´ma
stom´ach
stom´ach-ache
stom´ach-er
sto-mach´ic
stom´a-ta
stone´bass
stone´boat
stone crush´er
stone´cut-ter
stoned
Stone´henge
stone´ma-son
stone proof
stone´wall
stone´ware
stone´work
ston´i-ly
ston´i-ness
ston´ing
ston´y
stop´gap
stop´page
stopped
stop´per
stop´ping
stop´watch
stor´age
sto´rax
stored
store´house
store´keep-er
store´room
sto´ried
stor´ing
stork
storm´i-ly
storm´i-ness
storm´proof
storm´y
sto´ry
sto´ry-tell-er
stout´ness

stove´pipe
sto´ver
stow´age
stow´away
stra-bis´mal
stra-bis´mus
strad´dle
strad´dler
strad´dling
Stradi-var´i-us
strafed
straf´ing
strag´gle
strag´gler
strag´gling
strag´gly
straight
straight´away
straight´edge
straight´en
straight´en-er
straight´for´ward
strained
strain´er
strait
strait´en
strait´ened
strait´jacket
strait´laced
strand´er
strange´ly
strange´ness
stran´ger
stran´gle
stran´gler
stran´gling
stran´gu-late
stran-gu-la´tion
strapped
strap´ping
stra´ta
strat´a-gem
stra-te´gic
stra-te´gi-cal
strat´e-gist
strat´e-gy
Strat´ford
stra-tic´u-late
strat-i-fi-ca´tion

strat´i-fied
strat´i-fy
strat´i-fy-ing
strat´i-graph´ic
stra-tig´ra-phy
strat´o-cu´mu-lus
strat´o-sphere
strat´o-spher´ic
stra´tum
stra´tus
straw˝ber-ry
straw˝board
stray´er
stray´ing
streak´i-ness
streak´y
stream
stream´er
stream˝let
stream˝line
stream˝lined
street
street˝car
strength
strength´en
strength´en-ing
strength˝less
stren´u-ous
strep´ta-mine
strep´to-coc´cic
strep-to-coc-co´sis
strep-to-coc´cus
strep-to-my´cin
stressed
stretch´er
strewed
strewn
stri´at´ed
stri-a´tion
strick´en
strick˝le
strict´ly
strict´ness
stric´ture
stri´dent
strid´er
strid´ing
strid´u-late
strid-u-la´tion

strid´u-la-to-ry
strid´u-lous
strife
strik´er
strik´ing
stringed
strin´gen-cy
strin´gent
string´er
string´i-ness
string´ing
string´piece
string´y
striped
strip´er
strip´ing
strip´ling
stripped
strip´ping
strive
striv´en
striv´ing
stro˝bo-scop´ic
stro˝bo-tron
stro´ga-noff
stroked
strok´er
strok´ing
stroll´er
strong´—arm
strong´box
strong´hold
strong´ly
strong´point
strong´room
strop´ping
struc´tur-al
struc´tur-al-ly
struc´ture
stru´del
strug´gle
strug´gled
strug´gling
strum´ming
strum´pet
strut´ted
strut´ting
strych´nine
strych´nin-ism

stubbed
stub˝ber
stub˝bi-ness
stub˝bing
stub˝ble
stub˝bly
stub˝born
stub˝born-ness
stub˝by
stuc´co
stuc´co-er
stuc´co-work
stuck´—up
stud´ded
stud´ding
Stu´de-bak-er
stu´dent
stud´ied
stud´ied-ly
stu´dio
stu´dious
stud´y
stud´y-ing
stuff
stuffed
stuff´i-ly
stuff´i-ness
stuff´ing
stuff´y
stul-ti-fi-ca´tion
stul´ti-fied
stul´ti-fy
stul´ti-fy-ing
stum˝ble
stum˝bling
stum˝bling block
stump´age
stump´y
stunned
stun´ning
stunt´ed
stu´pe-fied
stu´pe-fi-er
stu´pe-fy
stu´pe-fy-ing
stu-pen´dous
stu´pid
stu-pid´i-ty
stu´pid-ly

stu´por
stu´por-ous
stur´died
stur´di-ly
stur´di-ness
stur´dy
stur´geon
stut´ter
stut´tered
stut´ter-ing
Stutt´gart
Stuy´ve-sant
styled
sty´let
styl´ing
styl´ish
styl´ist
sty-lis´tic
sty´lite
styl-i-za´tion
styl´ize
sty´mie
sty´mied
sty´mie-ing
styp´tic
sty´rene
suave
suave´ly
suav´i-ty
sub-al´tern
sub-atom´ic
sub-ce-les´tial
sub´cel-lar
sub´cla´vi-an
sub´com-mit-tee
sub-con´scious
sub´con-trac-tor
sub´cu-ta´ne-ous
sub´di-vide
sub´di-vid-ing
sub´di-vi-sion
sub-due´
sub-du´ing
sub´ject
sub-jec´tion
sub-jec´tive
sub-jec´tiv-ism
sub-jec-tiv´i-ty
sub´join´

sub´ju-gate
sub´ju-gat-ing
sub´ju-ga´tion
sub´ju-ga-tor
sub-junc´tive
sub´lease´
sub´les´see´
sub´les´sor
sub´let´
sub´let´ting
sub´li-mate
sub´li-mat-ing
sub´li-ma´tion
sub-lime´
sub-lime´ly
sub-lim´in-al
sub-lim´i-ty
sub´ma-rine
sub-merge´
sub-merged´
sub-mer´gence
sub-mer´gible
sub-mer´sal
sub-merse´
sub-mersed´
sub-mers´ible
sub-mers´ing
sub-mer´sion
sub-mis´sion
sub-mis´sive
sub-mit´
sub-mit´ted
sub-mit´ting
sub-nor´mal
sub-nor-mal´i-ty
sub-or´di-nate
sub-or´di-nate-ly
sub-or´di-na´tion
sub-or´di-na-tive
sub-orn´
sub-or-na´tion
sub-pe´naed
sub-poe´na
sub-poe´naed
sub-poe´na-ing
sub´ro-gate
sub-ro-ga´tion
sub ro´sa
sub-scribe´

sub-scrib´er
sub-scrib´ing
sub-scrip´tion
sub-scrip´tive
sub´se-quence
sub´se-quent
sub´se-quen´tial
sub-ser´vi-ence
sub-ser´vi-ent
sub-serv´ing
sub-side´
sub-sid´ence
sub-sid´i-ary
sub-sid´ing
sub-si-di-za´tion
sub´si-dize
sub´si-dy
sub-sist´
sub-sist´ence
sub-sist´ent
sub-son´ic
sub´stance
sub-stan´tial
sub-stan-ti-al´i-ty
sub-stan´tial-ly
sub-stan´ti-ate
sub-stan-ti-a´tion
sub´stan-tive
sub´sta-tion
sub-stit´u-ent
sub´sti-tut-able
sub´sti-tute
sub´sti-tut-ed
sub´sti-tut-ing
sub-sti-tu´tion
sub´sti-tu-tive
sub´stratum
sub´struc´ture
sub-sump´tive
sub-tend´
sub´ter-fuge
sub-ter-ra´nean
sub-ter-ra´ne-ous
sub´tle
sub´tle-ty
sub´tly
sub-tract´
sub-tract´er
sub-trac´tion

sub-trac´tive
sub-trop´i-cal
sub´urb
sub-ur´ban
sub-ur´ban-ite
sub-ven´tion
sub-ver´sion
sub-ver´sion-ary
sub-ver´sive
sub-vert´
sub-vert´er
sub-vert´ible
sub´way
suc-ceed´
suc-cess´
suc-cess´ful
suc-cess´ful-ly
suc-ces´sion
suc-ces´sive
suc-ces´sor
suc-cinct´
suc-cinct´ly
suc-cin´ic
suc´cor
suc´co-ry
suc´co-tash
suc´cu-lent
suc-cumb´
suck´er
suck´le
suck´ler
suck´ling
Su´cre
su´crose
suc´tion
Su-dan´
sud´den
sud´den-ly
suds-y
sue
sued
suede
su´et
su´ety
Su´ez´
suf´fer
suf´fer-able
suf´fer-ance
suf´fer-er

suf´fer-ing
suf-fice´
suf-ficed´
suf-fic´er
suf-fi´cien-cy
suf-fi´cient
suf-fic´ing
suf´fix
suf´fo-cate
suf´fo-cat-ing
suf´fo-ca´tion
suf´fo-ca-tive
Suf´folk
suf´fra-gan
suf´frage
suf´frag-ette´
suf-frag-ett´ism
suf´frag-ist
suf-fus´able
suf-fuse´
suf-fus´ing
suf-fu´sion
suf-fu´sive
sug´ar
sug´ar beet
sug´ar-boat
sug´ar bush
sug´ar cane
sug´ared
sug´ar-i-ness
sug´ar-loaf
sug´ar ma´ple
sug´ar-plum
sug´ary
sug-gest´
sug-gest-ibil´i-ty
sug-gest´ible
sug-ges´tion
sug-ges´tive
su´i-ci´dal
su´i-ci´dal-ly
su´i-cide
su´ing
suit-abil´i-ty
suit´able
suit´ably
suit´case
suite
suit´ing

suit´or
su-ki-ya´ki
sul´fa
sul-fa-cet´a-mide
sul´fa-di´a-zine
sul-fa-gua´ni-dine
sul-fa-mer´a-zine
sul´fa-meth´y´thi´a-
  zole
sul´fam´ic
sulf-am´ide
sul-fam´o-yl
sul-fa-nil´a-mide
sul´fa-nil´ic
sul´fate
sul´fa-tize
sul´fide
sulf-ox´ide
sul´fur
sul´fu-rate
sul-fu´re-ous
sul-fu´ret-ed
sul-fu´ric
sul´fu-rize
sul´fu-rous
sul´fur-yl
sulk´i-ly
sulk´i-ness
sulk´y
sul´len
sul´len-ly
sul´len-ness
sul´lied
Sul´li-van
sul´ly
sul´tan
su-tan´a
sul´tan-ate
sul-tan´ic
sul´tri-er
sul´tri-ness
sul´try
su´mac
Su-ma´tra
Su-mer´i-an
sum´ma cum lau´de
sum-mar´i-ly
sum´ma-ri-za´tion
sum´ma-rize

sum´ma-ry
sum-ma´tion
sum´mer
sum´mer-house
sum´mer-time
sum´mery
sum´ming
sum´mit
sum´mit-ry
sum´mon
sum´moned
sum´mon-er
sum´mon-ing
sum´monsed
sump´ter
sump´tu-ary
sump-tu-os´i-ty
sump´tu-ous
sun´beam
sun´bon-net
sun´burn
sun´burned
sun´burst
sun´dae
Sun´day
sun´der
sun´der-ance
sun´dew
sun´di-al
sun´down
sun´down-er
sun´dries
sun´dry
sun´fast
sun´fish
sun´flow-er
sun´glass-es
sunk´en
sun´lamp
sun´less
sun´light
sun´lit
sun´ni-er
sun´ning
sun´ny
sun´rise
sun´set
sun´shine
sun´shiny

sun´spot
sun´stroke
sun´struck
sun´up
su´per
su-per-a-bil´i-ty
su´per-a-ble
su-per-abun´dance
su-per-abun´dant
su-per-an´nu-ate
su-per-an´nu-at-ed
su-per-an-nu-a´tion
su-perb´
su-perb´ly
su´per-car-go
su-per-cil´i-ary
su-per-cil´i-ous
su-per-co-lum´nar
su-per-er´o-gate
su-per-er-o-ga´tion
su´per-erog´a-to-ry
su´per-fe-ta´tion
su-per-fi´cial
su-per-fi-ci-al´i-ty
su-per-fi´cial-ly
su-per-fi´cies
su´per-fine
su-per-flu´i-ty
su´per-flu-ous
su´per-heat´ed
su´per-hu´man
su´per-im-pose´
su´per-im-po-si´tion
su-per-in-duce´
su´per-in-tend´
su-per-in-tend´en-cy
su-per-in-tend´ent
su-pe´ri-or
su-pe-ri-or´i-ty
su´per´la-tive
su´per-man
su´per-mar-ket
su-per´nal
su´per-na´tant
su-per-nat´u-ral
su´per-nat´u-ral-is´tic
su´per-nu´mer-ary
su´per-pose
su-per-po-si´tion

su´per-pow-er
su´per-sat´u-rate
su-per-sat-u-ra´tion
su-per-scrip´tion
su-per-sede´
su´per-sed´ing
su-per-sen´si-ble
su-per-sen´si-tive
su-per-sen´so-ry
su-per-son´ic
su´per-star
su-per-sti´tion
su-per-sti´tious
su´per-struc´ture
su´per-tank-er
su-per-vene´
su-per-ve´nience
su´per-ven´ing
su-per-ven´tion
su´per-vise
su´per-vis-ing
su´per-vi´sion
su´per-vi-sor
su´per-vi´so-ry
su´per-volt-age
su´per-weap-on
su´per-wom-an
su-pine´
sup´per
sup´per-time
sup-plant´
sup-plan-ta´tion
sup-plant´er
sup´ple
sup´ple-ment
sup´ple-men´tal
sup´ple-men-tar´i-ly
sup´ple-men´tary
sup-ple-men-ta´tion
sup´ple-ness
sup-ple´tive
sup´pli-ance
sup´pli-ant
sup´pli-cant
sup´pli-cate
sup´pli-cat-ing
sup-pli-ca´tion
sup´pli-ca-to-ry
sup-plied´

sup-pli´er
sup-ply´
sup-ply´ing
sup-port´
sup-port-abil´i-ty
sup-port´able
sup-port´er
sup-port´ing
sup-port´ive
sup-pos´able
sup-pos´al
sup-pose´
sup-posed´
sup-pos´ing
sup-po-si´tion
sup´po-si´tion-al-ly
sup-pos´i-ti´tious
sup-pos´i-to-ry
sup-press´
sup-press´ible
sup-pres´sion
sup-pres´sor
sup´pu-rate
sup´pu-rat-ing
sup-pu-ra´tion
sup´pu-ra-tive
sup´pu-ta´tion
su´pra
su´pra-re´nal
su-prem´a-cy
su-preme´
su´ra
su´ral
sur´base
sur-cease´
sur´charge
sur´cin-gle
sur´coat
sure´fire´
sure´foot-ed
sure´ly
sure´ness
sur´er
sur´est
sure´ty
sur´face
sur´faced
sur´fac-er
sur´fac-ing

sur-fac´tant
sur´feit
surf´y
surge
sur´geon
sur´gery
sur´gi-cal
surg´ing
su´ri-cate
Su´ri-nam
sur´li-ly
sur´li-ness
sur´ly
sur-mis´able
sur-mise´
sur-mis´ing
sur-mount´
sur-mount´able
sur-mount´ed
sur´name
sur-pass´
sur-pass´ing
sur´plice
sur´plus
sur´plus-age
sur-pris´able
sur-pris´al
sur-prise´
sur-prised´
sur-pris´ed-ly
sur-pris´ing
sur-re´al-ism
sur-re´al-ist
sur-re´al-is´tic
sur-ren´der
sur-rep-ti´tious
sur´rey
sur´ro-gate
sur´ro-gat-ed
sur´ro-gat-ing
sur-round´
sur-round´ed
sur-round´ing
sur´tax
sur-tout´
sur-veil´lance
sur-veil´lant
sur-vey´
sur-vey´ing

sur-vey´or
sur-viv´al
sur-vive´
sur-vi´vor
sur-vi´vor-ship
sus-cep-ti-bil´i-ty
sus-cep´ti-ble
sus´pect
sus-pend´
sus-pend´ed
sus-pend´er
sus-pend´ible
sus-pense´
sus-pen´si-ble
sus-pen´sion
sus-pen´so-ry
sus-pi´cion
sus-pi´cious
Sus´que-han´na
Sus´sex
sus-tain´
sus-tained´
sus-tain´ing
sus-tain´ment
sus´te-nance
sus´ten-tac´u-lar
sus´ten-ta´tion
sus´ten-ta-tive
sut-tee´
su´ture
su´tur-ing
su´ze-rain
su´ze-rain-ty
svelte
swabbed
swab´bing
swab´ble
Swa´bia
swad´dle
swad´dled
swad´dling
swag´ger
swal´low
swal´low-tail
swa´mi
swamp
swamp´er
swamp´land
swamp´y

| | | |
|---|---|---|
| swank´i-ness | swerved | syl-lab-i-fi-ca´tion |
| swank´y | swerv´ing | syl-lab´i-fied |
| swan´like | swift´er | syl-lab´i-fy |
| swan´nery | swift´ly | syl-lab´i-fy-ing |
| swans´down | swift´ness | syl´la-bize |
| swarmed | swim´mer | syl´la-ble |
| swarm´er | swim´mer-et´ | syl´la-bus |
| swarm´ing | swim´ming | syl-lep´sis |
| swarth´i-ly | swim´ming-ly | syl´lo-gism |
| swarth´i-ness | swin´dle | syl-lo-gis´ti-cal |
| swarth´y | swin´dler | syl´van |
| swash´buck-ler | swin´dling | sym-bi´o-sis |
| swas´ti-ka | swing´ing | sym´bi-ot´ic |
| swatch | swin´ish | sym´bol |
| swath | swiped | sym-bol´ic |
| swathe | swip´ing | sym-bol´i-cal |
| sway´backed | swirl´ing | sym´bol-ism |
| sway´ing | switch | sym´bol-is´tic |
| Swa´zi-land | switch´back | sym-bol-iza´tion |
| swear´ing | switch´board | sym´bol-ize |
| sweat´er | switch´er | sym-bol´o-gy |
| sweat´i-ly | switch´man | sym-met´ri-cal |
| sweat´i-ness | Switz´er-land | sym´me-trize |
| sweat´shop | swiv´el | sym´me-try |
| sweat´y | swiv´eled | sym´pa-thet´ic |
| Swe´den | swiv´el-ing | sym´pa-thize |
| swee´ny | swol´len | sym´pa-thiz-er |
| sweep´er | swoon | sym´pa-thiz-ing |
| sweep´ing | swoon´ing | sym´pa-tho-lyt´ic |
| sweep´stakes | swoop | sym´pa-thy |
| sweet´bread | sword | sym-phon´ic |
| sweet´bri-er | sword´fish | sym-pho´ni-ous |
| sweet corn | sword grass | sym´pho-nize |
| sweet´en | sword knot | sym´pho-ny |
| sweet´ened | sword´play | sym-po´di-um |
| sweet´en-ing | swords´man | sym-po´si-ac |
| sweet flag | swords´man-ship | sym-po´si-um |
| sweet´heart | sworn | symp´tom |
| sweet´ish | syc´a-more | symp-to-mat´ic |
| sweet´ly | sych´no-car´pous | symp-to-mat´i-cal-ly |
| sweet´meats | sy-co´ni-um | symp´tom-a-tize |
| sweet´ness | syc´o-phan-cy | symp-tom-a-tol´o-gy |
| sweet pea | syc´o-phant | syn´a-gogue |
| sweet´shop | sy-co´sis | syn´apse |
| swelled | Syd´ney | syn´ar-thro´sis |
| swell´ing | syl-lab´ic | syn-chon-drot´o-my |
| swel´ter | syl-lab´i-cate | syn´chro-nism |
| swel´ter-ing | syl-lab´i-cat-ing | syn´chro-nis´tic |
| swerve | syl-lab-i-ca´tion | syn-chro-ni-za´tion |

syn´chro-nize
syn´chro-niz-er
syn´chro-niz-ing
syn-chron´o-graph
syn´chro-nous
syn´chro-ny
syn´chro-scope
syn´chro-tron
syn´cline
syn´co-pate
syn´co-pat-ed
syn´co-pat-ing
syn´co-pa´tion
syn´co-pa-tor
syn´co-pe
syn-cop´ic
syn´di-cal-ism
syn´di-cate
syn´di-cat-ing
syn´di-ca´tion
syn´di-ca-tor
syn´drome
syn-er´e-sis
syn-er´gic
syn´er-gism
syn-er-gis´ti-cal
syn-i-ze´sis
syn´od
syn´od-al
syn-od´i-cal
syn-od´i-cal-ly
syn-oe´cious
syn´o-nym
syn´o-nym´ic
syn-o-nym´i-ty
syn-on´y-mous
syn-on´y-my
syn-op´sis
syn-op´tic
syn-tac´ti-cal
syn´tax
syn-tec´tic
syn´the-sis
syn´the-sist
syn´the-size
syn´the-siz-er
syn´the-siz-ing
syn-thet´ic
syn-thet´i-cal

syn-thet´i-cal-ly
syn´the-tize
syn´thol
syph´i-lis
syph´i-lit´ic
sy´phon
Syr´a-cuse
Syr´ia
sy-ringe´
sy-rin´ge-al
sy-rin´gic
sy-rin´gin
syr-in-gi´tis
syr´up
sys´tem
sys´tem-at´ic
sys´tem-at´i-cal-ly
sys´tem-a-ti-za´tion
sys´tem-a-tize
sys-tem´ic
sys-tem-iza´tion
sys´tem-ize
sys´to-le
sys-tol´ic

T

tabbed
tab´bing
tab´by
tab´er-na-cle
tab´er-nac´u-lar
Tab´i-tha
ta´ble
tab´leau
tab´leaux
ta´ble-cloth
ta´ble d´hôte´
ta´ble-land
ta´ble-spoon
ta´ble-spoon-ful
tab´let
ta´ble-ware
ta´bling
tab´loid
ta-boo´
ta´bor
tab´u-lar
tab´u-late

tab´u-lat-ing
tab-u-la´tion
tab´u-la-tor
ta-chom´e-ter
tach´o-met´ric
ta-chom´e-try
tac´it
tac´it-ly
tac´i-turn
tac-i-tur´ni-ty
tack´le
tack´ler
tack´ling
tack´y
Ta-co´ma
tact´ful
tact´ful-ly
tac´ti-cal
tac´ti-cal-ly
tac-ti´cian
tac-tic´i-ty
tac´tics
tac´tile
tac-til´i-ty
tact´less
tac-tom´e-ter
tac´tu-al
tad´pole
taf´fe-ta
taf´fy
Ta-ga´log
tagged
tag´ging
Ta-hi´ti
Ta´hoe
tail´board
tail´er
tail´less
tail´light
tai´lor
tai´lored
tai´lor-ing
tai´lor—made´
tail´piece
tail´race
tail´spin
taint
Tai´pei´
Tai´wan´

take´down
tak´en
take´off
tak´er
tak´ing
talc
tal´cum
tale´bear-er
tal´ent
tal´ent-ed
ta´les
tales´man
tal´i-on
tal´is-man
talk´a-thon
talk´a-tive
talk´er
Tal´la-has´see
tal´lied
tal´low
tal´ly
Tal´mud
Tal-mud´ic
Tal´mud-ist
tal´on
ta-lon´ic
Ta´los
tam´able
ta-ma´le
tam´a-rack
tam´a-rind
tam´a-risk
tam´bour
tam´bou-rine´
tame´able
tamed
tame´ness
tam´er
tam´ing
Tam´ma-ny
tam´—o´—shan-ter
Tam´pa
tamp´er
Tam-pi´co
tam´pon
tan´a-ger
Tan´a-gra
Ta-nan´a-rive
tan´bark

tan´dem
Tan´gan-yi´ka
tan´ge-lo
tan´ge-los
tan´gent
tan-gen´tial
tan-ger-e´tin
tan´ger-ine´
tan-gi-bil´i-ty
tan´gi-ble
Tan-gier´
tan´gle
tan´gled
tan´gling
tan´go
tan´goed
tang´y
tank´age
tan´kard
tank´er
tanned
tan´ner
tan´nery
tan´nic
tan´nin
tan´ning
tan-tal´ic
tan´ta-lite
tan´ta-lize
tan´ta-liz-er
tan´ta-lum
tant´amount
tan´trum
Tan-za-ni´a
Tao´ism
taped
tape´line
tape mea´sure
ta´per
ta´per-ing
tap´es-try
ta-pe´tum
tape´worm
tap-i-o´ca
ta´pir
tap-is´
tapped
tap´ping
tap´room

tap´root
tap´ster
tar-an-tel´la
ta-ran´tu-la
tar´di-ly
tar´di-ness
tar´dy
tar´get
tar´ge-teer´
tar´iff
Tar´king-ton
tar´nish
tar´nish-able
ta´ro
tar-pau´lin
tar´pon
tar´ra-gon
tarred
tar´ried
tar´ring
tar´ry
tar´ry-ing
tar´sal
tar´sus
tar´tan
tar´tar
Tar-tar´ian
tar-tar´ic
Tar´ta-ry
task´mas-ter
Tas-ma´nia
tas´ma-nite
tas´sel
tas´seled
tas´sel-ing
taste´ful
taste´less
tast´er
tast´i-ness
tast´ing
tast´y
Ta´tar
tat´ter
tat´tered
tat´tle
tat´tler
tat´tle-tale
tat-too´
tat-too´er

taught
taunt
taunt´er
taunt´ing
taunt´ing-ly
Taun´ton
taupe
Tau´rus
tav´ern
taw´dri-ness
taw´dry
tawn´i-er
tawn´y
tax-abil´i-ty
tax´able
tax-a´tion
tax´—ex-empt´
tax´i-cab
tax´i-der´mic
tax´i-der-mist
tax´i-der-my
tax´ied
tax´i-me-ter
tax´ing
tax´o-nom´ic
tax-on´o-my
tax´pay-er
Tchai-kov´sky
teach´able
teach´er
teach´ing
tea´cup
tea´house
tea´ket-tle
teal
team´mate
team´ster
team´work
tea par´ty
tea´pot
tear´ful
tear gas
tear´ing
tear´less
tea´room
tear sheet
teased
teas´er
teas´ing

tea´spoon
tea´spoon-ful
tea´time
tech-ne´ti-um
tech´ni-cal
tech-ni-cal´i-ty
tech-ni´cian
Tech´ni-col-or
tech´nics
tech-nique´
tech-noc´ra-cy
tech´no-crat
tech-nog´ra-phy
tech-no-log´i-cal
tech-nol´o-gy
Te-cum´seh
te´di-ous
te´di-um
teen´—ag´er
tee´ter
teethed
teeth´ing
tee´to-tal-er
Tef´lon
teg-men´tal
teg´mi-nal
teg´u-men
teg´u-ment
teg´u-men´tary
Te-he-ran´
Teh-ran´
Te-huan´te-pec
Tel-Au´to-graph
Tel´ Aviv´
tel´e-cast
tel´e-gram
tel´e-graph
te-leg´ra-pher
tel´e-graph´ic
te-leg´ra-phy
tele-ki-ne´sis
tel´e-me-ter
tel´e-met´ric
te-lem´e-try
tel´e-mo-tor
tel´e-path´ic
te-lep´a-thy
tel´e-phone
tel´e-phon´ic

te-leph´o-ny
tel´e-pho´to
tel´e-pho-tog´ra-phy
Tel´e-Promp´Ter
tel´e-scope
tel´e-scop´ic
tel´e-scop´i-cal-ly
te-les´co-py
tel´e-sis
Tel´e-type
tel´e-typ-ist
tel´e-vise
tel´e-vi-sion
tel´e-vi-sor
tell´er
tell´tale
tel-lu´ri-an
tel-lu´ric
tel´lu-ride
tel-lu´ri-um
tem´per
tem´pera
tem´per-a-ment
tem´per-a-men´tal
tem´per-ance
tem´per-ate
tem´per-a-ture
tem´pered
tem´per-er
tem´pest
tem-pes´tu-ous
tem´plar
tem´plate
tem´ple
tem´plet
tem´po
tem´po-ral
tem-po-ral´i-ty
tem-po-rar´i-ly
tem´po-rary
tem´po-rize
tem´po-riz-er
tempt
tempt´able
temp-ta´tion
tempt´er
tempt´ing
tempt´ress
tem´pus fu´git

ten-a-bil´i-ty
ten´a-ble
te-na´cious
te-nac´i-ty
te-nac´u-lum
ten´an-cy
ten´ant
ten´ant-able
ten´ant-ry
tend´ance
tend´en-cy
tend´er
ten´der-foot
ten´der-heart-ed
ten´der-iz-er
ten´der-loin
ten´der-ness
ten-di-ni´tis
ten´di-nous
ten´don
ten´dril
Ten´e-brae
Te-ne-ri´fe
ten´et
ten´fold
Ten´ite
Ten´nes-see´
ten´nis
Ten´ny-son
ten´on
ten´or
ten´pen-ny
ten´pins
ten´si-ble
ten´sile
ten´sion
ten´son
ten´sor
ten-so´ri-al
ten´—strike
ten´ta-cle
ten-tac´u-lar
tent´age
ten´ta-tive
tent´ed
tent´er
ten´ter-hook
te-nu´i-ty
ten´u-ous

ten´ure
te´pee
tep´id
te-pid´i-ty
te-qui´la
ter´a-con´ic
ter´a-cryl´ic
Ter´ence
ter´gite
ter´gum
term´er
ter´mi-na-ble
ter´mi-nal
ter´mi-nate
ter-mi-na´tion
ter´mi-na-tor
ter´mi-ni
ter-mi-nol´o-gy
ter´mi-nus
ter´mite
ter´mor
Terp-sich´o-re
terp´si-cho-re´an
ter´race
ter´ra—cot´ta
ter´ra fir´ma
ter-rain´
Ter-ra-my´cin
ter´ra-pin
terr-a´que-ous
ter-rar´i-um
ter-raz´zo
Ter´re Haute
ter-rene´
ter-res´tri-al
ter´ri-ble
ter´ri-bly
ter´ri-er
ter-rif´ic
ter-rif´i-cal-ly
ter´ri-fied
ter´ri-fy
ter´ri-to´ri-al
ter´ri-to-ry
ter´ror
ter´ror-ism
ter´ror-ist
ter´ror-ize
ter´ry-cloth

terse
terse´ly
terse´ness
ter´tiary
Ter-tul´lian
tes´sel-late
tes´sel-lat-ed
tes-sel-la´tion
tes´ta
test´able
tes´ta-cy
tes´ta-ment
tes´tate
tes´ta-tor
tes-ta´trix
test´er
tes´ti-cle
tes-tic´u-lar
tes-ti-fi-ca´tion
tes´ti-fy
tes-ti-mo´ni-al
tes´ti-mo-ny
tes´ti-ness
tes´tis
tes-tos´ter-one
test tube
tes-tu´di-nal
tes-tu-di-nar´i-ous
tes´ty
tet´a-nus
tet´a-ny
te-tar´to-he´dral
te´tar-toi´dal
tête—à—tête
teth´er
teth´ered
tet-ra-cy´cline
tet´ra-eth´yl
tet´ra-gon
te-tram´er-ous
te-tram´e-ter
tet´ra-mine
tet´ra-zine
tet-ra-zo´li-um
te-traz´o-lyl
tet´ra-zone
tet´ri-tol
te-tron´ic
tet´rose

te-trox´ide
tet´ryl
Teu´ton
Tex´an
Tex-ar-kan´a
Tex´as
text´book
tex´tile
tex´tu-al
tex´tu-ary
tex´tur-al
tex´ture
Thack´er-ay
Thai´land
tha-lam´ic
thal´a-mus
tha-las´sic
Tha´les
tha-lid´o-mide
thal-lif´er-ous
thal´line
thal´li-um
thal´lo-phyte
thal´lus
Thames
thank´ful
thank´ful-ness
thank´less
thanks´giv´ing
thatch´er
thau´ma-site
the´ar-chy
the´a-ter
the-at´ri-cal
The´ban
Thebes
thegn
the´ism
the´ist
the-is´tic
the-mat´ic
them-selves´
thence´forth
thence´for´ward
then´o-yl
the-oc´ra-cy
the´o-crat´ic
The-oc´ri-tus
the-od´i-cy

the-od´o-lite
the-od´o-lit´ic
The´o-dore
The´o-do´sia
the´o-gon´ic
the-og´o-ny
the-o-lo´gian
the´o-log´i-cal
the-ol´o-gize
the-ol´o-gy
the-om´a-chy
the´o-mor´phic
the´o-pa-thet´ic
the´o-path´ic
the-op´a-thy
the-oph´a-ny
the´o-rem
the´o-re-mat´ic
the´o-ret´i-cal
the-o-re-ti´cian
the´o-rist
the-o-ri-za´tion
the´o-rize
the´o-ry
the´o-soph´ic
the-os´o-phist
the-os´o-phy
ther´a-peu´tic
ther´a-peu´ti-cal-ly
ther´a-pist
ther´a-py
there´abouts
there´af´ter
there´by´
there´fore´
there-in´
there-of´
there-on´
The-re´sa
there´upon´
there´with´
ther´mal
ther´mi-cal-ly
Ther´mi-dor
therm´i´on
therm´ion´ic
therm´is´tor
ther´mite
ther´mo-chro-mism

the ...
ther´...
ther´mo-...
ther´mo-...
ther-mog´ra...
ther´mo-graph´ic
ther´mol´y-sis
ther´mo-lyt´ic
ther-mom´e-ter
ther´mo-met´ric
ther´mo-met´ri-cal-ly
ther-mom´e-try
ther´mo-nu´cle-ar
ther-moph´i-ly
ther´mo-pile
Ther´mos
ther´mo-scop´ic
ther´mo-stat
ther´mo-stat´ic
ther´mo-ther´a-py
ther-mot´ro-pism
the-sau´rus
the´ses
the´sis
Thes´pi-an
Thes´sa-lo´ni-an
Thes´sa-ly
the´tin
the-ur´gic
the´ur-gy
the-ve´tin
thi-am´ide
thi-am´l-nase
thi-am´ine
thia-naph´thene
thi-an´threne
thi´a-zole
thi-az´o-line
thi´a-zol-sul´fone
thick´en
thick´en-ing
thick´et
thick´ness
thick´set´
thick´—skinned´
thief
thiev´ery
thieves
thiev´ing

...ish
...gh˝bone
thim˝ble
thim˝ble-ful
thi-mer´o-sal
think´er
think´ing
thin´ner
thin´ness
thin´—skinned´
thi´o-fla´vine
third
third´ly
thirst
thirst´i-ly
thirst´i-ness
thirst´y
thir˝teen´
thir´ti-eth
thir´ty
this˝tle
this´tle-down
thith´er
thi-u-ro´ni-um
thix-ot´ro-py
Thom´as
thong
tho-rac´ic
tho-rac´i-co-lum˝bar
tho-ra´co-scope
tho-ra-cos´to-my
tho´rax
Tho-reau´
thor´ic
tho-rif´er-ous
tho´rite
tho´ri-um
thorn´y
tho´ron
thor´ough
thor´ough-bred
thor´ough-fare
thor´ough-go-ing
thor´ough-ly
thor´ough-ness
though
thought´ful
thought´ful-ly
thought´ful-ness

thought´less
thought´less-ness
thou´sand
thou´sand-fold
thou´sandth
thrall´dom
thrash´er
thra-son´i-cal
thread´bare
thread´cr
thread´worm
thread´y
threat´en
threat´en-ing
three´fold
three´pence
three´score
three´some
thre´i-tol
thre´node
thre-nod´ic
thren´o-dist
thren´o-dy
thre´o-nine
thresh´er
thresh´old
threw
thrift´i-er
thrift´i-ly
thrift´i-ness
thrift´less
thrift´y
thrill´er
thrill´ing
thrips
thrive
thriv´ing
throat
throat´i-ness
throat´y
throb˝bing
throe
throm˝bin
throm˝bo-an´gi-i´tis
throm-bo-cy-to´sis
throm-bo-plas´tin
throm-bo´sis
throm-bot´ic
throm˝bus

throng
throt´tle
throt´tled
through
through-out´
throw
thrush
thrust´er
thrust´ing
thud˝ding
thu´le
thu´li-um
thumb´nail
thumb˝screw
thump´er
thun˝der
thun˝der-bird
thun˝der-bolt
thun˝der-cloud
thun˝der-er
thun˝der-head
thun˝der-ous
thun˝der-ous-ly
thun˝der-show-er
thun˝der-storm
thun˝der-struck
Thurs´day
thwart
thyme
thy´mic
thy´mine
thy´mol
thy´mus
thy´roid
thy-roi´dal
thy-roid-ec´to-my
thy-roid-i´tis
thy´ro-nine
thy-rot´ro-phin
thy-rox´ine
thyr´soid
thyr´sus
thy´sa-nu´ran
thy´sa-nu´rous
ti-ar´a
Ti˝ber
Ti-bet´
tib´ia
tib´i-al

tick´er
tick´et
tick´et-er
tick´i-ci´dal
tick´i-cide
tick´ing
tick´le
tick´ler
tick´lish
Ti-con-der-o´ga
tid´al
tid´bit
tid´dly-winks
tide´wa-ter
ti´di-ly
ti´di-ness
ti´ding
ti´dy
tie´—in
tie´mann-ite
Tien´tsin´
tier
Tier´ra del Fue´go
tie´—up
tif´fa-ny
tif´fin
ti´ger
ti´ger-ish
ti´ger lily
tight´en
tight´en-er
tight´en-ing
tight´rope
tight´wad
ti´gress
Ti´gris
til´de
Til´den
tiled
til´ing
till´able
till´age
till´er
tilt´er
tim´ber
tim´bered
tim´ber-man
tim´ber wolf
tim´ber-work

tim´bre
tim´brel
tim´brelled
Tim´buk-tu´
time´—hon´ored
time´keep-er
time´li-er
time´li-ness
time´ly
time´piece
tim´er
time´ta-ble
tim´id
ti-mid´i-ty
tim´ing
tim´o-rous
tim´o-thy
tim´pa-ni
tim´pa-nist
tinc´ture
tin´der
tin´foil
tinge´ing
tin´gle
tin´gled
tin´gling
ti´ni-er
tin´ker
tin´kle
tin´kling
tin´ner
tin´ni-er
tin´ny
tin´sel
tin´seled
tin´smith
tint´er
tin-tin-nab-u-la´tion
tin-tin-nab´u-lous
tint-om´c-ter
tin´type
tin´ware
ti´ny
tip´off
Tip-pe-ca-noe´
tip´per
Tip-pe-rar´y
tip´pet
tip´ping

tip´ple
tip´si-ly
tip´staff
tip´ster
tip´sy
tip´toe
tip´—top
ti-rade´
Ti-ra´ne
tired´ly
tire´less
tire´some
tir´ing
Tish-chen´ko
tis´sue
ti´tan
ti´ta-nate
ti-ta´nia
ti-tan´ic
ti-ta-nif´er-ous
ti´ta-nite
ti-ta´ni-um
ti-tan´ous
ti´ter
tith´able
tithe
tith´er
tith´ing
Ti´tian
ti´tian-esque
Ti´ti-ca´ca
tit´il-late
tit´i-vate
ti´tle
ti´tled
tit´mouse
Ti´to-ism
ti´trate
ti-tra´tion
tit´ter
tit-u-ba´tion
tit´u-lar
tit´u-lary
toad´stool
toad´y
toast´er
toast´mas-ter
to-bac´co
to-bac´co-n

to-bac´cos
To-ba´go
to-bog´gan
to-bog´gan-er
to-col´o-gy
to-coph´er-ol
toc´sin
to-day´
tod´dle
tod´dler
tod´dy
tof´fee
to´ga
to´gaed
to´gat-ed
to-geth´er
to-geth´er-ness
tog´ging
tog´gle
tog´gler
To´go
toil´er
toi´let
toi´let-ry
toi-lette´
toil´some
toil´worn
To´kay´
to´ken
To´kyo
To-le´do
tol´er-a-ble
tol´er-a-bly
tol´er-ance
tol´er-ant
tol´er-ate
tol-er-a´tion
toll´booth
toll´gate
Tol´stoy
to´lu
tol´u-ate
tol´u-ene
tol´yl-ene
tom´a-hawk
to-ma´to
ײma´toes
ײboy
ײstone

tom´cat
tom-fool´ery
to-mog´ra-phy
to-mor´row
tom´—tom
ton´al
to-nal´i-ty
tone´less
ton´er
to-net´ics
Ton´ga
tongue
tongue´less
tongu´er
tongue´—tied
tongu´ing
ton´ic
to-nic´i-ty
to-night
to´nite
ton´nage
ton-neau´
ton´o-log´i-cal
to-nom´e-ter
ton´o-met´ric
to-nom´e-try
ton´sil
ton-sil-lec´to-my
ton-sil-li´tis
ton-sil-lot´o-my
ton-so´ri-al
ton´sure
ton´tine
tool´box
tool crib
tool´er
tool´hold-er
tool´ing
tool kit
tool´room
tooth´ache
tooth´brush
tooth´less
tooth´paste
tooth´pick
tooth pow-der
tooth´some
to´paz
to´paz-ine

top´coat
to-pec´to-my
to-pee´
To-pe´ka
top´er
top´flight´
top-gal´lant
top hat
top´—heavy
to´pi-ary
top´ic
top´i-cal
top´knot
top´mast
top´most
top´—notch´
top´o-deme
to-pog´ra-pher
topo-graph´i-cal
topo-graph´i-cal-ly
to-pog´ra-phy
top´o-log´i-cal
top´per
top´ping
top´ple
top´pling
top´sail
top´side
top´soil
top´sy—tur´vy
toque
To´rah
torch´bear-er
torch´light
torch´wood
to´re-ador
to-reu´tic
to´ric
to´rii
to-rin´gin
tor-ment´
tor-men´tor
tor-na´do
tor-na´does
to´roid
to-roi´dal
To-ron´to
tor-pe´do
tor-pe´do boat

tor-pe´does
tor´pid
tor-pid´i-ty
tor´por
tor´por-if´ic
torque
torque´me-ter
Tor´rens
tor´rent
tor-ren´tial
tor´rid
tor-si-om´e-ter
tor´sion
tor´so
tort
tor´te
tor-ti´lla
tor´tious
tor´toise
tor´toise-shell
tor-tu-os´i-ty
tor´tu-ous
tor´tu-ous-ly
tor´ture
tor´tur-er
tor´tur-ing-ly
tor´tur-ous
toss´ing
toss´—up
tot´able
to´tal
to´taled
to´tal-ing
to-tal-i-tar´i-an
to-tal-i-tar´i-an-ism
to-tal´i-ty
to´tal-i-za-tor
to´tal-ize
to´tal-iz-er
to´tal-ly
to´tem
to´tem-ism
tot´ing
tot´ter
tou´can
touch´down
tou-ché´
touch-i-ly
touch´i-ness

touch´ing
touch´stone
touch´y
tough
tough´en
tough´ness
Tou-lon´
Tou-louse´
tou-pee´
tour´ism
tour´ist
tour´ma-line
tour´na-ment
tour´ney
tour´ni-quet
tou´sle
tou´sled
tout´er
tow´age
to´ward
tow´boat
tow´el
tow´eled
tow´el-ing
tow´er
tow´ered
tow´er-ing
tow´head
tow´line
town´ house
towns´folk
town´ship
towns´man
towns´peo-ple
tow´path
tow´rope
tox-e´mia
tox-e´mic
tox´ic
tox-ic´i-ty
tox´i-co-log´i-cal
tox-i-col´o-gist
tox-i-col´o-gy
tox-i-co´sis
tox-if´er-ous
tox´i-ge-nic´i-ty
tox´in
tox´i-pho´bia
tox-oph´i-lite

tra-bec´u-la
trace´able
trac´er
trac´ery
tra´chea
tra´che-al
tra-che´idal
tra-che-i´tis
tra-che-ot´o-my
tra-cho´ma
tra-chom´a-tous
tra-chyt´ic
trac´ing
track´age
track´er
track´less
track´man
track´walk-er
trac-ta-bil´i-ty
trac´ta-ble
trac´tion
trac´tive
trac´tor
trade´—in
trade´—last
trade´mark
trade name
trad´er
trade school
trades´man
trade un´ion
trade wind
trad´ing
tra-di´tion
tra-di´tion-al
tra-di´tion-ary
trad´i-tive
trad´i-tor
tra-duce´
tra-duc´er
tra-duc´ible
Tra-fal´gar
traf´fic
traf´fic-able
traf´ficked
traf´fick-er
traf´fick-ing
tra-ge´di-an
tra-ge´di-enne

trag´e-dy
trag´ic
trag´i-cal
trag´i-cal-ly
trag´i-com´e-dy
trail´er
train´ee´
train´er
train´ing
train´load
train´man
trait
trai´tor
trai´tor-ous
trai´tress
traj´ect
tra-jec´tile
tra-jec´to-ry
tram´mel
tram´meled
tram´mel-ing
tramp´er
tram´ple
tram´pling
tram´po-line´
tram´way
tran´quil
tran´quil-ize
tran´quil-iz-er
tran´quil´li-ty
trans-act´
trans-ac´tion
trans´at-lan´tic
trans-ceiv´er
tran-scend´
tran-scen´den-cy
tran-scen´dent
tran´scen-den´tal
tran´scen-den´tal-ism
trans-con-ti-nen´tal
tran-scribe´
tran-scrib´er
tran´script
tran-scrip´tion
trans-duc´er
trans-duc´tor
tran-sect´
tran´sept
trans´e-unt

trans´fer
trans-fer´able
trans´fer-ase
trans´fer-ee´
trans-fer´ence
trans-fer-en´tial
trans-ferred´
trans-fer´rer
trans-fer´ring
trans-fig-u-ra´tion
trans-fig´ure
trans-fix´
trans-fix´ion
trans-form´
trans-for-ma´tion
trans-for-ma´tion-al
trans-form´a-tive
trans-form´er
trans-fus´able
trans-fuse´
trans-fu´sion
trans-gress´
trans-gres´sion
trans-gres´sor
trans-hu´mance
tran´sien-cy
tran´sient
tran-sil´ience
tran-sil´ient
tran-sis´tor
tran-sis´tor-ize
tran´sit
tran´sit-er
tran-si´tion
tran-si´tion-al
tran´si-tive
tran´si-to-ry
trans-late´
trans-la´tion
trans-la´tor
trans-lit´er-ate
trans-lit´er-a-tor
trans-lu´cence
trans-lu´cen-cy
trans-lu´cent
trans-mi´grate
trana-mi-gra´tion
trano-mi´gra-to-ry
trans-mis´si-ble

trans-mis´sion
trans-mit´
trans-mit´ta-ble
trans-mit´tal
trans-mit´ter
trans-mut-abil´i-ty
trans-mut´able
trans-mu-ta´tion
trans-mute´
trans-oce-an´ic
tran´som
trano-pa-cif´ic
trans-par´en-cy
trans-par´ent
tran-spir´able
tran-spi-ra´tion
tran-spir´a-to-ry
tran-spire´
tran-spi-rom´e-ter
trans-plant´
trans-plan-ta´tion
tran-spon´der
trans-port´
trans-por-ta´tion
trans-pose´
trans-po-si´tion
trans-sex´u-al
trans-sex´u-al-ism
trans-ship´
trans-ship´ping
trans-ver´sal
trans-verse´
trans-vert´er
trans-vert´ible
trans-ves´tism
trans-ves´tite
trap´door
tra-peze´
tra-pe´zi-form
tra-pe´zi-um
trap´e-zoid
trap´e-zoi´dal
trap´per
trap´pings
Trap´pist
trap´shoot-ing
trash´y
trau´ma
trau-mat´ic

trau´ma-tism
trau´ma-tize
travail´
trav´el
trav´eled
trav´el-er
trav´el-ing
trav´el-og
trav´el-ogue
tra-vers´able
tra-vers´al
trav´erse
trav´er-tine
trav´ois
trawl´er
treach´er-ous
treach´ery
trea´cle
tread´ing
trea´dle
tread´mill
trea´son
trea´son-able
trea´son-ous
trea´sure
trea´sur-er
trea´sure trove
trea´sury
treat
treat´er
trea´ties
trea´tise
treat´ment
trea´ty
tre´ble
tre´bled
troc fern
tree frog
tree´ing
tree´less
tree´nail
tree toad
tree´top
tre´foil
trek´king
trel´lis
trel´lised
trel´lis-work
trem´ble

trem´bling
trem´bling-ly
tre-men´dous
tre-men´dous-ly
trem´or
trem´u-lous
trench
tren´chan-cy
tren´chant
tren´cher
Tren´ton
tre-pan´
trep-a-na´tion
tre-pan´ning
tre-phine´
trep-i-da´tion
tre-pid´i-ty
tres´pass
tres´pass-er
tres´tle
tres´tle-man
tri´ad
tri´al
tri´an-gle
tri-an´gu-lar
tri-an´gu-late
tri-an-gu-la´tion
trib´al
tribe
tribes´man
trib-u-la´tion
tribu´nal
trib´u-nate
trib´une
trib´u-ni´cial
trib´u-tary
trib´ute
tri´ceps
trich-i-no´sis
tri-chlo´ride
tri-cho´sis
tri-chot´o-my
trick´ery
trick´i-ly
trick´i-ness
trick´le
trick´ster
trick´y
tri´col-or

tri´cot
tri-crot´ic
tri´cro-tism
tri-cus´pid
tri´cy-cle
tri-cy´clic
tri´dent
tri´er
Trier
Tri-este´
tri´fle
tri´fler
tri´fling
tri-fo´cal
tri-fo´li-ate
tri-fo´li-o-late
trig´ger
tri´gon
trig´o-nal
tri-go-ni´tis
trig-o-nom´e-ter
trig-o-no-met´ric
trig-o-nom´e-try
tri-lat´er-al
tril´lion
tril´li-um
tri´lo-bite
tri-log´ic
tril´o-gy
tri´mer-ide
trim´er-ous
tri-mes´ic
trim´e-ter
trim´mer
trim´ming
tri´na-ry
Trin´i-dad
Trin´i-ty
trin´ket
tri-no´mi-al
tri´o
Tri´o-nal
tri-par´ti-ble
tri-par´tite
tri-par-ti´tion
tri´pe-dal
trip´—ham-mer
tri´ple
tri-ple´gia

trip´let
trip´lex
trip´li-cate
trip-li-ca´tion
tri-plic´i-ty
tri´pod
trip´o-dal
tri-pod´ic
Trip´o-li
trip´ping-ly
tri´reme
tri-sect´
tri-sec´tion
tri-se´mic
tri-so´mic
tris´ti-chous
Tris´tram
tri-syl-lab´ic
tri-syl´la-ble
trite´ness
trit´i-um
tri´ton
tri´umph
tri-um´phal
tri-um´phant
tri´umph-ing
tri-um´vir
tri-um´vir-al
tri-um´vi-rate
tri´une
tri-va´lence
tri-va´lent
triv´et
triv´ia
triv´i-al
triv-i-al´i-ty
triv´i-um
tro´car
tro-cha´ic
tro-chan´ter
tro´che
troch-e-am´e-ter
tro´chee
troch´i-lus
troch´le-ar
tro-choi´dal
tro-chom´e-ter
trod´den
trog´lo-dyte

Troi´lus
Tro´jan
troll´er
trol´ley
trol´lop
Trol´lope
trom-bi-di´a-sis
trom-bone´
trom-bon´ist
tro-mom´e-ter
tro-nom´e-ter
troop
troop´er
troop´ship
tro-pae´o-lin
tro´pane
trope
troph´ic
tro´phied
tro´phy
trop´ic
trop´ic acid
trop´i-cal
tro´pism
tro-pol´o-gy
trop´o-lone
tro-pom´e-ter
trop´o-phyte
tro´po-sphere
trop-tom´e-ter
Trot´sky
trot´ter
trot´ting
trou´ba-dour
trou´ble
trou´bled
trou´bler
trou´ble-some
trou´blous
trough
trounce
troupe
troup´er
troup´i-al
trou´sers
trous´seau
trou-vère´
tro´ver
trow´el

trow´eled
tru´an-cy
tru´ant
Truck´ee
truck´er
truck´le
truck´ling
truck´man
truc´u-lence
truc´u-lent
trudge
trud´gen
trudg´ing
tru´est
truf´fle
tru´ism
tru-is´tic
tru´ly
trum´pery
trum´pet
trum´pet-er
trun´cate
trun´cat-ed
trun-ca´tion
trun´cheon
trun´dle
trunk´ful
trunk line
trun´nion
truss´ing
trust´ee´
trust-ee´ship
trust´ful
trust´i-ly
trust´ing
trust´wor-thi-ness
trust´wor-thy
trust´y
truth´ful
truth´ful-ness
try´ing
try´out
try´sail
try square
tryst
tryst´er
tsar
tset´se
tu´ba

tub´al
tub´ba-ble
tu´ber
tu´ber-cle
tu-ber´cu-lar
tu-ber´cu-lin
tu-ber-cu-lo´sis
tu-ber´cu-lous
tube´rose
tu´ber-ous
tub´ing
tu´bu-lar
tu-bu-la´tion
tu´bule
tuck´er
Tuc-son´
Tu´dor
Tues´day
tu´fa
tuft´ed
tuft´er
tug´boat
tug´—of—war´
tu-i´tion
tu-la-re´mia
tu´lip
tu´lip-wood
Tul´sa
tum´ble
tum´ble-down
tum´bler
tum´ble-weed
tum´bling
tum´brel
tu´mid
tu´mor
tu´mult
tu-mul´tu-ous
tu´mu-lus
tu´na
tun´able
tun´dra
tune´ful
tune´less
tung´sten
tung´stic
tu´nic
tu´nicked
tun´ing

tun´ing fork
Tu´nis
Tu-ni´sia
tun´nel
tun´neled
tun´nel-er
tun´ny
tu´pe-lo
tur´ban
tur´baned
tur´bid
tur-bid´i-ty
tur´bi-nal
tur´bi-nate
tur´bine
tur´bo-charg-er
tur´bo-jet
tur´bo-prop
tur´bot
tur´bu-la-tor
tur´bu-lence
tur´bu-lent
tu-reen´
turf´man
tur´gen-cy
Tur-ge´nev
tur´gent-ly
tur-ges´cence
tur-ges´cent
tur´gid
tur-gid´i-ty
tur´gor
Tur-got´
Tu´rin
Tur´ke-stan´
tur´key
tur´keys
Turk´ish
tur´mer-ic
tur´moil
turn´buck-le
Turn´bull
turn´coat
turn´down
Tur´ner
turn´er
tur´nip
turn´key
turn´out

turn´over
turn´pike
turn´spit
turn´stile
turn´ta-ble
tur´pen-tine
tur´pi-tude
tur´quoise
tur´ret
tur´ri-lite
tur´tle
tur´tle-dove
Tus´ca-loo´sa
Tus´can
Tus´ca-ny
Tus-ke´gee
tusk´er
tus´sle
tu´te-lage
tu´te-lar
tu´te-lary
tu´tor
tu´tored
tu-to´ri-al
tu-to´ri-al-ly
tut´ti—frut´ti
Tu-tu-i´lan
tux-e´do
tu-yere´
twad´dle
twan´gle
twang´y
tweet´er
twecz´ers
twelfth
twen´ti-eth
twen´ty
twid´dle
twi´light
twing´ing
twi´—night
twin´ing
twin´kle
twin´kling
twin´ning
twist´er
twitch
twitch´er
Twitch´ell

twit´ter
twit´ting
two´fold
two´pence
two´some
two´—step
tycoon´
ty´ing
Ty´ler
tym-pan´ic
tym´pa-nist
tym-pa-ni´tes
tym´pa-nit´ic
tym´pa-num
tym´pa-ny
Tyn´dall
typ´able
type´cast
type´found-er
type met´al
type´script
type´set-ter
type wash
type´write
type´writ-er
type´writ-ing
type´writ-ten
typh-li´tis
typh-lol´o-gy
ty´phoid
ty-phoi´dal
ty-phoi´din
ty-phon´ic
ty-phoon´
ty´phous
ty´phus
typ´i-cal
typ-i-fi-ca´tion
typ´i-fy
typ´ist
ty-pog´ra-pher
ty-po-graph´ic
ty-po-graph´i-cal
ty-pog´ra-phy
ty-ran´ni-cal
ty-ran´ni-cide
tyr´an-nize
tyr´an-nous
tyr´an-nous-ly

tyr´an-ny
ty´rant
ty´ro
Tyrol´
Tyro´le-an
Tyr´o-lese´
Ty-rone´
ty´ro-sine
tyro-sin-o´sis

## U

Uban´gi
ubi´e-ty
ubiq´ui-tar´i-an
ubiq´ui-tary
ubiq´ui-tous
ubi´qui-ty
ud´der
udom´e-ter
u´do-me´tric
Ugan´da
ug´li-fy
ug´li-ness
ug´ly
ukase´
Ukraine´
Ukrain´ian
uku-le´le
u´la-ma´
ul´cer
ul´cer-ate
ul-cer-a´tion
ul´cer-a-tive
ul´cer-ous
ul´na
ul´nar
ul-nar´e
ul´ster
ul-te´ri-or
ul´ti-ma
ul´ti-ma-cy
ul´ti-mate
ul-ti-ma´tum
ul´ti-mo
ul´tra
ul´tra-ism
ul´tra-ma-rine´
ul-tra-mon´tan-ism

ul´tra-mun´dane´
ul-tra-son´ic
ul-tra-vi´o-let
ul´tra vi´res
ul´tra-vi´rus
ul´u-lant
ul´u-late
ul´u-la´tion
Ulys´ses
um´ber
um-bil´i-cal
um-bil´i-cus
um´bra
um´brage
um´bra´geous
um-brel´la
Um´bri-an
um´pir-age
um´pire
un-abat´ed
un-a´ble
un-abridged´
un-ac-cept´able
un-ac-com´pa-nied
un-ac-count´able
un-ac-cus´tomed
un-ac-quaint´ed
un-adorned´
un-adul´ter-at-ed
un-af-fect´ed
un-afraid´
un-aid´ed
un-al´loyed
un-al´ter-able
un-al´tered
un-am-bi´tious
un—Amer´i-can
un-a´mi-able
un-aneled´
una-nim´i-ty
unan´i-mous
un-an-nounced´
un-an´swer-able
un-ap-proach´able
un-ar´gued
un-armed´
u´na-ry
un-ashamed´
un-asked´

un-as-sail´able
un-as-sist´ed
un-as-sum´ing
un-at-tached´
un-at-tain´able
un-at-tend´ed
un-at-trac´tive
un-au´tho-rized
un-avail´ing
un-avoid´able
un-aware´
un-bal´anced
un-bear´able
un-beat´en
un-be-com´ing
un-be-lief´
un-be-liev´able
un-be-liev´er
un-be-liev´ing
un-bend´
un-bend´ing
un-ben´e-ficed
un-bent´
un-bi´ased
un-bid´den
un-bind´
un-blam´able
un-bleached´
un-blem´ished
un-blink´ing
un-blush´ing
un-bolt´ed
un-born´
un-bos´om
un-bound´
un-bound´ed
un-break´able
un-bri´dled
un-bro´ken
un-buck´le
un-bur´den
un-but´ton
un-called—for
un-can´ny
un-ceas´ing
un-cer-e-mo´ni-ous
un-cer´tain
un-cer´tain-ty
un-chained´

un-chal´lenged
un-change´able
un-changed´
un-char´i-ta-ble
un-chart´ed
un-chaste´
un-checked´
un-chris´tian
un´cial
un-cir´cum-cised
un-civ´il
un-civ´il-ized
un-clad´
un-clasped´
un´cle
un-clean´
un-cloud´ed
un-com´fort-able
un-com´mon
un-com-mu´ni-ca-tive
un-com-plain´ing
un-com´pro-mis-ing
un-con-cern´
un-con-ccrued´
un-con-di´tion-al
un-con´quer-able
un-con´quered
un-con´scio-na-ble
un-con´scious
un-con´scious-ness
un-con-sti-tu´tion-al
un-con-trol´la-ble
un-con-trolled´
un-con-ven´tion-al
un-cor-rupt´ed
un-count´ed
un-cou´ple
un-couth´
un-cov´er
un-cov´ered
un-crowned´
unc´tion
unc´tu-ous
un-cul´ti-vat-ed
un-cul´tured
un-cured´
un-daunt´ed
un-de-cid´ed
un-dec´yl-ene

un-dec´y-len´ic
un-de-feat´ed
un-de-filed´
un-de-fined´
un-dem-o-crat´ic
un-de-mon´stra-ble
un-de-mon´stra-tive
un-de-ni´able
un´der
un´der-brush
un´der-clothes
un´der-cloth´ing
un´der-cov´er
un´der-cur-rent
un´der-cut
un´der-dog
un-der-es´ti-mate
un´der-foot´
un´der-glaze
un´der-go´
un´der-gone´
un-der-grad´u-ate
un´der-ground
un´der-growth
un´der-hand-ed
un´der-line
un´der-ling
un´der-ly-ing
un´der-mine´
un´der-neath´
un-der-nour´ished
un´der-paid´
un´der-pass
un-dcr-priv´i-lcged
un´der-rate´
un´der-score
un´der-sec´re-tary
un´der-sell´
un´der-shirt
un´der-side
un´der-signed
un´der-sized
un´der-slung
un´der-stand´
un-der-stand´able
un-der-stand´ing
un´der-state-ment
un´der-stood´
un´der-study

un´der-take
un´der-tak-er
un´der-tak´ing
un´der-tone
un´der-took´
un´der-tow
un-der-val-u-a´tion
un´der-wa´ter
un´der-wear
un´der-weight
un´der-went´
un´der-world
un´der-write
un´der-writ-er
un´der-writ´ten
un-de-served´
un-de-sir´able
un-de-vel´oped
un-dis´ci-plined
un-dis-cov´ered
un-dis-mayed´
un-dis-put´ed
un-dis-turbed´
un-di-ver´si-fied
un-di-vid´ed
un-do´
un-do´ing
un-done´
un-doubt´ed-ly
un-dreamed´
un-dress´
un-due´
un´du-lant
un´du-late
un´du-lat-ed
un-du-la´tion
un´du-la-to-ry
un-du´ly
un-dy´ing
un-earned´
un-earth´
un-earth´ly
un-eas´i-ly
un-eas´i-ness
un-eas'y
un-ed´u-cat-ed
un-em-ployed´
un´em-ploy´ment
un-end´ing

un-en-dur´able
un-e´qual
un-e´qualed
un-equiv´o-cal
un-err´ing
un-e´ven
un-e´ven-ness
un-event´ful
un-ex-am´pled
un-ex-cep´tion-al
un-ex-pect´ed
un-ex-plained´
un-ex-plored´
un-ex´pur-gat-ed
un-fail´ing
un-fair´
un-faith´ful
un-fa-mil´iar
un-fas´ten
un-fath´om-able
un-fa´vor-able
un-feel´ing
un-feigned´
un-feign´ed-ly
un-fet´tered
un-fil´ial
un-fin´ished
un-fit´
un-fit´ted
un-fit´ting
un-flag´ging
un-fledged´
un-flinch´ing
un-fold´
un-fore-seen´
un-for-get´ta-ble
un-for-giv´able
un-for´tu-nate
un-found´ed
un-fre´quent-ed
un-friend´ly
un´ful-filled´
un-furl´
un-fur´nished
un-gain´ly
un-gen´er-ous
un-god´ly
un-gov´ern-able
un-gra´cious

un-grate´ful
un-ground´ed
un´gual
un-guard´ed
un´guent
un´guen-tary
un-guen´tous
un´gu-la
un´gu-lar
un´gu-late
un-hal´lowed
un-ham´pered
un-hap´pi-ly
un-hap´pi-ness
un-hap´py
un-harmed´
un-har´ness
un-health´y
un-heard´
un-heed´ed
un-heed´ing
un-hes´i-tat-ing-ly
un-hinge´
un-ho´ly
un-hon´ored
un-horse´
un-hur´ried
un-hurt´
u´ni-bi´va´lent
u´ni-cel´lu-lar
u´ni-corn
un-iden´ti-fied
u´ni-fi-able
uni-fi-ca´tion
unif´ic
u´ni-fied
uni-fo´li-o-late
u´ni-form
u´ni-form-i-tar´i-an
uni-form´i-ty
u´ni-fy
u´ni-fy-ing
uni-ju´gate
uni-lat´er-al
un-imag´i-na-tive
un-im-paired´
un-im-peach´able
un-im-por´tance
un-im-por´tant

un-im-proved´
un-in-cor´po-rat-ed
un-in-flam´ma-ble
un-in-formed´
un-in-hab´it-ed
un-in-i´ti-at-ed
un-in´jured
un-in-tel´li-gi-ble
un-in-ten´tion-al
un-in´ter-est-ed
un-in-ter-rupt´ed
un-in-vit´ed
un´ion
un´ion-ism
un´ion-ist
un´ion-ize
unip´a-rous
uni-pla´nar
unip´o-tent
unique´
unique´ly
u´ni-son
unis´o-nance
unis´o-nous
u´nit
unit´able
Uni-tar´i-an
u´ni-tary
unite´
unit´ed
unit´ing
u´ni-tive
u´nit-ize
u´ni-ty
u´ni-va´lence
u´ni-va´lent
u´ni-valve
u´ni-ver´sal
uni-ver-sal´i-ty
u´ni-verse
uni-ver´si-ty
univ´o-cal
un-just´
un-jus´ti-fi-able
un-kempt´
un-kind´
un-kind´li-ness
un-kind´ness
un-known´

un-lace´
un-law´ful
un-learned´
un-leash´
un-leav´ened
un-less´
un-let´tered
un-like´
un-like´li-hood
un-like´ly
un-lim´ber
un-lim´it-ed
un-liq´ui-dat-ed
un-list´ed
un-load´
un-lock´
un-loose´
un-luck´y
un-man´age-able
un-man´ly
un-man´ner-ly
un-mar´ried
un-masked´
un-mea´sur-able
un-mel´lowed
un-mend´able
un-men´tion-able
un-mer´chant-able
un-mer´ci-ful
un-mis-tak´able
un-mit´i-gat-ed
un-mixed´
un-mor´al
un-mort´gaged
un-moved´
un-nat´u-ral
un-nec-es-sar´i-ly
un-nec´es-sary
un-nerve´
un-no´ticed
un-ob-served´
un-ob-tru´sive
un-oc´cu-pied
un-of-fi´cial
un-o´pened
un-or´ga-nized
un-orig´i-nal
un-or´tho-dox
un-os´ten-ta´tious

un-pack´
un-paid´
un-pal´at-able
un-par´al-leled
un-par´don-able
un-par-lia-men´ta-ry
un-per´fo-rat-ed
un-per-turbed´
un-pleas´ant
un-pleas´ant-ness
un-pol´ished
un-pop´u-lar
un-pop-u-lar´i-ty
un-prac´ti-cal
un-prec´e-dent-ed
un-pre-dict´able
un-prej´u-diced
un-pre-med´i-tat-ed
un-pre-pared´
un-pre-ten´tious
un-prin´ci-pled
un-print´able
un-proc´essed
un-pro-duc´tive
un-pro-fes´sion-al
un-prof´it-able
un-pro-pi´tious
un-pro-tect´ed
un-pro-voked´
un-pub´lished
un-pun´ished
un-qual´i-fied
un-quench´able
un-ques´tion-able
un-ques´tioned
un-qui´et
un-quote´
un-rav´el
un-read´y
un-re´al
un-re-al´i-ty
un-rea´son-able
un-rec´og-niz-able
un-re-con-struct´ed
un-reel´
un-re-flec´tive
un-re-gen´er-ate
un-re-lent´ing
un-re-li´able

un-re-li´gious
un-re-mit´ting
un-re-mu´ner-at-ed
un-re-mu´ner-a-tive
un-rep-re-sent´a-tive
un-re-quit´able
un-re-quit´ed
un-re-served´
un-rest´
un-re-strained´
un-re-strict´ed
un-rid´dle
un-righ´teous
un-ripe´
un-ri´valed
un-roll´
un-ruf´fled
un-ru´ly
un-safe´
un-sal´able
un-san´i-tary
un-sat-is-fac´to-ry
un-sat´is-fied
un-sat´u-rat-ed
un-sa´vory
un-scathed´
un-schol´ar-ly
un-sci-en-tif´ic
un-scram´ble
un-scru´pu-lous
un-search´able
un-sea´son-able
un-seat´
un-seem´ly
un-seen´
un-self´ish
un-self´ish-ness
un-set´tled
un-shak´able
un-shak´en
un-shav´en
un-sheathe´
un-shod´
un-sight´ly
un-signed´
un-skilled´
un-skill´ful
un-snarl´
un-so´cia-ble

un-sol´der
un-so-lic´it-ed
un-so-lic´i-tous
un-so-phis´ti-cat-ed
un´sound´
un-spar´ing
un-speak´able
un-spe´cial-ized
un-spec´u-la-tive
un-spoiled´
un-spot´ted
un-sta´ble
un-stained´
un-stead´i-ly
un-stead´y
un-strung´
un-stud´ied
un-sub-stan´tial
un-suc-cess´ful
un-suit´able
un-suit´ed
un-sul´lied
un-sup-port´ed
un-sur-passed´
un-sus-pect´ed
un-sym-pa-thet´ic
un-taint´ed
un-tam´able
un-tamed´
un-tan´gle
un-tar´nished
un-taught´
un-ten´able
Un´ter-mey-er
un-think´able
un-think´ing
un-ti´dy
un-tie´
un-til´
un-time´ly
un-tir´ing
un-ti´tled
un-told´
un-touch´able
un-touched´
un-to´ward
un-trained´
un-tram´meled
un´trans-lat´able

un-tra-vers´able
un-tried´
un-trou´bled
un-true´
un-truth´ful
un-tu´tored
un-used´
un-u´su-al
un-u´su-al-ness
un-ut´ter-able
un-var´nished
un-var´y-ing
un-veil´
un-ven´ti-lat-ed
un-ver´i-fied
un-vir´tu-ous-ly
un-vit´ri-fied
un-want´ed
un-war´i-ly
un-war´rant-able
un-war´rant-ed
un-war´y
un-washed´
un-wa´ver-ing
un-wea´ried
un-wel´come
un-whole´some
un-wield´y
un-will´ing
un-will´ing-ness
un-wise´
un-wit´ting
un-wont´ed
un-work´able
un-world´ly
un-wor´thi-ness
un-wor´thy
un-wo´ven
un-wrap´
un-writ´ten
un-yield´ing
up´braid´
up´bring-ing
up´—coun´try
up´date
up´end´
up´grade´
up-heav´al
up-held´

up-hill´
up-hold´
up-hol´ster
up-hol´ster-er
up-hol´stery
up´keep
up´land
up´lift
upon´
up´per
up´per-cut
up´per-most
up´right
up´right-ness
up´ris-ing
up´roar
up-roar´i-ous
up-roar´i-ous-ly
up´root
up´set
up-set´
up´shot
up´si-lon
up´stage
up´stairs´
up-stand´ing
up´start
up´state´
up´stat-er
up´stream´
up´stroke
up´thrust
up´—to—date´
up´turn
up´ward
U´ral
ural´i-tize
Ura´nia
Ura´nian
uran´ic
u´ra-nin
u´ra-nin-ite
ura´ni-um
U´ra-nus
ur´ban
ur´bane´
ur-ban´i-ty
ur´chin
ure´a

ure-am´e-ter
ure´mia
ure´mic
ure-om´e-ter
ure´ter
ure´ter-al
u´re-thane
ure´thra
ure-thri´tis
uret´ic
ure´yl-ene
ur´gen-cy
ur´gent
ur´gent-ly
urg´ing
u´ri-nal
uri-nal´y-sis
u´ri-nary
u´ri-nate
uri-na´tion
u´rine
u´ri-nol´o-gy
u´ro-fla´vin
u´ro-gen´i-tal
urog´ra-phy
u´ro-leu´cic
uro-li-thi´a-sis
uro-li-thol´o-gy
u´ro-log´ic
urol´o-gist
urol´o-gy
uro-poi-e´sis
u´ro-poi´et´ic
uros´co-py
ur´si-gram
ur´sine
Ur´su-la
Ur´su-line
ur-ti-ca´ceous
ur-ti-car´ia
ur-ti-ca´tion
U´ru-guay
us-abil´i-ty
us´able
us´age
us´ance
use´ful
use´ful-ness
use´less

use´less-ness
us´er
ush´er
u´su-al
u´su-al-ly
u´su-rer
usu´ri-ous
usurp´
usur-pa´tion
usurp´er
u´su-ry
U´tah
uten´sil
u´ter-ine
u´ter-us
U´ti-ca
util-i-tar´i-an
util-i-tar´i-an-ism
util´i-ty
u´ti-li-za´tion
u´ti-lize
u´ti-liz-er
ut´most
Uto´pia
uto´pi-an
u´tri-cle
utric´u-lar
utric´u-li-form
ut´ter
ut´ter-ance
ut´ter-most
uva´rov-ite
u´vea
uve-i´tis
uvi-ton´ic
u´vu-la
u´vu-lar
uvu-li´tis
ux´o´ri-al
ux-or´i-cide

# V

va´can-cy
va´cant
va´cate
va´cat-ing
va-ca´tion
va-ca´tion-ist

vac´ci-nal
vac´ci-nate
vac-ci-na´tion
vac´ci-na-tor
vac-cine´
vac´il-late
vac´il-lat-ing
vac-il-la´tion
vac´il-la-to-ry
vac´u-ist
va-cu´i-ty
vac-u-o-la´tion
vac-u-om´e-ter
vac´u-ous
vac´u-ous-ly
vac´u-um
vag´a-bond
vag´a-bond-age
va-gar´i-ous
va´gary
va-gil´i-ty
va-gi´na
vagi´nal
vag´i-nate
vag-i-nec´to-my
vag-i-ni´tis
va-got´o-my
va´gran-cy
va´grant
vague
vague´ly
va´guish
va´gus
vain-glo´ri-ous
vain´glo-ry
vain´ness
val´ance
val-e-dic´tion
val-e-dic-to´ri-an
val´e-dic´to-ry
va´lence
Va-len´cia
val´en-tine
Va-le´ra
val´et
Val-hal´la
val´iant
val´id
val´i-date

val-i-da´tion
va-lid´i-ty
val´ine
va-lise´
val´ley
val´leys
val´or
va´o-ri-za´tion
val´o-rize
val´or-ous
val´or-ous-ly
Val´pa-rai´so
val´u-able
val´u-ably
val-u-a´tion
val´ue
val´ued
val´ue-less
val´u-ing
val´val
val´vate
valve
val´vu-lar
val´vu-late
vam´pire
vam´pir-ism
va-na´di-um
Van Bu´ren
Van-cou´ver
van´dal
van´dal-ism
van-dyke´
Va-nes´sa
van´guard
va-nil´la
va-nil´lic
vanil´lin
van´ish
van´i-ty
van´quish
van´quish-er
van´tage
vap´id
va-pid´i-ty
vap´id-ly
va-pog´ra-phy
va´por
va-por-es´cence
va´por-if´ic

va-por-im´e-ter
va´por-iz-able
va-por-iza´tion
va´por-ize
va´por-iz-er
va´por-ous
va-que´ro
var-i-a-bil´i-ty
var´i-a-ble
var´i-ance
var´i-ant
var´i-at-ed
var-i-a´tion
var´i-cel´la
var´i-col-ored
var´i-cose
var-i-co´sis
var-i-cos´i-ty
var´ied
var´ie-gate
var´ie-gat-ed
var-ie-ga´tion
va-ri´e-tal
va-ri´e-ty
var´i-form
va-ri´o-la
var´i-o-late
var-i-o-la´tion
var´i-o-lite
var´i-o-lit´ic
var´i-o-loid
va-ri´o-lous
var-i-om´e-ter
var-i-o´rum
var´i-ous
var´i-ous-ly
var´i-type
var´let
var´nish
var´nish-er
var´si-ty
var´us
var´y
vas´cu-lar
vas-cu-lar´i-ty
vas-ec´to-my
Vas´e-line
vas´sal
vas´sal-age

Vas´sar
vas´ti-tude
vast´ly
vast´ness
vat´ic
Vat´i-can
va-tic´i-nal
va-tic-i-na´tion
va-tic´i-na-tor
vaude´ville
vault´ing
vaunt´ing
vav´a-sor
vec´tion
vec´tor
vec-to´ri-al
veer´ing-ly
vee´ry
veg´e-ta-ble
veg´e-tal
veg-e-tar´i-an
veg-e-tar´i-an-ism
veg´e-tate
veg-e-ta´tion
veg-e-ta´tion-al
veg´c-ta-tive
veg´e-tism
veg´e-tive
ve´he-mence
ve´he-ment
ve´he-ment-ly
ve´hi-cle
ve-hic´u-lar
veil´ing
veined
vein´ing
ve-la´men
ve´lar
ve-lar´i-um
Ve-las´quez
veldt
ve´li-ca´tion
vel´lum
ve-loc´i-pede
ve-loc´i-ty
ve-lom´e-ter
ve-lour´
ve´lum
ve-lu´men

vel´vet
vel´vet-een´
vel´vety
ve´nal
ve-nal´i-ty
ve-nat´ic
ve-na´tion
ven´dace
ven´dage
vend´er
ven-det´ta
ven-det´tist
vend´ible
ven-di´tion
ven´dor
ve-neer´
ve-neer´er
ven´er-able
ven´er-ate
ven-er-a´tion
ven´er-a-tor
ve-ne´re-al
ve-ne-re-ol´o-gy
Ve-ne´tian
Ven-e-zu-e´la
ven´geance
venge´ful
ve´nial
Ven´ice
ven´i-son
ven´om
ven´om-ous
ve-nos´i-ty
ve´nous
ve´nous-ly
vent´er
ven´ti-late
ven-ti-la´tion
ven´ti-la-tor
ven´tral
ven´tri-cle
ven-tric´u-lar
ven´tri-lo´qui-al
ven-tril´o-quism
ven-tril´o-quist
ven-tril´o-quis´tic
ven-tril´o-quy
ven´ture
ven´tur-er

ven´ture-some
ven-tu´ri
ven´tur-ing
ven´tur-ous
Ve´nus
ve-ra´cious
ve-ra´cious-ly
ve-rac´i-ty
Ve´ra-cruz
ve-ran´da
ver´a-scope
ver´bal
ver-bal´i-ty
ver-bal-iza´tion
ver´bal-ize
ver´bal-iz-er
ver´bal-ly
ver-ba´tim
ver´bi-age
verb´ify
ver-bose´
ver-bos´i-ty
ver-bo´ten
ver´dan-cy
ver´dant
ver´der-er
Ver´di
ver´dict
ver´di-gris
ver´din
ver´di-ter
Ver-dun´
ver´dure
ver´dur-ous
ver´dur-ous-ness
ver´e-cund
verge
verg´er
Ver´gil
verg´ing
ver´i-fi-able
ver-i-fi-ca´tion
ver´i-fied
ver´i-fy
ver´i-ly
ve´rism
ver´i-ta-ble
ver´i-tas
ver´i-ty

ver´meil
ver-mi-cel´li
ver´mi-cide
ver-mic´u-lar
ver-mic-u-la´tion
ver-mic´u-lite
ver´mi-form
ver´mif´u-gal
ver´mi-fuge
ver-mil´ion
ver´min
ver-mi-na´tion
ver-mi-no´sis
ver´min-ous
ver´min-ous-ly
Vermont´
ver-mouth´
ver-nac´u-lar
ver-nac´u-lar-ism
ver´nal
ver-na´i-za´tion
ver´nal-ize
ver´nal-ly
ver-na´tion
Ver´ner
ver´ni-er
Ver´non
Ve-ro´na
ve-ron´i-ca
Ver-sailles´
ver´sa-tile
ver´sa-tile-ly
ver-sa-til´i-ty
versed
ver-si-fi-ca´tion
ver´si-fied
ver´si-fi-er
ver´si-fy
ver´sion
ver´sus
ver´te-bra
ver´te-brae
ver´te-bral
ver´te-brate
ver´tex
ver´ti-cal
ver´ti-cal-ly
ver´ti-ces
ver´ticil´late

ver-tic´i-ty
ver´ti-go
verve
ver´y
ves´i-cant
ves´i-cate
ves´i-cle
ve-sic´u-lar
Ves-pa´sian
ves´per
ves´per-al
Ves-puc´ci
ves´sel
Ves´ta
ves´tal
vest´ed
vest-ee´
ves´ti-ary
ves-tib´u-lar
ves´ti-bule
ves´tige
ves-tig´ial
ves-tig´ial-ly
vest´ment
ves´try
ves´try-man
ves´tur-al
ves´ture
Ve-su´vi-us
vetch
vet´er-an
vet-er-i-nar´i-an
vet´er-i-nary
ve´to
ve´toed
ve´to-er
ve´toes
ve´to-ing
vex-a´tion
vex-a´tious
vex´ed-ly
vex´il-lary
vi´a
vi-a-bil´i-ty
vi´able
vi´a-duct
vi´al
vi-a´tor
vi´bran-cy

vi´brant
vi´brate
vi´brat-ing
vi-bra´tion
vi-bra´tion-al
vi-bra´to
vi´bra-tor
vi´bra-to-ry
vib´rio
vib´ri-on´ic
vib-ri-o´sis
vic´ar
vic´ar-age
vic´ar—gen´er-al
vi-car´i-al
vi-car´i-ate
vi-car´i-ous
vi-car´i-ous-ly
vice ad´mi-ral
vice—chan´cel-lor
vice—con´sul
vice—pres´i-den-cy
vice—pres´i-dent
vice´roy
vice´roy-al-ty
vi´ce ver´sa
Vi´chy
vi-chys-soise´
Vi´ci
vi-cin´i-ty
vi´cious
vi´cious-ness
vic´tim
vic´tim-ize
vic´tor
Vic-to´ria
vic-to´ri-ous
vic´to-ry
Vic-tro´la
vict´ual
vict´ualed
vict´ual-er
vi-cu´na
vid´eo
Vi-en´na
Vi´en-nese´
Viet´nam´
view´point
vig´il

vig´i-lance
vig´i-lant
vig-i-lan´te
vig-i-lan´tism
vi-gnette´
vi-gnet´ter
vig´or
vig´or-ous
vi´king
vile´ly
vile´ness
vil-i-fi-ca´tion
vil´i-fi-er
vil´i-fy
vil´i-fy-ing
vil´i-pend
vil´la
vil´lage
vil´lag-er
vil´lain
vil´lain-ous
vil´lainy
vil-la-nel´la
vil-la-nelle´
vil-lat´ic
vil´lein
vil´li
vil´li-form
vil-los´i-ty
vil´lus
Vil´na
vi´na
vin-ai-grette´
Vin-cennes´
Vin´cent
vin-ci-bil´i-ty
vin´ci-ble
vin´di-ca-ble
vin´di-cate
vin-di-ca´tion
vin´di-ca-tive
vin´di-ca-tor
vin´di-ca-to-ry
vin-dic´tive
vin-dic´tive-ly
vin´e-gar
vin´e-gary
vin´ery
vine´yard

vi´nic
vin-i-fi-ca´tion
vi´nous
vin´tage
vin´tag-er
vint´ner
vin´y
vi´nyl
vi´nyl-a´tion
vi´nyl-ene
Vi´nyl-ite
Vin´yon
vi´ol
vi-o´la
vi´ol-able
vi´o-la´ceous
vi´o-late
vi-o-la´tion
vi´o-la-tor
vi´o-lence
vi´o-lent
vi´o-let
vi-o-lin´
vi-o-lin´ist
vi-o-lon-cel´list
vi´per
vi´per-ous
vi-ra´go
vi´ral
vir´eo
vi-res´cence
vi-res´cent
Vir´gil
vir´gin
vir´gin-al
Vir-gin´ia
vir-gin´i-ty
vir-gin´i-um
vir´i-al
vi´ri-ci´dal
vir´i-des´cent
vi-rid´i-ty
vir´ile
vir´il-ism
vi-ril´i-ty
vi-rol´o-gy
vi-ro´sis
vir-tu´
vir´tu-al

vir-tu-al´i-ty
vir´tue
vir-tu-os´i-ty
vir-tu-o´so
vir´tu-ous
vir´u-lence
vir´u-lent
vi´rus
vi´sa
vis´age
vis´aged
vis´—à—vis´
vis´cera
vis´cer-al
vis´cid
vis-cid´i-ty
vis´cin
Vis´co-liz-er
vis-com´e-ter
vis´co-scope
vis´cose
vis-co-sim´e-ter
vis-cos´i-ty
vis´count
vis´count-ess
vis´cous
Vish´nu
vis-i-bil´i-ty
vis´i-ble
Vis´i-goth
vi´sion
vi´sion-ary
vi´sioned
vis´it
vis´i-tant
vis-i-ta´tion
vis´i-tor
vi´sor
vis´ta
Vis´tu-la
vi´su-al
vis-u-al´i-ty
vi-su-al-iza´tion
vi´su-al-ize
vi´su-al-iz-er
vi´su-al-ly
vi-ta´ceous
vi´tal
vi-tal´i-ty

vi-tal-iza´tion
vi´tal-ize
vi´ta-min
vi´ta-scope
vi´ti-ate
vi´ti-at-ed
vi-ti-a´tion
vi´ti-a-tor
vit´i-cul-ture
vit´i-cul´tur-ist
vit´rain
vit´re-ous
vi-tres´cence
vi-tres´cent
vi-tres´ci-ble
vit´ri-fi-able
vit-ri-fi-ca´tion
vit´ri-form
vit´ri-fy
vit´ri-ol
vit´ri-o-lat-ed
vit´ri-ol´ic
vit-ri-os´i-ty
vit´u-line
vi-tu´per-ate
vi-tu-per-a´tion
vi-tu´per-a-tive
vi´va
vi-va´cious
vi-va´cious-ly
vi-vac´i-ty
vi´van-dier´
vi´vant´
vi-var´i-um
vi´va vo´ce
Viv´i-an
viv´id
vi-vid´i-ty
viv´id-ly
viv´id-ness
viv-i-fi-ca´tion
viv´i-fied
viv´i-fy
vivi-par´i-ty
vi-vip´a-rous
vi-vip´a-rous-ly
viv´i-sect
viv´i-sec´tion
vix´en

vix´en-ish
viz´ard
vi-zier´
vizs´la
Vlad´i-vos-tok´
vo´ca-ble
vo-cab´u-lary
vo´cal
vo´cal-ist
vo-cal-iza´tion
vo´cal-ize
vo´cal-iz-er
vo-ca´tion
vo-ca´tion-al
voc´a-tive
voc´a-tive-ly
vo-cif´er-ant
vo-cif´er-ate
vo-cif-er-a´tion
vo-cif´er-ous
vo-cif´er-ous-ly
vo-cod´er
vod´ka
vogue
voice´less
voic´ing
void´able
voile
vo´lant
vo´lar
vol´a-tile
vo´a-til´i-ty
vo´a-til-iza´tion
vol´a-til-ize
vol-can´ic
vol-ca´no
vol-ca´noes
vol´ca-nol´o-gy
vo-lem´i-tol
Vol´ga
vol-i-ta´tion
vo-li´tion
vol´i-tive
vol´ley
vol´ley-ball
vol´plane
vol´plan-ist
Vol´stead-ism
Vol´ta

volt´age
vol-ta´ic
Vol-taire´
vol-tam´e-ter
vol´ta-met´ric
volt´—am´me-ter
volt´me-ter
vo´u-bil´i-ty
vol´u-ble
vol´ume
vol-u-me-nom´e-ter
vo-lu´me-ter
vol´u-met´ric
vo-lu-mi-nos´i-ty
vo-lu´mi-nous
vol´un-tar´i-ly
vol´un-ta-rism
vol´un-tary
vol´un-tary-isin
vol´un-teer´
vol´un-teered
vo-lup´tu-ary
vo-lup´tu-ous
vo-lup´tu-ous-ly
vo-lup´tu-ous-ness
vo-lu´tion
vol´vu-lus
vom´it
vom´it-er
voo´doo
voo´doo-ism
vo-ra´cious
vo-rac´i-ty
vo-ra´go
vor´tex
vor´ti-cal-ly
vor-ti-cel´la
vor´ti-ces
vor-tic´i-ty
Vosges
vot´able
vo´ta-ress
vo´ta-rist
vo´ta-ry
vot´er
vot´ing
vo´tive
vouch´er
vouch-safe´

vow´el
vox po´pu-li
voy´age
voy´ag-er
voy´a-geur´
Vul´can
vul´can-ite
vul-can-iza´tion
vul´can-ize
vul´can-iz-er
vul´gar
vul-gar´i-an
vul´gar-ism
vu´gar´i-ty
vul´gar-iza´tion
vul´gar-ize
vul´gar-ly
vul-ner-a-bil´i-ty
vul´ner-a-ble
vul´ner-ary
vul´pine
vul´ture
vul´tur-ous
vul´va
vul´var
vul-vi´tis
vy´ing

**W**

Wa´bash
wab´ble
wack´y
wad´ding
wad´dle
wad´dled
wad´dling
wad´er
wad´ing
wa´fer
waf´fle
waft´age
waft´er
wag´er
wag´es
wage´work-er
wag´gish
wag´gle
wag´gling

wag´ing
Wag´ner
Wag´ner-ism
wag´on
wag´on-er
wag´on-ette´
wag´on-load
wag´tail
wa-hi´ne
waif
Wai-ki-ki´
wail´ing
wain´scot
wain´wright
waist´band
waist´coat
waist´line
wait´er
wait´ing room
wait´ress
waive
waiv´er
wake´ful
wake´ful-ness
wak´en
wak´en-er
wak´en-ing
Wa-la´chi-an
Wal´den
Wal´den´si-an
Wal´do
Wal´dorf
walk´away
walk´er
walk´ie—talk´ic
walk´ing
walk´out
wal´la-by
Wal´lace
Wal-la´chia
wall´board
Wal´len-stein
Wal´ler
wal´let
wall´eyed
wall´flow-er
Wal-loon´
wal´lop
wal´lop-er

wal´lop-ing
wal´low
wall´paper
wal´nut
Wal´pole
wal´rus
Wal´ter
Wal´tham
Wal´ton
waltz
waltz´er
wam´pum
wan´der
wan´der-er
wan´der-ing
wan´der-lust
wan´gle
wan´gled
wan´gling
wan´ing
wan´ly
wan´ness
want´ing
wan´ton
wan´ton-ly
wan´ton-ness
wap´en-take
wap´i-ti
war´ble
war´bler
war´bling
war cry
war´den
war´denship
ward´er
war´der-ship
ward´robe
ward´room
ward´ship
ware´house
ware´room
war´fare
war´fa-rin
war´i-ly
war´i-ness
war´like
war´lock
warm´er
warm´heart-ed

war´monger
warmth
warn´er
warn´ing
warp
warp´age
war´path
warp´ing
war´ra-gal
war´rant
war´rant-ee´
war´rant-er
war´ran-tor´
war´ran-ty
war´ren
war´rior
War´saw
war´ship
war´time
wart´y
War´wick
war´y
wash´able
wash´ba-sin
wash´board
wash´bowl
wash´cloth
washed—out
wash´er
wash´er-wom-an
wash´ing
Wash´ing-ton
wash´out
wash´room
wash´stand
wash´tub
wasp´ish
was´sail
was´sail-er
Was´ser-mann
wast´age
waste´bas-ket
waste´ful
waste´land
waste´pa-per
wast´er
wast´ing
was´trel
watch´case

watch´dog
watch´er
watch´ful
watch´ful-ness
watch´mak-er
watch´man
watch´tow-er
watch´word
wa´ter
wa´ter bug
Wa´ter-bury
wa´ter clock
wa´ter-col-or
wa´ter-course
wa´ter-cress
wa´ter-fall
wa´ter-fowl
wa´ter-front
wa´ter gap
wa´ter gas
wa´ter-glass
wa´ter lev-el
wa´ter lily
wa´ter-line
wa´ter-log
wa´ter-logged
Wa´ter-loo´
wa´ter main
wa´ter-man
wa´ter-mark
wa´ter-mel-on
wa´ter me-ter
wa´ter mill
wa´ter pipe
wa´ter po-lo
wa´ter-pow-er
wa´ter-proof
wa´ter rat
wa´ter-shed
wa´ter-side
wa´ter snake
wa´ter-spout
wa´ter ta-ble
wa´ter-tight
wa´ter tow-er
wa´ter wag-on
wa´ter-way
wa´ter-wheel
wa´ter-works

wa´tery
watt´age
Wat-teau´
watt´tle
watt´me-ter
Wau-ke´gan
Wau´sau
wave´length
wave´let
wave´me-ter
wav´er
wa´ver
wa´ver-er
wa´ver-ing
wa´ver-ing-ly
Wa´ver-ley
wav´i-est
wav´ing
wav´y
wax´en
wax´i-est
wax´i-ness
wax´ing
wax pa-per
wax´works
wax´y
way´bill
way´far-er
way´far-ing
way´laid
way´lay
way´side
way´ward
way´worn
wayz´goose
weak
weak´en
weak´ened
weak´fish
weak´ling
weak´—mind-ed
weak´ness
wealth
wealth´i-er
wealth´y
wean´er
weap´on
weap´on-eer´
wear´able

wear´er
wea´ri-ful
wea´ri-less
wea´ri-ly
wea´ri-ness
wear´ing
wea´ri-some
wea´ri-some-ly
wea´ry
wea´sand
wea´sel
wea´seled
weath´er
weath´er—beat-en
weath´er-board
weath´er-cock
weath´ered
weath´er-ing
weath´er-man
weath´er-proof
weath´er—strip
weath´cr vane
weave
weav´er
weav´er-bird
weav´ing
webbed
web´bing
We´ber
web´—foot-ed
Web´ster
wed´ded
wed´ding
wedge—shaped
wedg´ing
Wedg´wood
wed´lock
Wednes´day
weed´er
weed´y
week
week´day
week´end
week´ly
weep´er
weep´ing
wee´vil
weigh
weight

weight´i-ness
weight´y
weir
weird
weird´ly
weird´ness
wel´come
weld´er
wel´fare
wel´kin
well—bal´anced
well—be-haved´
well´—be´ing
well´born
well´bred´
Wel´ling-ton
well´—known´
well´—nigh´
wells´ite
well´spring
well´—to—do´
well´—
   trained´welsh´er
Welsh´man
wel´ter
wel´ter-weight
wend´ing
were´wolf
Wes´ley
Wes´sex
West Ches´ter
west´er
woot´or ly
west´ern
west´ern-er
West In´dies
West´ing-house
West´min-ster
West´more-land
West-pha´lia
West Vir-gin´ia
west´ward
wet´back
weth´er
wet´ness
wet´ting
Wey´mouth
whack´ing
whale´back

whale´boat
whale´bone
whal´er
whal´ery
whal´ing
wharf
wharf´age
wharf´in-ger
Whar´ton
wharves
what-ev´er
what´not
what-so-ev-er
wheat´en
whee´dle
whee´dled
wheel´bar-row
wheel´base
wheeled
wheel´er
wheel´horse
wheel´house
Wheel´ing
wheel´wright
wheeze
wheez´i-ly
wheez´i-ness
wheez´ing-ly
wheez´y
whelp
when´as´
whence
when-ev´cr
when´so-ev´er
where´abouts
where´as´
where´at´
where´by´
where´fore´
where´in´
where´of
where´so-ev´er
where´upon´
wher-ev´er
where´with´
where´with-al
wher´ry
wher´ry-man
wheth´er

whet´stone
whet´ting
whey
which-ev´er
which´so-ev´er
whif´fen-poof
whif´fet
whif´fle
whif´fle-tree
while
whi´lom
whim´per
whim´pered
whim´per-ing
whim´si-cal
whim-si-cal´i-ty
whim´sy
whined
whin´ing
whin´ing-ly
whin´nied
whin´ny
whip´cord
whip hand
whip´lash
whip´per-snap-per
whip´pet
whip´ping
whip´poor-will
whip´saw
whip´stitch
whirl´er
whirl´i-gig
whirl´pool
whirl´wind
whirl´y-bird
whir´ring
whisk´er
whisk´ered
whis´key
whis´kies
whis´ky
whis´per
whis´pered
whis´per-ing
whist
whis´tle
whis´tler
Whis-tle´ri-an

whis´tling
white´bait
white´cap
white´—col´lar
white´fish
White´hall
white´—hot´
white lead
white´ly
whit´en
white´ness
whit´en-ing
white´wall
white´wash
white wa´ter
white´wood
whith´er
whit´ing
whit´ish
whit´low
Whit´man
Whit´ti-er
whit´tle
whit´tled
whit´tling
whiz´zer
who-dun´it
who-ev´er
whole´heart-ed
whole´sale
whole´sal-er
whole´some
whole wheat
whol´ly
whom-so-ev´er
whoop
whoop´ee
whoop´ing
whoop´ing cough
whop´per
whop´ping
whore
whorl
who-so-ev´er
Wich´i-ta
wick´ed
wick´ed-ly
wick´ed-ness
wick´er

wick´ered
wick´er-work
wick´et
wick´i-up
wide´—eyed
wid´en
wide´spread
wid´geon
wid´get
wid´ow
wid´ow-er
wid´ow-hood
width
wield
wield´er
wield´y
wie´ner
wie´ner schnit´zel
Wies´ba-den
wife
wife´ly
wigged
wig´gle
wig´gling
wig´gly
wig´wag
wig´wam
wild´cat
Wilde
Wil´der
wil´der-ness
wild´—eyed
wild´fire
wild´fowl
wild´ness
wild´wood
wil´ful
Wil´helm
Wil´helms-ha-ven
wil´i-ly
wil´i-ness
Wilkes—Bar´re
Wil-lam´ette
wil´lem-ite
will´ful
will´ful-ly
will´ful-ness
Wil´liam
Wil´liams-burg

will´ing
will´ing-ness
will´—o´—the—wisp
wil´low
wil´lowy
wil´ly—nil´ly
Wil´ming-ton
Wil´son
Wil´ton
wil´y
wim´ble
wim´ple
wince
Win´ches-ter
winc´ing
wind´age
wind´bag
wind´blown
wind´break
wind´break-er
wind´ed
wind´er
Win´der merc
wind´fall
wind´flow-er
wind´i-er
wind´i-ness
wind´ing
wind´ing—sheet
wind´jam-mer
wind´lass
win´dle
wind´less
win´dle-straw
wind´mill
win´dow
win´dow-pane
win´dow—shop-ping
win´dow-sill
wind´pipe
wind´row
wind´shield
Wind´sor
wind´storm
wind´up
wind´ward
wind´y
wine cel´lar
wine´glass

wine´grow-er
wine´press
win´ery
Wine´sap
wine´skin
winged
wing´ed
wing´ed-ly
wing´less
wing´spread
wink´ing
win´kle
Win-ne-ba´go
win´ner
win´ning
Win´ni-peg
win´now
win´now-er
Wins´low
win´some
win´some-ness
Win´ston—Sa´lem
win´ter
win´ter-green
win´ter-ize
win´ter-time
win´try
win´y
wip´er
wip´ing
wire´less
wire´pho-to
wir´er
wire´weed
wir´i-ness
wir´ing
wir´y
Wis-con´sin
wis´dom
wise´acre
wise´crack
wise´ly
wis´est
wish´bone
wish´ful
wish´y—washy
wisp´y
wis-tar´ia
Wis-te´ria

wist´ful
wist´ful-ly
wi´tan
witch´craft
witch´ery
witch ha-zel
witch´ing
with-al´
with-draw´
with-draw´al
with-drawn´
with-drew´
with´er
with´ered
with´er-ing
with-held´
with-hold´
with-hold´ing
with-in´
with-out´
with-stand´
with-stand´ing
with´y
wit´less
wit´ness
wit ti-cism
wit´ti-ly
wit´ting-ly
wit´ty
wiz´ard
wiz´ard-ry
wiz´ened
woad
wob´ble
wob´bly
wob´bu-la-tor
woe´be-gone
woe´ful
woe´ful-ness
wolf
Wolfe
Wolff´ian
wolf´hound
wolf´ish
wolf´ish-ly
Wol´sey
wol´ver-ine´
wolves
wom´an

wom´an-hood
wom´an-ish
wom´an-kind
wom´an-like
wom´an-ly
womb
wom´bat
wom´en
wom´en-folk
won´der
won´dered
won´der-ful
won´der-land
won´der-ment
won´der—work-er
won´drous
won´drous-ly
wont
wood´bine
wood´chuck
wood´cock
wood´craft
wood´cut
wood´cut-ter
wood´ed
wood´en
wood´en-ware
wood´i-er
wood´land
wood´lot
wood´man
wood´peck-er
wood´pile
wood pulp
wood´ruff
wood´shed
woods´man
Wood´stock
woods´y
wood´work
wood´y
woo´er
woof
woof´er
wool´en
wool´gath-er-ing
wool´li-ness
wool´ly
wool´sack

Wool´worth
Worces´ter
word´age
word´i-est
word´i-ly
word´ing
word´less
word´ster
Words´worth
word´y
work-abil´i-ty
work´able
work´a-day
work´bas-ket
work´bench
work´book
work´box
work´day
work´er
work´horse
work´house
work´ing
work´ing-man
work´man
work´man-like
work´man-ship
work´men
work´out
work´room
work´shop
work´ta-ble
work´week
world´li-ness
world´ling
world´ly
world´ly—wise
world´wide´
worm´hole
worm´wood
worm´y
worn—out
wor´ried
wor´ri-ment
wor´ri-some
wor´ry
wor´ry-ing
wors´en
wor´ship
wor´shiped

wor´ship-er
wor´ship-ful
wor´ship-ing
worst´ed
wor´sted
wor´thi-ly
wor´thi-ness
worth´less
worth´while´
wor´thy
would
wound
wound´ed
wo´ven
wrack
wraith
wran´gle
wran´gler
wran´gling
wrap´per
wrap´ping
wrath´ful
wrath´i-ly
wreak
wreath
wreathe
wreath´ing
wreck
wreck´age
wreck´er
wrench
wrest
wres´tle
wres´tler
wres´tling
wretch
wretch´ed
wretch´ed-ness
wrig´gle
wrig´gler
wrig´gly
wright
wring´er
wring´ing
wrin´kle
wrin´kled
wrin´kling
wrin´kly
wrist

wrist´band
wrist´let
wrist´lock
wrist pin
wrist´watch
write´—off
writ´er
write´—up
writhe
writhed
writh´er
writh´ing
writ´ing
writ´ten
wrong
wrong´do-er
wrong´do-ing
wrong´ful
wrong´ly
wroth
wrought
wrought iron
wry´ly
Wurt´tem-berg
Wy´an-dotte
Wyc´liffe
Wy´lie
Wy-o´ming

X

xan´the-nyl
xan´thine
Xan-thip´pe
xan´tho-gen-ate
xan-tho-ma-to´sis
xan´thom´a-tous
xan-thom´e-ter
xan´thous
xan-thox-y-le´tin
xan-thy´drol
Xav´i-er
xe´bec
xe´nia
xe´nial
xe-nog´a-my
xen´o-gen´e-sis
xen´o-ge-net´ic
xen´o-lith

xe´non
xeno-pho´bia
xeno-pho´bic
Xen´o-phon
xe´ric
xer´o-graph´ic
xe-rog´ra-phy
xe´ro-phyte
xe´ro-phyt´ic
xe´ro-sere
xe-ro´sis
Xer´xes
x ray
xy´lem
xy´lene
xy´le-nol
xy´le-nyl
xy´lic
xy´lo-graph´ic
xy-log´ra-phy
xy´loid
xy-lol´o-gy
xy-lom´e-ter
xy-loph´a-gous
xy´lo-phone
xy´lo-phon-ist
xy´lo-side
xy-lot´o-my
xy´lo-yl
xy´lu-lose
xy´lyl-ene
Xy´ris

Y

yacht
yacht´ing
yachts´man
Yah´weh
yak
Yak´i-ma
yam
Yang´tze´
Yan´kee
yap´ping
Ya´qui
yard´age
yard´arm
yard´stick

yar´row
yaw´ing
yawl
yaw´me-ter
yawn
yawn´ing-ly
year´book
year´ling
year´long
year´ly
yearn
yearn´ing
yeast
yeast´i-ness
yeast-y
yel´low
yel´low-bird
yel´low fe´ver
yel´low-fin
yel´low-ish
yel´low jack-et
Yel´low-stone
yelp´er
Yem´en
yeo´man
yeo´man-ry
yes´ter-day
yes´ter-morn
yes´ter-year
yew
Yid´dish
yield
yield´able
yield´ing
yip´ping
yo´del
yo´del-er
yo´del-ing
yo´ga
yo´gi
yo´gurt
yoke
yo´kel
Yo´ko-ha´ma
yolk
Yom Kip´pur
yon´der
Yon´kers
yore

York´shire
Yo-sem´i-te
young
young´ber-ry
young´ish
young´ling
young´ster
Youngs´town
youn´ker
your-self´
youth´ful
youth´ful-ly
Yo´—Yo
yt-ter´bi-um
yt-ter´bous
yt-trif´er-ous
yt´tri-um
Yu´ca-tan´
yuc´ca
Yu-go-slav´ia
Yu´kon
Yule
Yule´tide

Z

Zach-a-ri´ah
Zaire
Zam´bia
za´ny
Zan´zi-bar´
Zea´land
zeal´ot
zeal´ot-ry
zeal´ous
Zeb´e-dee

ze´bra
ze´bu
Zech-a-ri´ah
ze´nith
Ze´no
ze´o-lite
ze-ol´i-tize
zeph´yr
zeph´yr-e´an
Zep´pe-lin
ze´ro
ze´roes
ze´ro-ize
ze´ros
zest
zest´ful
zig´zag
zig´zag-ging
Zim-ba´bwe
zinc
zinc´ate
zinc´ic
zinc´i-fy
Zin´fan-del
zin´nia
Zi´on
Zi´on-ism
Zi´on-ist
zip´per
zip´py
zir´con
zir´con-ate
zir-co´ni-um
zith´er
zo´di-ac
zo-di´a-cal

zom´bi
zon´al
zoned
zon´ing
zo-og´a-my
zo´o-ge´o-graph´ic
zo´o-ge-og´ra-phy
zo-og´ra-pher
zo-og´ra-phy
zo-ol´a-ter
zo-o-log´i-cal
zo-ol´o-gist
zo-ol´o-gy
zo-om´e-ter
zo´o-spo-ran´gi-um
zo´o-spore
Zo´ro-as-ter
Zo´ro-as´tri-an
Zo-ys´ia
zuc-chi´ni
Zu´lu
Zu´ñi
zun´yite
Zu´rich
zwie´back
Zwing´li
Zwing´li-an-ism
zy´go-mat´ic
zy´gote
zy-got´ic
zy-mol´o-gy
zy´mo-plas´tic
zy´mos-then´ic
zy-mot´ic
zy´mur-gy